McGraw-Hill
Mathematics

McGraw-Hill
School Division

New York   Farmington

Senior Consulting Authors

Gunnar Carlsson, Ph.D.
Professor of Mathematics
Stanford University
Stanford, California

Ralph L. Cohen, Ph.D.
Professor of Mathematics
Stanford University
Stanford, California

Program Authors

Douglas H. Clements, Ph.D.
Professor of Mathematics Education
State University of New York at Buffalo
Buffalo, New York

Lois Gordon Moseley, M.S.
Mathematics Consultant
Houston, Texas

Carol E. Malloy, Ph.D.
Assistant Professor of Mathematics Education
University of North Carolina at Chapel Hill
Chapel Hill, North Carolina

Robyn R. Silbey, M.S.
Montgomery County Public Schools
Rockville, Maryland

McGraw-Hill School Division

A Division of The McGraw-Hill Companies

McGraw-Hill School Division
Two Penn Plaza
New York, New York 10121-2298

Printed in the United States of America
ISBN 0-02-100126-X

2 3 4 5 6 7 8 9 071/043 05 04 03 02 01

Contributing Authors

Mary Behr Altieri, M.S.
Mathematics Teacher
1993 Presidential Awardee
Lakeland Central School District
Shrub Oak, New York

Barbara W. Ferguson, Ph.D.
Assistant Professor of Mathematics
and Mathematics Education
Kennesaw State University
Kennesaw, Georgia

Nadine Bezuk, Ph.D.
Professor of Mathematics Education
San Diego State University
San Diego, California

Carol P. Harrell, Ph.D.
Professor of English and English Education
Kennesaw State University
Kennesaw, Georgia

Pam B. Cole, Ph.D.
Associate Professor of
Middle Grades English Education
Kennesaw State University
Kennesaw, Georgia

Donna Harrell Lubcker, M.S.
Assistant Professor of Education
and Early Childhood
East Texas Baptist University
Marshall, Texas

Chung-Hsing OuYang, Ph.D.
Assistant Professor of Mathematics
California State University, Hayward
Hayward, California

Contents

Chapter 1:
Place Value and Money
Theme: Games

Chapter 2: Add Whole Numbers
Theme: Creature Features

Chapter 3:
Subtract Whole Numbers
Theme: Let it Grow

Chapter 4: Time, Data, and Graphs

Theme: All about You

Chapter 5:
Multiplication Concepts
Theme: Performing Arts

Chapter 6:
Multiplication Facts

Theme: Here, There, and Everywhere

Chapter 7: Division Concepts

Theme: Outer Space

Chapter 8:
Division Facts

Theme: Our Earth

Chapter 9: Multiply by 1-digit Numbers
Theme: Cool Collections

Chapter 10:
Divide by 1-Digit Numbers
Theme: Work Together

Chapter 11: Measurement

Theme: Sports and Fitness

Chapter 12: Geometry

Theme: Houses and Homes

CLUSTER **A** Learning Geometry

CLUSTER **B** Using Geometry

S.O.S.

Chapter 13:
Fractions and Probability
Theme: Let's Eat

Chapter 14: Relate Fractions and Decimals

Theme: Inventions and Discoveries

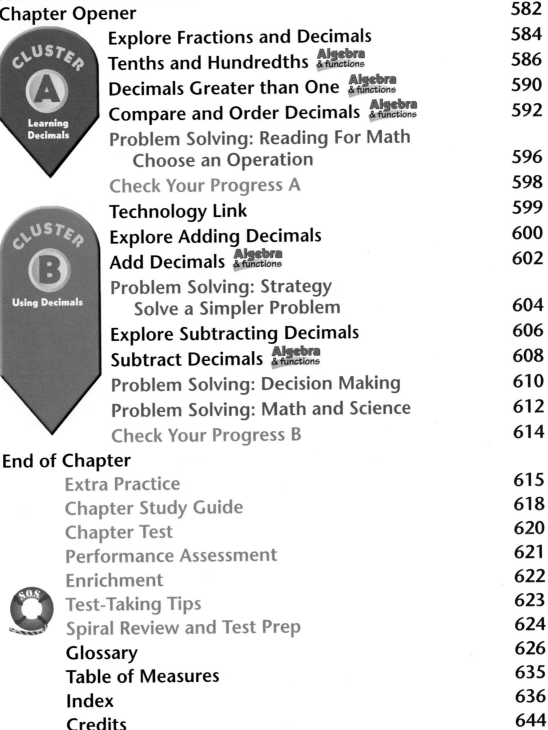

Place Value and Money

Theme: Games

Use the Data

Biggest Games

Game	Largest Number of Participants
Pass the Parcel	3,464 people
Bingo	15,756 people
Board Game "Goose"	1,631 people

Source: Guinness Book of World Records

- What is the word name for the number of people in the biggest game of Bingo?
- How can you arrange the data so that the games are in order from greatest to least?

What You Will Learn

In this chapter you will learn how to
- read and write whole numbers up to 1 million.
- compare, order, and round whole numbers.
- count money and make change.
- use strategies to solve problems.

Additional activities at
www.mhschool.com/math

1·1 ▶ Explore Place Value

Learn

Math Word

place value the value given to a digit by its place in a number

You can use place-value models to explore showing the place value of 526.

Work Together

▶ Show 526 as many ways as you can. Record your work on a **place-value** chart. Use
  • only tens and ones.
  • hundreds, tens, and ones.

You Will Need

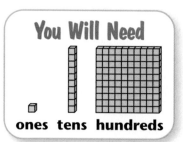

ones tens hundreds

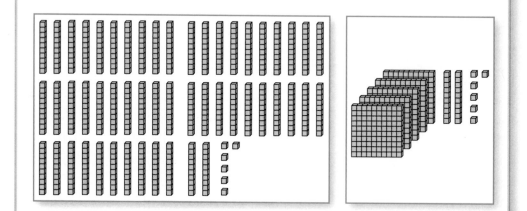

▶ Use place-value models to show each number. Record your work on a place-value chart. Compare your models and charts with those of other students.
  264   207   435   551
▶ 1,000 is ten hundreds. Use hundreds place-value models to show this number.

Make Connections

You can use a place-value chart to understand numbers greater than 100. What number do the models show?

Think:
How many hundreds?
How many tens?
How many ones?

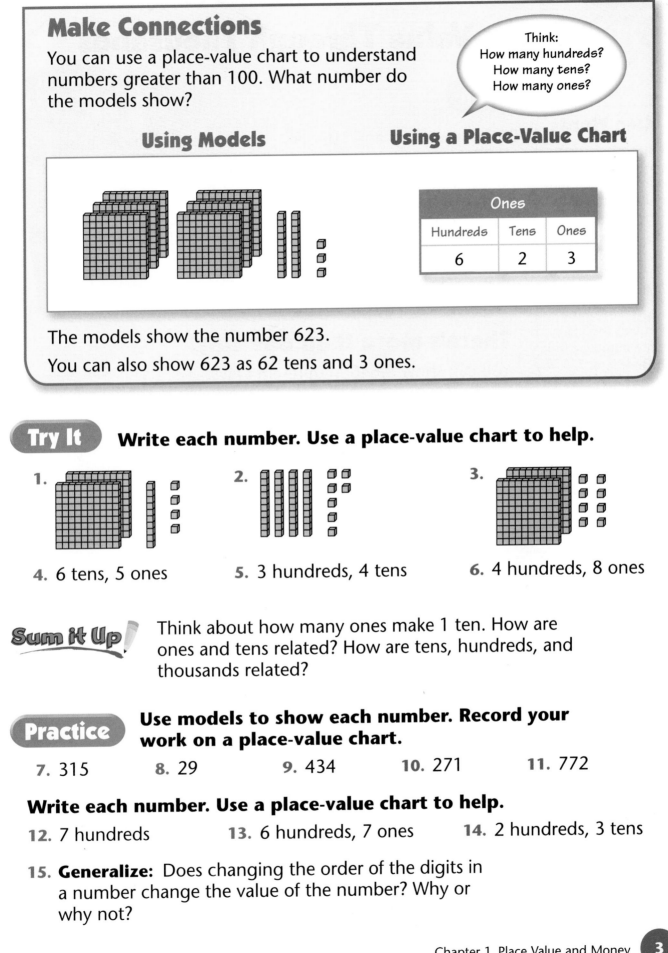

Using Models

Using a Place-Value Chart

Ones		
Hundreds	Tens	Ones
6	2	3

The models show the number 623.

You can also show 623 as 62 tens and 3 ones.

Try It Write each number. Use a place-value chart to help.

1.

2.

3.

4. 6 tens, 5 ones

5. 3 hundreds, 4 tens

6. 4 hundreds, 8 ones

Sum it Up! Think about how many ones make 1 ten. How are ones and tens related? How are tens, hundreds, and thousands related?

Practice Use models to show each number. Record your work on a place-value chart.

7. 315   8. 29   9. 434   10. 271   11. 772

Write each number. Use a place-value chart to help.

12. 7 hundreds   13. 6 hundreds, 7 ones   14. 2 hundreds, 3 tens

15. **Generalize:** Does changing the order of the digits in a number change the value of the number? Why or why not?

1·2 Place Value Through Thousands

She ran 2,640 feet!

Math Words

expanded form
a way of writing a number as the sum of the values of its digits

standard form
a way of writing a number that shows only its digits

digit any of the symbols used to write numbers: 0, 1, 2, 3, 4, 5, 6, 7, 8, 9

Learn

Britni Browning, age 10, is a prize-winning dogsled racer. Once Britni fell and had to run half a mile to catch up to her dogs. We will use many different ways to show the number of feet Britni ran to catch up to her dogs.

There's more than one way!

You can show 2,640 in different ways.

Method A

Use models to show 2,640.

Expanded form:
2,000 + 600 + 40

Standard form:
2,640

Method B

Use the place-value chart to show 2,640. Show each **digit**.

Thousands			Ones		
Hundreds	Tens	Ones	Hundreds	Tens	Ones
0	0	2	6	4	0

Word name: two thousand six hundred forty

Try It   Write each number in standard form.

1.

2.

3. 3 thousands, 4 hundreds, 5 ones

4. 2,000 + 100 + 60 + 6

 How do you use place value to name numbers?

Write each number in standard form.

5.

6.

★**7.** 7 + 100 + 40   ★**8.** 30 + 4 + 400 + 2,000   ★**9.** 800 + 7,000 + 30 + 2

Write the word name for each number.

10. 561   **11.** 408   **12.** 1,243   **13.** 4,320   **14.** 8,054

Write each number in expanded form.

15. 974   **16.** 807   **17.** 4,123   **18.** 3,007

Problem Solving

Use data from *Did You Know?* for problem 19.

19. Music: Musical chairs is a game played all over the world. Read about the biggest game of musical chairs. How can you write that number of people in expanded form? as a word name?

20. Compare: How is expanded form similar to standard form? How is it different?

★**21.** What number has 4 thousands, 3 more hundreds than thousands, 2 more tens than hundreds, and no ones?

Did You KNOW?

The biggest game of musical chairs was played in Singapore on August 5, 1989. There were 8,238 people in the game.

Spiral Review and Test Prep

Skip-count to find each missing number. Tell how you skip-counted.

22. 19, ▮, 23, ▮, 27   **23.** 144, ▮, ▮, 444, 544   **24.** 80, 85, 90, ▮, ▮

Choose the correct answer.

25. Suppose you have 2 quarters, 1 nickel, and 1 penny. How much do you have?

   A. 61 cents   **C.** 56 cents
   B. 59 cents   **D.** Not Here

26. Matt wakes up at 8:15 A.M. School starts in one hour. At what time must Matt be at school?

   F. 9:15 A.M.   **H.** 9:00 A.M.
   G. 7:15 A.M.   **J.** 8:30 A.M.

1·3

Place Value Through Hundred Thousands

Math Word

period each group of three digits in a place-value chart

Learn

Have you ever used a computer? If so, you have probably used a computer software program. The chart shows sales of popular software programs. What is the value of each digit in the number of units Techmaker sold?

Software Publishers

Publisher	Number of Units Sold
Spark	753,543
Vision Systems	923,162
Techmaker	529,355

Example

You can use a place-value chart to find the value of each digit. Commas are used to separate **periods**.

Thousands			Ones		
Hundreds	Tens	Ones	Hundreds	Tens	Ones
5	2	9	3	5	5

The chart shows the value of each digit in 529,355.

You can use expanded form to show each digit's value:

500,000 + 20,000 + 9,000 + 300 + 50 + 5

Try It
Write the value of each underlined digit. Use a place-value chart to help.

1. 2,456   2. 8,358   3. 5,582   4. 83,035   5. 45,679

6. 876,654   7. 263,475   8. 341,567   9. 543,654   10. 68,403

 Sum It Up! How does place value help you find the value of each digit in a number?

Practice Write the value of each underlined digit.

11. 2<u>3</u>
12. <u>4</u>56
13. 80<u>7</u>
14. <u>1</u>,543
15. 2,4<u>5</u>6

16. <u>2</u>1,435
17. 35,<u>5</u>66
18. <u>1</u>00,765
19. 987,<u>6</u>54
20. 4<u>3</u>2,543

Write the value of 5 in each number.

21. 35
22. 502
23. 52,312
24. 256,762
25. 512,478

Write the digit in each place named.

26. 659 (hundreds)
27. 34,782 (ten thousands)
28. 123,476 (tens)

Algebra & functions Complete the table.

29. What is 1,000 more?

Input	Output
2,987	
4,321	
7,001	

★ 30. What is 10,000 less?

Input	Output
21,098	
43,145	
90,500	

Problem Solving

31. Flight Maker sells 196,227 computer games. Show the number of games sold in expanded form.

★32. Name a six-digit number in which the sum of its digits is odd and less than 6.

Journal 33. **Analyze:** Name some things counted in hundred thousands. Find examples in books, newspapers, or magazines.

Spiral Review and Test Prep

34. 9 + 3
35. 18 − 9
36. 13 − 4
37. 6 + 4

Choose the correct answer.

38. Amy, Bob, and Carl are standing in line. Nobody else is in line with them. How many different ways can they stand in line?
    A. 4 ways
    C. 5 ways
    B. 6 ways
    D. 8 ways

39. April caught 4 fish. Oscar caught 6 fish. How many fish did they catch altogether?
    F. 2
    H. 24
    G. 8
    J. Not Here

1.4 Compare and Order Whole Numbers

Algebra & functions   **Learn**

Board Game Sales
June 1 – June 30

Game	Number Sold
Mancala	114
Checkers	110

Math Words

< means "is less than"

> means "is greater than"

Toys for Kids keeps a record of game sales each month. Did Mancala or Checkers have greater sales in June?

There's more than one way!

Method A

You can solve this problem by using a number line.
Compare the numbers.

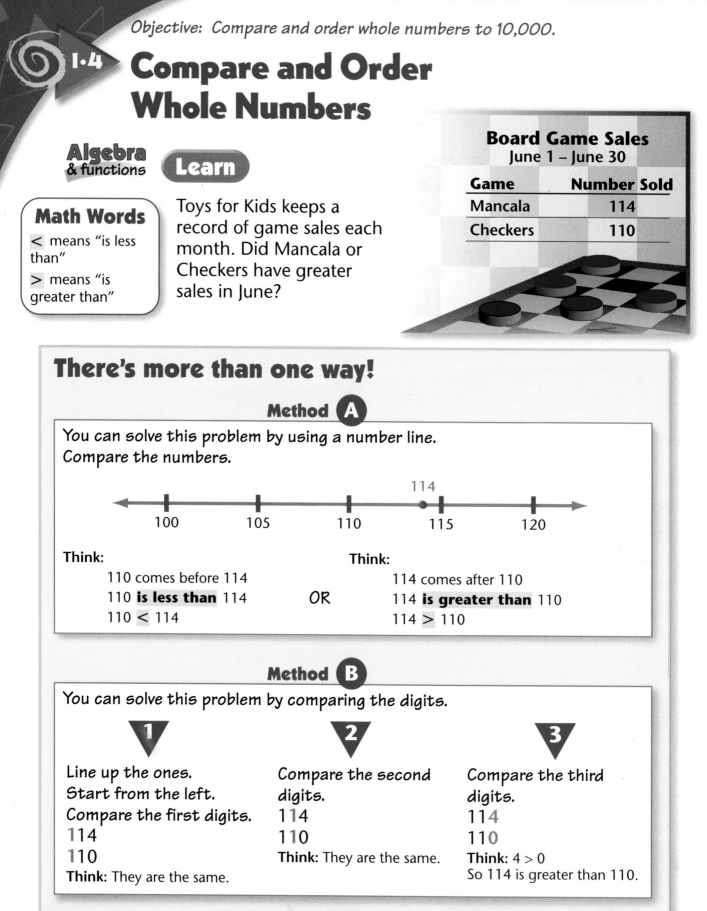

Think:

110 comes before 114

110 **is less than** 114

110 < 114

OR

Think:

114 comes after 110

114 **is greater than** 110

114 > 110

Method B

You can solve this problem by comparing the digits.

1

Line up the ones. Start from the left. Compare the first digits.

114
110

Think: They are the same.

2

Compare the second digits.

114
110

Think: They are the same.

3

Compare the third digits.

114
110

Think: 4 > 0
So 114 is greater than 110.

More Mancala games were sold than Checkers games.

Use the table. List the top three games sold in order from greatest to least.

One Year Sales Report

Game	Number
Chess	1,124
Dominoes	1,056
Checkers	1,137

Example

You can order numbers by comparing the digits.

1

Line up the ones. Start from the left. Compare the first digits.

1,124
1,056
1,137

Think: They are the same.

2

Compare the second digits.

1,124
1,056
1,137

Think: 0 < 1

So 1,056 is least.

3

Compare the third digits.

1,124
1,137

Think: 3 > 2

So 1,137 > 1,124.

Therefore, 1,137 is the greatest.

Games in order from greatest to least:

Checkers   1,137   Chess   1,124   Dominoes   1,056

Try It   **Compare. Write >, <, or =.**

1. 67 ● 76   2. 116 ● 99   3. 544 ● 544   4. 193 ● 139

5. 676 ● 643   6. 2,134 ● 2,233   7. 5,034 ● 5,028   8. 6,081 ● 6,111

Order from least to greatest.

9. 2,312; 2,245; 1,765   10. 4,214; 3,124; 3,289   11. 1,110; 1,101; 1,011

12. 5,432; 5,321; 5,429   13. 6,324; 6,257; 6,145   14. 8,099; 8,136; 8,089

Sum It Up!   Is a 2-digit number always greater or always less than a 3-digit number? Explain how you know.

Compare. Write >, <, or =.

15. 55 ● 44   16. 19 ● 91   17. 65 ● 56   18. 103 ● 93
19. 67 ● 114   20. 201 ● 89   21. 66 ● 616   22. 193 ● 193
23. 96 ● 201   24. 3,041 ● 3,014   25. 58 ● 508   26. 4,006 ● 409
27. 804 ● 488   28. 997 ● 979   29. 101 ● 110   30. 701 ● 770
★31. 3 ● 2 ● 1   ★32. 12 ● 9 ● 6   ★33. 14 ● 12 ● 17   ★34. 24 ● 21 ● 28

Order from least to greatest.

35. 234; 1,245; 789   36. 6,245; 6,134; 7,098   37. 2,010; 2,245; 2,209
38. 6,543; 6,553; 6,453   39. 1,207; 1,341; 1,118   40. 4,110; 4,101; 4,001

Order from greatest to least.

41. 678; 3,411; 2,187   42. 3,098; 3,678; 4,109   43. 7,709; 7,699; 7,832
44. 5,423; 5,487; 5,421   45. 8,340; 8,304; 8,309   46. 9,099; 9,900; 9,090

47.

Make it RIGHT

567
97
9 > 5
so 97 > 561

Here's how Parth compared 567 to 97. Tell what mistake he made. Explain how to correct it.

★48. There is a 3-digit mystery number. The sum of its digits is 13. The first digit is less than the second digit. The last digit is 2. The first two digits have a difference of 3. What number is it?

49. Which of these two prizes is greater: two thousand, five hundred fifty dollars or $2,500?

Problem Solving

50. Megan scored 125 points in a board game. Leroy scored 152 and Eli scored 129. Who won the game? How can you tell?

★51. Logical Reasoning: Use any four digits from those listed below to make the greatest whole number that you can. Use each digit only once. Explain your reasoning.

   5   8   4   9   7   2

Use data from the chart for problems 52–55.

52. Miko played in the game of chess that took the longest time to finish. In which game did Miko play?

53. Which game took the least amount of time to play?

54. Analyze: How can you tell which game took the least amount of time without comparing the value of each digit?

Chess Game Time Records	
Game Number	Number of Minutes from Start to Finish
1	118
2	109
3	98
4	120

55. Create a problem using the data from the chart. Solve it. Ask others to solve it.

★56. The highest score for one turn in a spelling game is 392. The highest score for the first move in the game is 124. Which is worth more? How can you tell? How much more is it worth?

Spiral Review and Test Prep

Fill in the missing number.

57. 99, , 101   **58.** 33, ▮, 35   **59.** 70, ▮, 72   **60.** 44, ▮, 46

Choose the correct answer.

61. Ella is taller than Tina. Kito is shorter than Marc and Tina. Kito is not taller than Ella. Who is the shortest?

  A. Ella   **C.** Tina

  B. Kito   **D.** Marc

62. Use skip-counting to fill in the blank.

  11, 13, ▮, 17, 19

  F. 16   **H.** 14

  G. 15   **J.** Not Here

1·5 Problem Solving: Reading for Math
Using the Four-Step Process

Word Wonder Winners!

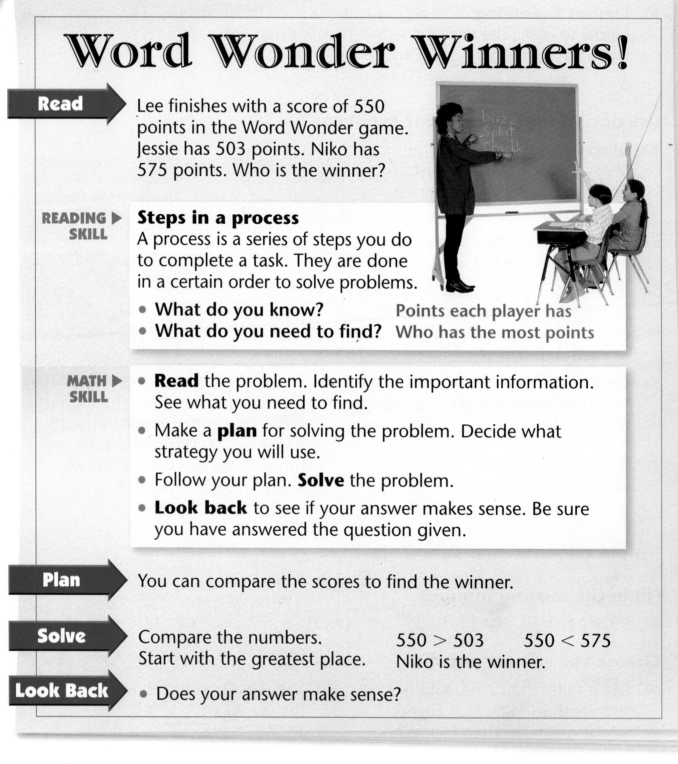

Read ▶ Lee finishes with a score of 550 points in the Word Wonder game. Jessie has 503 points. Niko has 575 points. Who is the winner?

READING ▶ SKILL

Steps in a process
A process is a series of steps you do to complete a task. They are done in a certain order to solve problems.

- **What do you know?**   Points each player has
- **What do you need to find?**   Who has the most points

MATH ▶ SKILL

- **Read** the problem. Identify the important information. See what you need to find.

- Make a **plan** for solving the problem. Decide what strategy you will use.

- Follow your plan. **Solve** the problem.

- **Look back** to see if your answer makes sense. Be sure you have answered the question given.

Plan ▶ You can compare the scores to find the winner.

Solve ▶ Compare the numbers.   550 > 503   550 < 575
Start with the greatest place.   Niko is the winner.

Look Back ▶ • Does your answer make sense?

Sum it Up! How did using the four-step process help you solve this problem?

Practice **Solve. Use the four-step process.**

1. Ann's game piece is on Box 10 of a board game. She moves it ahead 10 boxes, and then 10 more boxes. Where is her game piece now?

2. Justin has 200 points. He scores 200 points three more times. How many points does he have now?

3. In one round of a game, Ted wins $200 in play money. In 3 more rounds, Ted wins $100 in each round. How much play money does Ted win in 4 rounds?

4. Lon has 350 points. Hanna has 200 more points than Lon. Toni has 100 points less than Lon. How many points does each player have? Who is the winner?

Use data from Student Scores for problems 5–8.

5. Who has the highest score so far?

6. Tami plays three more games. She gets 100 points added to her score for each game. What is her new score?

7. Ed loses 200 points in the next game. What is his new score?

8. Ben scores 200 points in the next game. Suni scores 100 points. Who has the most points?

Student Scores	
Name	**Score**
Ben	780 points
Ed	640 points
Suni	820 points
Tami	230 points

Spiral Review and Test Prep

Choose the correct answer.

Maria starts a round in a game with 1,470 points. During the round she receives 100 points. What is her score at the end of the round?

9. Which of these statements is true?
   A. Maria won the game.
   B. Maria starts the round with 1,470 points.
   C. Maria ends the game with 100 points.

10. Which plan will help you solve the problem?
   F. Compare 1,470 and 100.
   G. Increase 1,470 by 100.
   H. Decrease 1,470 by 100.

1·6 Round to Tens, Hundreds, and Thousands

Pinball Game	Times Played Each Week
Castle Capers	118
Space Race	179

Math Word

round to find the nearest value of a number based on a given place value

Learn

Have you ever played a pinball machine? Each machine keeps track of the number of times it has been played each week. About how many times have Castle Capers and Space Race been played?

Example 1

You can **round** to the nearest hundred to tell about how many. Use a number line to help.

Find the two hundreds 118 and 179 are between. Then see which hundred they are closer to.

118 is between 100 and 200. It is closer to 100.
179 is between 100 and 200. It is closer to 200.

Castle Capers has been played about 100 times and Space Race has been played about 200 times.

More Examples

A Round to the nearest ten or ten dollars.

671	$35	298
1 < 5	5 = 5,	8 > 5
so 671 rounds down to 670.	so $35 rounds up to $40.	so 298 rounds up to 300.

B Round to the nearest hundred or hundred dollars.

$734	174	950
3 < 5	7 > 5,	5 = 5
so $734 rounds down to 700.	so 174 rounds up to 200.	so 950 rounds up to 1,000.

A total of 2,180 pinball games were played in one week at Pinball Plaza. To the nearest thousand, how many games were played?

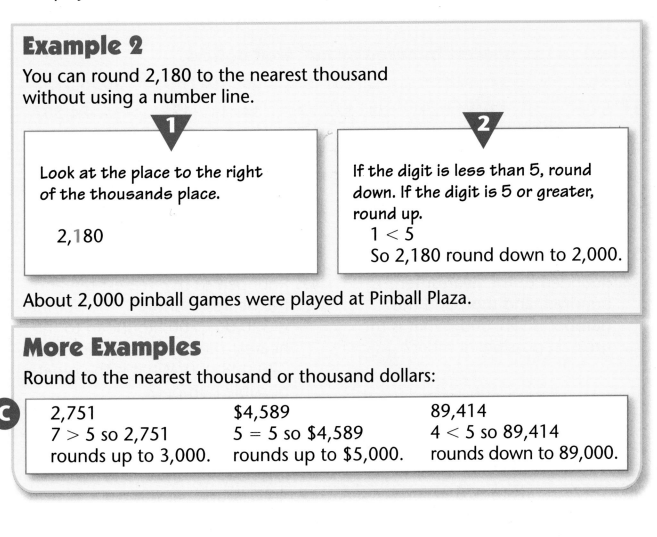

Example 2
You can round 2,180 to the nearest thousand without using a number line.

1

Look at the place to the right of the thousands place.

2,180

2

If the digit is less than 5, round down. If the digit is 5 or greater, round up.

1 < 5

So 2,180 round down to 2,000.

About 2,000 pinball games were played at Pinball Plaza.

More Examples
Round to the nearest thousand or thousand dollars:

C

| 2,751 | $4,589 | 89,414 |
| 7 > 5 so 2,751 rounds up to 3,000. | 5 = 5 so $4,589 rounds up to $5,000. | 4 < 5 so 89,414 rounds down to 89,000. |

Try It Round to the nearest ten or ten dollars.

1. 33　　　2. 49　　　3. $14　　　4. 126　　　5. $469

Round to the nearest hundred or hundred dollars.

6. 459　　　7. $381　　　8. $901　　　9. $1,254　　　10. 6,782

Round to the nearest thousand or thousand dollars.

11. $1,254　　12. 3,541　　13. 8,932　　14. 21,562　　15. $76,123

Sum it Up Explain why the number 158 can be rounded to 160 or to 200.

Round to the nearest ten or ten dollars.

16. 48	**17.** 89	**18.** $70	**19.** 148	**20.** $451
21. 592	**22.** 1,234	**23.** $5,001	**24.** 1,193	**25.** 9,892

Round to the nearest hundred or hundred dollars.

26. 312	**27.** $782	**28.** 201	**29.** $911	**30.** 6,555
31. 8,067	**32.** $4,029	**33.** $7,777	**34.** 11,742	**35.** 24,567

Round to the nearest thousand or thousand dollars.

36. $2,234	**37.** 3,842	**38.** 8,912	**39.** 1,510	**40.** $7,223
41. 12,371	**42.** $25,672	**43.** 55,555	**44.** $10,934	**45.** 89,954

Solve each number riddle.

★ **46.** Rounded to the nearest ten, hundred, and thousand the number is 921,000. What is the greatest possible number?

★ **47.** Rounded to the nearest ten and the nearest hundred, the number is 320,007,700. Rounded to the nearest thousand, the number is 320,008,000. What is the greatest possible number?

Algebra & functions **Find the missing digits to make the following sentences true.**

48. 3 ▮ 7 rounds to 320

49. 4 ▮ 5 rounds to 500

50. ▮,356 rounds to 2,000

51. 5,▮56 rounds to 5,000

52.

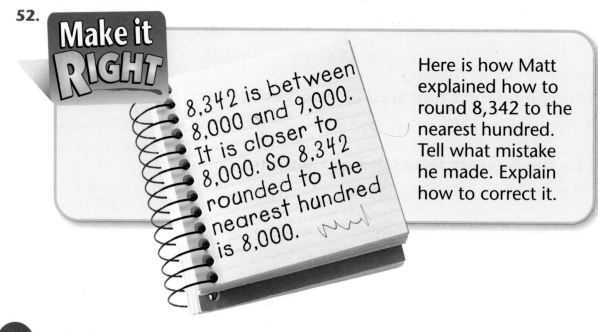

Make it RIGHT

8,342 is between 8,000 and 9,000. It is closer to 8,000. So 8,342 rounded to the nearest hundred is 8,000.

Here is how Matt explained how to round 8,342 to the nearest hundred. Tell what mistake he made. Explain how to correct it.

Problem Solving

53. **Generalize:** Write about when you would use rounded numbers and when you would use exact numbers.

Use data from the sign for problems 54–55.

54. What is the price of the video game player rounded to the nearest hundred?

55. What is the price of the video game 10-pack rounded to the nearest ten?

56. **Number Sense:** Copy and complete with numbers that make sense: Every year the toy store in our town sells about ____ video games. Each game costs about ____ dollars. In my school, ____ students have their own video game players.

57. **Create a problem** about rounding. Solve it. Ask others to solve it.

Use data from *Did You Know?* for problems 58–59.

58. **Science:** How often does an adult's heart beat an hour when rounded to the nearest hundred? thousand?

59. Whose heart beats more in an hour?

ON SALE TODAY!

$199
Video Game Player

$312
10-Pack Video Games

Did You KNOW?

An adult's heart beats about 4,320 times an hour. A newborn baby's heart beats about 7,200 times an hour.

Spiral Review and Test Prep

60. 48 + 10   61. 66 − 20   62. 60 + 15   63. 95 − 10

Choose the correct answer.

64. Which number has 3 tens and no hundreds?

    A. 301   **C.** 3

    B. 37   **D.** 130

65. Which is not equal to 14?

    F. 10 + 3   **H.** 7 + 7

    G. 8 + 6   **J.** 5 + 9

Write the word name for each number. (pages 4–5)

1. 342   2. 506   3. 2,220   4. 3,508   5. 4,071

Write the value of each underlined digit. (pages 6–7)

6. 3,<u>4</u>97   7. 1<u>2</u>,489   8. 2<u>3</u>4,558   9. <u>4</u>98,641

Compare. Write >, <, or =. (pages 8–11)

10. 44 ● 84   11. 92 ● 103   12. 300 ● 30   13. 128 ● 128

Order from least to greatest. (pages 8–11)

14. 3,105; 2,756; 4,567   15. 1,345; 1,435; 2,451   16. 6,548; 5,639; 6,539

Round each number to the nearest ten or ten dollars. (pages 14–17)

17. 85   18. 25   19. $395   20. 831   21. 929

Round each number to the nearest hundred or hundred dollars. (pages 14–17)

22. 592   23. $731   24. $1,676   25. 6,102   26. $8,531

Round each number to the nearest thousand or thousand dollars. (pages 14–17)

27. $4,831   28. 9,431   29. 48,011   30. $78,357   31. 83,560

Solve.

32. Here is a number sentence: $3,000 + \blacksquare + 70 + 8 = 3,578$. What number should go where the blank is to make the sentence true?

Journal

33. **Generalize:** Explain how you can use comparing numbers to round a number to the nearest thousand. Give an example.

Additional activities at www.mhschool.com/math

Place-Value Models

Tricia has 1,254 stickers in her sticker album. How many thousands of stickers does she have? How many hundreds? How many tens? How many ones?

You can build a model of the number of stickers in Tricia's album using place-value or base-ten models.

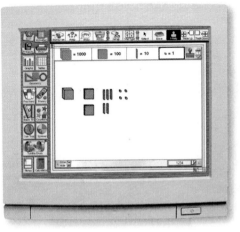

- Start with the 4. Stamp out that many ones.

- Move to the 5 and stamp out that many tens.

- Move to the 2 and stamp out that many hundreds.

- Move to the 1 and stamp out that many thousands.

The number box keeps count as you stamp.

How many thousands does she have? how many hundreds? how many tens? how many ones?

Use the computer to model each number. Then name the value of each digit.

1. 1,432   2. 2,581   3. 4,173   4. 6,108

Solve.

5. Mrs. Arnold's class has collected 2,315 nuts for a class project. How many thousands of nuts do they have? how many hundreds? how many tens? how many ones?

6. **Analyze:** How does using the model help you name the value of each digit in the number?

For more practice, use Math Traveler™.

Objective: Solve a problem by making a table.

1·7 Problem Solving: Strategy
Make a Table

Read ▸ **Read the problem carefully.**

Mr. Bing has to pick a game for his gym class to play. He knows the class's three favorite games. Which game should he pick?

- **What do you know?** The three favorite games
- **What do you need to find out?** Which game he should pick

Plan ▸ Collect and organize data to find out which game the students like most.

Solve ▸ Organize the results in a table.

Mr. Bing will pick soccer.

Survey Results		
Game	Tally	Number
Kickball	卌 IIII	9
Dodge Ball	卌 III	8
Soccer	卌 卌 II	12

Write your name under your favorite game

Kickball

John Kim Juan	May Kito Kwang	Chuck Leon Cara

Dodge Ball

Jess Sara Rod Bob	Gary Sofia Nero Ashley

Soccer

Lars Tom Paco Del	Zoe Tia Fred Bill	Ollie Joan Alan Claire

Look Back ▸ Does the answer make sense? How can you tell?

Sum it Up! How does making a table help you solve a problem?

Practice **Make a table to solve. Use data from the table to solve problems 1–3.**

1. Which day had the most sign-ups?

2. Which day had the least sign-ups?

3. **What if** 3 students change their day to Tuesday instead of Monday? Then which day will have the most sign-ups? the least?

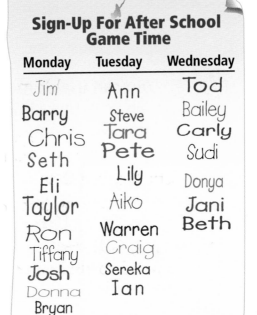

Sign-Up For After School Game Time

Monday	Tuesday	Wednesday
Jim	Ann	Tod
Barry	Steve	Bailey
Chris	Tara	Carly
Seth	Pete	Sudi
Eli	Lily	
Taylor	Aiko	Donya
Ron	Warren	Jani
Tiffany	Craig	Beth
Josh	Sereka	
Donna	Ian	
Bryan		

Mixed Strategy Review

Use data from the table on page 20 for problems 4–6.

4. How many more votes did the most popular game get than the least popular game?

★5. Some students changed their minds about which game to play. Now there is a tie between two of the games. How could the votes change so that two games are tied?

6. How many students voted in the survey?

CHOOSE A STRATEGY
- Find a Pattern
- Work Backward
- Use Logical Reasoning
- Write a Number Sentence
- Make a Table or List
- Guess and Check
- Make a Graph
- Solve a Simpler Problem
- Act it out

7. **Create a problem** using the data in your table. Solve the problem and show your work.

8. **Collect data** for your own survey. Ask friends to name their favorite outdoor games. Make a table to organize your data. Create a problem that uses the data. Ask a friend to solve it.

9. **Social Studies:** In the year 2010, Lake Compounce Amusement Park, the oldest amusement park in the United States, will be 164 years old. How old was it in the year 2000?

Objective: Count bills and coins to find money amounts.

1·8

Explore Money

Learn

You can use coins and bills to explore finding money amounts.

Work Together

▶ Use play money bills and coins to buy each item. Record your work in a table.

You Will Need
- **play money— bills and coins**

BINGO
BINGO •$3.57

Jacks •$1.89

•$4.32

- Take turns buying the items.
- Use bills and coins to buy the games. How many of each will you need?
- What if you use a five-dollar bill to pay for each game? What change will you receive?
- Have your partner use play money to count out the change. Which coins and bills will you get back as change?
- Copy and complete to record your work in a table.

Cost of Item	Coins and Bills	
	Amount Paid	Change

Make Connections

Here's how you can count change with money. Find the change if you use a five-dollar bill to pay for a travel game that costs $3.68.

Count Up

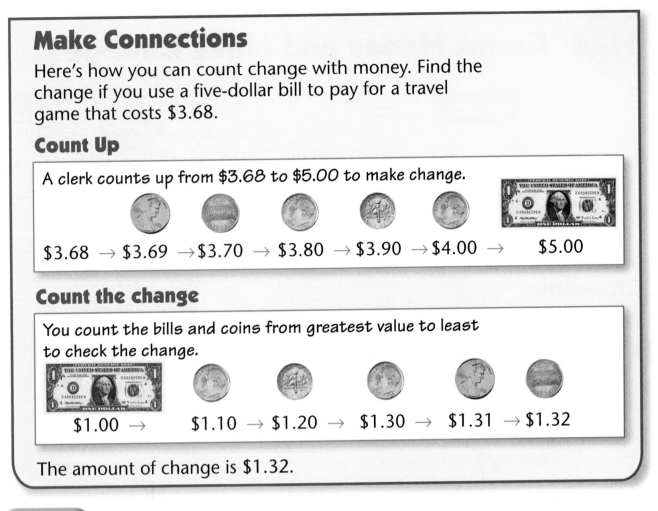

A clerk counts up from $3.68 to $5.00 to make change.

$3.68 → $3.69 → $3.70 → $3.80 → $3.90 → $4.00 → $5.00

Count the change

You count the bills and coins from greatest value to least to check the change.

$1.00 → $1.10 → $1.20 → $1.30 → $1.31 → $1.32

The amount of change is $1.32.

Try It Complete the table. Use play money to help.

Toy or Game	Cost	You Give	Change
1. Backgammon	$4.66	$5.00	
2. Parcheesi	$3.25	$5.00	

Sum it Up What two steps do you follow to find the correct change?

Practice Complete the table. Use play money to help.

Game	Cost	You Give	Change
3. Battleship	$2.32	$5.00	
4. Top	$0.67	$1.00	
5. Yo-Yo	$1.79	$5.00	
6. Puzzle	$3.99	$5.00	

7. **Analyze:** How could you use only quarters and pennies to give change for the Puzzle above?

1·9 Count Money and Make Change

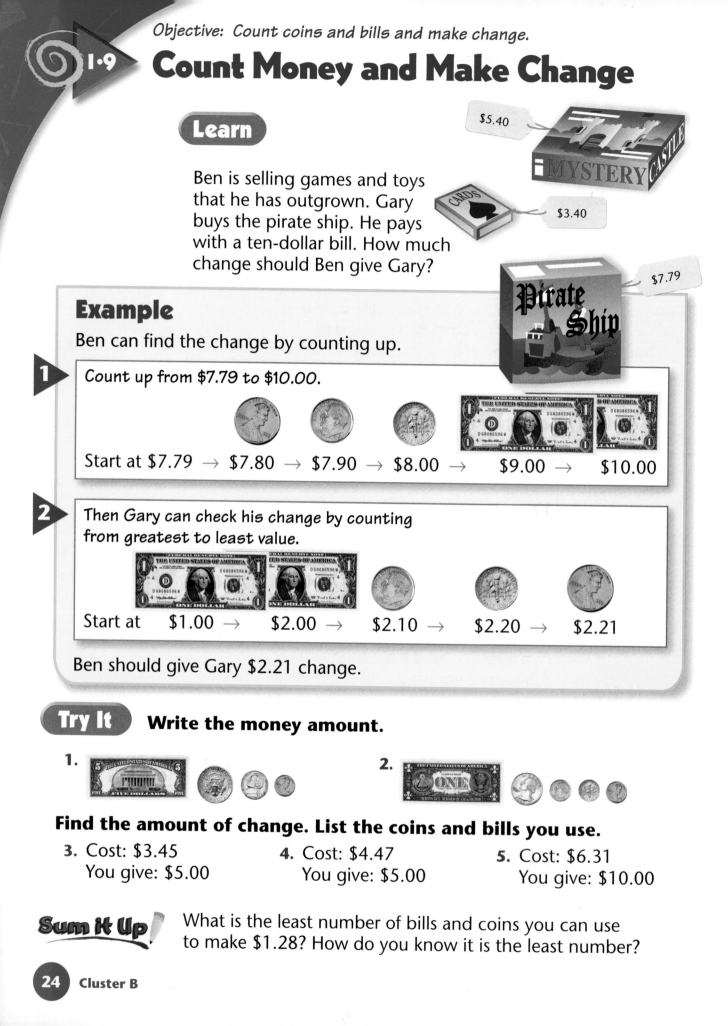

Learn

$5.40

MYSTERY CASTLE

Ben is selling games and toys that he has outgrown. Gary buys the pirate ship. He pays with a ten-dollar bill. How much change should Ben give Gary?

CARDS $3.40

Pirate Ship $7.79

Example

Ben can find the change by counting up.

1 Count up from $7.79 to $10.00.

Start at $7.79 → $7.80 → $7.90 → $8.00 → $9.00 → $10.00

2 Then Gary can check his change by counting from greatest to least value.

Start at $1.00 → $2.00 → $2.10 → $2.20 → $2.21

Ben should give Gary $2.21 change.

Try It — Write the money amount.

1.

2.

Find the amount of change. List the coins and bills you use.

3. Cost: $3.45
   You give: $5.00

4. Cost: $4.47
   You give: $5.00

5. Cost: $6.31
   You give: $10.00

Sum It Up What is the least number of bills and coins you can use to make $1.28? How do you know it is the least number?

6.

7.

Find the amount of change. List the coins and bills you use.

8. Cost: $2.13
   You give: $5.00

9. Cost: $4.09
   You give: $5.00

10. Cost: $8.88
    You give: $10.00

11. Cost: $4.19
    You give: $10.00

12. Cost: $2.99
    You give: $10.00

13. Cost: $7.02
    You give: $10.00

Find the amount of change without using quarters. List the coins and bills you use.

★14. Cost: $1.19
   You give: $2.00

★15. Cost: $3.07
   You give: $5.00

★16. Cost: $4.25
   You give: $10.00

Algebra & functions Compare. Write >, <, or =.

17. $1.54 ● $1.14

18. $3.00 ● $2.99

19. $5.47 ● $6.01

Problem Solving

20. **Analyze:** Marco paid $1.00 to buy a ball for $0.40. The coins show how Camille counted up to find the change for Marco. What is her mistake? What should Marco's change be?

21. **Collect data** from newspaper advertisements for items costing less than $10.00. Find how much change you will get for each item if you pay with a ten-dollar bill.

Spiral Review and Test Prep

Write the number that is 10 more than each number.

22. 45   23. 90   24. 134   25. 431   26. 709

Choose the correct answer.

27. Which set shows all odd numbers?

    A. 1, 2, 3   C. 3, 2, 1

    B. 9, 7, 5   D. 3, 4, 5

28. What is the missing number that makes the sentence true?
    $5 + 6 + 3 = \blacksquare + 3 + 5$

    F. 6   H. 3

    G. 5   J. Not Here

1·10 **Compare and Order Money**

Algebra & functions

Learn

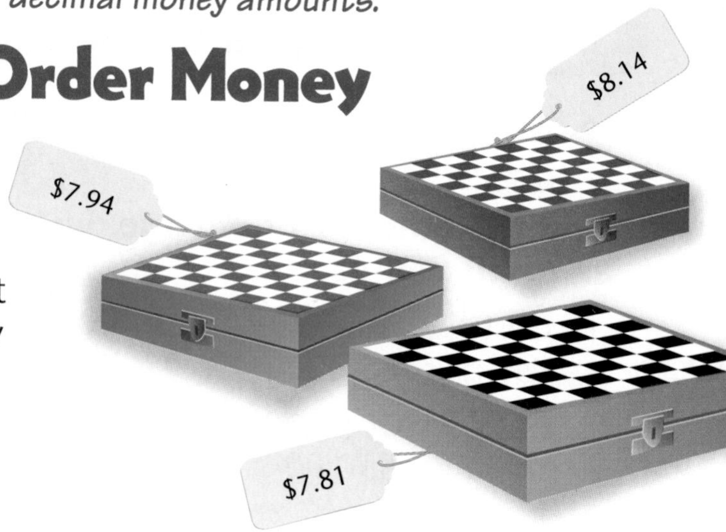

You want to be a smart shopper when you buy games. Which chess game costs the most? Which costs the least?

$8.14

$7.94

$7.81

Example

You can solve this problem by comparing the money amounts.

1

Line up the amounts. Compare the ones.

$7.81
$8.14
$7.94

Think:
8 > 7 so
$8.14 > $7.81 and
$8.14 > $7.94

2

Compare the decimals in the other two amounts.

$7.81

$7.94

Think:
9 > 8 so
$7.94 > $7.81

3

Write the amounts in order from greatest to least.

$8.14, $7.94, $7.81

The chess game that is $8.14 costs the most.
The one that is $7.81 costs the least.

Try It   **Compare. Write >, <, or =.**

1. $5.51 ● $1.55   2. $1.21 ● $1.12   3. $7.08 ● $7.80

Write in order from greatest to least.

4. $5.62; $7.12; $4.32   5. $7.77; $6.81; $7.72

6. $4.45; $3.35; $4.55   7. $6.75; $6.82; $6.63

Sum It Up   How would you compare $7.15 and $9.15 using >, <, or =?

Compare. Write >, <, or =.

8. $4.41 ⬤ $1.44

9. $2.32 ⬤ $2.23

10. $6.09 ⬤ $6.90

11. $7.99 ⬤ $7.99

12. $0.98 ⬤ $1.11

13. $3.33 ⬤ $3.30

Write in order from greatest to least.

14. $6.24; $5.99; $7.00

15. $5.11; $4.99; $5.09

16. $8.77; $8.54; $9.12

17. $9.21; $9.12; $9.09

18. $0.96; $1.16; $1.06

19. $3.33; $3.31; $3.35

★20. $125.67; $152.12; $99.99

★21. $102.56; $120.65; $102.65

Problem Solving

22. Steven saved $2.33 to buy a game. The money to the right shows how much his sister, Sara, saved. Who has more money? How can you tell?

23. **Compare:** How is comparing money amounts the same as comparing whole numbers? How is it different?

24. Kailey bought a travel game of checkers for $2.72. She paid with a five-dollar bill. How much change should she get?

25. **Health:** Sam learned in science that boys his age should eat about 2,800 calories each day. He usually eats 100 fewer calories than this. How many calories does Sam eat each day?

Spiral Review and Test Prep

Round to the nearest hundred.

26. 345

27. 789

28. 1,156

29. 4,671

30. 12,754

Choose the correct answer.

31. Which number is missing in this skip-counting pattern?
3, ▮, 7, 9, 11

A. 4

C. 6

B. 5

D. 8

32. Greg has a one-dollar bill, 4 quarters, 3 nickels, and 2 pennies. How much money does he have?

F. $1.43

H. $2.17

G. $1.72

J. $2.32

1·11 A

Problem Solving: Application

Decision Making

Broadway Elementary School is having a tag sale. Hector and Dora each have money to buy toys and games.

Should Hector and Dora put their money together and share what they buy or buy their own toys and games, each using his or her own money?

You Decide!

What will they do with their money?

Hector's money

Dora's money

Broadway Elementary School Tag Sale

All Board Games	$1.25
All Computer Games	$7.50
All Video Games	$10.00
Yo-Yos	$0.75
Balls	$0.25
All Other Games and Toys	$0.50 – $3.00 (Check tags for price.)

$1.25

$7.50

$10.00

$0.75

$0.25

$1.25

Read for Understanding

1. How much money does Hector have in all? How much does Dora have?

2. Which games or toys cost the most? Which cost the least?

3. If Dora buys a game of checkers, how much will she spend?

4. If Hector buys a yo-yo, how much will he spend?

5. Can Dora buy a computer game? Why or why not? Can Hector?

6. Can Hector buy a video game? Why or why not? Can Dora?

Make Decisions

7. **What if** Dora decides to buy her own toys and games? Which kinds can she buy? Which can't she buy?

8. What if Hector decides to buy his own toys and games? Which kind can he buy? Which can't he buy?

9. What are some advantages for Dora and Hector to put their money together? What are some disadvantages?

10. What information should Dora and Hector know about each other before they decide to put their money together and share?

11. Dora does not own a computer. She does have a video game player. Should she put her money together with Hector? Why or why not?

12. Hector has a computer. He is getting a video game player next month for his birthday. Should he put his money together with Dora? Why or why not?

13. If you had the same amount of money as Dora, which game or toy would you buy? Would you have any money left over? How much?

14. If you had the same amount of money as Hector, which game or toy would you buy? How much money would you have left?

15. If Dora and Hector put their money together, how much will they have in all?

16. What are some games and toys Dora and Hector can buy and share together?

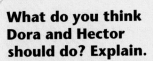 What do you think Dora and Hector should do? Explain.

Problem Solving: Math and Science
Which arm is stronger—your left or your right?

A baseball rolls toward you and stops at your feet. You pick it up and throw it back to the team. Which arm do you use?

Most people are either right- or left-handed. Since they do most things with that arm, it often grows stronger.

You Will Need
- paper ball
- heavy book
- ruler
- timer or clock
- meterstick (optional)

Hypothesize

Which arm do you think will be stronger?

Safety

Work away from other people. Never throw toward other people.

Procedure

1. Work with a partner. Take turns.

2. Throw the paper ball with your left arm, and measure how far it traveled.

3. Do the same with your right arm.

4. Hold the book in your left hand, and count how many times you can raise it straight overhead in 30 seconds.

5. Do the same with your right arm.

Copy and complete the table to record how far the paper ball traveled and the number of book lifts.

	Left Arm	Right Arm
Paper Ball		
Book Lifts		

Conclude and Apply

1. Which arm could throw farther? How do you know?

2. Which arm could do more book lifts? How do you know?

3. Compare your left and right arms. Which one is stronger?

4. A football player does 42 push-ups. Another football player does 97. Which person probably used more energy?

Did You KNOW?

Your body uses food for energy. Your muscles use the energy to throw, push, pull, and lift. The more you exercise, the more energy you use.

Going Further

Design and complete an activity to decide which leg is stronger.

Design and complete an activity to compare how well you see using only your left or right eye.

Problem Solving

Write the money amount. (pages 24–25)

1.

2.

3. 1 five-dollar bill, 4 one-dollar bills, 4 dimes

4. 2 one-dollar bills, 5 quarters, 2 pennies

Find the amount of change. List the coins and bills you use. (pages 24–25)

5. Cost: $2.56
You give: $5.00

6. Cost: $3.19
You give: $5.00

7. Cost: $8.34
You give: $10.00

Compare. Write >, <, or =. (pages 26–27)

8. $6.33 ● $6.33

9. $4.24 ● $4.42

10. $7.71 ● $7.71

11. $5.51 ● $5.15

12. $0.94 ● $1.04

13. $1.41 ● $1.14

Write in order from greatest to least. (pages 26–27)

14. $4.34; $6.20; $4.99

15. $8.14; $7.09; $7.92

16. $3.21; $ 3.12; $3.31

Copy and complete the data for problems 17–19. Solve. (pages 20–21)

17. Which team won the most baseball games?

18. Which team won the fewest baseball games?

19. Write the teams' names in order from fewest games won to most games won.

20. **Generalize:** What are some other reasons for comparing and ordering numbers in sports? Write about one example.

Number of Baseball Games Won		
Team	Tally	Number of Games
Cardinals	卌 卌 ‖	12
Royals	卌 ‖‖	8
Tigers	卌 卌	10
Lions	卌 卌 卌	
Hawks	卌 卌 卌 ‖‖	

Additional activities at
www.mhschool.com/math

Extra Practice

Place Value Through Thousands (pages 4–5)

Write each number in expanded form.

1. 5,146 2. 379 3. 4,600 4. 405 5. 6,038

Write each number in standard form.

6. 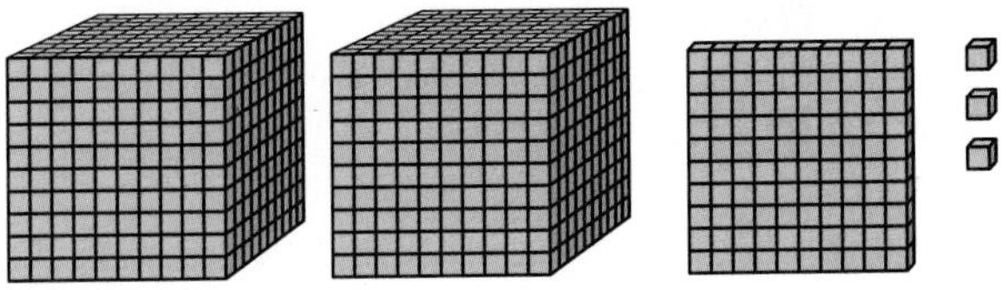

7. 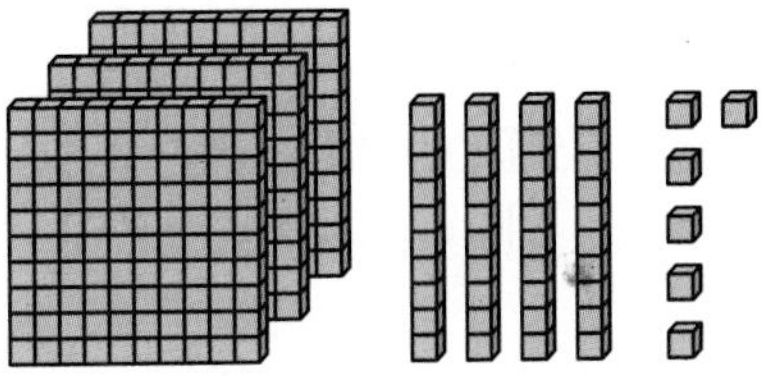

Write the word name for each number.

8. 683 9. 2,490 10. 8,761 11. 3,019 12. 570

Place Value Through Hundred Thousands (pages 6–7)

Write the value of the underlined digit.

1. 3$\underline{2}$5,000 2. 4$\underline{9}$ 3. 3,$\underline{5}$62 4. 2$\underline{4}$,032 5. 9$\underline{8}$5

6. $\underline{7}$52,603 7. $\underline{3}$6,980 8. 12$\underline{6}$,305 9. 5,69$\underline{1}$ 10. 7,$\underline{8}$62

Write the value of the digit 3 in each number.

11. 163,402 12. 377 13. 325,000 14. 232,601 15. 37

Write the digit in each place named.

16. 6,742 (hundreds) 17. 30,740 (ten thousands) 18. 146,198 (tens)

Compare and Order Whole Numbers (pages 8–11)

Compare. Write >, <, or =.

1. 89 ● 98 2. 391 ● 319 3. 420 ● 42 4. 532 ● 532

5. 115 ● 105 6. 301 ● 103 7. 612 ● 621 8. 626 ● 266

Order from least to greatest.

9. 132; 3,210; 689 10. 4,345; 4,145; 5,621 11. 3,609; 3,215; 3,208

12. 5,988; 5,918; 5889 13. 6,034; 6,430; 6,403 14. 8,060; 8,600; 8,006

Extra Practice

Solve. Tell how you used four steps to solve.

1. Betty has 150 points in a game. Jeri has 100 points less than Betty. Sara has 200 more points than Jeri. How many points does each player have? Who is the winner?

2. Harry has 580 points. He loses 300 points in the next turn. What is his new score?

3. Matty has 760 points. George has 400 fewer points than Matty. How many points does George have?

Round to Tens, Hundreds, and Thousands (pages 14–17)

Round to the nearest ten or ten dollars.

1. $32	**2.** 77	**3.** $86	**4.** 153	**5.** 366
6. 622	**7.** $3,214	**8.** 6,008	**9.** $4,391	**10.** 8,336

Round to the nearest hundred or hundred dollars.

11. 421	**12.** $678	**13.** 332	**14.** 816	**15.** $5,689
16. $4,038	**17.** 7,662	**18.** 8,728	**19.** $15,648	**20.** 32,774

Round to the nearest thousand or thousand dollars.

21. 3,625	**22.** $5,489	**23.** 7,362	**24.** $1,552	**25.** 6,214
26. 14,724	**27.** 28,841	**28.** $62,457	**29.** 33,118	**30.** $88,701

Extra Practice

Problem Solving: Strategy
Make a Table (pages 20–21)

Use data from the table for problems 1–4.

1. Which player got the most points?

2. How many more points did the winner get than the second-place player?

3. Write the scores in order from least to greatest.

4. How many more points did Carol get than Ben?

Math Game Scores	
Players	Scores
Alano	54
Ben	22
Carol	30

Count Money and Make Change (pages 24–25)

Find the amount of change. List the coins and bills.

1. Cost: $3.87
   You give: $5.00

2. Cost: $2.76
   You give: $5.00

3. Cost: $4.08
   You give: $5.00

4. Cost: $8.42
   You give: $10.00

5. Cost: $7.15
   You give: $10.00

6. Cost: $3.56
   You give: $10.00

Algebra: Compare and Order Money (pages 26–27)

Compare. Write >, <, or =.

1. $0.76 ● $0.67
2. $5.64 ● $5.46
3. $1.20 ● .12
4. $8.54 ● $8.54
5. $5.15 ● $5.05
6. $7.01 ● $1.07
7. $2.45 ● $2.54
8. $3.43 ● $3.34

Order from least to greatest.

9. $3.65; $3.57; $5.89
10. $8.75; $0.99; $3.25
11. $3.60; $3.21; $3.20

Order from greatest to least.

12. $0.92; $6.12; $3.17
13. $2.46; $2.60; $3.71
14. $1.28; $1.34; $1.51

Chapter Study Guide

Language and Math

Complete. Use a word from the list.

1. The ____ for 340 is 300 + 40.

2. The ____ for five hundred two is 502.

3. Each group of three digits in a place-value chart is called a ____.

Skills and Applications

Read and write whole numbers up to 1 million. (pages 2–7)

Example

Write the expanded form and the word name for the number 2,673.

Solution

Show the number in a place-value chart.

Thousands			Ones		
Hundreds	Tens	Ones	Hundreds	Tens	Ones
0	0	2	6	7	3

2,000 + 600 + 70 + 3 is the expanded form.
Two thousand, six hundred, seventy-three is the word name.

Write each number in standard form.

4. three thousand, forty-five

5. one thousand, four hundred, seventy-four

6. eighteen thousand, ninety-seven

Write the expanded form for each number.

7. 1,532

8. 81,479

Find the value of each underlined digit.

9. 65,1<u>9</u>3

10. <u>2</u>31,768

Compare, order, and round whole numbers and money. (pages 8–11, 14–17, 26–27)

Example

Write the numbers in order from least to greatest.
2,176; 1,892; 2,078

Solution

Line up the numbers. Compare the digits, one place at a time.
2,176
1,892   1 < 2 so 1,892 is least
2,078   1 > 0 so 2,176 is
          greatest
Least to greatest:
1,892; 2,078; 2,176

Write the numbers in order from least to greatest.

11. 689, 547, 559

12. $356; $3,800; $3,785

13. 2,576; 2,412; 1,999

Round each number to the nearest hundred.

14. 859   15. 547

16. 3,642   17. 7,481

18. $7,318   19. $4,623

Count money and make change. (pages 22–25)

Example

Cost: $3.74   You give: $5.00
What is your change?

Solution

Count up from $3.74 to $5.00.

$3.75 → $4.00 → $5.00

Change: $1.26

Find the change.

20. Cost: $1.78
    You give:
    $5.00

21. Cost: $4.52
    You give:
    $5.00

22. Cost: $8.89
    You give:
    $10.00

23. Cost: $3.72
    You give:
    $10.00

Use strategies to solve problems. (pages 12–13, 20–21)

Example

Which game had the most players?

Solution

Look at the table.
12 > 2; 12 > 5
12 is next to
the game Tag.
Tag had the
most players.

Games People Played	
Game	Number of Players
Checkers	2
Hopscotch	5
Tag	12

Use data from the table for problems 24–25.

24. Which game had the least number of players?

25. Write the number of players who played Tag in expanded form.

Chapter Test

Write the number in expanded form.

1. 434
2. 301
3. 1,163
4. 7,820

Write the digit in each place named.

5. 751
   (hundreds)
6. 4,784
   (thousands)
7. 3,416
   (tens)
8. 12,580
   (ten thousands)

Compare. Write >, <, or =.

9. 3,567 ● 3,740
10. 832 ● 823
11. 259 ● 259

Order from greatest to least.

12. $178, $411, $218
13. 402, 98, 410
14. 8,674; 8,701; 8,107
15. 7,712; 6,699; 7,800

Round to the nearest hundred.

16. 222
17. 855
18. 3,458

Round to the nearest thousand.

19. 7,809
20. 12,671

Use data from the table to solve problems 21–25.

21. List the games in order from the most to the least number sold.

22. List the games in order from most expensive to least expensive.

23. Which bills and coins would you use to pay for a game of Chess?

24. If you paid for a game of Mancala with a ten-dollar bill, how much change should you get back?

25. If 100 more games of Mancala are sold in June than in May, how many are sold in June?

Game Warehouse Inventory May 1 – May 31		
Game	Price	Number Sold
Mancala	$3.77	187
Checkers	$7.99	92
Chess	$5.49	103
Battleship	$8.05	211

Performance Assessment

You are designing a game for your class. Here are the facts you need to make and play the game.

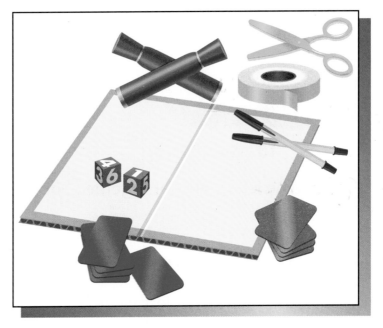

- The game board uses small squares numbered from 1 to 100.

- There are two sets of game cards numbered by 2s from 2 to 20. Each card has one number. One set is red. The other set is green.

- There are two sets of game cards numbered by 5s from 5 to 25. Each card has one number. One set is red. The other set is green.

- You can also use a number cube and some small objects for playing pieces.

Include in your game rules

- counting by 2s, 5s, and 10s.
- forward and backward moves.
- ways to win.
- comparing final scores.
- rounding numbers.

Journal

A Good Answer

- has clear rules for the game.
- shows a game board that is correctly numbered.
- uses counting by 2s, 5s, and 10s.

Portfolio

You may want to save this work in your portfolio.

Enrichment
Roman Numerals

In ancient Rome people used letters to name numbers.

I   5   10   50 100

When the same letters appear together, add to find the number.

II

Think: 1 + 1 = 2

XX

Think: 10 + 10 = 20

III

Think: 1 + 1 + 1 = 3

When a letter (or letters) of less value is to the right of a letter of greater value, add.

VI

Think: 5 + 1 = 6

XII

Think: 10 + 1 + 1 = 12

LXI

Think: 50 + 10 + 1 = 61

When a letter of less value is to the left of a letter of greater value, subtract.

IV

Think: 5 − 1 = 4

IX

Think: 10 − 1 = 9

XL

Think: 50 − 10 = 40

Write the number.

1. VII
2. XXIV
3. LVI
4. XLI
5. XIX
6. LXIII
7. LII
8. LXXIV

Write the Roman numeral.

9. 4
10. 36
11. 53
12. 59
13. 90
14. 73
15. 64
16. 81

17. Write and solve an addition problem using Roman numerals.

18. How is place value in our system similar to using Roman numerals?

Test-Taking Tips

Sometimes you have answers to choose from when you take a test. It helps to eliminate the answers that you know right away are not correct. This is called the **process of elimination.**

Cara has 100 beads on her necklace. Every tenth bead is blue. What number bead is the sixth blue bead?

A. 20   **C.** 60

B. 45   **D.** 62

You know that the answer has to be a ten.

You can eliminate choices B and D.

Now you have only two choices, A and C.

This gives you a better chance of choosing the correct answer, C.

Check for Success

Before turning in a test, go back one last time to check.

☑ I understood and answered the questions asked.

☑ I checked my work for errors.

☑ My answers make sense.

Read each problem. Eliminate any answer choices you know are wrong. Choose the letter of the correct answer.

1. 88 is less than ▮.

   A. 42   **C.** 82

   B. 55   **D.** 98

2. Which is 100 more than 5,421?

   F. 6,421   **H.** 5,431

   G. 5,521   **J.** 5,321

3. 487 rounded to the nearest ten is ▮.

   A. 400   **C.** 490

   B. 450   **D.** 500

4. Which is not less than 4,127?

   F. 105   **H.** 2,063

   G. 697   **J.** 5,111

5. What number is missing?

   15, 20, 25, 30, ▮, 40

   A. 10   **C.** 45

   B. 35   **D.** 62

6. $892 rounded to the nearest hundred dollars is ▮.

   F. $1,000   **H.** $900

   G. $982   **J.** $800

Test Prep

Spiral Review and Test Prep
Chapter 1

Choose the correct answer.

Number Sense

1. Which is the greatest number?
- **A.** 8 tens
- **C.** 9 tens
- **B.** 8 hundreds
- **D.** 9 hundreds

2. Players can score 12 points in the first round and 12 points in the second round. How many points can players score in the game altogether?
- **F.** 12 points
- **H.** 24 points
- **G.** 20 points
- **J.** 28 points

3. Which shows 3 dimes and 4 pennies?
- **A.** $0.34
- **C.** $0.07
- **B.** $0.19
- **D.** Not Here

4. The player with the most points is the winner. Which player came in second place?

Arthur 136

Chun   156

Brooke 132

Devon 158

Explain how you found your answer.

Algebra and Functions

5. Skip-count to complete the pattern.
35, 40, 45, ▮, 55, 60
- **A.** 65
- **C.** 48
- **B.** 50
- **D.** 30

6. Game cards follow this pattern: 10, 20, 30, 40, and so on. Which of the following cards could be part of the game?

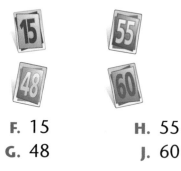

- **F.** 15
- **H.** 55
- **G.** 48
- **J.** 60

7. What is the rule for this table?

Input	1	3	5	7
Output	8	10	12	14

- **A.** Add 6
- **C.** Add 7
- **B.** Subtract 6
- **D.** Subtract 7

8. What does this number line show?

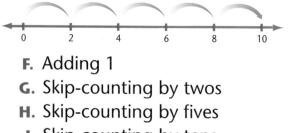

- **F.** Adding 1
- **G.** Skip-counting by twos
- **H.** Skip-counting by fives
- **J.** Skip-counting by tens

Measurement and Geometry

9. Which item weighs less than 1 pound?

A.

C.

B.

D.

10. Which is true about this figure?

F. It is a square.
G. It is a trapezoid.
H. It has 3 sides.
J. It has 4 sides.

11. Jenna is playing a game with her brother. Which game piece is shaped like a rectangle?

A.

C.

B.

D.

12. What time is shown on this clock?

F. 12:00
G. 12:30
H. 1:30
J. Not Here

Statistics, Data Analysis, and Probability

Use data from the table for problems 13–16.

Points Scored in Kickball	
Class	Number of Points
Room A	9
Room B	5
Room C	4
Room D	7

13. Which class scored the least number of points?

A. Room A
B. Room B
C. Room C
D. Room D

14. How many more points did Room A score than Room B?

F. 5 points
G. 3 points
H. 6 points
J. 4 points

15. How many points did Rooms A and B score altogether?

A. 12 points
B. 14 points
C. 16 points
D. 13 points

16. Which shows the room numbers in order from least to greatest number of points?

F. A, B, C, D
G. A, D, B, C
H. C, B, D, A
J. B, C, D, A

Theme: Creature Features

Use the Data

Some Endangered Species in the United States

Group	Number of Species
Reptiles	14
Amphibians	7
Snails	15
Arachnids	5

Source: World Almanac and Book of Facts.

- How many endangered species are listed in all? How can you use addition to find the answer?

What You Will Learn
In this chapter you will learn how to
- add using mental math strategies.
- use the properties of addition.
- find the sum of whole numbers.
- estimate sums, including money amounts.
- use strategies to solve problems.

Additional activities at
www.mhschool.com/math

Objective: Use properties and strategies to add.

 2·1 # Addition Properties

Algebra & functions

Learn

Math Words

addend a number to be added

sum the answer in addition

Commutative Property when adding, the order of the numbers can change but the sum is the same

Identity Property when one of the two addends is zero, the sum is the same as the other addend

What is your favorite animal at the zoo? At the San Diego Zoo in California, 15 monkeys were doing tricks. Then the 2 monkeys shown in the picture joined them. How many monkeys were doing tricks in all?

Example 1

Find 15 + 2 to solve the problem.

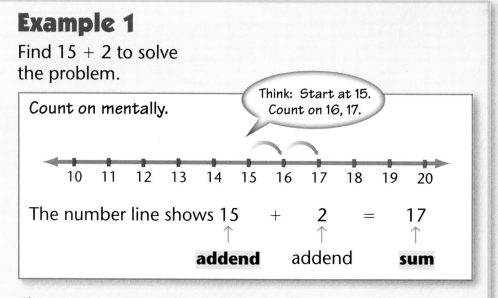

Count on mentally.

Think: Start at 15. Count on 16, 17.

10 11 12 13 14 15 16 17 18 19 20

The number line shows 15 + 2 = 17

addend   addend   sum

There were 17 monkeys doing tricks.

One monkey ate 7 bananas and another monkey ate 8 bananas. How many bananas did they eat in all?

Example 2

Find 7 + 8 to solve the problem.

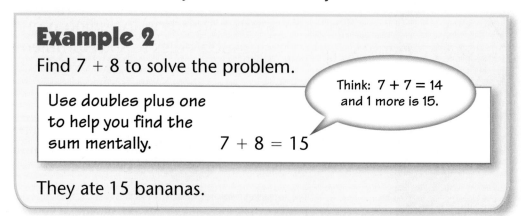

Use doubles plus one to help you find the sum mentally.

Think: 7 + 7 = 14 and 1 more is 15.

$7 + 8 = 15$

They ate 15 bananas.

What if 3 monkeys are doing tricks and 5 more monkeys join them to do tricks. No more monkeys come. How many monkeys are doing tricks?

More Examples

These addition properties can help you add mentally.

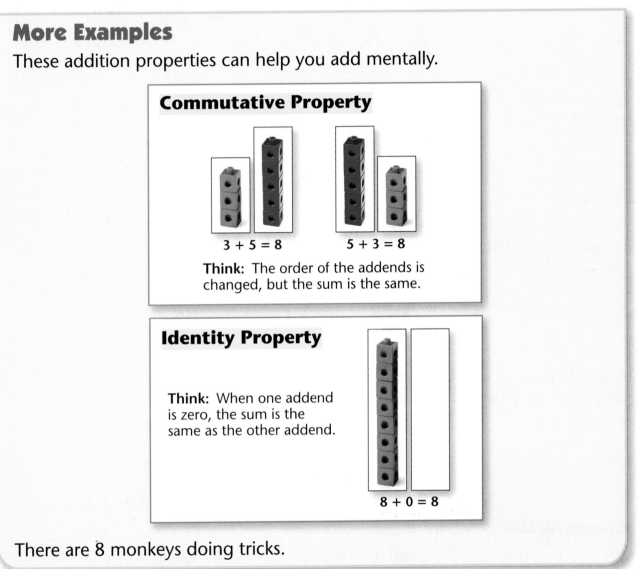

Commutative Property

3 + 5 = 8   5 + 3 = 8

Think: The order of the addends is changed, but the sum is the same.

Identity Property

Think: When one addend is zero, the sum is the same as the other addend.

8 + 0 = 8

There are 8 monkeys doing tricks.

Try It   **Add. Use mental math.**

1. 7 + 2   2. 5 + 0   3. 6 + 5   4. 0 + 9

5. 8 + 7   6. 4 + 13   7. 5 + 1   8. 0 + 3

9.   14   10.   18   11.   6   12.   34
   + 5   + 2   +7   + 6

Sum it Up!   Explain how you added in problems 1–3 above.

Add. Use mental math.

13. 7 + 4   **14.** 9 + 4   **15.** 8 + 5   **16.** 6 + 0   **17.** 14 + 8

18. 6 + 9   **19.** 23 + 7   **20.** 9 + 9   **21.** 8 + 7   **22.** 0 + 2

23.   4   **24.**   8   **25.**   8   **26.**   6   **27.**   7
$\quad\underline{+22}$ $\quad\underline{+1}$ $\quad\underline{+8}$ $\quad\underline{+14}$ $\quad\underline{+0}$

28.   7   **29.**   9   **30.**   6   **31.**   8   **32.**   9
$\quad\underline{+7}$ $\quad\underline{+7}$ $\quad\underline{+6}$ $\quad\underline{+0}$ $\quad\underline{+6}$

Find each missing number.
Name the addition property you used.

> You can use a letter to stand for a missing number.

33. $9 + 1 = 1 + t$ **34.** $4 + s = 4$ **35.** $5 + 6 = a + 5$

36. $c + 4 = 4 + 3$ **37.** $2 + g = 5 + 2$ ★**38.** $0 + n = 25$

Add. Then use the Commutative Property
to write a different addition sentence.

39. 3 + 2   **40.** 2 + 0   **41.** 6 + 7   **42.** 0 + 4

43. 7 + 4   **44.** 11 + 0   **45.** 6 + 9   **46.** 0 + 1

Compare. Use >, <, or = .

47. 7 + 0 ● 0 + 6   **48.** 5 + 6 ● 4 + 5   **49.** 8 + 4 ● 4 + 8

50.

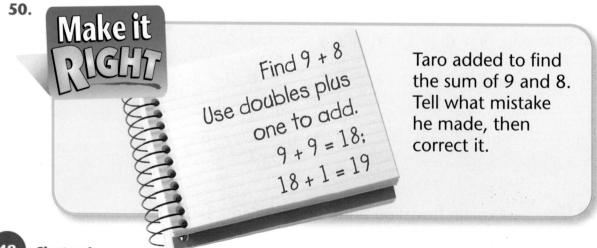

Make it RIGHT

Find 9 + 8
Use doubles plus one to add.
9 + 9 = 18;
18 + 1 = 19

Taro added to find the sum of 9 and 8. Tell what mistake he made, then correct it.

Problem Solving

Use data from the table for problems 51–52.

51. How many visitors did the Tampa Bay Zoo and the Lincoln Park Zoo have altogether?

52. What if The New York Aquarium has as many visitors as National Zoological Park and Living Seas Aquarium together? How many visitors did the New York Aquarium have?

Zoo and Aquarium Visits

Place	Number of Visitors
Tampa Bay Zoo	4 million
Lincoln Park Zoo	3 million
National Zoological Park	3 million
Living Seas Aquarium	6 million

Source: Top Ten of Everything

53. Career: Pat walks dogs as part of his pet-sitting business. On Monday he walks 5 dogs. On Tuesday he walks 2 more dogs than on Monday. How many dogs does he walk altogether on both days?

54. Logical Reasoning: Name this 2-digit number: The sum of the digits is 8, and the difference is 4. The ones digit is greater than the tens digit.

55. Create a problem about addition using the table. Solve it. Ask others to solve it.

Journal

56. Analyze: How could you use the Commutative Property to find $3 + 8$?

57. Mental Math: There were 6 bears inside the cave and 7 more outside. How many bears were there in all? Explain how you added.

Spiral Review and Test Prep

Round to the nearest hundred.

58. 549 **59.** 791 **60.** 1,297 **61.** 3,333 **62.** 23,764

Choose the correct answer.

63. What is the missing number?

$n + 6 = 13$ $6 + n = 13$

A. 19   **C.** 7

B. 8   **D.** 3

64. Which is the same as 12?

F. $7 + 7$ **H.** $8 + 3$

G. $6 + 7$ **J.** $5 + 7$

Objective: *To review adding three or more numbers and define and use the Associative Property.*

Add 3 or More Numbers

Algebra
& functions

Learn

Math Word

Associative Property When adding, the grouping of numbers can change but the sum is the same.

$(5 + 5) + 6$
$10 + 6 = 16$

$5 + (5 + 6)$
$5 + 11 = 16$

May helps take care of the animals in her classroom's Animal Corner. There are 2 turtles, 7 fish, and the 3 birds shown in the picture. How many animals are there altogether?

Example

Find: $2 + 7 + 3$

You can use the Commutative Property and the **Associative Property** to make addition easier. Use the Associative Property to add two numbers at a time.

$3 + 7 + 2 =$ ← Use the Commutative Property to change the order.

$(3 + 7) + 2 =$ ← Group the numbers. You can use parentheses to show how you grouped them.

$10 + 2 = 12$ ← Make a 10. Add mentally.

There are 12 animals altogether.

Try It
Add. Show how you used the Associative Property.

1. $6 + 3 + 5$ **2.** $4 + 1 + 7$ **3.** $2 + 5 + 3$ **4.** $4 + 0 + 6$

Sum It Up

How can you use the Commutative Property and the Associative Property to add $6 + 8 + 4$ mentally?

Add. Show how you used the Associative Property.

5. $1 + 6 + 7$ **6.** $3 + 6 + 0$ **7.** $8 + 4 + 2$ **8.** $2 + 9 + 4$

Use the Commutative Property and the Associative Property to add mentally. Explain what you did.

9. $3 + 5 + 3$ **10.** $8 + 5 + 2$ **11.** $4 + 3 + 6$ **12.** $5 + 7 + 5$

13. $6 + 2 + 4 + 1$ **14.** $1 + 7 + 1 + 3$ **15.** $2 + 6 + 8 + 0$ **16.** $1 + 2 + 9 + 2$

17. $4 + 6 + 7 + 1$ **18.** $1 + 8 + 2 + 2$ **19.** $7 + 6 + 3 + 4$ **20.** $2 + 8 + 3 + 1$

Find each missing number.

21. $(3 + 4) + 7 = d + (4 + 7)$ **22.** $7 + r + 9 = 16$

★23. $m + 6 + 2 = 6 + 10$ **★24.** $(5 + 4) + (2 + 6) = 10 + p$

Problem Solving

25. In another classroom the Animal Corner has 4 fish, 3 turtles, 6 mice, and 2 parakeets. How many animals are there altogether?

26. Science: Tina read that some whales migrate 2,775 miles from cold Alaskan waters to the warmer oceans near Hawaii. Write the distance they travel in expanded form.

27. Analyze: Which property can you use to find the missing number? Explain how.

$4 + 7 + 8 = 7 + 4 + \blacksquare$

Spiral Review and Test Prep

Compare. Write $>$, $<$, or $=$.

28. $57 \bullet 34$ **29.** $103 \bullet 301$ **30.** $284 \bullet 289$ **31.** $4,910 \bullet 4,091$

Choose the correct answer.

32. Which number rounds to 500?

   A. 431   **C.** 566

   B. 495   **D.** 585

33. What is the value of the 9 in 2,936?

   F. 9,000   **H.** 900

   G. 90   **J.** Not Here

2·3 **Addition Patterns**

Algebra
& functions

Learn

Math Word

pattern a series of numbers or figures that follows a rule

Marisa learned that ants are social insects. They live in communities or groups. She estimates there are 800 ants in one colony and 500 in another colony. How many ants are in both colonies?

Example 1

Find: 800 + 500

> You can use facts and **patterns** to find sums mentally.
>
> | | |
> |---|---|
> | 8 + 5 = 13 | **Think:** 8 ones + 5 ones = 13 ones |
> | 80 + 50 = 130 | 8 tens + 5 tens = 13 tens |
> | 800 + 500 = 1,300 | 8 hundreds + 5 hundreds = 13 hundreds |

There are 1,300 ants in both colonies.

Try It **Write the number that makes each sentence true.**

1.   4 + 5 = a   **2.**   r + 4 = 11   **3.**   3 + n = 8
   40 + 50 = b   s + 40 = 110   30 + p = 80
  400 + 500 = c   t + 400 = 1,100   300 + q = 800

 Show how you use facts and patterns to find 500 + 400 mentally.

Write the number that makes each sentence true.

4.
$3 + 6 = z$
$30 + 60 = t$
$300 + 600 = s$

5.
$b + 7 = 15$
$p + 70 = 150$
$g + 700 = 1,500$

6.
$4 + s = 8$
$40 + h = 80$
$400 + a = 800$

Add. Use mental math.

7. $200 + 800$ **8.** $200 + 900$ **9.** $700 + 600$ **10.** $800 + 800$

11. $4,000 + 1,000$ **12.** $3,000 + 4,000$ **13.** $500 + 60 + 20$ **14.** $300 + 70 + 30$

Find the missing digit.

★**15.** $6\blacksquare + 34 = 94$ ★**16.** $30 + \blacksquare1 = 121$ ★**17.** $\blacksquare30 + 700 = 1,430$

Problem Solving

Use data from the bar graph for problems 18–20.

18. Mental Math: Which two animals got 1,400 votes altogether?

19. Which animal got the most votes? How do you know?

20. Did dogs and cats together get more or less votes than horses and cows together?

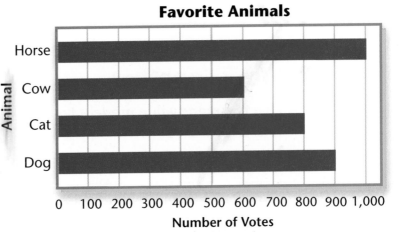

Favorite Animals

21. Analyze: How would you add $300 + 72$ mentally?

22. Beth had 105 dog stickers and 50 cat stickers. How many items did she have altogether?

Spiral Review and Test Prep

23. $8 + 4$ **24.** $3 + 6$ **25.** $9 + 7$ **26.** $6 + 9$ **27.** $2 + 5$

Choose the correct answer.

28. Laura buys a toy for her pet parakeet. She pays with a one-dollar bill and gets back a quarter and a dime for change. How much did the toy cost?

A. $0.35   **C.** $0.70

B. $0.65   **D.** $1.00

29. What is the value of the underlined digit in 5<u>4</u>,048?

F. 4 ten thousands

G. 4 thousands

H. 4 hundreds

J. 4 tens

Objective: Use place value models to review adding numbers with regrouping.

2•4
Explore Regrouping in Addition

Learn

Math Word

regroup to name a number in a different way

You can use place value models to explore regrouping in addition.

What is 278 + 549?

Work Together

► Use the place value models to find 278 + 549.

You Will Need
- **place value models**

- Show 278 using 2 hundreds, 7 tens, and 8 ones.

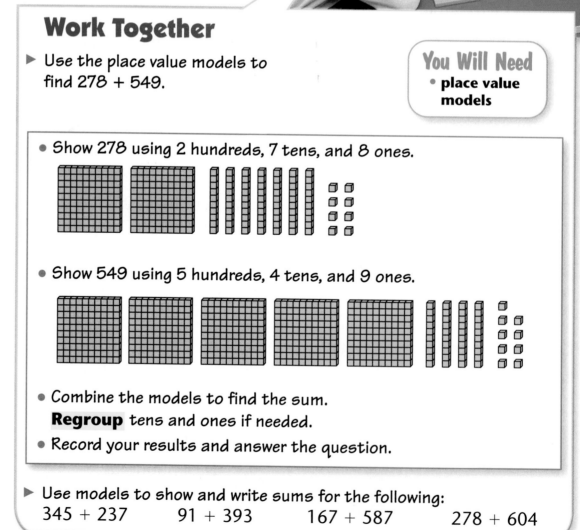

- Show 549 using 5 hundreds, 4 tens, and 9 ones.

- Combine the models to find the sum.
  Regroup tens and ones if needed.
- Record your results and answer the question.

► Use models to show and write sums for the following:

| 345 + 237 | 91 + 393 | 167 + 587 | 278 + 604 |

54 Cluster A

Make Connections

Here is how you can add numbers with regrouping.

Find: 354 + 237

Using Models	Using Paper and Pencil

1 Show 354 and 237.

Write the problem in vertical form:

$$354$$
$$+237$$

Add the ones.
Think: 4 + 7 = 11

2 Regroup 11 ones as 1 ten and 1 one.

Regroup 11 ones as 1 ten and 1 one.

$$\overset{1}{3}54$$
$$+237$$
$$\overline{1}$$

3 Combine the tens. Combine the hundreds.

Add the tens. Add the hundreds.

$$\overset{1}{3}54$$
$$+237$$
$$\overline{591}$$

Try It **Find each sum. You may use models.**

1. 61 + 13   2. 74 + 17   3. 217 + 36   4. 436 + 93

Sum it Up When do you need to regroup ones? tens?

Practice **Find each sum. You may use models.**

5. 725 + 135   6. 303 + 189   7. 89 + 89   8. 98 + 55

9. **Compare:** How is regrouping ones the same as regrouping tens? How is it different?

2·5 Add Whole Numbers

Learn

Alligators can be dangerous when protecting their nests. In Central Florida, 278 American alligator nests were counted. In South Florida, 456 American alligator nests were counted. How many were counted in all?

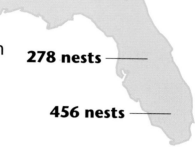

278 nests ———

456 nests ———

Example 1

Find 456 + 278 to solve this problem.

1 Add the ones. Regroup if necessary.

$$\begin{array}{r} \overset{1}{}456 \\ +278 \\ \hline 4 \end{array}$$

Think: 14 ones = 1 ten 4 ones

2 Add all the tens. Regroup if necessary.

$$\begin{array}{r} \overset{11}{}456 \\ +278 \\ \hline 34 \end{array}$$

Think: 13 tens = 1 hundred 3 tens

3 Add the hundreds.

$$\begin{array}{r} \overset{11}{}456 \\ +278 \\ \hline 734 \end{array}$$

Think: 13 ones = 1 ten 3 ones

So 734 nests were counted.

A nature photographer spent $978 on new equipment to photograph alligators. He spent $94 on film. How much did he spend in all?

Example 2

Find $978 + $94 to solve the problem.

1

Add the ones.
Regroup if necessary.

$$\begin{array}{r} {\scriptstyle 1} \\ \$97\overset{}{8} \\ +\ \ 94 \\ \hline 2 \end{array}$$

Think:
12 ones = 1 ten
2 ones

2

Add all the tens.
Regroup if necessary.

$$\begin{array}{r} {\scriptstyle 1\ 1} \\ \$978 \\ +\ \ 94 \\ \hline 72 \end{array}$$

Think:
17 tens = 1 hundred
7 tens

3

Add all the hundreds.
Regroup if necessary.

$$\begin{array}{r} {\scriptstyle 1\ 1} \\ \$978 \\ +\ \ 94 \\ \hline \$1,072 \end{array}$$

The nature photographer spent $1,072 in all.

More Examples

A

$$\begin{array}{r} {\scriptstyle 1\ 1} \\ 968 \\ +\ \ 98 \\ \hline 1,066 \end{array}$$

B

$$\begin{array}{r} \$2.12 \\ +\ \ 5.78 \\ \hline \$7.90 \end{array}$$

You can add money as you would whole numbers. Do not forget to write the dollar sign and the decimal point.

Try It   **Find each sum.**

1. $\begin{array}{r} 689 \\ +\ 49 \\ \hline \end{array}$

2. $\begin{array}{r} 857 \\ +603 \\ \hline \end{array}$

3. $\begin{array}{r} 905 \\ +812 \\ \hline \end{array}$

4. $\begin{array}{r} \$8.74 \\ +\ 7.29 \\ \hline \end{array}$

5. $\begin{array}{r} \$9.83 \\ +\ 9.76 \\ \hline \end{array}$

6. $\begin{array}{r} 44 \\ +26 \\ \hline \end{array}$

7. $\begin{array}{r} 23 \\ +74 \\ \hline \end{array}$

8. $\begin{array}{r} \$6.50 \\ +\ 2.75 \\ \hline \end{array}$

9. $\begin{array}{r} \$3.92 \\ +\ 3.92 \\ \hline \end{array}$

10. $\begin{array}{r} 404 \\ +782 \\ \hline \end{array}$

11. $\begin{array}{r} 154 \\ +\ 62 \\ \hline \end{array}$

12. $\begin{array}{r} \$5.47 \\ +0.76 \\ \hline \end{array}$

13. $\begin{array}{r} 86 \\ +599 \\ \hline \end{array}$

14. $\begin{array}{r} 65 \\ +454 \\ \hline \end{array}$

15. $\begin{array}{r} \$3.21 \\ +\ 4.67 \\ \hline \end{array}$

Sum it Up!   Explain the steps you would use to add 365 + 208.

Find each sum.

16. $512
    + 309

17. 472
    +803

18. 905
    +398

19. $9.76
    + 5.40

20. 485
    + 80

21. 167
    +708

22. $156
    + 999

23. $8.87
    + 2.05

24. 320
    +675

25. $7.79
    + 1.01

26. 147
    + 88

27. 915
    +207

28. 236
    + 19

29. $5.02
    + 4.39

30. 608
    + 94

31. $8.09
    + 0.71

32. $76.40 + $34.27
33. 789 + 657
34. 870 + 456
35. 456 + 654
36. $141 + $299
37. 186 + 876
38. $6.10 + $3.61
39. $147 + $508

Algebra & functions Find each missing digit.

40. 456
    +65■
    ─────
    1,110

41. ■27
    +670
    ─────
    1,197

42. 7■2
    +594
    ─────
    1,376

43. 5■8
    +■4■
    ─────
    1,187

44. **Make it RIGHT**

   1
   936
   +599
   ─────
   1,525

Look at Hal's work to the left. What was his mistake? Show how to correct it.

Problem Solving

45. **Career:** Anna works as a tour guide at the zoo for the summer. In July she earned $547. In August she earned $568. How much did she earn in all?

★ 46. **Measurement:** A one-year-old American alligator weighs about 4 pounds. A two-year-old American alligator can weigh between 9 and 12 pounds. What is the most weight an American alligator can gain in one year?

Use data from the table for problems 47–48.

47. The Photo Store keeps a record of all items it sells. How many camera cases altogether do they have available for sale?

48. **Create a problem** that must be solved by using addition with the information from the table. Solve your problem, then trade problems with another student.

Photo Store Inventory

Item	Number Available
Waterproof camera cases	357
35-millimeter cameras	589
Boxes of 24-exposure film	702
Canvas camera cases	803

49. The Photo Store sells about 150 tripods each week. They have 92 four-foot tripods and 71 five-foot tripods in stock. Do they have enough for one week? How do you know?

★ 50. **Number Sense:** Sue estimates she has about 300 cat toys left to sell. To get this estimate she rounded the exact number to the nearest hundred. What are the possible exact numbers?

Journal 51. **Explain** how to use mental math to add $504 + 403$.

52. Jon bought frames that cost $2.78 and $3.65. What is the total cost?

Spiral Review and Test Prep

53. $12 + 9$ 54. $24 + 11$ 55. $35 + 14$ 56. $53 + 47$

Find each missing number. Tell what property you used.

57. $m + 0 = 5$ 58. $2 + (3 + 4) = 2 + (4 + s)$ 59. $(5 + 6) + r = 5 + (p + 7)$

Choose the correct answer.

60. Which problem has a sum of about 500?
    A. $297 + 352$ C. $520 + 189$
    B. $387 + 264$ D. $198 + 267$

61. What is the order from least to greatest of 564, 463, 465?
    F. 564, 463, 465   H. 465, 564, 463
    G. 463, 465, 564   J. 463, 564, 465

62. What is 6,463 rounded to the nearest ten?
    A. 6,460   C. 6,500
    B. 6,400   D. 6,000

63. Quentin has $10 to spend on his garden. He buys 2 new bushes at $4 each. How much will be left?
    F. $8   H. $4
    G. $6   J. $2

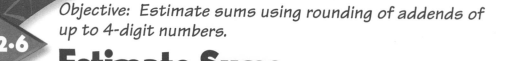

2·6

Estimate Sums

Learn

Math Word

estimate to find an answer that is close to the exact answer

Veterinarians care for animals. If veterinarians at an animal clinic see 349 animals in one week and 364 animals another week, about how many animals will they see altogether in 2 weeks?

Lauren Davidson is a veterinarian.

Example

Sometimes an exact sum is not needed. You can **estimate** to solve this problem.

Estimate: 349 + 364

So 349 + 364 is about 700.

Think: 349 + 364
↓   ↓
300 + 400 = 700

Round to the nearest hundred.

The veterinarians will see about 700 animals.

More Examples

A
89 + 902
90 + 900 = 990

Think: Round each addend to the nearest ten.

B
1,543 + 2,087
2,000 + 2,000 = 4,000

Think: Round each addend to the nearest thousand.

Try It **Estimate each sum. Tell how you rounded.**

1. 46 + 38   **2.** 220 + 370   **3.** 1,345 + 507

How can you estimate 278 + 79 two different ways?

Estimate each sum.

| 4. 1,432
 +6,573 | 5. 5,385
 +3,710 | 6. 6,321
 + 515 | 7. 387
 166
 +295 | 8. 1,064
 2,890
 + 901 |

9. 13 + 72   10. 417 + 523   11. 345 + 710   12. 781 + 15   13. 813 + 942

★14. 23,034 + 12,987   ★15. 31,256 + 57,009   ★16. 87,231 + 10,123

Algebra & functions **Estimate. Write > or < to make true sentences. Explain your reasoning.**

17. 48 + 17 ● 70   18. 376 + 497 ● 800   19. 613 + 821 ● 1,500

Pick pairs of numbers from the box.

★20. With a sum > 1,200.   ★21. With a sum < 800.

| 119 | 432 | 680 |
| 75 | 744 | 838 |

Problem Solving
Use data from *Did You Know?* for problem 22.

22. If a cheetah could keep up that speed, about how many kilometers would it travel in 2 hours? Explain how you estimated your answer.

23. **Analyze:** Sam says that 108 + 55 is about 170. Would 200 also be a reasonable estimate? Explain.

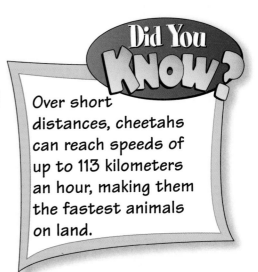

Did You KNOW?

Over short distances, cheetahs can reach speeds of up to 113 kilometers an hour, making them the fastest animals on land.

Spiral Review and Test Prep

Describe and complete the skip-counting pattern.

24. 70, ▮, 80, ▮, 90, ▮, 100   25. 11, ▮, 15, 17, 19, ▮, ▮

Choose the correct answer.

26. Which shape is not a rectangle?

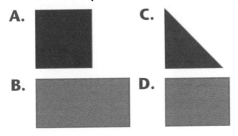

A.   C.

B.   D.

27. There are 9 goldfish and 4 guppies in a fish tank. Which number sentence shows how many fish in all?

   F. 9 + 4 = 13   H. 13 + 4 = 17

   G. 13 + 9 = 22   J. 4 + 9 = 12

2·7

Objective: Form conclusions about whether to estimate or find an exact answer.

Problem Solving: Reading for Math
Estimate or Exact Answer

About 500 Animals Saved

Read ▶ There are 212 dogs at the animal shelter. There are also 199 cats and 98 rabbits. About how many animals are in the shelter? Is the headline reasonable?

READING SKILL ▶ **Form a Conclusion**

You form a conclusion when you make a decision. The decision is based on past experience and the information given.

- **What do you know?** The exact number of animals; the headline says 500 animals

- **What do you need to find?** How the actual number compares to the headline

MATH SKILL ▶ **Estimate or Exact Answer**

Sometimes you need an exact answer. Sometimes an estimate is enough.

Plan ▶ Decide if you need to estimate or find an exact sum.

Solve ▶ The headline reads "about 500." This is not an exact number. You can estimate to see if it is reasonable.
212 rounds to 200. 198 rounds to 200. 98 rounds to 100.

Add: $200 + 200 + 100 = 500$

There are about 500 animals. The headline is reasonable.

Look Back ▶ • Is your answer reasonable? Why or why not?

Sum it Up Rewrite the problem above so an exact answer is needed. Explain why it is needed.

Practice

Solve. Explain why you gave an estimated or exact answer.

1. Last month 262 puppies were brought to the shelter. The same month, the shelter received 179 cats. Altogether, how many puppies and cats were brought to the shelter last month?

2. In May the shelter took in 19 cats. In June the shelter took in 22 cats. In July only 9 cats came to the shelter. Did the shelter take in more than 40 cats during May, June, and July?

Use data from the table for problems 3–8.

3. Green Willow Farm is next to the animal shelter. Many animals live there, too. How many horses and cows are at Green Willow Farm?

Animals at Green Willow Farm

Animal	Number of Animals
Chicken	203
Cow	62
Duck	231
Horse	89
Pig	208
Sheep	197

4. Risha feeds the chickens and ducks each day. Does he feed more than 400 of them a day?

5. How many horses, cows, and sheep live at the farm?

6. Seth will visit Green Willow Farm tomorrow. Will he see more than 400 pigs and ducks?

7. About how many animals at the farm have 4 legs?

8. About how many animals are at Green Willow Farm?

Spiral Review and Test Prep

Choose the correct answer.

On Monday morning there were 24 birds in the shelter. During the week 18 more birds were rescued. Are there more than 30 birds in the shelter now?

9. Which statement is true?
   A. There are 30 birds in the shelter now.
   B. Ten more birds were rescued.
   C. There were 24 birds on Monday.

10. Which number sentence will help you solve the problem?
   F. $30 - 24 = 6$
   G. $24 + 18 > 30$
   H. $30 - 18 > 6$

Add. (pages 46–49)

1. $19 + 9$ **2.** $8 + 7$ **3.** $0 + 6$ **4.** $14 + 6$ **5.** $15 + 6$

Add. Tell which properties you used to make it easier.
(pages 50–51)

6. $9 + 0$ **7.** $3 + 5 + 7$ **8.** $5 + 0 + 2$

9. $1 + 8 + 7 + 2$ **10.** $3 + 5 + 2 + 6$

Write the number that makes each sentence true. (pages 52–53)

11. $6 + 2 = a$ **12.** $4 + r = 13$ **13.** $5 + k = 12$
$60 + 20 = d$ $s + 90 = z$ $50 + m = w$
$600 + 200 = g$ $p + q = 1{,}300$ $q + c = b$

Add. (pages 56–59)

14. $924 + 253$ **15.** $\$25 + \$758$ **16.** $412 + 591$ **17.** $645 + 291$

Estimate each sum. (pages 60–61)

18. $19 + 71$ **19.** $527 + 563$ **20.** $457 + 810$ **21.** $483 + 15 + 42$

Solve. (pages 46–63)

22. Number Sense: Write an addition sentence that has 3 addends with a total that is the same number as $7 + 7$.

23. Social Studies: India has 3 amphibian species listed as "threatened." Japan has 7 more listed than India. How many amphibian species are listed as "threatened" in Japan?

24. Kyle has 6 mollies and 7 guppies in his fish tank. Seth has 3 more fish than Kyle. How many fish does Seth have?

Journal

25. Summarize: When do you use the Commutative Property to help you add? When do you use the Associative Property?

Additional activities at
www.mhschool.com/math

TECHNOLOGY LINK

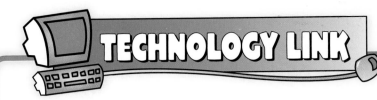

Model Properties of Addition

Ramon has 17 apples in one bag and 5 apples in another bag. Write two different number sentences that show the total number of apples.

You can use counters to stamp out a model of 17 + 5 and 5 + 17.

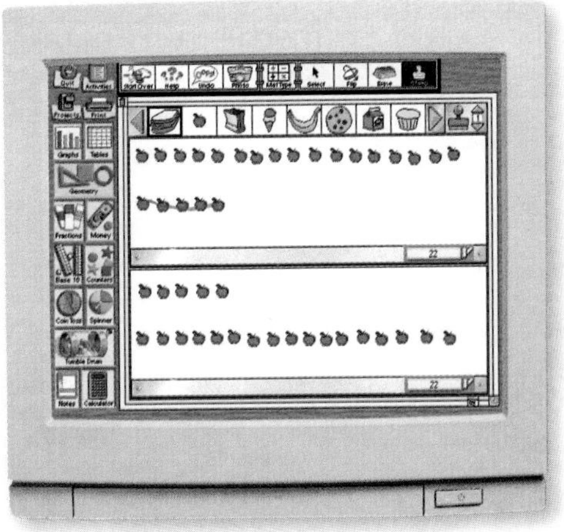

- Use a mat with two sections open.
- In the top section, stamp out 17 apples in the first row.
- Stamp out 5 apples in the second row.
- In the bottom section, stamp out 5 apples in the first row.
- Stamp out 17 apples in the second row.

The number boxes keep count as you stamp.

What pair of addition sentences can you write?

Use the computer to complete each number sentence.

1. 10 + 4 = ■	**2.** 8 + 15 = ■	**3.** 4 + 16 = ■	**4.** 6 + 18 = ■
4 + 10 = ■	15 + 8 = ■	16 + 4 = ■	18 + 6 = ■

Solve.

5. Miguel has 16 marbles in one box and 9 marbles in another. Write two different number sentences that show the total number of marbles.

6. **Analyze:** How does using the model help you decide if the order in which two numbers are added changes the sum?

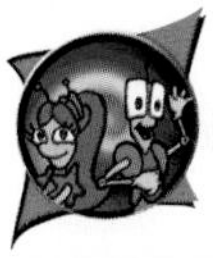

For more practice, use Math Traveler™.

2·8

Add Greater Numbers

6,713 bats

Learn

What kind of animal sleeps upside down? Little brown bats sleep as they cling to the ceilings of caves. There are 6,713 bats in one cave. In another cave nearby there are 5,389 bats. How many bats live in the two caves altogether?

Example

Find 6,713 + 5,389 to solve this problem.

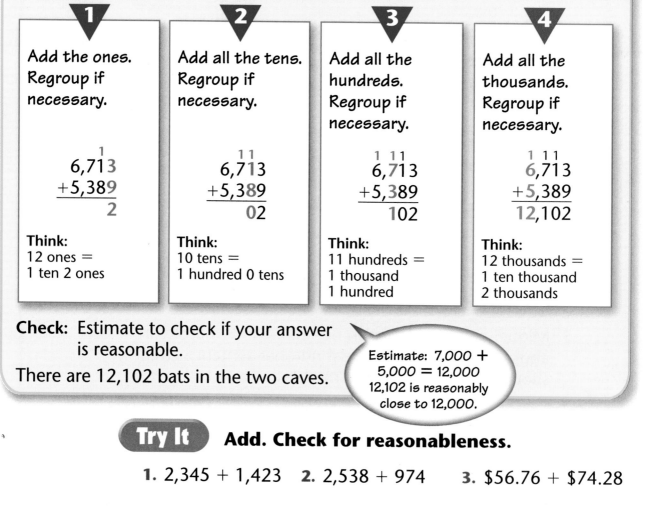

1	**2**	**3**	**4**
Add the ones. Regroup if necessary.	Add all the tens. Regroup if necessary.	Add all the hundreds. Regroup if necessary.	Add all the thousands. Regroup if necessary.
$\begin{array}{r}\overset{1}{6,713}\\ +5,389\\ \hline 2\end{array}$	$\begin{array}{r}\overset{11}{6,713}\\ +5,389\\ \hline 02\end{array}$	$\begin{array}{r}\overset{1\,11}{6,713}\\ +5,389\\ \hline 102\end{array}$	$\begin{array}{r}\overset{1\,11}{6,713}\\ +5,389\\ \hline 12,102\end{array}$
Think: 12 ones = 1 ten 2 ones	**Think:** 10 tens = 1 hundred 0 tens	**Think:** 11 hundreds = 1 thousand 1 hundred	**Think:** 12 thousands = 1 ten thousand 2 thousands

Check: Estimate to check if your answer is reasonable.

There are 12,102 bats in the two caves.

> Estimate: 7,000 + 5,000 = 12,000 12,102 is reasonably close to 12,000.

Try It   Add. Check for reasonableness.

1. 2,345 + 1,423   **2.** 2,538 + 974   **3.** $56.76 + $74.28

Sum it Up Explain how you would find the sum of 1,765 + 2,098.

Add. Check for reasonableness.

4. 3,434
    +2,324

5. 4,567
    +2,837

6. 5,856
    +7,594

7. 3,685
    + 886

8. $65.64
    + 47.73

9. 9,756
    + 574

10. $64.87
    + 8.36

11. 9,475
    +8,869

12. $87.89
    + 15.47

13. 9,758
    + 876

14. 4,251 + 6,729

15. $53.62 + $8.38

★ 16. 9,762 + 5,618

★ 17. 34,364 + 77,612

★ 18. $476.39 + $86.43

★ 19. 245,769 + 84,967

Algebra & functions **Complete. Write > or <.**

20. 5,324 + 6,912 ● 4,798 + 8,145

21. 4,813 + 5,124 ● 3,789 + 5,485

22. 9,352 + 1,942 ● 8,978 + 2,003

23. 6,786 + 987 ● 997 + 7,034

Problem Solving

24. **Music:** One of the top ten songs of 1968 was "I Heard It Through the Grapevine." In what year will this song reach its 50th anniversary?

25. Hank pays $1,198 for some new cameras to photograph bats. He pays $2,976 for a special night lens. How much did he spend?

Journal 26. **Explain** why you want to use estimation to check that your answer is reasonable.

27. **Science:** A bottlenosed dolphin may dive up to 1,476 feet below the ocean's surface. What is that depth to the nearest 10? nearest 1,000?

Spiral Review and Test Prep

Round to the nearest thousand.

28. 5,497   29. 791   30. 1,697   31. 3,333   32. 23,764

Choose the correct answer.

33. What is the missing number?

    $n + 6 = 14$ $6 + n = 14$

    A. 19   C. 7

    B. 8   D. 3

34. Which is another name for 120?

    F. 12 + 10   H. 100 + 2

    G. 10 + 20   J. 100 + 20

2·9 Problem Solving: Strategy
Write a Number Sentence

Read ➤ **Read the problem carefully.**

The table shows how much time certain animals usually spend asleep. A koala sleeps 8 hours more than a hamster. How many hours does a koala spend asleep each day?

Sleepy Animals

Animals	Average Hours Sleeping Each Day
Sloth	20
Opossum	19
Hamster	14
Cat	13

Source: The Top Ten of Everything

- **What do you know?** A koala sleeps 8 hours more than a hamster; a hamster sleeps 14 hours each day.

- **What do you need to find out?** How many hours a koala sleeps

Plan ➤ Since you are finding the total of unequal groups you can add. Write an addition sentence.

Solve ➤ Write a number sentence and solve.

number of hours a hamster sleeps	+ 8 =	number of hours a koala sleeps
14	+ 8 =	22

A koala spends 22 hours asleep each day.

Look Back ➤ Does your answer make sense?

Sum it Up! Tell when you would add to solve a problem.

Use data from the table on page 68 for problem 1. Write a number sentence to solve.

1. Which two animals combined spend 27 hours sleeping?

2. There are 12 baby deer and 48 grown deer eating grass. How many deer are there altogether?

3. There are 26 ducks and 37 swans swimming in a pond. How many birds are in the pond?

4. Max has a box of dog treats. In it there are 6 chicken-flavored, 4 liver-flavored, and 3 beef-flavored. How many treats are there?

Mixed Strategy Review

5. Meg works at an animal shelter. She gave water to 46 dogs and 56 cats. How many animals needed water?

6. Mila saw 7 birds in her backyard and 8 more in her front yard. Then 6 birds landed on the roof of her house. How many birds did she see altogether?

CHOOSE A STRATEGY
- Logical Reasoning
- Draw a Picture
- Make a Graph
- Act It Out
- Make a Table or List
- Find a Pattern
- Guess and Check
- Write a Number Sentence
- Work Backward
- Solve a Simpler Problem

Use data from the survey for problems 7–9.

7. Show one way to organize the results of the survey.

8. How many pets are there in all?

9. List the pets in order from greatest number to least.

SURVEY: What pets do you have?	
Jan	2 dogs
Randy	1 cat
Allan	1 dog
Len	1 goldfish
Phil	5 goldfish
Sara	2 dogs
Anita	3 cats
Yoshi	3 dogs

Collect data for problems 10–12.

10. Ask students in your class what kind of pets they have. How will you organize your results?

11. **Language Arts:** Write a paragraph describing the pets in your class.

12. **Create a problem** that must be solved by writing a number sentence with the data you collected. Solve it. Ask others to solve it.

Problem Solving

Add More Than Two Numbers

2·10

Learn

Whoa! Rory's cattle ranch has 1,887 cows, 165 horses, and 463 calves. How many animals are on the ranch?

Rory has 165 horses on his ranch.

Example

Find: 1,887 + 165 + 463

You can use the Commutative Property and the Associative Property to help you look for tens and doubles.

1

Add the ones. Regroup if necessary.

$$\begin{array}{r} \overset{1}{} \\ 1,88\mathbf{7} \\ 16\mathbf{5} \\ +\ \ 46\mathbf{3} \\ \hline 5 \end{array}$$

Think: Make a ten.
$7 + 5 + 3$
$= 7 + 3 + 5$
$= 10 + 5 = 15$

2

Add all the tens. Regroup if necessary.

$$\begin{array}{r} ^{2\,1} \\ 1,8\mathbf{8}7 \\ 1\mathbf{6}5 \\ +\ \ 4\mathbf{6}3 \\ \hline 15 \end{array}$$

Think: Use doubles.
$6 + 6 = 12$
$12 + 8 = 20$
$20 + 1 = 21$

3

Add all the hundreds. Regroup if necessary.

$$\begin{array}{r} ^{2\,1} \\ 1,\mathbf{8}87 \\ \mathbf{1}65 \\ +\ \ \mathbf{4}63 \\ \hline 515 \end{array}$$

Think:
$8 + 2 = 10$
$1 + 4 = 5$
$10 + 5 = 15$

4

Add all the thousands. Regroup if necessary.

$$\begin{array}{r} ^{1\ 2\,1} \\ \mathbf{1},887 \\ 165 \\ +\ \ 463 \\ \hline 2,515 \end{array}$$

Think:
$1 + 1 = 2$

Check for reasonableness: Estimate: $2,000 + 200 + 500 = 2,700$
2,515 is reasonably close to 2,700.

There are 2,515 animals on the ranch.

 Try It **Add. Check for reasonableness.**

1. $97 + 423 + 89$

2. $5,782 + 348 + 230$

 Does it matter which number you add first in each column? Why or why not?

Add. Check for reasonableness.

3. $6,145
     39
+   462

4.   545
  102
+733

5. $7.04
  2.64
+ 5.39

6. 8,276
  114
+ 892

7.   473
   68
7,272
+ 354

8. $52 + $423 + $4,897

9. $5.97 + $6.73 + $5.89

10. 510 + 630 + 6,865

11. 49 + 9,911 + 97 + 98

Find each missing number so that the sum of all the numbers is 1,030.

★**12.**

255	261
▨	250

★**13.**

▨	256
253	263

★**14.**

252	▨
259	257

Problem Solving

Use data from *Did You Know?* for problem 15.

15. Estimate how much one bull and one cow would weigh together. How did you make your estimate?

16. **Create a problem** adding more than two numbers. Solve it. Ask others to solve it.

17. **Analyze:** Explain how you can check the sum in an addition problem with more than two numbers.

Did You KNOW?

The smallest breed of cattle is the Ovambo. Bulls weigh about 496 pounds and cows weigh about 353 pounds.

Spiral Review and Test Prep

Write each missing number in the counting patterns.

18. 56, 57, ▨, 59

19. 777, 778, ▨, 780

20. 989, ▨, 991, 992

Choose the correct answer.

21. Which is another name for 205?
   A. 20 + 5   C. 200 + 50
   B. 200 + 5   D. 20 + 50

22. Which is the missing number?
25, ▨, 21, 19, 17, 15
   F. 23   H. 18
   G. 20   J. 22

Problem Solving: Application
Decision Making

You Decide!

Which pet should Lisa adopt?

Lisa's dad said she could adopt a pet. Lisa is not sure whether she wants a dog or a cat. She went to the animal shelter to find out more about owning each type of pet.

How to Care for Your New Cat
Food and Water:
- Canned: 1-2 cans each day.......... $0.50 each can
- Treats: as needed........................$2.00 each box
- Always keep water bowl filled

Supplies:
- Cat litter: 5-Lb bag each month...$3.99
- Litterpan:...................................$10 - $25

How to Care for Your New Dog
Food and Water:
- Canned: 2-4 cans each day
  (depending on size of dog)........$1.00 each can
- Treats: as needed......................$2.00 each box
- Always keep water bowl filled

Supplies:
- Leash and collar.........................$9.25

Shots
Cats $30 - $65
Dogs $40 - $75

Animal Shelter Cat
Name: Cally

Breed: calico

Weight: 9 lb   Age: 1 year

Vaccinations: Yes **X**   No___

Date Arrived: Aug. 5

Additional Information: _____
    Loves to play, purrs often

Daily feeding: 1 can

Animal Shelter Dog
Name: Puffy

Breed: terrier mix

Weight: 45 lb   Age: 4 years

Vaccinations: Yes **X**   No___

Date Arrived: Aug. 1

Additional Information: _____
    Loves kids, housebroken

Daily feeding: 2 cans

Read for Understanding

1. How much food will Puffy need each day? How much will Cally need?

2. Which pet weighs less? How much does it weigh?

3. Which pet is older? by how much?

4. About how much does a litter pan and 1 bag of litter cost?

5. How much does it cost a year for shots for each pet?

6. What is the cost of a leash and collar for the dog?

7. What breed of dog is Puffy? What breed of cat is Cally?

8. How much would a box of treats for Cally or Puffy cost?

9. How much would it cost to feed Cally for 2 days if you gave Cally 2 cans a day?

10. How much would it cost to feed Puffy for 2 days?

Make Decisions

11. **What if** Lisa decides to adopt Puffy? How much change would she get from $10 if she buys a collar and leash?

12. How many five-dollar bills would Lisa need if she adopts Cally and buys the most expensive litter pan?

13. If Lisa adopts Cally, how much will it cost to feed Cally for 1 week, including treats?

14. If Lisa adopts Puffy, how much will it cost to feed Puffy for 1 week including treats?

15. What are some advantages and disadvantages of adopting Puffy?

16. What are some advantages and disadvantages of adopting Cally?

17. What other expenses might there be for either pet that aren't listed on the bulletin board?

Which pet should Lisa adopt? Why? Your Decision!

Objective: *Apply adding whole numbers to investigate science concepts.*

Problem Solving: Math and Science
How do you build a tall tower?

What if you were asked to build a tower? It must be very tall without falling over.

In this activity, you will build a tower and decide the best way to make it tall and strong.

You Will Need
- **80 connecting cubes**

Hypothesize

Study the pieces your teacher has given you. Talk with your group and make a plan for building a tall, strong tower.

Procedure

1. Build a tower. (Use a black line master of tower and moat.)

2. The tower must be as tall as possible. Use as many pieces as you can.

3. The tower must fit inside the moat.

4. If your tower falls (it probably will—many times!), count the number of pieces you used.

5. Try again. If the tower falls, count and record the number of pieces you used.

6. Keep trying. Don't stop until you build the tallest possible tower.

Copy and complete the chart to record the number of cubes you use in each tower.

	Cubes		Cubes
Tower 1		Tower 6	
Tower 2		Tower 7	
Tower 3		Tower 8	
Tower 4		Tower 9	
Tower 5		Tower 10	

Problem Solving

Conclude and Apply

- What was the greatest number of pieces you used in a tower?

- Describe the building strategy that worked best for making your tower.

- Thinking about your building strategies, how do you think designers and builders planned the construction of the Sears Tower?

Did You KNOW?

The tallest building in North America is the Sears Tower in Chicago. It stands 1,454 feet high.

Going Further

1. Make a strong bridge. How is your building strategy different? What is the greatest number of pieces you can use in your bridge? Do you need any extra objects to build the bridge?

Estimate each sum. (pages 66–69)

1. 4,124 + 3,245
2. 363 + 636
3. 3,425 + 1,082
4. 7,538 +493

Add. Check for reasonableness. (pages 66–69; 70–71)

5. 125 + 895
6. 310 + 628 + 942 + 864
7. 4,826 + 596
8. 7,538 + 499
9. 521 + 673
10. 30 + 31 + 40 + 14
11. 5,436 + 689
12. $8.95 + $7.05 + $5.98
13. 34 + 509 + 162
14. 4,432 + 567
15. 993 + 231 + 888
16. 1,072 + 97 + 440
17. 6,345 + 567

18.
```
   $787
    84
+  142
```

19.
```
   633
    75
+   92
```

20.
```
   $18.50
    1.05
    10.17
+    0.33
```

21.
```
   2,536
    166
   3,005
+    24
```

Solve. (pages 66–71)

22. There are 945 customers at the pet supply store on Monday, 832 on Tuesday, and 915 on Wednesday. How many customers were in the store during these three days?

23. Ned needs 275 pounds of chicken feed for his farm. Chicken feed comes in 75-pound, 125-pound, and 175-pound sacks. Which sacks should he buy?

24. Matt and Guy want to buy a book about animals. Each boy agrees to chip in $7.75 for the book. What is the most the book could cost?

Journal
25. **Summarize:** How do you decide when to add mentally, estimate a sum, or use paper and pencil to add?

Additional activities at www.mhschool.com/math

Extra Practice

Addition Properties (pages 46–49)

Add. Then use the Commutative Property to write a different addition sentence.

1. $7 + 5$
2. $9 + 7$
3. $8 + 3$
4. $6 + 0$
5. $16 + 4$
6. $6 + 3$
7. $8 + 9$
8. $13 + 6$

Add 3 or More Numbers (pages 50–51)

Use the Commutative Property and the Associative Property to add mentally. Explain what you did.

1. $3 + 8 + 4$
2. $6 + 8 + 4$
3. $9 + 3 + 4 + 1$
4. $7 + 5 + 7 + 2$

Solve.

5. Nan's snake grew 2 inches, then 2 more inches. The snake was 6 inches long when she got it. How long is it now?

6. Paco has 3 turtles, 4 snakes, and 2 lizards. How many animals does he have in all?

Addition Patterns (pages 52–53)

Write the number that makes each sentence true.

1. $5 + 6 = c$
$50 + 60 = g$
$500 + 600 = m$

2. $6 + 8 = p$
$60 + 80 = r$
$600 + 800 = t$

3. $3 + s = 12$
$30 + z = 120$
$300 + n = 1{,}200$

Solve.

4. One zoo has 300 species of birds. Another has 800 different species of birds. How many species are in both zoos together?

5. Paul has taken 60 photos of butterflies and 40 photos of spiders. How many photos has he taken altogether?

Add Whole Numbers (pages 56–59)

Add. Check for reasonableness.

1. $\$324 + \$108$
2. $385 + 611$
3. $\$7.22 + \$5.68$
4. $795 + 462$
5. $\$2.31 + \$2.04$
6. $275 + 718$

Extra Practice

Estimate each sum. Tell how you rounded.

1. 21 + 67
2. 339 + 578
3. 683 + 509
4. 458 + 27
5. 789 + 667
6. 1,567 + 4,356
7. 3,780 + 5,705
8. 8,425 + 378

Solve.

9. Leo the lion weighs 432 pounds and Tigger the tiger weighs 661 pounds. About how much do both weigh together?

10. One baboon at the zoo is 39 inches tall. The gorilla at the zoo is about twice as tall. About how tall is the gorilla?

Problem Solving: Reading for Math
Estimate or Exact Answer (pages 62–63)

Solve.

1. On June 10 a veterinarian saw 4 cats. On the same day the vet saw 9 dogs. How many animals did the veterinarian see on June 10 altogether?

2. In a week the veterinarian saw 21 cats and 35 dogs. About how many animals did the veterinarian see in a week?

3. Mr. Jones has 8 pigs and 13 cows on his farm. How many animals does he have altogether?

4. Mr. Jones also has 19 chickens and 31 sheep. About how many animals does Mr. Jones have?

Add Greater Numbers (pages 66–67)

1. 3,126 +2,324
2. $80.76 + 16.06
3. 4,005 +3,687
4. 7,651 + 1,368
5. $27.65 + $37.31
6. 9,241 + 1,436

Solve.

7. A pet supply store has 576 cans of dog food and 864 cans of cat food on shelves. How many cans of pet food are on shelves in all?

8. Thursday 4,328 people visited the zoo. Friday 5,006 people visited the zoo. How many people visited the zoo on those days?

Extra Practice

Problem Solving Strategy: Write a Number Sentence (pages 68–69)

1. Rebecca has 5 goldfish, 1 dog, and 2 cats. How many pets does she have?

2. Rebecca's friend John has 3 cats, 2 gerbils, and 21 fish. How many pets does John have?

3. Jason works at an animal shelter. He feeds 22 cats and 17 dogs. How many animals did he feed?

4. Emma also works at an animal shelter. She gives 34 cats and 38 dogs water. How many animals need water?

Add More Than Two Numbers (pages 70–71)

Add. Check for reasonableness.

1.
$$\begin{array}{r} \$136 \\ 27 \\ + \ 251 \\ \hline \end{array}$$

2.
$$\begin{array}{r} 4,229 \\ 3,303 \\ +1,464 \\ \hline \end{array}$$

3.
$$\begin{array}{r} 811 \\ 347 \\ +633 \\ \hline \end{array}$$

4.
$$\begin{array}{r} \$3.19 \\ 0.47 \\ + \ 2.51 \\ \hline \end{array}$$

5. 5,365 + 59 + 432

6. $0.63 + $3.84 + $7.85

7. 394 + 7,778 + 466

8. $0.42 + $1.30

9. $2.47 + $6.33

10. $0.49 + $0.79 + $3.49

Solve.

11. Joni's farm has 1,298 chickens, 357 cows, and 23 horses. How many animals were on the farm altogether?

12. Ray bought a hamster for $8.79, a cage for $12.95, and a bag of wood shavings for $5.25. How much did he spend altogether?

13. On vacation Marty visited zoos, parks, and aquariums. The first week he traveled 428 miles, the second week he traveled 512 miles, and the third week he traveled 391 miles. How far did he travel altogether?

14. Kay wants a dog stamp that costs $1.29, a cat stamp that costs $1.15, a bird stamp that costs $0.89, and an ink pad that costs $1.79. She has $5.00 to spend. Does she have enough money? Why or why not?

Chapter Study Guide

Language and Math

Complete. Use a word or words from the list.

1. The ____ of 6 + 7 is 13.

2. The ____ shows that 7 + 8 = 8 + 7.

3. The ____ shows that when zero is added to a number the answer is always that number.

4. To ____ a sum you can round the numbers, then add.

5. To add three or more numbers, use the ____.

Math Words

addend
Associative
  Property
Commutative
  Property
estimate
Identity Property
sum

Skills and Applications

Add using mental math strategies. (pages 46–53)

Example
Find: 800 + 700

Solution
Use basic facts and patterns to add mentally.

Think:
$$8 + 7 = 15$$
$$80 + 70 = 150$$
$$800 + 700 = 1,500$$

Add. Use mental math.

6. 90 + 10

7. 120 + 40

8. 800 + 400

9. 1,300 + 700

Use the properties of addition. (pages 46–53)

Example
Add. Tell what properties you used.
2 + 5 + 8

Solution
Use the Commutative
Property   2 + 8 + 5
Use the Associative
Property   (2 + 8) + 5
                         10 + 5 = 15

Add. Then write a different addition sentence.

10. 15 + 0

11. 5 + 3 + 2

Add. Tell what properties you used.

12. 8 + 0 + 12

13. 3 + 8 + 7 + 5

Find the sum of whole numbers. (pages 46–71)

Example
Find: $674 + 148$
Solution
Add the numbers in each place. Regroup if necessary.

$$\begin{array}{r} {\scriptstyle 1\ 1} \\ 674 \\ +148 \\ \hline 822 \end{array}$$

Add.

14. $546 + 178$

15. $764 + 187 + 32$

16. $467 + 77 + 1{,}012$

17. $\$605 + \$234 + \$371$

18. $\$8.24 + \$3.19$

19. $\$2.65 + \$0.43 + \$13.39$

Estimate sums, including money amounts. (pages 60–63)

Example
Estimate: $281 + 637$
Solution
Round each number.

Think: $281 + 637$
$\qquad \downarrow \qquad \downarrow$
$\qquad 300 + 600 = 900$

So $281 + 637$ is about 900.

Estimate each sum.

20. $482 + 135$

21. $2{,}062 + 817$

22. $\$9.98 + \$8.25$

23. $\$4.78 + \$2.23$

Use strategies to solve problems. (pages 62–63, 68–69)

Example
Margo has a job walking dogs. She walks 7 dogs in the morning and 5 more in the afternoon. How many dogs does she walk in a day?
Solution
Since you need to find a total you can add. Write and solve a number sentence to show how many dogs in all.
$7 + 5 = 12$
She walks 12 dogs in a day.

Solve.

24. There are 12 doves on a telephone wire. They are joined by 15 pigeons and 8 crows. How many birds are on the wire altogether?

25. Colin has 12 neon tetras, 16 mollies, and 8 tangs in his aquarium. Does he have more than 30 fish in his aquarium?

Chapter Test

Add. Use mental math. Tell what strategy you used.

1. 9 + 8   **2.** 4 + 0   **3.** 60 + 70   **4.** 300 + 800

Add. Tell what addition properties you used.

5. 1 + 8 + 9   **6.** 12 + 9 + 0   **7.** 4 + 5 + 5   **8.** 2 + 6 + 7 + 4

Add.

9. 54 + 25 + 92   **10.** $1,164 + $906   **11.** 3,568 + 264

12. 760 + 99   **13.** $8,991 + $536 + $33   **14.** 1,776 + 1,812 + 1,933

15. $1.56 + $0.74   **16.** $5.66 + $3.74 + $15.22   **17.** $9.05 + $0.07 + $0.25

Estimate each sum.

18. 56 + 32   **19.** 714 + 298   **20.** 2,398 + 732   **21.** 6,020 + 1,987

Solve.

22. Ted collects pictures of butterflies. He already has 47 pictures in his scrapbook. How many pictures will he have if he adds 58 more pictures?

23. Anne bathed her dog for 30 minutes on Sunday. She walked the dog for 15 minutes on Sunday morning and 20 minutes on Sunday afternoon. How many minutes did Anne spend caring for her dog on Sunday?

24. Cat food costs $6.75 for a small bag, $8.99 for a medium bag, and $9.99 for a large bag. Is $25.00 enough to buy all three sizes? Explain.

25. Roy bought 2 dog collars on sale for $5.49 each. The usual price was $6.99. The tax was $0.43. How much did Roy spend altogether?

Performance Assessment

The children's museum is planning to add more toy animals to its collection. They have 57 animals now.

57 toy animals

During the next 5 years the museum will add animals every year. They can't buy any more than 60 new animals a year. Each year they must buy a different number of new animals.

Choose the number of animals bought each year. Then copy and complete the chart.

The museum can spend $5,555 for each of the five years. How much will be spent in all? Show how you found the total.

Year	Starting Number of Animals	Number of New Animals	Total Number of Animals
1	57		
2			
3			
4			
5			

Journal

A Good Answer

- has a completed chart.
- shows a different number of animals bought each year.
- shows the steps you followed to find the total number of animals for each year.
- shows the total number of dollars spent.

Portfolio

You may want to save this work for your portfolio.

Assessment

Enrichment

Front-End Estimation

You know how to use rounding to estimate sums.

Here is another way to estimate. It is called **front-end estimation**.

To use front-end estimation, look at the digit in the greatest place. Think of it as the "front" digit. The underlined digits in the numbers below are the "front" digits.

2̲3   9̲9   1̲56   3̲48   8̲01

Here's how to use the front-end estimation:

Estimate: 423 + 766 + 528

423 + 766 + 528	Find the front-end digits.
↓ ↓ ↓	Rewrite the numbers. Use the front-end digits. Use zeros for the other digits.
400 + 700 + 500	
400 + 700 + 500 = 1,600	Add to find the estimate

Estimate each sum. Use front-end estimation.

1. 39 + 31
2. 44 + 92
3. 75 + 22
4. 54 + 85 + 13
5. 56 + 23
6. 67 + 11 + 34
7. 506 + 243
8. 56 + 23 + 93 + 81
9. 180 + 420 + 310
10. 491 + 350 + 207
11. 723 + 507
12. 88 + 51 + 66 + 81

Solve.

13. **Generalize:** Will a front-end estimation be greater or less than the actual sum? Explain.

14. Give an example of when you might use front-end estimation. When would using front-end estimation not make sense?

Test-Taking Tips

When you are taking a test, it is important to **read carefully**. It helps to read each item more than once.

Sparkle design pencils cost $0.75. They are also sold in packs of 3 for $2.00. What is the least 5 pencils can cost?

A. $3.00   **C.** $3.50

B. $3.25   **D.** $3.75

When you read the problem the first time, you might think the answer is choice D, $3.75.

$0.75 + $0.75 + $0.75 + $0.75 + $0.75 = $3.75
If you read the problem again, you might notice that you can buy 3 pencils for $2.00.

$2.00 + $0.75 + $0.75 = $3.50
The correct choice is C.

Check for Success

Before turning in a test, go back one last time to check.

☑ I understood and answered the questions asked.

☑ I checked my work for errors.

☑ My answers make sense.

Read each problem carefully. Think about how you would answer it. Then read the problem again. Choose the letter of the correct answer.

0 1 2 3 4 5 6 7 8 9 10 11 12 13 14 15 16 17 18 19 20 21 22 23 24 25

1. The number 111 is 10 more than which number?

   A. 10   **C.** 101

   B. 91   **D.** 110

2. Dena had 2 cents on Monday. She doubled it every day after that. How much did she have on Friday?

   F. $0.04   **H.** $0.32

   G. $0.10   **J.** $0.64

3. Which number is the arrow pointing to?

   A. 5   **C.** 20

   B. 17   **D.** 22

4. What is the eighth number in this skip-counting pattern?

   3, 6, 9, 12, 15, 18

   F. 19   **H.** 24

   G. 21   **J.** 27

Test Prep

Spiral Review and Test Prep
Chapters 1-2

Choose the correct answer.

Number Sense

1. A haddock fish is about 100 centimeters in length and a cod fish is about 200 centimeters. The length of an Atlantic salmon is between these two lengths. What could the length of a salmon be?

A. 150 centimeters

B. 98 centimeters

C. 210 centimeters

D. 205 centimeters

2. Which symbol makes the number sentence true?

3,658 ● 3,685

F. >　　　　　**H.** =

G. <　　　　　**J.** Not Here

3. At the aquarium there is an adult male seal lion that weighs 678 pounds. What is its weight rounded to the nearest hundred?

A. 600 pounds　**C.** 670 pounds

B. 700 pounds　**D.** 680 pounds

4. Cara has three one-dollar bills, 2 quarters, 1 dime, and a penny. How much does she have?

F. $1.51　　　**H.** $3.61

G. $3.51　　　**J.** $4.61

Algebra and Functions

5. Find the missing number.

32 + ▮ = 12 + 32

A. 20　　　　**C.** 12

B. 32　　　　**D.** 10

6. Which basic fact could you use to find the sum of 200 + 700?

F. 7 + 7　　　**H.** 20 + 700

G. 200 + 70　　**J.** 2 + 7

7. The table shows the number of baby animals born each year at a zoo. If this pattern continues, how many babies could be born in the fifth year?

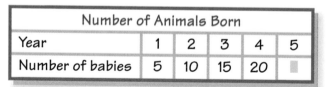

Number of Animals Born					
Year	1	2	3	4	5
Number of babies	5	10	15	20	▮

A. 25　　　　**C.** 22

B. 24　　　　**D.** 18

8. Find the numeral that means 8 hundred, 4 tens, and 7 ones.

F. 84　　　　**H.** 811

G. 847　　　**J.** 8,047

Statistics, Data Analysis, and Probability

Use data from the table for questions 9–12.

Species of Reptiles	
Animal Group	Number of Species
Turtles/Tortoises	215
Crocodiles/Alligators	25
Lizards	3,000
Snakes	2,700

9. Which group has the least number of species?
   - **A.** Lizards
   - **B.** Turtles/Tortoises
   - **C.** Snakes
   - **D.** Crocodiles/Alligators

10. How many species of snakes and lizards are there?
    - **F.** 240
    - **G.** 3,215
    - **H.** 5,700
    - **J.** 2,725

11. Which two groups have the closest number of species?
    - **A.** Turtles/Tortoises and Crocodiles/Alligators
    - **B.** Snakes and Crocodiles/Alligators
    - **C.** Lizards and Turtles/Tortoises
    - **D.** Lizards and Snakes

12. Which is the closest estimate for the number of species of reptiles in all?
    - **F.** 6,200
    - **G.** 6,000
    - **H.** 5,900
    - **J.** 5,700

Mathematical Reasoning

13. A number has 3 digits. The ones digit is greatest. The tens digit is two times the hundreds digit. What is the number?
    - **A.** 242
    - **B.** 638
    - **C.** 366
    - **D.** Not Here

14. Pat buys new fish for her tank each week. The first week she bought 4 fish, the second week she bought 8 fish, and last week she bought 12 fish. If the pattern continues, how many fish could she buy this week?
    - **F.** 24
    - **G.** 20
    - **H.** 16
    - **J.** 6

15. Will's dad is building a pen for Will's turtles. It is in the shape of a rectangle. It is 6 feet long and 3 feet wide. Which shows how much fencing is needed for the pen?
    - **A.** $6 + 3$
    - **B.** 6×3
    - **C.** $6 + 3 + 6 + 3$
    - **D.** Not Here

16. One sea turtle nest had 185 hatched eggs. Another nest had 145. About how many hatched in all? Explain.

Subtract Whole Numbers

Theme: Let It Grow!

Use the Data
Top 5 Fruit Crops in the World

Crop	Tons Produced
Oranges	66 million
Bananas	64 million
Grapes	63 million
Apples	60 million
Watermelons	51 million

Source: Top Ten of Everything 1999

- How many more tons of grapes were produced than watermelons?

- How did you use subtraction to solve the problem?

What You Will Learn
In this chapter you will learn how to
- subtract using mental math strategies.
- use inverse operations.
- subtract whole numbers.
- estimate differences.
- use strategies to solve problems.

Additional activities at
www.mhschool.com/math

Objective: Complete fact families and find missing addends and solve problems involving numeric equations or inequalities.

3·1

Relate Addition and Subtraction

Algebra & functions   **Learn**

Math Words

related facts basic facts using the same numbers

fact families a group of related facts using the same numbers

Yum! Fresh vegetables from the garden! Ian picks 11 tomatoes and 4 green peppers. How many vegetables did he pick? How many more tomatoes than green peppers did Ian pick?

Example 1

You can use **related facts** from a **fact family** to answer the questions.

Add to find how many vegetables are in the garden.	Subtract to find how many more tomatoes than green peppers he picked.
$11 + 4 = 15$ or $4 + 11 = 15$	$11 - 4 = 7$

Think: You can use a related fact to check your answer. $11 - 7 = 4$

Ian picked 15 tomatoes and green peppers.

Ian picked 4 more tomatoes than green peppers.

More Examples

Fact families are made from related sentences.

Related sentences apply to more than just facts.

A
$7 + 6 = 13$
$6 + 7 = 13$
$13 - 6 = 7$
$13 - 7 = 6$

B
$15 + 2 = 17$
$2 + 15 = 17$
$17 - 15 = 2$
$17 - 2 = 15$

C
$18 + 0 = 18$
$0 + 18 = 18$
$18 - 0 = 18$
$18 - 18 = 0$

D
$15 + 15 = 30$
$30 - 15 = 15$

What if 8 of 17 vegetables are ready to be picked?
How many are not ready to be picked?

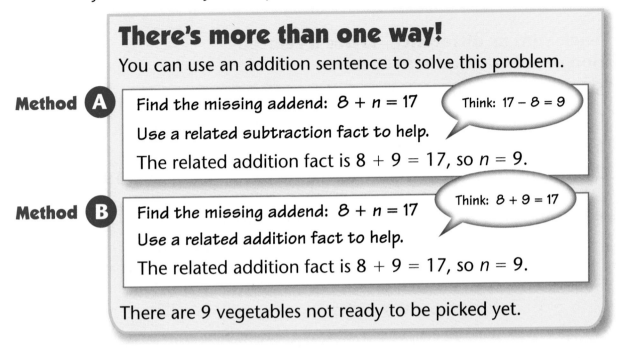

There's more than one way!

You can use an addition sentence to solve this problem.

Method A

Find the missing addend: $8 + n = 17$

Think: $17 - 8 = 9$

Use a related subtraction fact to help.

The related addition fact is $8 + 9 = 17$, so $n = 9$.

Method B

Find the missing addend: $8 + n = 17$

Think: $8 + 9 = 17$

Use a related addition fact to help.

The related addition fact is $8 + 9 = 17$, so $n = 9$.

There are 9 vegetables not ready to be picked yet.

 Try It **Write a group of related sentences for each group of numbers.**

1. 5, 8, 13
2. 5, 0, 5
3. 6, 6, 12
4. 23, 9, 14
5. 7, 13, 20
6. 8, 1, 9
7. 6, 15, 21
8. 5, 9, 14
9. 7, 11, 18
10. 3, 19, 22

Write the missing number in each fact family.

11. $4 + 6 = k$
    $m + 4 = 10$
    $10 - n = 4$
    $10 - 4 = p$

12. $2 + v = 9$
    $2 + 7 = t$
    $r - 7 = 2$
    $9 - s = 7$

13. $4 + 0 = w$
    $x + 0 = 4$
    $4 - y = 4$
    $z - 4 = 0$

Find each missing addend.

14. $8 + n = 12$
15. $x + 14 = 20$
16. $5 + y = 12$
17. $w + 12 = 19$
18. $6 + g = 11$
19. $17 + t = 24$
20. $8 + m = 12$
21. $r + 22 = 24$

22. $\begin{array}{r} t \\ +13 \\ \hline 22 \end{array}$

23. $\begin{array}{r} n \\ +5 \\ \hline 11 \end{array}$

24. $\begin{array}{r} 8 \\ +r \\ \hline 16 \end{array}$

25. $\begin{array}{r} 15 \\ +z \\ \hline 20 \end{array}$

 How did you find the missing addend for problem 11 above?

Write a group of related sentences for each group of numbers.

26. 7, 11, 18 **27.** 4, 9, 13   **28.** 9, 9, 18   **29.** 2, 2, 0   **30.** 6, 21, 15

Find each sum or difference. Write a related addition or subtraction sentence.

31. $15 - 4$ **32.** $9 + 0$ **33.** $16 + 8$ **34.** $7 - 7$ **35.** $22 - 7$

36. $16 - 8$ **37.** $3 + 17$ **38.** $17 - 9$ **39.** $16 - 3$ **40.** $18 - 9$

41. $15 - 5$ **42.** $8 - 6$ **43.** $18 - 4$ **44.** $14 - 6$ **45.** $4 + 7$

★**46.** $321 - 292$ ★**47.** $108 + 982$ ★**48.** $458 - 191$

Write the missing numbers in each fact family.

49. $3 + 6 = x$ **50.** $8 + m = 8$ **51.** $n + 8 = 12$
     $z + 3 = 9$ $0 + y = 8$ $8 + n = 12$
     $9 - z = 3$ $y - 0 = 8$ $12 - r = 4$
     $x - 6 = 3$ $y - 8 = 0$ $12 - n = 8$

Find each missing addend. Tell which method you used.

52. $7 + n = 15$ **53.** $e + 2 = 2$ **54.** $4 + f = 8$ **55.** $n + 2 = 11$

56. $\begin{array}{r} 7 \\ +v \\ \hline 12 \end{array}$ **57.** $\begin{array}{r} s \\ +7 \\ \hline 14 \end{array}$ **58.** $\begin{array}{r} 8 \\ +s \\ \hline 15 \end{array}$ **59.** $\begin{array}{r} f \\ +6 \\ \hline 14 \end{array}$

Find the missing number. Explain what you did.

60. $12 - n = 9$ **61.** $7 - l = 6$ **62.** $x - 4 = 2$ **63.** $k - 9 = 8$

64. $24 - y = 18$ **65.** $r - 7 = 4$ **66.** $8 - g = 8$ **67.** $25 - x = 21$

68.

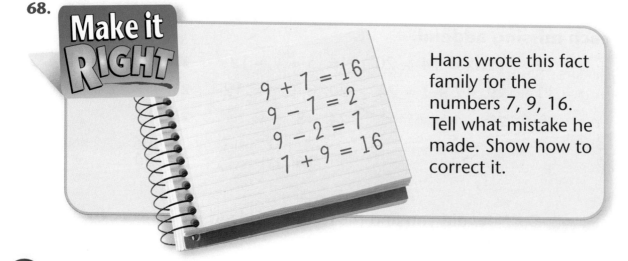

Hans wrote this fact family for the numbers 7, 9, 16. Tell what mistake he made. Show how to correct it.

$9 + 7 = 16$
$9 - 7 = 2$
$9 - 2 = 7$
$7 + 9 = 16$

Problem Solving

Use data from the sign for problems 69–70.

69. Erin buys 1 rose bush and 2 marigolds. How much does she spend?

70. **Language Arts:** You buy a Bird of Paradise plant from Sal and Marge. You pay with a ten-dollar bill. Write an entry in your diary telling what you bought and how much change you got back. Describe your new plant.

SAL & MARGE'S PLANT SHOP

Just in:

Birds of Paradise	$8.99 each
Rose bushes	$7.95 each
Marigolds	$1.29 each

Use data in *Did You Know?* for problems 71–72.

71. Nan read that petals of some sunflowers can be up to 4 inches long. Which flower has longer petals? How much longer?

72. **Measurement:** Which of these is about as wide as a rafflesia flower—a mouse pad, a doorway, a movie screen?

73. **Explain:** Do 3, 4, and 7 make up a fact family? Do 1, 3, and 6 make up a fact family? Explain how you decided.

74. **Create a problem** that can be solved by addition. Then change the problem so it can be solved using a related fact.

Did You KNOW?

The largest flower in the world belongs to a kind of rafflesia plant. The pink flower can grow up to 36 inches wide and can weigh as much as 15 pounds. Each of its 5 petals is about 1 inch thick and 18 inches long.

Spiral Review and Test Prep

Write the change.

75. Cost: $2.85
    You give: $5.00

76. Cost: $0.32
    You give: $1.00

77. Cost: $3.79
    You give: $4.00

Choose the correct answer.

78. What number will make the number sentence true?
    $(5 + 3) + w = 5 + (3 + 8)$
    A. 3
    B. 7
    C. 5
    D. 8

79. Skip-count to find the missing number: 21, 18, 15, m
    F. 12
    G. 14
    H. 10
    J. Not Here

Extra Practice, page 121

3·2 Problem Solving: Reading for Math
Identify Extra Information

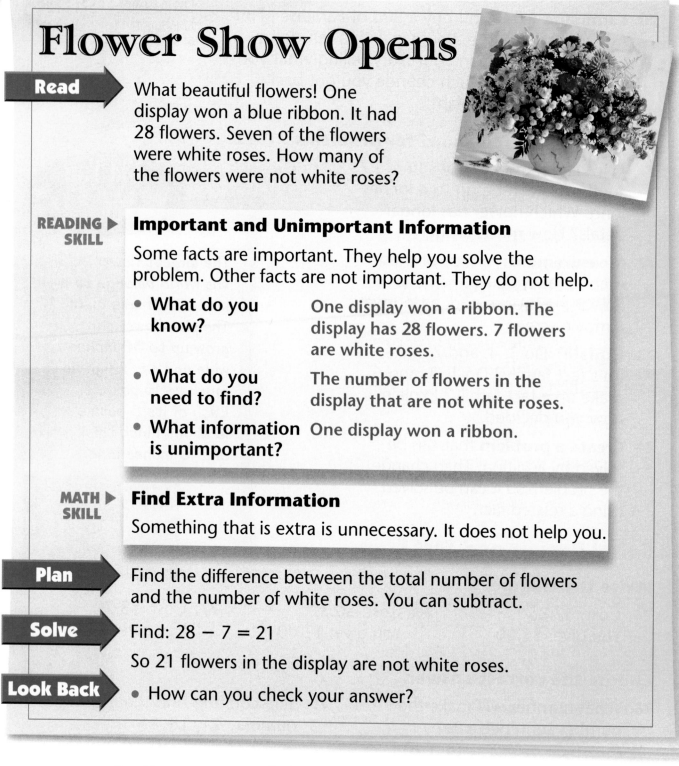

Flower Show Opens

Read ▶ What beautiful flowers! One display won a blue ribbon. It had 28 flowers. Seven of the flowers were white roses. How many of the flowers were not white roses?

READING SKILL ▶ **Important and Unimportant Information**

Some facts are important. They help you solve the problem. Other facts are not important. They do not help.

- **What do you know?**

  One display won a ribbon. The display has 28 flowers. 7 flowers are white roses.

- **What do you need to find?**

  The number of flowers in the display that are not white roses.

- **What information is unimportant?**

  One display won a ribbon.

MATH SKILL ▶ **Find Extra Information**

Something that is extra is unnecessary. It does not help you.

Plan ▶ Find the difference between the total number of flowers and the number of white roses. You can subtract.

Solve ▶ Find: $28 - 7 = 21$

So 21 flowers in the display are not white roses.

Look Back ▶ • How can you check your answer?

Sum it Up How can you tell if information in a problem is unimportant or extra?

Solve. Identify the extra information.

1. The Garden Club made 18 displays for the show. One is a flag made with red, white, and blue flowers. The flag has 17 flowers in it. There are 6 red flowers and 8 white flowers. How many blue flowers are there?

2. Another display at the show has the same number of daisies and buttercups. Daisies at the show cost $1.00 each. There are 18 flowers in the display. How many buttercups are in this display?

3. Mrs. Potter won 14 ribbons. Mr. Dubois won 15 first-place ribbons and 2 second-place ribbons. How many ribbons did Mr. Dubois win in all?

4. It took Nancy 5 hours to make her display. She used 43 roses, 36 daisies, and 20 lilies. How many flowers did Nancy use in her display?

Use data from the Garden Club News for problems 5–8.

5. There are 27 more maple trees than peach trees. How many more maple trees than oak trees are at the show?

6. There are 18 fewer cherry trees than apple trees. How many more maple trees than cherry trees are at the show?

7. How many fruit trees are there altogether?

8. There are the same number of cherry trees as there are peach trees. Which two kinds of trees equal the total number of maple trees in the display?

Garden Club News

Tree	Number of Trees
Apple	26
Cherry	8
Peach	8
Maple	35
Oak	9

Spiral Review and Test Prep

Choose the correct answer.

One display at the Garden Club was made by 3 people. It has 15 light flowers and 17 dark flowers. How many flowers are there altogether?

9. Which of these statements is true?
   A. There are exactly 30 flowers.
   B. There are 17 light flowers.
   C. There are 17 dark flowers.

10. What information is extra?
   F. There are 15 light flowers.
   G. Three people made the display.
   H. There are 17 dark flowers.

Chapter 3 Subtract Whole Numbers **95**

Problem Solving

3·3

Subtraction Patterns

Algebra & functions

Learn

There are 300 tickets still available for Sunday's Orchard show. How many tickets have been sold?

Orchard SHOW

Tickets	
$5.25	adults
$4.75	children under 12

Limited: 800 tickets available for Sunday's show

Example

Find $800 - 300$ to solve.

You can use patterns to find differences mentally.

$$8 - 3 = 5$$
$$80 - 30 = 50$$
$$800 - 300 = 500$$

Think: 8 ones − 3 ones = 5 ones
8 tens − 3 tens = 5 tens
8 hundreds − 3 hundreds = 5 hundreds

A total of 500 tickets have been sold.

More Examples

A
$$10 - 5 = 5$$
$$100 - 50 = 50$$
$$1,000 - 500 = 500$$

Think: 10 ones − 5 ones = 5 ones
10 tens − 5 tens = 5 tens
10 hundreds − 5 hundreds = 5 hundreds

B
$$20 - 10 = 10$$
$$200 - 100 = 100$$
$$2,000 - 1,000 = 1,000$$

Think: 20 ones − 10 ones = 10 ones
20 tens − 10 tens = 10 tens
20 hundreds − 10 hundreds = 10 hundreds

Try It **Write the number that makes each sentence true.**

1. $7 - 5 = n$
$70 - 50 = m$
$700 - 500 = p$

2. $9 - 4 = t$
$90 - 40 = c$
$900 - 400 = w$

3. $13 - f = 8$
$130 - r = 80$
$1,300 - z = 800$

 Sum it Up! Explain how to use subtraction facts and patterns to find $70 - 40$ mentally.

Write the number that makes each sentence true.

4.
$$7 - 6 = q$$
$$70 - 60 = r$$
$$700 - 600 = s$$

5.
$$8 - 2 = k$$
$$80 - 20 = l$$
$$800 - 200 = m$$

6.
$$10 - p = 8$$
$$100 - e = 80$$
$$1,000 - t = 800$$

Subtract mentally.

7. $1,400 - 700$ 8. $780 - 600$
9. $120 - 60$ 10. $624 - 300$
11. $80 - 20$ 12. $1,100 - 1,100$
13. $640 - 400$ 14. $937 - 607$

Find the missing digit.

★15. $\blacksquare31 - 200 = 731$ ★16. $120 - \blacksquare0 = 50$ ★17. $1,\blacksquare30 - 700 = 630$

Problem Solving

Use data from the table for problem 18.

18. **Career:** Jared is a sales clerk at Land and Lawn Garden Center. He hoped to work 110 hours during June. Did he work more or fewer hours than he hoped? how many more or fewer hours?

19. **Create a problem** that can be solved by subtracting mentally. Solve it. Ask others to solve it.

★20. Rick's father bought one adult ticket at $5.25 and one child's ticket at $4.75 for the Orchard Show. How much change did his father get if he paid for the tickets with a twenty-dollar bill?

June Work Schedule Employee: Jared Armonk	
Week	Number of hours
June 1–5	20
June 8–12	30
June 15–19	20
June 22–26	10

21. **Generalize:** When is it easy to subtract mentally?

Spiral Review and Test Prep

22. $9 + 4$ 23. $18 + 0$ 24. $8 + 8 + 3$ 25. $7 + 6$ 26. $2 + 12 + 1$

Choose the correct answer.

27. Which number is closest to this sum? $49 + 37$

   A. 70   C. 90
   B. 80   D. 100

28. Mr. Harper works in his garden for 45 minutes every day. How long did he work altogether from Monday through Wednesday?

   F. 45 minutes   H. 90 minutes
   G. 145 minutes   J. 135 minutes

3·4

Explore Regrouping in Subtraction

Learn

Math Word

regroup to name a number in a different way

You can use place value models to explore regrouping in subtraction. What is 362 − 148?

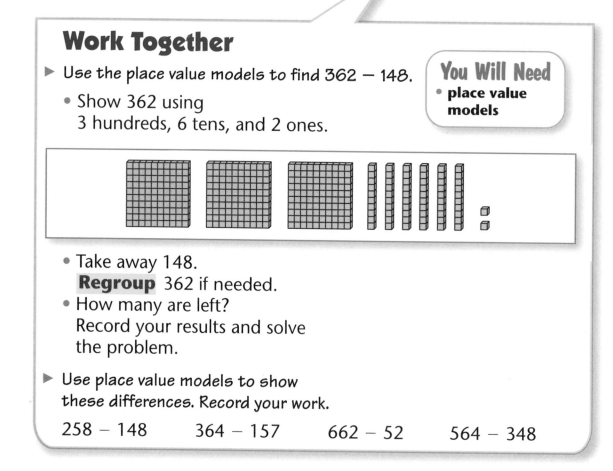

Work Together

▶ Use the place value models to find 362 − 148.

You Will Need
- place value models

- Show 362 using 3 hundreds, 6 tens, and 2 ones.

- Take away 148.
  Regroup 362 if needed.
- How many are left?
  Record your results and solve the problem.

▶ Use place value models to show these differences. Record your work.

258 − 148   364 − 157   662 − 52   564 − 348

Make Connections

Here are ways you can subtract numbers with regrouping. Find: 272 − 137

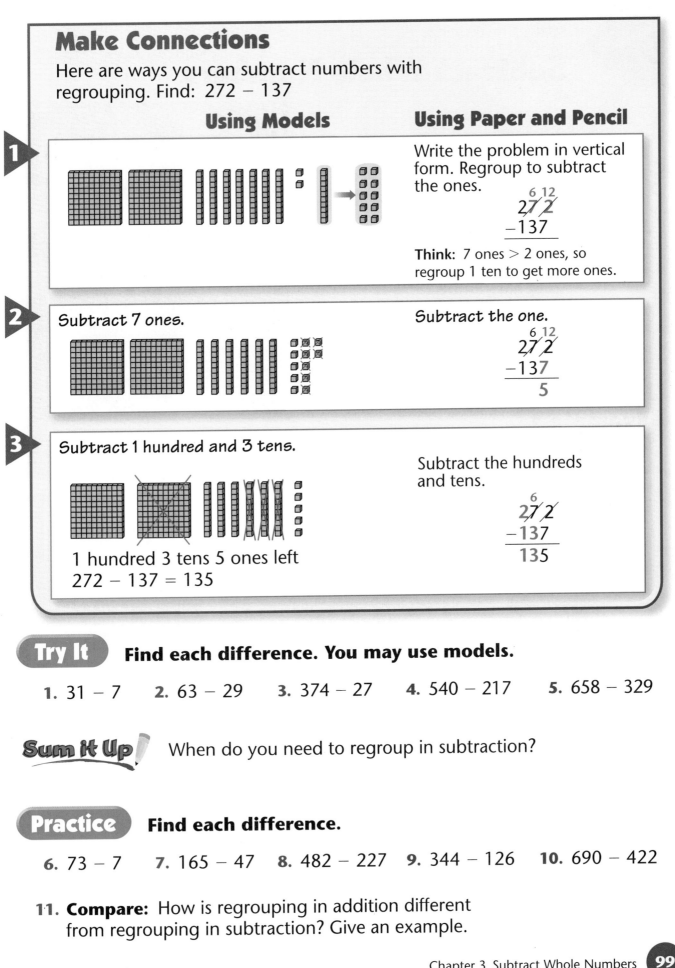

Using Models   **Using Paper and Pencil**

1 Write the problem in vertical form. Regroup to subtract the ones.

$$\begin{array}{r} {\scriptstyle 6\ 12} \\ 2\cancel{7}\cancel{2} \\ -137 \\ \hline \end{array}$$

Think: 7 ones > 2 ones, so regroup 1 ten to get more ones.

2 Subtract 7 ones.

Subtract the one.

$$\begin{array}{r} {\scriptstyle 6\ 12} \\ 2\cancel{7}\cancel{2} \\ -137 \\ \hline 5 \end{array}$$

3 Subtract 1 hundred and 3 tens.

1 hundred 3 tens 5 ones left
272 − 137 = 135

Subtract the hundreds and tens.

$$\begin{array}{r} {\scriptstyle 6} \\ \cancel{2}\cancel{7}2 \\ -137 \\ \hline 135 \end{array}$$

Try It   **Find each difference. You may use models.**

1. 31 − 7   **2.** 63 − 29   **3.** 374 − 27   **4.** 540 − 217   **5.** 658 − 329

Sum it Up   When do you need to regroup in subtraction?

Practice   **Find each difference.**

6. 73 − 7   **7.** 165 − 47   **8.** 482 − 227   **9.** 344 − 126   **10.** 690 − 422

11. Compare: How is regrouping in addition different from regrouping in subtraction? Give an example.

Objective: Subtract 2-, and 3- digit numbers with and without regrouping.

Subtract Whole Numbers

Learn

Strangler figs climb on trees in order to reach for the sun. If a tree is 267 feet tall and the strangler fig vine has climbed 196 feet, how much farther does it have to climb?

267 foot tall tree

196 foot tall strangler fig

Example 1

You can find 267 − 196 to solve this problem.

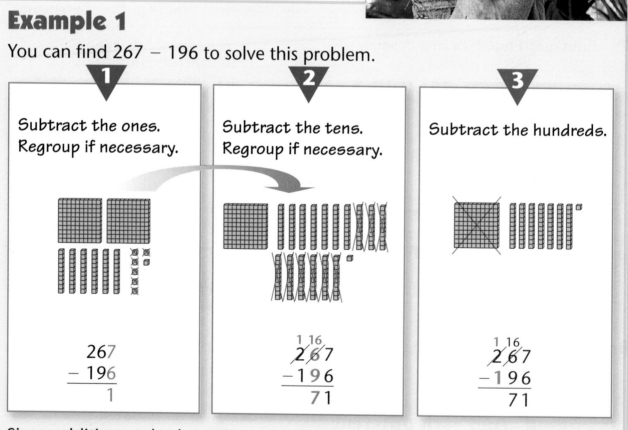

1

Subtract the ones. Regroup if necessary.

```
  267
- 196
─────
    1
```

2

Subtract the tens. Regroup if necessary.

```
  1 16
  2̸6̸7
- 196
─────
   71
```

3

Subtract the hundreds.

```
  1 16
  2̸6̸7
- 196
─────
   71
```

Since addition and subtraction are inverse operations, you can add to check: 71 + 196 = 267.

The vine has to grow 71 feet to reach the top of the tree.

Today ticket sales were $938 for the forest exhibit at the nature preserve. Yesterday they were $719. How much more money was collected today?

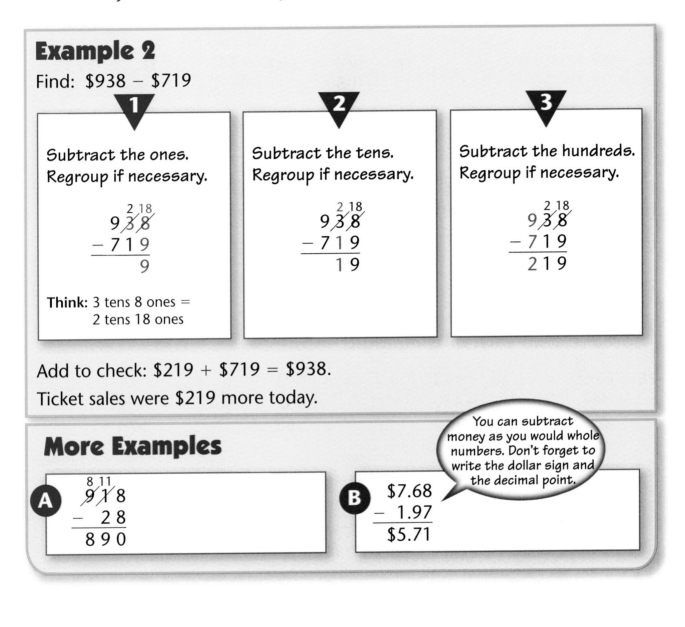

Example 2

Find: $938 − $719

1 Subtract the ones. Regroup if necessary.

$$\begin{array}{r} 9\overset{2\ 18}{\cancel{3}\cancel{8}} \\ -\ 7\ 1\ 9 \\ \hline 9 \end{array}$$

Think: 3 tens 8 ones = 2 tens 18 ones

2 Subtract the tens. Regroup if necessary.

$$\begin{array}{r} 9\overset{2\ 18}{\cancel{3}\cancel{8}} \\ -\ 7\ 1\ 9 \\ \hline 1\ 9 \end{array}$$

3 Subtract the hundreds. Regroup if necessary.

$$\begin{array}{r} 9\overset{2\ 18}{\cancel{3}\cancel{8}} \\ -\ 7\ 1\ 9 \\ \hline 2\ 1\ 9 \end{array}$$

Add to check: $219 + $719 = $938.

Ticket sales were $219 more today.

More Examples

A
$$\begin{array}{r} \overset{8\ 11}{9\cancel{1}\ 8} \\ -\ \ \ 2\ 8 \\ \hline 8\ 9\ 0 \end{array}$$

B
$$\begin{array}{r} \$7.68 \\ -\ 1.97 \\ \hline \$5.71 \end{array}$$

You can subtract money as you would whole numbers. Don't forget to write the dollar sign and the decimal point.

Try It Subtract. Check your answer.

1. 651 − 392   2. $812 − $576   3. $9.06 − $5.92   4. $5.31 − $4.99

5. $7.34 − $2.86   6. $917 − $473   7. 525 − 169   8. $7.14 − $5.57

 Make up a subtraction problem in which you subtract two 3-digit numbers and must regroup the tens and the hundreds. Explain how to solve the problem.

Subtract. Remember to check.

9. 764
    −592

10. 552
    −493

11. 347
    −256

12. 992
    −985

13. $9.13
    − 4.79

14. $9.42
    − 8.46

15. 264
    −120

16. 527
    −308

17. $412
    − 205

18. 523
    −103

19. 971 − 398

20. 836 − 654

21. $3.58 − $1.18

22. 556 − 357

23. 887 − 708

24. 672 − 486

Pick pairs of numbers from the set below that have a difference closest to the given target number.

973   371   829   104   281   173   874

★**25.** Target number: 800   ★**26.** Target number: 500   ★**27.** Target number: 200

Algebra & functions **Find each missing digit.**

28. 616
    −34■
    269

29. ■43
    −430
    113

30. 5■3
    −465
    48

★**31.** ■6■
    −1■9
    573

32.

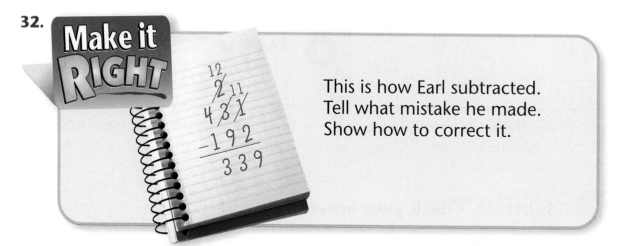

This is how Earl subtracted. Tell what mistake he made. Show how to correct it.

Problem Solving

Journal **33. Analyze:** When you subtract 89 from 351, why do you have to regroup twice in the tens place?

34. Each year the Pottstown Garden Club collects a total of $1,245 in dues. So far members have paid $848 in dues. How much more must the Garden Club collect in dues?

Use data from the table for problems 35–38.

35. List the beans in order from greatest to least number of calories in a cup.

36. How many more or fewer calories are in a cup of green beans than in a cup of great northern beans?

37. For lunch Andy had a hamburger, a cup of black beans, and a cup of mashed potatoes. The meal had 745 calories. How many calories did the hamburger have?

38. **Create a problem** using the data from the table. The problem should be able to be solved by subtraction. Solve it. Ask others to solve it.

39. **Time:** Mr. Young started weeding his garden at 7:00 A.M. The clock shows the time he finished that morning. For how long did Mr. Young weed his garden?

40. In May tulip bulbs cost $10.45 for a case. In July, tulip bulbs were on sale for $6.80. How much less did the tulip bulbs cost in July than in May?

★41. There are 365 days in a year. Grace shops at the garden center between 98 and 129 days each year. What is the least number of days in a year that Grace is not shopping at the garden center?

Calorie Count	
Vegetable (1 Cup)	**Calories**
green beans	35
black beans	225
green peas	125
mashed potatoes	160
great northern beans	210

Source: World Almanac and Book of Facts

Spiral Review and Test Prep

42. 15 − 8   **43.** 11 − 9   **44.** 13 − 8   **45.** 14 − 7

Choose the correct answer.

46. Which number is the same as 40,000 + 2,000 + 600 + 7?

    A. 402,607   **C.** 42,607

    B. 42,670   **D.** 42,067

47. Find the missing number.
6,783 + n = 6,793

    F. 0   **H.** 100

    G. 10   **J.** 6,783

Check Your Progress A

Subtract. (pages 90–93)

1. 12
   − 8

2. 14
   − 9

3. 4
   −4

4. 20
   − 1

Write a group of related sentences for each group of numbers. (pages 90–93)

5. 6, 8, 14

6. 12, 7, 19

7. 4 , 8, 12

8. 4, 17, 13

Copy and complete. (pages 96–97)

9.
$$9 - 4 = n$$
$$90 - 40 = t$$
$$900 - 400 = p$$

10.
$$r - 7 = 1$$
$$k - 70 = 10$$
$$m - 700 = 100$$

11.
$$10 - f = 4$$
$$100 - d = 40$$
$$1,000 - v = 400$$

Subtract. (pages 100–103)

12. $63 - 22$

13. $587 - 503$

14. $215 - 90$

15. $\$8.31 - \$2.53$

16. $589 - 431$

17. $843 - 578$

18. $\$7.65 - \$5.76$

19. $542 - 521$

20. $957 - 78$

21. $\$6.23 - \$3.98$

Solve. (pages 90–103)

22. Nina picked 15 daisies. She gave 8 to her mother. How many daisies did she have left?

23. Jared counted 127 flowers and 84 trees in the park. About how many more flowers than trees did he count?

24. On one day a plant nursery sold 34 small trees, 125 flowering plants, and 47 cactus plants. How many flowering plants and cactus plants were sold altogether?

25. **Summarize:** How does knowing one addition fact help you subtract?

Additional activities at www.mhschool.com/math

TECHNOLOGY LINK

Use the Internet

Tara is gathering data on high and low temperatures for different parts of the world. She needs to find data for four different locations. She will use the data she collects to complete the following table. How can she use the Internet to gather the data to copy and complete the table?

Location	High Temperature	Low Temperature	Difference

- Go to www.mhschool.com/math
- Find the list of sites that provide weather data. Click on a link.
- Find the data on high and low temperatures. Choose four locations for which data is given.
- Copy the table. Write in the names of the locations you chose.
- Record in the table the high and low temperatures for each location.
- Find the difference between the high and low temperatures for each location. Record the difference in the table.

1. Which location has the greatest difference between the high and low temperatures? the least difference?

2. **Analyze:** Why does using the Internet make more sense than using another source to find the data.

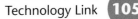 For more practice, use Math Traveler™.

3·6

Regroup Across Zeros

Learn

The Tree Musketeers plant trees to block pollution. If the Tree Musketeers need to plant 203 trees this year and they already planted 125 trees, how many trees do they still need to plant?

Math in ACTION

The Tree Musketeers is a group run entirely by kids.

Example

You can subtract 125 from 203 to solve this problem.

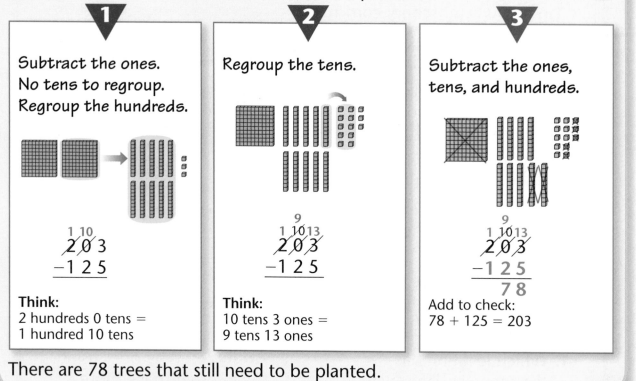

1

Subtract the ones. No tens to regroup. Regroup the hundreds.

$$\begin{array}{r} \overset{1\ 10}{2\ \cancel{0}\ 3} \\ -1\ 2\ 5 \\ \hline \end{array}$$

Think:
2 hundreds 0 tens =
1 hundred 10 tens

2

Regroup the tens.

$$\begin{array}{r} \overset{9}{\underset{}{}}\\ \overset{1\ \cancel{10}\ 13}{2\ \cancel{0}\ \cancel{3}} \\ -1\ 2\ 5 \\ \hline \end{array}$$

Think:
10 tens 3 ones =
9 tens 13 ones

3

Subtract the ones, tens, and hundreds.

$$\begin{array}{r} \overset{9}{\underset{}{}}\\ \overset{1\ \cancel{10}\ 13}{2\ \cancel{0}\ \cancel{3}} \\ -1\ 2\ 5 \\ \hline 7\ 8 \end{array}$$

Add to check:
78 + 125 = 203

There are 78 trees that still need to be planted.

Try It **Subtract. Check your answer.**

1. 307 − 39   **2.** $2.07 − $0.35   **3.** 302 − 199

Sum It Up Explain the steps to follow to subtract 506 − 248.

Practice

Subtract. Add to check.

4. 106
    − 27

5. 703
    −147

6. $201
    − 31

7. 500
    −317

8. 506
    −257

9. 802 − 704

10. 600 − 312

11. 401 − 294

12. 205 − 118

13. 401 − 57

14. $605 − $339

Algebra & functions   Use the rule to find the difference.

15.

| Rule: Subtract 445 | |
Input	Output
851	
704	
900	

16.

| Rule: Subtract 354 | |
Input	Output
412	
603	
701	

17.

| Rule: Subtract 109 | |
Input	Output
320	
345	
657	

Problem Solving

Use data from the graph for problems 18–19.

18. The local newspaper surveyed 800 gardeners. How many more gardeners prefer to grow annual flowers rather than perennials?

★19. **What if** 40 of the gardeners who chose vegetables change their minds and vote for perennials? How will this change the survey results?

| Which do you prefer to grow? Survey Results | |
Kind of plant	Number of votes
Annual flowers	300
Perennial flowers	270
Vegetables	230

20. **Analyze:** Which is a more accurate way to check a subtraction answer, estimation or addition? Why?

Spiral Review and Test Prep

What is the value of the underlined digit in each number?

21. 4<u>2</u>1

22. <u>6</u>,302

23. 13,0<u>3</u>1

24. 1<u>2</u>4,512

Choose the correct answer.

25. Which belongs in the same fact family as 6 + 3 = 9?

  A. 9 + 3 = 12   C. 12 − 3 = 9

  B. 9 − 3 = 6   D. 6 − 3 = 3

26. Which has an estimated sum of 400?

  F. 191 + 231   H. 270 + 301

  G. 312 + 187   J. 221 + 115

3·7

Estimate Differences

Learn

Math Word

estimate to find an answer that is close to the exact answer

"This must be the tallest tree in the world!" Craig shouted to Ray. "No," said Ray. "A redwood tree in California is much taller!" About how much taller than Greg's tree is the California redwood?

150 feet

Redwood
368 feet

Example

You can **estimate** the difference to solve this problem.

Estimate: 368 − 150
Round each number so you can subtract mentally.

Think: 368 − 150.
        ↓   ↓

            Round to the
            nearest hundred.

400 − 200 = 200

So 368 − 150 is about 200.

The world's tallest tree is about 200 feet taller.

More Examples

Estimate.

A   88 − 28
     ↓   ↓

        Round to the
        nearest ten.

90 − 30 = 60

B   3,643 − 1,087
     ↓   ↓

            Round to the
            nearest thousand.

4,000 − 1,000 = 3,000

Try It   **Estimate each difference. Tell how you rounded.**

1. 49 − 31 2. 420 − 170 3. 1,450 − 607 4. 8,513 − 2,807

 Sum it Up   How can you estimate 386 − 75 two different ways?

Estimate each difference.

5. 83 − 62   **6.** 616 − 423   **7.** 1,245 − 710   **8.** 381 − 15

9. 1,144 − 272   **10.** 4,432 − 1,673 **11.** 9,385 − 5,730 **12.** 4,211 − 115

13. 3,024 − 917   **14.** 9,256 − 7,009 **15.** 7,512 − 2,097 **16.** 5,193 − 3,579

Algebra & functions **Write > or < to make a true sentence.**

17. 38 − 17 ⚫ 30   **18.** 416 − 197 ⚫ 300   **19.** 1,121 − 612 ⚫ 400

★**20.** 94 − 36 ⚫ 83 − 39   ★**21.** 84 − 21 ⚫ 77 − 36   ★**22.** 156 − 85 ⚫ 178 − 93

Problem Solving
Use data from the photo for problem 23.

23. Science: If a saguaro cactus is 103 years old, about how many more years might it live? Explain.

24. Pablo and Jamie each counted the number of flowering desert bushes they saw. Pablo saw 98 bushes and Jamie saw 133. How many did they see altogether?

25. Analyze: Sandy estimates 872 − 312 is about 600. How did she round the numbers? Is this estimate greater or less than the exact answer? Explain.

The saguaro cactus can live for up to 200 years and grow to 50 feet tall.

Spiral Review and Test Prep

Find the missing addends.

26. 9 + n = 10   **27.** t + 7 = 11   **28.** 3 + 4 + k = 12 **29.** p + 6 + 2 = 18

Choose the correct answer.

30. Greg planted 15 tulips on Monday and another 7 tulips on Tuesday. Which number sentence tells how many tulips Greg planted?
   A. 15 − 7 = 8   **C.** 7 + 8 = 15
   B. 15 − 8 = 7   **D.** Not Here

31. Lester lives 482 miles from the desert. What is that number rounded to the nearest hundred?
   F. 500   **H.** 400
   G. 480   **J.** 490

3·8 Problem Solving: Strategy
Write a Number Sentence

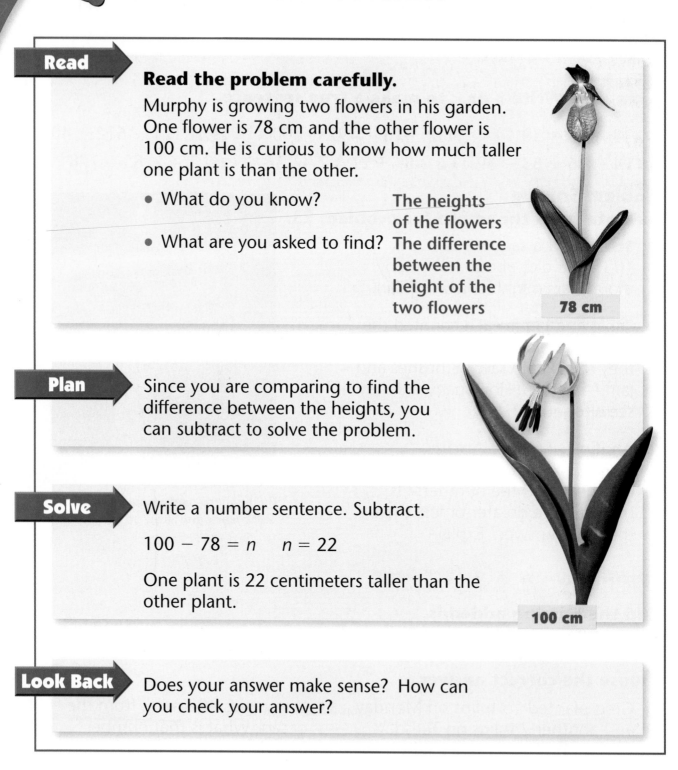

Read

Read the problem carefully.

Murphy is growing two flowers in his garden. One flower is 78 cm and the other flower is 100 cm. He is curious to know how much taller one plant is than the other.

- What do you know? — The heights of the flowers
- What are you asked to find? — The difference between the height of the two flowers

78 cm

Plan

Since you are comparing to find the difference between the heights, you can subtract to solve the problem.

Solve

Write a number sentence. Subtract.

$100 - 78 = n$ $n = 22$

One plant is 22 centimeters taller than the other plant.

100 cm

Look Back

Does your answer make sense? How can you check your answer?

Sum it Up Tell how you know when to use a subtraction sentence to solve a problem.

Write a number sentence to solve.

1. A Douglas fir is 100 meters tall and a Ponderosa pine is 68 meters tall. How much taller is the Douglas fir than the Ponderosa pine?

2. In Littleton Park there are 1,128 trees. Clarksville Common has 840 trees. How many fewer trees are in Clarksville Common?

3. A Grand fir tree can grow to be 72 meters tall. The Coast redwood tree can grow to be 17 meters taller. How tall can the Coast redwood tree grow?

4. Last year Broad Street School raised $1,016 for the library by selling plants. They hope to raise at least $175 more this year. What is the least amount they can raise to meet their goal?

Mixed Strategy Review

Solve.

5. Laura buys a packet of seeds. She pays with a dollar and gets back a quarter and a dime for change. How much did the seeds cost?

6. **Science:** A pine cone releases 2 seeds from each of its scales. One pine cone has 81 scales. How many seeds can it release? Explain how you got your answer.

CHOOSE A STRATEGY
- Logical Reasoning
- Draw a Picture
- Make a Graph
- Act It Out
- Make a Table or List
- Find a Pattern
- Guess and Check
- Write a Number Sentence
- Work Backward
- Solve a Simpler Problem

Use data from the survey for problems 7–10.

7. **Language Arts:** Write a notice for the Watertown paper that summarizes the results of the survey.

8. How many more votes did the winning flower get than the one with the least number of votes?

★9. If you round all the votes to the nearest hundred, can you still tell which flower won? Can you tell which came in second? Why or why not?

10. **Create a problem** using the information from the chart. Solve it. Then give it to a friend to solve.

Watertown Official Town Flower Survey

Flower	Number of Votes
Rose	1,345
Tulip	978
Daisy	1,008
Tiger Lily	749

3·9 Subtract Greater Numbers

Learn

Look at all those flowers! The Botanical Gardens creates a special display with 2,238 red roses and 1,319 pink roses. How many more red roses are there than pink roses?

2,238 red roses | **1,319 pink roses**

Example 1

Find: 2,238 − 1,319

1

Subtract the ones. Regroup if necessary.

$$
\begin{array}{r}
2,2\overset{2\ 18}{\cancel{3}\cancel{8}} \\
-1,3\,1\,9 \\
\hline
9
\end{array}
$$

Think:
3 tens 8 ones =
2 tens 18 ones

2

Subtract the tens. Regroup if necessary.

$$
\begin{array}{r}
2,2\overset{2\ 18}{\cancel{3}\cancel{8}} \\
-1,3\,1\,9 \\
\hline
1\,9
\end{array}
$$

3

Subtract the hundreds. Regroup if necessary.

$$
\begin{array}{r}
\overset{1\ 12\ 2\ 18}{2,\cancel{2}\cancel{3}\cancel{8}} \\
-1,3\,1\,9 \\
\hline
9\,1\,9
\end{array}
$$

Think:
2 thousands
2 hundreds =
1 thousand
12 hundreds

4

Subtract the thousands.

$$
\begin{array}{r}
\overset{1\ 12\ 2\ 18}{2,\cancel{2}\cancel{3}\cancel{8}} \\
-1,3\,1\,9 \\
\hline
9\,1\,9
\end{array}
$$

Estimate:
2,000 − 1,000 = 1,000
919 is reasonably close to 1,000.

Check: You can estimate to check whether your answer is reasonable.

There are 919 more red roses than pink roses.

The regular admission price to the Botanical Gardens is $10.00. Jean has a discount coupon worth $2.25 off the price. How much will Jean pay?

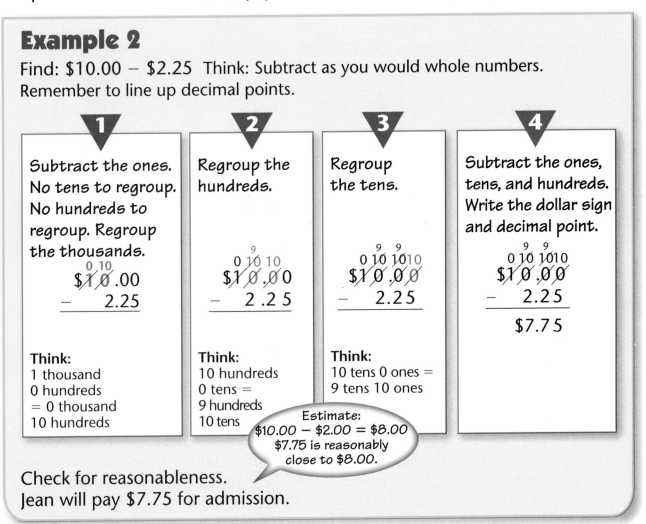

Example 2

Find: $10.00 − $2.25 Think: Subtract as you would whole numbers. Remember to line up decimal points.

1

Subtract the ones. No tens to regroup. No hundreds to regroup. Regroup the thousands.

$$\begin{array}{r} {}^{0\ 10}\\ \$\cancel{10}.00 \\ -\ \ 2.25 \\ \hline \end{array}$$

Think:
1 thousand
0 hundreds
= 0 thousand
10 hundreds

2

Regroup the hundreds.

$$\begin{array}{r} {}^{0\ 10\ 10}\\ \$\cancel{10}.\cancel{0}0 \\ -\ \ 2.25 \\ \hline \end{array}$$

Think:
10 hundreds
0 tens =
9 hundreds
10 tens

3

Regroup the tens.

$$\begin{array}{r} {}^{9\ \ 9}\\ {}^{0\ 10\ 10\,10}\\ \$\cancel{10}.\cancel{0}\cancel{0} \\ -\ \ 2.25 \\ \hline \end{array}$$

Think:
10 tens 0 ones =
9 tens 10 ones

Estimate:
$10.00 − $2.00 = $8.00
$7.75 is reasonably close to $8.00.

4

Subtract the ones, tens, and hundreds. Write the dollar sign and decimal point.

$$\begin{array}{r} {}^{9\ \ 9}\\ {}^{0\ 10\ 10\,10}\\ \$\cancel{10}.\cancel{0}\cancel{0} \\ -\ \ 2.25 \\ \hline \$7.75 \end{array}$$

Check for reasonableness.
Jean will pay $7.75 for admission.

Try It   **Subtract. Check that each answer is reasonable.**

1. 3,435
  −1,423

2. 4,436
  −1,628

3. 6,027
  −4,538

4. 1,004
  − 868

5. $70.98
  − 64.99

6. 2,670
  − 657

7. $10.59
  − 7.68

8. 5,098
  −4,913

9. $31.24
  − 19.54

10. 7,639
  −3,564

11. 2,346 − 1,538 12. $12.18 − $9.56 13. 8,139 − 893 14. $60.77 − $33.45

Sum it Up!   Explain the steps to follow to subtract 3,006 − 1,345.

Subtract. Check that each answer is reasonable.

15. 4,568
   −2,423

16. 3,567
   −1,887

17. 8,435
   −7,598

18. 3,574
   − 896

19. $75.53
   − 38.75

20. 1,202
   − 673

21. $20.76
   − 9.36

22. 9,004
   −8,757

23. $76.08
   − 16.87

24. 8,008
   − 986

25. 6,251 − 6,251

26. $62.74 − $7.55

27. 8,004 − 7,695

28. $90.69 − $17.89

★29. 77,364 − 34,612

★30. 90,005 − 9,769

★31. $400.48 − $176.49

★32. 100,000 − 99,348

Algebra & functions **Write + or − to make a true number sentence.**

33. 3,945 ● 396 = 3,549

34. 4,003 ● 2,673 = 6,676

35. 6,004 ● 3,239 = 2,765

36. 5,734 ● 1,517 = 4,217

37.

Make it RIGHT

$$\begin{array}{r}\overset{9}{\cancel{10}}\overset{9}{\cancel{10}}12\\ 3,\cancel{0}\cancel{0}2\\ -1,764\\ \hline 2,238\end{array}$$

Here is how Helen subtracted 3,002 − 1,764. Tell what mistake Helen made. Show how to correct it.

Problem Solving

38. An adult ticket for a movie about a garden costs $12.75. A child's ticket costs $1.85 less. What is the cost of a child's ticket?

39. **Logical Reasoning:** How many cuts are needed in a log to get 4 pieces? 5 pieces? 6 pieces? What do you notice? Predict the number of cuts needed to get 27 pieces.

40. **Summarize:** Tell how to subtract two numbers no matter how many digits they have.

41. Eli buys a flower pot for $11.94. Jen buys a flower pot for $10.58. How much more did Eli spend?

Use data from the table for problems 42–44.

42. If you buy two different plants, which will give you the most change from a twenty-dollar bill? How much change?

43. Paul buys one of each type of plant. He gives the clerk $30. How much change should he get?

44. **Create a problem** using the data from the table. The problem should be able to be solved by subtraction. Solve it. Ask others to solve it.

Plant Sale

Tulips $11.35

Violets $8.75

Daisies $7.35

Use data from *Did You Know?* for problems 45 and 46.

45. How much taller is the Nepenthes plant than a pitcher plant?

46. During a nature program, Paco saw a patch of 24 pitcher plants. Insects were trapped by 9 of the plants. How many plants did not trap an insect?

Did You Know?

Carnivorous plants eat animals. Most eat insects, but some occasionally eat frogs or small rodents. Over 600 species of carnivorous plants exist, including the 49-foot Nepenthes and the 3-foot pitcher plant.

![spiral icon] **Spiral Review and Test Prep**

Write the digit in the thousands place.

47. 5,604   48. 10,641   49. 74,001   50. 123,627   51. 407,231

Choose the correct answer.

52. Which number has exactly 1 hundred thousand, 1 ten thousand, and 1 hundred?
    A. 100,100   C. 111,001
    B. 110,100   D. 10,100

53. It is 8 o'clock now. Pete will walk his dog in two hours. At what time will Pete walk his dog?
    F. 1 o'clock   H. 2 o'clock
    G. 9 o'clock   J. 10 o'clock

3·10 A

Problem Solving: Application
Decision Making

Which vegetable plants should he buy and how can he arrange them?

Aaron wants to plant vegetables in his garden. He has $10 to spend on plants. He will use plants that have already been started.

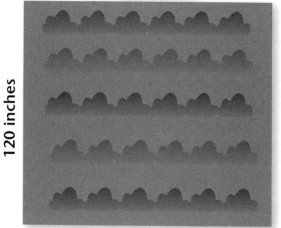

144 inches

120 inches

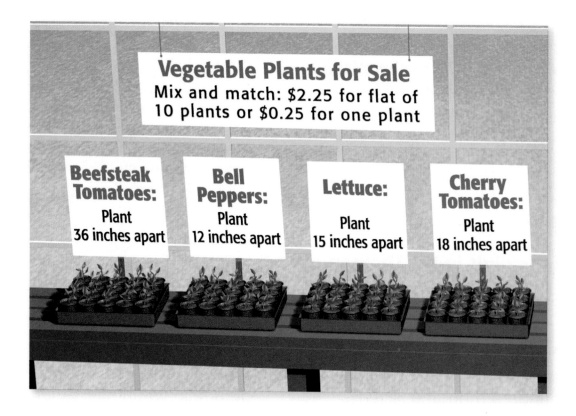

Vegetable Plants for Sale
Mix and match: $2.25 for flat of
10 plants or $0.25 for one plant

Beefsteak Tomatoes:
Plant
36 inches apart

Bell Peppers:
Plant
12 inches apart

Lettuce:
Plant
15 inches apart

Cherry Tomatoes:
Plant
18 inches apart

Read for Understanding

1. How long is Aaron's garden? How wide is it?

2. What is the cost of a flat of plants?

3. How many kinds of vegetable plants are there to choose from?

4. How far apart should beefsteak tomatoes be planted?

5. How far apart should cherry tomatoes be planted?

6. Which needs more space between each plant, lettuce or bell peppers?

Make Decisions

7. Which vegetables can be planted closest together?

8. How much more space is needed between beefsteak tomatoes than between cherry tomatoes?

9. Can Aaron buy 4 flats of plants? How can you tell?

10. If Aaron buys 4 flats of plants, how much money will he have left?

11. How many more plants can he buy with his change? How do you know?

12. Which needs more space between plants, beefsteak tomatoes or cherry tomatoes?

13. Is Aaron's garden long enough to plant 4 beefsteak tomato plants in a row? Explain.

14. Should Aaron place plants in the corners of his garden? Why or why not?

15. How many lettuce plants can Aaron fit in one row of his garden if he starts in a corner?

16. What if Aaron wants to buy only cherry tomato plants. How many plants can he fit in his garden?

17. Based on your diagram, does Aaron have enough money to buy all the plants he needs?

18. What are some advantages and disadvantages of buying only one kind of vegetable plant for his garden?

Your Decision!
Which plants should Aaron buy? How should he arrange them in his garden? Draw a diagram to show your decision.

Problem Solving: Math and Science
How does forest size affect the animals that live there?

You Will Need
- **5 big paper clips**
- **20 small paper clips**
- **shoe box with a cover**
- **large carton with a cover**

In the forest, foxes sometimes eat rabbits for food. Rabbits need space to run and hide from the foxes.

You will investigate what happens to the foxes and rabbits if the forest is big or small. You will use big paper clips as the foxes and small paper clips as the rabbits.

Foxes and rabbits live in the forest. The size of the forest can affect how they live.

Hypothesize

Will it be hard or easy for foxes to find rabbits in a big forest? in a small forest?

Procedure

1. Put all the paper clips in the shoe box. Close the box.
2. Gently shake the box side to side and up and down.
3. Open the box. Take out any small clips that touch big ones.
4. Close the box and shake again. Take out the small clips that are touching the big ones.
5. Repeat until all of the small clips are gone.
6. Tally how many times it takes to take out all of the small clips.
7. Repeat the activity using the large carton.

Data

Copy and complete the charts to record how many times it took to remove all of the small clips. Keep a tally as you go.

Tally	
Small Box	Big Box

Total	
	Total Number of Times
Small box	
Big box	

Conclude and Apply

- How many times did it take to remove all of the small clips from the shoe box? the large carton?

- Did it take more times to remove the clips from the shoe box or from the large carton?

- Subtract to find exactly how many more times.

- Is this activity a good model for what happens in the forest? How is it good? How is it bad?

- Describe what might happen to the prey population if there were no predators in the forest.

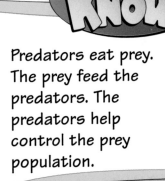

Did You KNOW?

Predators eat prey. The prey feed the predators. The predators help control the prey population.

Going Further

1. Repeat the activity with 10 big clips and 40 small clips. How did your answers change?

2. Wolves eat both foxes and rabbits. Design an activity to investigate this predator-prey relationship in small and large forests.

Subtract. Add to check. (pages 106–107)

1. 50 − 27
2. 405 − 25
3. 860 − 114
4. 702 − 331
5. 501 − 306
6. 634 − 100
7. 980 − 90
8. 756 − 206

Estimate each difference. (pages 108–109)

9. 75 − 58
10. 832 − 309
11. 3,364 − 609
12. 289 − 37

Subtract. Check that each answer is reasonable. (pages 112–115)

13. 606 − 89
14. $6,340 − $284
15. 4,875 − 3,168
16. 882 − 256
17. 3,515 − 1,863
18. 943 − 678

19.
   $$\begin{array}{r} 407 \\ -\ 89 \\ \hline \end{array}$$

20.
   $$\begin{array}{r} \$21.90 \\ -\ 11.75 \\ \hline \end{array}$$

21.
   $$\begin{array}{r} \$7.46 \\ -\ 3.39 \\ \hline \end{array}$$

Solve. (pages 106 –115)

22. An oak tree is 78 feet tall. The fir tree next to the oak is 122 feet tall. How much taller is the fir tree? Write a number sentence.

23. A large bouquet of flowers costs $8.49. A small bouquet sells for $5.75. How much money will you save if you buy a small bouquet?

24. A nursery has 2,468 bushes in stock. At the end of the season there are 386 bushes left. Show how to estimate the number of bushes the nursery sold.

25. **Summarize:** What are three different ways you can use to solve a subtraction problem?

Additional activities at
www.mhschool.com/math

Extra Practice

Relate Addition and Subtraction (pages 90–93)

Write a group of related sentences for each group of numbers.

1. 15, 4, 19   **2.** 3, 9, 12   **3.** 5, 5, 10   **4.** 7, 9, 16

Find the sum or difference. Write a related addition or subtraction fact.

5. 24 + 7   **6.** 7 + 1   **7.** 38 − 2   **8.** 9 − 0

Find each missing addend.

9. 7 + r = 14   **10.** q + 7 = 13   **11.** 2 + z = 2   **12.** p + 7 = 15

Problem Solving: Reading for Math
Identify Extra Information (pages 94–95)

Solve. Identify the extra information.

1. Paul picks 14 apples from one tree. He picks 9 apples from another. He picks 8 pears. He picks 10 peaches. How many more apples did he pick than pears?

2. A bush has 12 flowers and 10 buds. If 5 buds open, how many buds are left unopened?

3. Clara buys 4 roses, 5 tulips, and 2 ferns. How many flowers did she buy?

Subtraction Patterns (pages 96–97)

Write the number sentence that makes each sentence true.

1. $9 - 5 = w$
$90 - 50 = x$
$900 - 500 = y$

2. $12 - 3 = a$
$120 - b = 90$
$c - 300 = 900$

3. $l - 3 = 8$
$110 - m = 80$
$1,100 - 300 = n$

Subtract. Use mental math.

4. 700 − 300   **5.** 815 − 300   **6.** 240 − 30   **7.** 432 − 200

Extra Practice

Subtract Whole Numbers (pages 100–103)

Subtract. Check your answer.

1. $333 − $101
2. 48 − 24
3. $312 − $73
4. 848 − 653
5. $768 − $215
6. 648 − 325
7. 842 − 273
8. 3,478 − 565

9. Tamika bought a plant for $6.57. How much change did she get from $10.00?

10. Rob bought one packet of seeds for $0.39 and one for $0.56. He had $0.95 in his pocket. How much money will he have left after paying for the seeds?

Regroup Across Zeros (pages 106–107)

Subtract. Check your answer.

1. 302 − 58
2. $4,008 − $279
3. 6,020 − 3,654
4. 950 − 472

5. 302
   − 19

6. 404
   −269

7. $3,050
   −   299

8. 8,000
   −4,233

Solve.

9. According to the United Nations, about 630 million tons of rice and 333 million tons of potatoes were produced worldwide in 1997. How many more millions of tons of rice were produced than potatoes?

10. In a survey, 1,008 people were asked what their favorite flower is and 456 named tulips. How many named another kind of flower?

Estimate Differences (pages 108–109)

Estimate each difference.

1. 972 − 513
2. 334 − 178
3. 668 − 26
4. 8,237 − 3,890
5. 841 − 589
6. 356 − 24
7. 1,538 − 589
8. 3,038 − 1,950

9. Both corn and bamboo are grasses. Giant bamboo can grow 164 feet tall. The tallest corn plants can grow 25 feet tall. About how much taller can giant bamboo grow than corn?

Extra Practice

Problem Solving: Strategy
Write a Number Sentence (pages 110–111)

Use data from the table for problems 1– 5.

1. How many more species of beech are there than magnolia?

2. How many fewer species of dogwoods are there than willows?

3. How many more species of willows are there than magnolia?

4. How many species are shown in the table altogether?

5. Is the number of species of beech trees greater or less than the combined total of the other species of trees? How much greater or less?

Tree Species

Tree	Estimated Number of Species
Magnolia	230
Beech	900
Willow	500
Dogwood	110

Subtract Greater Numbers (pages 112–115)

Subtract.

1. $\begin{array}{r} \$0.72 \\ -\ 0.38 \end{array}$

2. $\begin{array}{r} \$263.89 \\ -\ 134.95 \end{array}$

3. $\begin{array}{r} \$7.12 \\ -\ 2.65 \end{array}$

4. $\begin{array}{r} \$842.23 \\ -\ 599.57 \end{array}$

5. $6,365 - $407

6. $5,224 - 567$

7. $7,548 - 892$

8. $2,534 - 1,630$

9. $4,938 - 1,861$

10. $8,643 - 4,014$

Solve.

11. The annual Garden Show collected $3,324 from ticket sales. The expenses for the show were $1,025. How much money is left over?

12. Last week 892 people visited the local botanical garden. This week 1,651 people visited. How many more people visited this week than last week?

Chapter Study Guide

Language and Math
Complete. Use a word from the list.

Math Words

decimal point
difference
estimate
fact families
regroup
related facts

1. The answer in subtraction is the ____.

2. The ____ separates dollars from cents in a money amount.

3. If you have to subtract more ones than you have, you can ____ the tens to ones.

4. To ____ a difference you can round the number, then subtract.

5. ____ are made up of related facts.

Skills and Applications

Use mental math. (pages 96–97)

Example
Find: $1,300 - 700$
Solution
Use patterns to subtract mentally.

$$13 - 7 = 6$$
$$130 - 70 = 60$$
$$1,300 - 700 = 600$$

Subtract Use mental math.

6. $70 - 40$ 7. $90 - 50$

8. $50 - 40$ 9. $80 - 80$

10. $120 - 40$ 11. $800 - 400$

12. $1,100 - 600$ 13. $1,300 - 800$

Use inverse operations. (pages 90–93)

Example
Find the missing addend: $n + 5 = 12$
Solution
Use the related subtraction fact.
$12 - 5 = 7$, so $7 + 5 = 12$
The missing addend is 7.

Write a group of related sentences.

14. 2, 6, 8 15. 8, 8, 16

Find each missing addend.

16. $n + 4 = 11$ 17. $6 + m = 14$

18. $y + 7 = 7$ 19. $5 + b = 11$

Find each difference. Write a related addition fact.

20. $10 - 10$ 21. $15 - 7$

Subtract whole numbers. (pages 98–103, 106–107, 112–115)

Example
Find: 614 − 148
Solution
Subtract. Regroup if necessary.

$$
\begin{array}{r}
{\scriptstyle 5\;10\,14} \\
\cancel{6}\,\cancel{1}\,\cancel{4} \\
-\,1\,4\,8 \\
\hline
4\,6\,6
\end{array}
$$

Check: 466 + 148 = 614

Subtract. Check your answer.

22. 456 − 187   **23.** 2,345 − 709

24. 764 − 187   **25.** 5,070 − 651

26. 642 − 98   **27.** 1,012 − 78

28. $8.24 − $3.19 **29.** $4.02 − $0.87

30. $605 − $234

Estimate differences. (pages 108–109)

Example
Estimate: 821 − 367
Solution
Round each number.
Think: 821 − 367
         ↓   ↓
         800 − 400 = 400
So 821 − 367 is about 400.

Estimate each difference.

31. 678 − 324   **32.** 842 − 513

33. 756 − 678   **34.** 1,380 − 564

35. 1,602 − 178   **36.** 978 − 540

37. $6.98 − $2.85 **38.** $8.74 − $3.23

Use strategies to solve problems. (pages 94–95, 110–111)

Example
A farmer has room to plant 523 rows of corn. So far she has planted 187 rows. How many more rows of corn can she plant?
Solution
Write a number sentence.
523 − 187 = 336
She can plant 336 more rows of corn.

Solve.

39. The florist ordered 124 roses, 276 tulips, and 178 carnations. How many more carnations than roses were ordered?

40. A seed catalog offers 1,246 kinds of flower seeds and 382 kinds of vegetable seeds. About how many more kinds of flower seeds are offered?

Chapter Test

Subtract.

1. $18 - 3$
2. $11 - 0$
3. $10 - 10$
4. $17 - 9$

Write each missing number.
Then complete the fact family.

5. $11 + b = 14$
6. $n + 8 = 8$
7. $15 + 6 = q$
8. $9 + r = 18$

Subtract.

9. $3,568 - 264$
10. $\$4,156 - \$609$
11. $5,122 - 899$
12. $607 - 78$
13. $\$8,002 - \$423$
14. $9,876 - 5,678$
15. $\$1.56 - \$0.74$
16. $\$6.65 - \$1.37$
17. $\$9.05 - \$0.89$

Estimate each difference.

18. $563 - 320$
19. $734 - 398$
20. $1,489 - 823$
21. $6,020 - 1,987$

Solve.

22. Ned collects dried flowers. He has 74 flowers in an album. The album holds 120 flowers. How many more flowers can be put in the album?

23. Suppose you work in your garden for 90 minutes on Saturday. On Sunday you work 25 minutes more than on Saturday. How many minutes have you worked in two days?

24. Flower pots cost $4.75 for small, $5.99 for medium, and $9.99 for large. How much will a small and a large flower pot cost altogether?

25. Raymond bought 2 garden hoses for $6.95 each. How much change should he get back from a twenty-dollar bill?

Performance Assessment

Dave has $475 to spend on his garden this year. He wants to have between $30 and $35 left to paint the garden fence. Look at the items on sale at the garden shop. Which items can Dave buy?

Make a chart like the one below to help you keep track of how much money is left. Make your chart as long as you need to.

$55

$49

$17

$220

GRASS SEED

$65

$129

$23

$20

$49

Use your chart to help you answer these questions.

- How many different items can Dave buy?
- How much money does he have left?

Item	Cost	Money Left

Journal

A Good Answer
- shows a chart that is clearly filled in.
- shows the steps you followed to find the money left after each purchase.
- shows the right amount left.

Portfolio

 You may want to save this work in your portfolio.

Enrichment

Odd or Even Sums and Differences

Odd numbers end in 1, 3, 5, 7, or 9. 27 is an odd number.
Even numbers end in 0, 2, 4, 6, or 8. 46 is an even number.

Write if the number is odd or even.

1. 45
2. 1
3. 127
4. 94
5. 328

When you add or subtract even and odd numbers, can you predict what the sum will be? Will you get an odd number? Will you get an even number? You can make a table to look for patterns.

6. Make a table like the one below to find sums.

Numbers	Example	Sum	Odd or Even?
odd + odd	43 + 21		
odd + odd	11 + 85		
even + even	32 + 12		
even + even	44 + 30		
odd + even	15 + 8		
even + odd	16 + 33		

7. Make a table like the one below to find differences.

Numbers	Example	Difference	Odd or Even?
odd − odd	15 − 3		
odd − odd	67 − 41		
even − even	88 − 14		
even − even	96 − 30		
odd − even	13 − 4		
odd − even	25 − 22		
even − odd	14 − 7		
odd − even	17 − 12		

8. **Generalize:** What did you discover? Write a paragraph.

9. How can you use these generalizations to check that a sum or difference is reasonable?

Test-Taking Tips

S.O.S.

Here is another way to work with multiple-choice questions. After you read the problem, eliminate choices by first **estimating the answer.**

Carl spent $3.47 at the store. How much change should he get from $5.00?

A. $0.98   **C.** $1.63
B. $1.53   **D.** $2.53

Estimate the answer by rounding $3.47 to $3.50.

$5.00 − $3.50 = $1.50

You can eliminate choices A and D. Now find the exact answer.

$5.00 − $3.47 = $1.53.

B is the correct choice.

Check for Success

Before turning in a test, go back one last time to check.

☑ I understood and answered the questions asked.

☑ I checked my work for errors.

☑ My answers make sense.

Use estimation to eliminate choices.
Choose the correct answer.

1. 399 + 802
   A. 403   **C.** 1,191
   B. 1,101   **D.** 1,201

2. 119 less than 450 is ▌.
   F. 331   **H.** 349
   G. 341   **J.** 569

3. Val got $3.76 in change from a ten-dollar bill. How much did she spend?
   A. $4.24   **C.** $6.24
   B. $5.34   **D.** $6.34

4. 538 − 82
   F. 456   **H.** 610
   G. 506   **J.** 620

5. 822 − 396
   A. 426   **C.** 536
   B. 526   **D.** 1,208

6. There were 324 people at the concert on Tuesday, 478 people on Wednesday, and 389 on Thursday. How many people went to the concert?
   F. 1,071   **H.** 1,191
   G. 1,091   **J.** 1,312

Test Prep

Spiral Review and Test Prep
Chapters 1–3

Choose the correct answer.

Number Sense

1. On Saturday about 1,645 people attended the Flower Show. On Sunday about 1,654 people attended. On Monday 1,564 people attended. List the days in order of greatest to least attendance.
   - **A.** Saturday, Sunday, Monday
   - **B.** Sunday, Saturday, Monday
   - **C.** Monday, Saturday, Sunday
   - **D.** Sunday, Monday, Saturday

2. What place value does the number 7 hold in 576,890?
   - **F.** Thousands
   - **G.** Hundred-thousands
   - **H.** Ten-thousands
   - **J.** Tens

3. On the first day Joe made $886. On the other two days he made $679 and $528. About how much did he make altogether?
   - **A.** $1,800
   - **C.** $2,000
   - **B.** $1,900
   - **D.** $2,100

4. Write 32,506 in expanded form. What number is missing?
   $$30,000 + \blacksquare + 500 + 6$$
   - **F.** 20,000
   - **H.** 200
   - **G.** 2,000
   - **J.** 2

Algebra and Functions

5. By mistake Tracy erased part of her subtraction problem. What is the missing digit?
   $$4\blacksquare6 - 149 = 287$$
   - **F.** 6
   - **H.** 3
   - **G.** 2
   - **J.** 4

6. What is the missing number?
   $$7 + 5 = 12$$
   $$70 + 50 = 120$$
   $$700 + n = 1,200$$
   - **A.** 50
   - **C.** 500
   - **B.** 70
   - **D.** 700

7. What operation makes this number sentence true?
   $$88 \; \bullet \; 4 = 84$$
   - **F.** $+$
   - **H.** $\times$
   - **G.** $-$
   - **J.** $\div$

8. Which number sentence shows how to use the Associative Property to add in a different way?
   $$(6 + 4) + 3$$
   - **A.** $3 + 4 + 3$
   - **C.** $13 + 0$
   - **B.** $6 + (4 + 3)$
   - **D.** $10 + 3$

Measurement and Geometry

9. When Marco planted a tomato plant in the ground it was 8 inches high. Seven weeks later the plant was 56 inches high. How much did the plant grow in those seven weeks?

    A. 7 inches
    B. 48 inches
    C. 64 inches
    D. Not Here

10. Each trip to the plant store and back takes Kim 20 minutes. One day Kim made 3 trips to the plant store. Which answer tells how long it took her altogether?

    F. less than a half hour
    G. less than 1 hour
    H. exactly 1 hour
    J. more than 1 hour

11. A landscaper makes a bed in the shape of a trapezoid. Which figure shows how this bed would look?

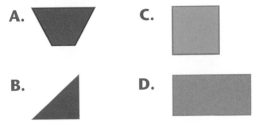

    A.   C.

    B.   D.

12. Green's Nursery has small carrying baskets for customers to use. Which item would not fit in a carrying basket?

    F. a bouquet of flowers
    G. an 8-foot maple tree
    H. a 12-inch shrub
    J. an 8-inch hanging plant

Statistics, Data Analysis, and Probability

Use the table for questions 13–16.

Flowering Herbs

Name	Height	Month It Flowers
Lavender	30 in.	June–July
Borage	16 in.	June–August
Catnip	14 in.	July–September
Chives	24 in.	June
Sage	18 in.	June

13. How many plants flower in June only?

    A. 1
    B. 2
    C. 3
    D. 4

14. How much taller are the chives than the catnip?

    F. 6 inches   H. 10 inches
    G. 8 inches   J. 12 inches

15. Which is the smallest plant?

    A. borage   C. chives
    B. sage   D. Not Here

16. Write a problem using data from the table. Explain how you would solve it.

Statistics, Data Analysis, and Probability

Use the table for problems 9–12.

Albert's Schedule	
7:30	Eat breakfast
8:00	Get ready for school
8:20	Leave for bus stop
8:30	Get on bus
8:45	Get to school

9. How much time does it take Albert to get ready for school?
   - **A.** 30 minutes
   - **B.** 20 minutes
   - **C.** 40 minutes
   - **D.** 10 minutes

10. How much time has passed from the time Albert starts breakfast to the time he leaves for the bus stop?
   - **F.** 1 hour 10 minutes
   - **G.** 1 hour
   - **H.** 60 minutes
   - **J.** 50 minutes

11. How long is the bus ride?
   - **A.** 5 minutes
   - **B.** 10 minutes
   - **C.** $\frac{1}{4}$ hour
   - **D.** $\frac{1}{2}$ hour

12. Albert makes a pictograph of his schedule. Each symbol stands for 5 minutes. How many symbols would he need to show the amount of time he spends on the bus?
   - **F.** 15
   - **G.** 10
   - **H.** 3
   - **J.** 1

Mathematical Reasoning

13. Which fact could you use to check $7 - 4 = 3$?
   - **A.** $7 + 4 = 3$
   - **B.** $3 + 4 = 7$
   - **C.** $3 + 7 = 10$
   - **D.** Not Here

14. Jerry's brother Dan is 14. His sister is 2 years older than Jerry and 3 years younger than Dan. How old is Jerry?
   - **F.** 9
   - **G.** 10
   - **H.** 11
   - **J.** 12

15. You spend $3.78 on a new toy. You pay with a five-dollar bill. What is your change?
   - **A.** $0.22
   - **B.** $1.22
   - **C.** $1.32
   - **D.** $2.22

16. The change in Matthew's pocket totals $0.39. What are the fewest coins he can have? How do you know?

Multiplication Concepts

Theme: Performing Arts

Use the Data

Longest-Running Broadway Musicals
(as of January 2000)

Musical	Number of Performances (Rounded to the Nearest Thousand)
Cats (1982–2000)	🎭🎭🎭🎭🎭🎭🎭
A Chorus Line (1975–1990)	🎭🎭🎭🎭🎭🎭
Les Miserables (1987–)	🎭🎭🎭🎭🎭
The Phantom of the Opera (1988–)	🎭🎭🎭🎭

Each 🎭 = 1,000 performances

Source: Top Ten of Everything

- For how many performances has the longest-running show run?

- How can multiplication help you solve this problem?

What You Will Learn
In this chapter you will learn how to
- multiply facts through 5.
- use the properties of multiplication.
- use strategies to solve problems.

Additional activities at
www.mhschool.com/math

5·1 Explore the Meaning of Multiplication

Algebra & functions

Learn

Math Words

multiplication an operation using at least two numbers to find another number, called a product

factor number that is multiplied to give a product.

product the answer in multiplication

You can use models to explore the meaning of multiplication. How many are in 4 groups of 6?

Work Together

► You can use **multiplication** to solve the problem.
Use cubes to model the problem.
Make a table like the one shown.

You Will Need
• connecting cubes

Number of Groups	Number in Each Group	Total
Factor	Factor	Product

• Make equal groups.
• Record the total in the table.
• Record the answer to the problem.

► Use cubes to solve these problems.

3 groups of 3	2 groups of 2	4 groups of 2
2 groups of 5	3 groups of 4	4 groups of 6

Make Connections

Here is how to find the product of 6 × 2.

Using Models

Using Paper and Pencil

Number of Groups		Number in Each Group		Product
6	×	2	=	12
↑		↑		↑
factor		**factor**		**product**

Try It Use models to find each total.

1. 3 groups of 3
2. 4 groups of 2
3. 2 groups of 5

Multiply. You may use models.

4. 3 × 5
5. 2 × 3
6. 3 × 6
7. 4 × 4
8. 3 × 3

 **Sum it Up** What happens to the product when the numbers listed for the number in each group and the number of groups are reversed?

Practice Use models to find each total.

9. 4 groups of 9
10. 7 groups of 3
11. 8 groups of 2
12. 8 groups of 4
13. 5 groups of 7
14. 1 group of 11

Multiply. You may use models.

15. 5 × 5
16. 6 × 4
17. 3 × 2
18. 9 × 3
19. 2 × 4
20. 2 × 7
21. 8 × 6
22. 9 × 2
23. 6 × 7
24. 1 × 8

25. **Generalize:** If you keep the product the same, what happens to the number of groups as the number in each group increases?

5·2 Relate Multiplication and Addition

Math in ACTION

Algebra & functions

Learn

Math Words

multiplication sentence a math statement that uses an equals symbol

multiple the product of a number and any whole number

Have you ever had to practice for a big performance? If Tatiana practices 3 hours each day for a week, how many hours will she practice altogether?

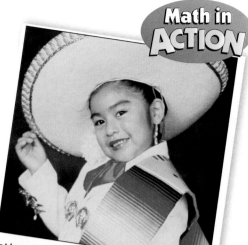

Tatiana is one of the youngest mariachi singers in California. She has been singing since she was three years old!

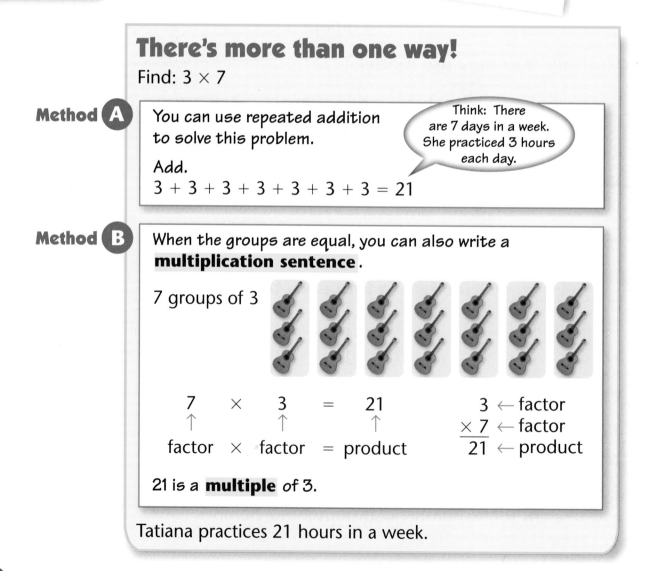

There's more than one way!

Find: 3 × 7

Method A

You can use repeated addition to solve this problem.

Add.

3 + 3 + 3 + 3 + 3 + 3 + 3 = 21

Think: There are 7 days in a week. She practiced 3 hours each day.

Method B

When the groups are equal, you can also write a **multiplication sentence**.

7 groups of 3

$$
\begin{array}{ccccc}
7 & \times & 3 & = & 21 \\
\uparrow & & \uparrow & & \uparrow \\
\text{factor} & \times & \text{factor} & = & \text{product}
\end{array}
$$

3 ← factor
× 7 ← factor
21 ← product

21 is a **multiple** of 3.

Tatiana practices 21 hours in a week.

If Tatiana's show goes on 4 times a week for 3 weeks, how many shows will there be?

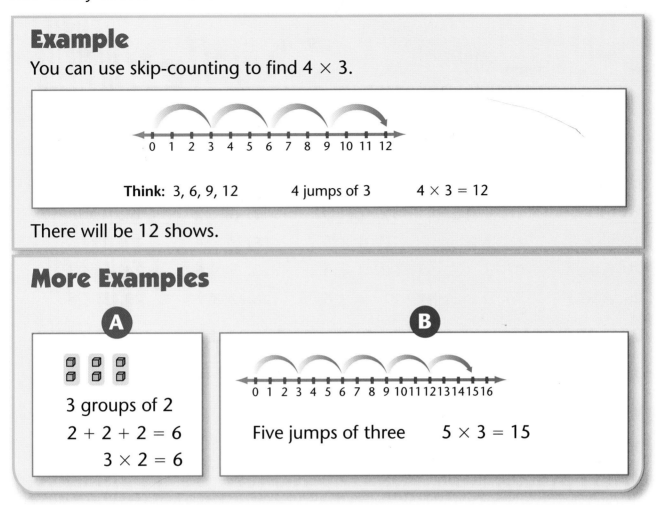

Example

You can use skip-counting to find 4×3.

Think: 3, 6, 9, 12   4 jumps of 3 $4 \times 3 = 12$

There will be 12 shows.

More Examples

A

3 groups of 2
$2 + 2 + 2 = 6$
$3 \times 2 = 6$

B

Five jumps of three $5 \times 3 = 15$

Try It **Find each total. Write an addition sentence and a multiplication sentence.**

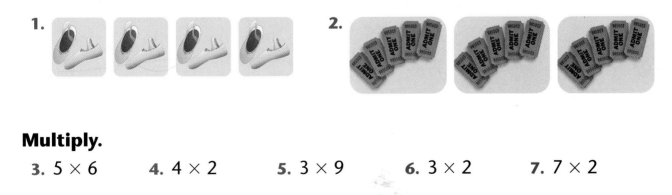

1.

2.

Multiply.

3. 5×6 **4.** 4×2 **5.** 3×9 **6.** 3×2 **7.** 7×2

When can you write a multiplication sentence or an addition sentence to solve a problem? When can you write only an addition sentence? Give examples for both.

 **Find each total. Write an addition sentence and a multiplication sentence.**

8.

9.

Multiply.

10. 3×2	**11.** 4×5	**12.** 2×9	**13.** 6×2	**14.** 4×4
15. 2×8	**16.** 3×3	**17.** 4×5	**18.** 2×4	**19.** 4×3
20. 5×1	**21.** 3×4	**22.** 2×6	**23.** 5×6	**24.** 5×3
25. 4×3	**26.** 3×5	**27.** 3×6	**28.** 2×7	**29.** 3×8

Describe and complete each skip-counting pattern.

30. 3, 6, 9, 12, 15, 18, ___

31. 4, 8, 12, 16, ___

Write + or × to make each sentence true.

★**32.** 2 ● 7 = 7 ● 7

★**33.** 6 ● 2 = 3 ● 4

34.

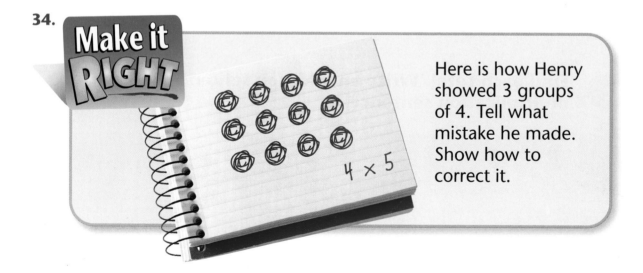

Here is how Henry showed 3 groups of 4. Tell what mistake he made. Show how to correct it.

Problem Solving

35. A sign painter takes 5 minutes to sketch each dancer's face on a sign. How long does it take to sketch 5 faces?

★**36.** Tickets for the school play cost $5 for adults and $2 for students. How much do 3 adult and 2 student tickets cost?

Use data from illustration for problem 37.

37. Spatial Reasoning: Make three squares by changing two wands.

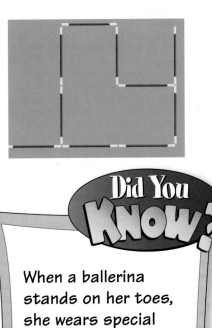

Use data from *Did You Know?* for problem 38.

38. Music: *The Nutcracker* is a ballet written by Peter Tchaikovsky. Marissa is dancing the role of the Sugarplum Fairy. About how many pairs of pointe shoes does she need for 3 weeks of performances?

39. Logical Reasoning: Lon, Jamie, and Rosie each like different kinds of plays—drama, comedy, and musical. Lon likes singing. Jamie likes to laugh. Which kind of play does Rosie like?

40. Number Sense: The circus puts on 2 shows each day. Does each show last for 12, 120, or 1,200 minutes? How can you tell?

41. Create a problem that uses equal numbers of groups. Solve it. Ask others to solve it.

42. Tickets to the dance cost $5. How much do 4 tickets cost?

Did You KNOW?

When a ballerina stands on her toes, she wears special shoes called pointe shoes. Professional ballerinas go through about 3 pairs of shoes in one week of performances.

Spiral Review and Test Prep

43.
$$
\begin{array}{r} 5{,}687 \\ -\ 367 \\ \hline \end{array}
$$

44.
$$
\begin{array}{r} 14 \\ 3 \\ +\ 29 \\ \hline \end{array}
$$

45.
$$
\begin{array}{r} 468 \\ 92 \\ +\ 174 \\ \hline \end{array}
$$

46.
$$
\begin{array}{r} 346 \\ +\ 145 \\ \hline \end{array}
$$

Choose the correct answer.

47. You read a book for 45 minutes. Which is true?
- **A.** You read for less than $\frac{1}{2}$ hour.
- **B.** You read for more than 1 hour.
- **C.** You read for exactly $\frac{1}{4}$ hour.
- **D.** You read for more than $\frac{1}{2}$ hour.

48. Andy's party is December 18. Today is December 4. How long is it until Andy's party?
- **F.** 22 days
- **G.** 2 weeks
- **H.** 3 weeks
- **J.** Not Here

5·3 Multiplication: Explore Using Arrays

Math Words

array objects or symbols displayed in rows and columns

Commutative Property of Multiplication When multiplying, the order of factors does not change the result.

Learn

You can use arrays to explore multiplication.

What is the product of 5×3?

Work Together

▶ Use counters to make an **array** model for the problem.

- How many rows will you make?
- How many counters will you show in each row?
- How many counters will you use altogether?
- What multiplication sentence does your array model show?
- Record the answer to the problem.

▶ What is the product of 3×5?

- Model the problem using counters and graph paper.
- How is this problem like the first? How is it different?
- What multiplication sentence does your array model show?
- Record the answer to the problem.

You Will Need
- counters
- graph paper

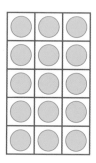

Make Connections

Find 6 × 4 and 4 × 6.

	Using Models	**Using Paper and Pencil**

- To show 6 × 4, make 6 rows of 4 counters.

$$\underset{\substack{\uparrow \\ \text{number} \\ \text{of rows}}}{6} \quad \times \quad \underset{\substack{\uparrow \\ \text{number} \\ \text{in each row}}}{4} \quad = \quad \underset{\substack{\uparrow \\ \text{product}}}{24}$$

$$\underset{\substack{\uparrow \\ \text{number} \\ \text{of rows}}}{4} \quad \times \quad \underset{\substack{\uparrow \\ \text{number} \\ \text{in each row}}}{6} \quad = \quad \underset{\substack{\uparrow \\ \text{product}}}{24}$$

- To show 4 × 6, make 4 rows of 6 counters.

The **Commutative Property of Multiplication** states that when the order of factors 6 and 4 is changed, the product is still 24.

Try It Write the multiplication sentence each array shows.

1.

2.

Find each product. Then use the Commutative Property to write a different multiplication sentence.

3. 2 × 3 4. 1 × 8 5. 4 × 5 6. 1 × 7 7. 3 × 4

Sum It Up! How are arrays for 4 × 5 and 5 × 4 alike? How are they different?

Practice **Find each product. Then use the Commutative Property to write a different multiplication sentence.**

8. 2 × 5 9. 6 × 2 10. 1 × 4 11. 4 × 3 12. 2 × 3

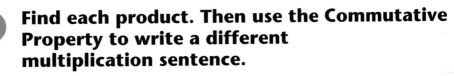

5·4

Problem Solving: Reading for Math
Choose an Operation

Let the Show Begin

Read ▶ Clark School is having a show. One act has 4 groups of dancers. There are 3 dancers in each group. How many dancers are in the act?

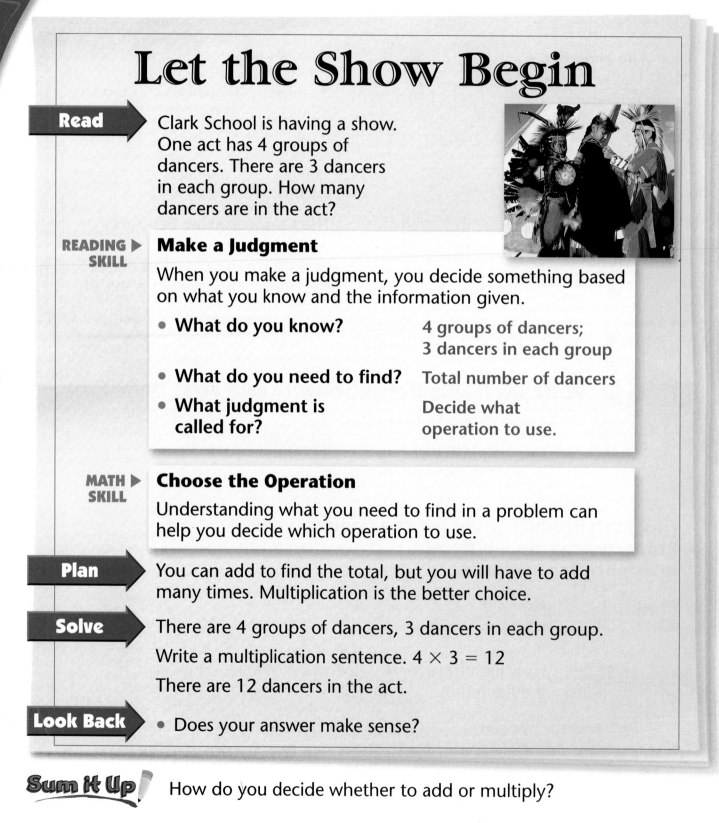

READING SKILL ▶ **Make a Judgment**

When you make a judgment, you decide something based on what you know and the information given.

- **What do you know?**   4 groups of dancers; 3 dancers in each group

- **What do you need to find?**   Total number of dancers

- **What judgment is called for?**   Decide what operation to use.

MATH SKILL ▶ **Choose the Operation**

Understanding what you need to find in a problem can help you decide which operation to use.

Plan ▶ You can add to find the total, but you will have to add many times. Multiplication is the better choice.

Solve ▶ There are 4 groups of dancers, 3 dancers in each group.

Write a multiplication sentence. $4 \times 3 = 12$

There are 12 dancers in the act.

Look Back ▶ • Does your answer make sense?

Sum it Up! How do you decide whether to add or multiply?

Solve. Tell how you chose the operation.

1. There are 8 students in a magic act. In another act, 6 students sing a song. Altogether, how many students are in these two acts?

2. A juggling act has 5 groups of students. Each group has 2 students. How many students are in the juggling act?

3. The balcony has 3 rows of seats. There are 6 seats in each row. How many seats are there in the balcony?

4. This year 8 boys and 9 girls joined the choir. Altogether how many boys and girls joined the choir this year?

Use data from the program for problems 5–10.

5. How many students are in Act 3?

6. How many students are in the skit performed as Act 4?

7. How many students are in Act 5?

8. Altogether, how many students are in both skits?

9. Which two acts contain the same number of students?

10. How many more students are in Act 4 than in Act 2?

Clark School Talent Show

Act 1	Song	3 groups of 3 students
Act 2	Skit	9 male students and 7 female students
Act 3	Dance	6 groups of 2 students
Act 4	Skit	7 third-grade students and 11 fourth-grade students
Act 5	Song	4 groups of 4 students

![Problem Solving sidebar label]

Spiral Review and Test Prep

Choose the correct answer.

Clarice buys 8 bags of bracelets for the show. Each bag holds 2 bracelets. How many bracelets did she buy?

11. Which of these statements is true?
    A. There are 16 bags of bracelets.
    B. Each bag holds 2 bracelets.
    C. A total of 8 bracelets were purchased for the show.

12. Which number sentence can you use to solve the problem?
    F. $8 + 2 = 10$
    G. $8 - 2 = 6$
    H. $8 \times 2 = 16$

Chapter 5 Multiplication Concepts

5·5 Multiply by 2 and 5

Learn

The Young Dancers are practicing for tonight's show. How many dancers are in the dance group if there are 2 rows of 4 dancers?

There's more than one way!

You can multiply to solve this problem.

The picture shows 2 groups of 4 dancers.

Find: 2×4

You can use the strategies you have learned to help you recall 2×4.

Method **A**

Skip-count by 2s to find the total number of dancers.

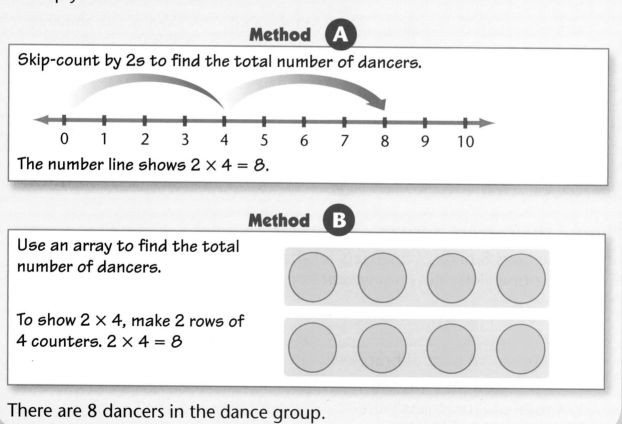

0 1 2 3 4 5 6 7 8 9 10

The number line shows $2 \times 4 = 8$.

Method **B**

Use an array to find the total number of dancers.

To show 2×4, make 2 rows of 4 counters. $2 \times 4 = 8$

There are 8 dancers in the dance group.

The dance show has 3 acts. If the show is performed for 5 days, how many acts are performed?

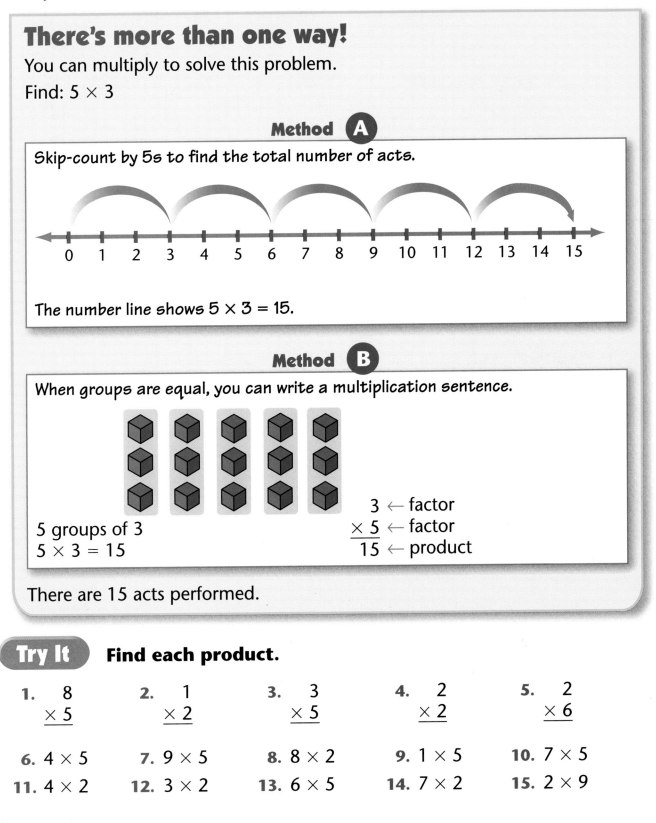

There's more than one way!

You can multiply to solve this problem.

Find: 5 × 3

Method A

Skip-count by 5s to find the total number of acts.

0 1 2 3 4 5 6 7 8 9 10 11 12 13 14 15

The number line shows 5 × 3 = 15.

Method B

When groups are equal, you can write a multiplication sentence.

5 groups of 3
5 × 3 = 15

$$\begin{array}{r} 3 \leftarrow \text{factor} \\ \times\ 5 \leftarrow \text{factor} \\ \hline 15 \leftarrow \text{product} \end{array}$$

There are 15 acts performed.

Try It Find each product.

1. $\begin{array}{r} 8 \\ \times\ 5 \\ \hline \end{array}$

2. $\begin{array}{r} 1 \\ \times\ 2 \\ \hline \end{array}$

3. $\begin{array}{r} 3 \\ \times\ 5 \\ \hline \end{array}$

4. $\begin{array}{r} 2 \\ \times\ 2 \\ \hline \end{array}$

5. $\begin{array}{r} 2 \\ \times\ 6 \\ \hline \end{array}$

6. 4 × 5

7. 9 × 5

8. 8 × 2

9. 1 × 5

10. 7 × 5

11. 4 × 2

12. 3 × 2

13. 6 × 5

14. 7 × 2

15. 2 × 9

Sum it Up What methods can you use to help you remember facts for multiplying 2?

Find each product.

16.	5 ×5	17.	7 ×5	18.	4 ×2	19.	9 ×5	20.	8 ×2	21.	2 ×2

22.	1 ×2	23.	2 ×4	24.	7 ×2	25.	5 ×3	26.	5 ×6	27.	5 ×8

28. 2×7 **29.** 2×5 **30.** 1×5 **31.** 2×6 **32.** 3×2

33. 5×3 **34.** 2×1 **35.** 2×4 **36.** 2×7 **37.** 9×2

38. 6×5 **39.** 2×3 **40.** 5×4 **41.** 3×5 **42.** 8×5

Algebra & functions **Complete the function tables.**

43.

Rule: Multiply by 5	
Input	Output
3	▦
5	▦
▦	35
▦	45

44.

Rule: Multiply by 2	
Input	Output
▦	4
4	▦
6	▦
▦	16

Find each total.

★**45.** $(2 + 1) \times 2$ ★**46.** $(1 + 1) \times 5$ ★**47.** $(5 + 1) \times 2$

★**48.** $(2 + 3) \times 5$ ★**49.** $(2 + 2) \times 4$ ★**50.** $(7 + 1) \times 5$

51.

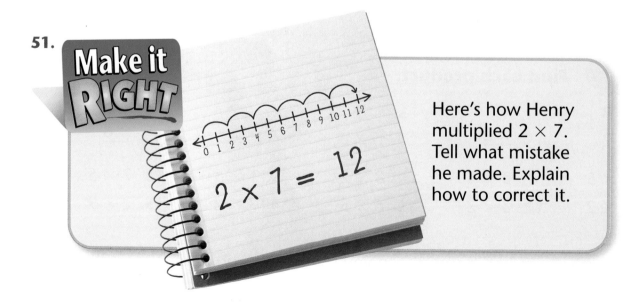

Make it RIGHT

$2 \times 7 = 12$

Here's how Henry multiplied 2×7. Tell what mistake he made. Explain how to correct it.

Problem Solving

52. There are 8 girls in Ms. Myers' ballet class. When they put on their ballet slippers, they leave their shoes at the door. How many shoes are at the door?

53. Music: Ballet folklorico is the traditional dance of Mexico. Dancers in a ballet folklorico company rehearse for 2 hours each day. How long will they rehearse from Monday through Friday?

★ **54.** On Monday 234 people came to see the Ballet Folklorico de Mexico. On Tuesday 72 more people came to see the show than on Monday. How many people in all saw the show in both days?

55. Explain which methods you use to help you remember facts for 5.

★ **56. Literature:** The book *Tuning in: The Sounds of the Radio,* by Eve and Albert Stwerka, has many experiments students can try with sound. In third grade, 5 students each did 3 experiments from the book. Two fourth-grade students each did 3 experiments. How many more experiments were done by third graders than by fourth graders?

57. Collect Data about favorite music groups from your friends. Show your data in a pictograph. Write a problem that uses the data. Challenge another student to solve it.

Spiral Review and Test Prep

58.
$$579 - 154$$

59.
$$1,324 + 231$$

60.
$$2,009 - 456$$

61.
$$3,891 + 768$$

Choose the correct answer.

62. Last month 2,431 tickets were sold for the ballet. What is this number rounded to the nearest hundred?

A. 2,400   C. 2,000

B. 2,300   D. Not Here

63. What is the missing number?
123, 223, ▌, 423, 523

F. 333   H. 323

G. 233   J. 343

Find each total. Write an addition sentence and a multiplication sentence. (pages 178–185)

1. ▯▯▯▯▯

2. ▯▯▯▯

3. 3×2

4. 2×8

5. 5×6

6. 7×5

7. 7×2

8. 8×2

9. $\begin{array}{r} 2 \\ \times\, 4 \\ \hline \end{array}$

10. $\begin{array}{r} 6 \\ \times\, 2 \\ \hline \end{array}$

11. $\begin{array}{r} 2 \\ \times\, 1 \\ \hline \end{array}$

12. $\begin{array}{r} 5 \\ \times\, 5 \\ \hline \end{array}$

13. $\begin{array}{r} 8 \\ \times\, 5 \\ \hline \end{array}$

14. $\begin{array}{r} 2 \\ \times\, 9 \\ \hline \end{array}$

15. $\begin{array}{r} 9 \\ \times\, 5 \\ \hline \end{array}$

16. $\begin{array}{r} 5 \\ \times\, 4 \\ \hline \end{array}$

17. $\begin{array}{r} 2 \\ \times\, 2 \\ \hline \end{array}$

18. $\begin{array}{r} 2 \\ \times\, 5 \\ \hline \end{array}$

19. $\begin{array}{r} 5 \\ \times\, 1 \\ \hline \end{array}$

20. $\begin{array}{r} 5 \\ \times\, 3 \\ \hline \end{array}$

21. $\begin{array}{r} 5 \\ \times\, 6 \\ \hline \end{array}$

Solve. (pages 178–191)

22. The chorus bus has 5 rows of seats. Each row has 4 seats. If 1 singer sits in each seat, can 18 singers fit on the bus? How can you tell?

23. Pablo and his 3 friends saw their favorite movie twice this week. How can you use addition to find the total number of movie tickets they bought this week? How can you use multiplication?

24. In a marching band, there are 5 rows with 3 band members in each row. How many members are in the band? Will you add or multiply to solve?

25. **Analyze:** What pattern do you find in the numbers when you skip-count by 2s?

Additional activities at
www.mhschool.com/math

TECHNOLOGY LINK

Model Multiplication

Marta's Pet Store has a new batch of puppies. Marta put the puppies in 4 different beds. There are 3 puppies in each bed. How many puppies does Marta have?

You can use counters to stamp out a model of 4 groups with 3 puppies in each group.

- Choose multiplication for the mat type.

- At the bottom of the screen, choose 4 in the box on the left and 3 in the box on the right.

The number boxes show that you are finding 4 groups of 3, or 4 × 3.

How many puppies does Marta have?

Use the computer to model each fact. Find the product.

1. 3 × 5   2. 8 × 2   3. 5 × 6   4. 7 × 3

Solve.

5. Kendra has 8 packages of baseball cards. There are 5 cards in each package. How many baseball cards does she have?

6. Mr. Montgomery has 4 cartons of water. There are 6 bottles in each carton. How many bottles of water does he have?

7. **Analyze:** How does using the models help you multiply?

For more practice, use Math Traveler™.

5·6 Multiply by 3 and 4

Learn

Have you ever been in a play? Each of these actors wears 3 costumes during the play. How many costumes are needed for the actors in this play?

Here are strategies you can use to help you remember how to multiply 3 and 4 so that you can recall facts quickly.

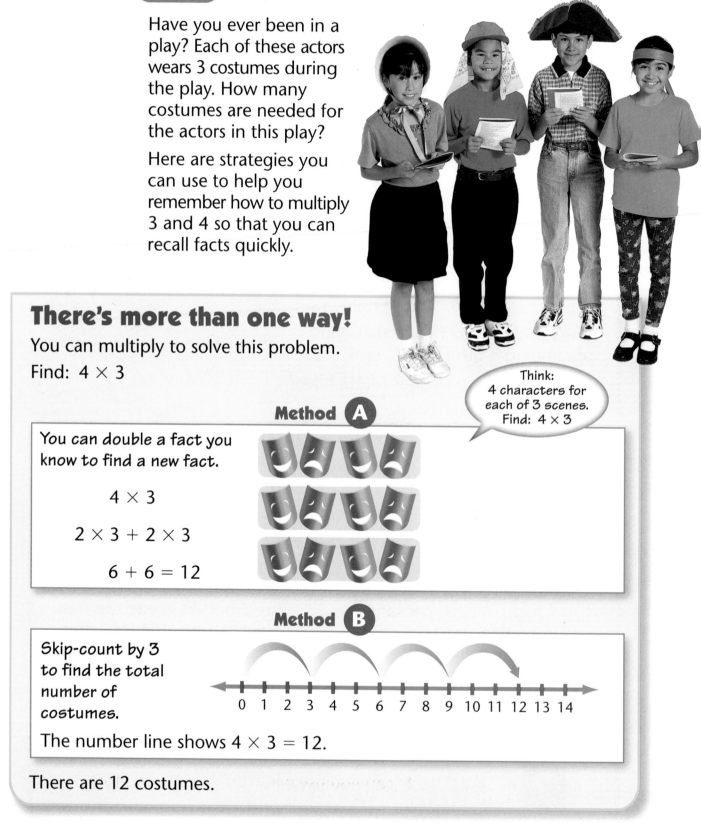

Think:
4 characters for each of 3 scenes.
Find: 4 × 3

There's more than one way!

You can multiply to solve this problem.

Find: 4 × 3

Method A

You can double a fact you know to find a new fact.

4 × 3

2 × 3 + 2 × 3

6 + 6 = 12

Method B

Skip-count by 3 to find the total number of costumes.

The number line shows 4 × 3 = 12.

There are 12 costumes.

How many people watch the play if there are 3 rows of 8 chairs each?

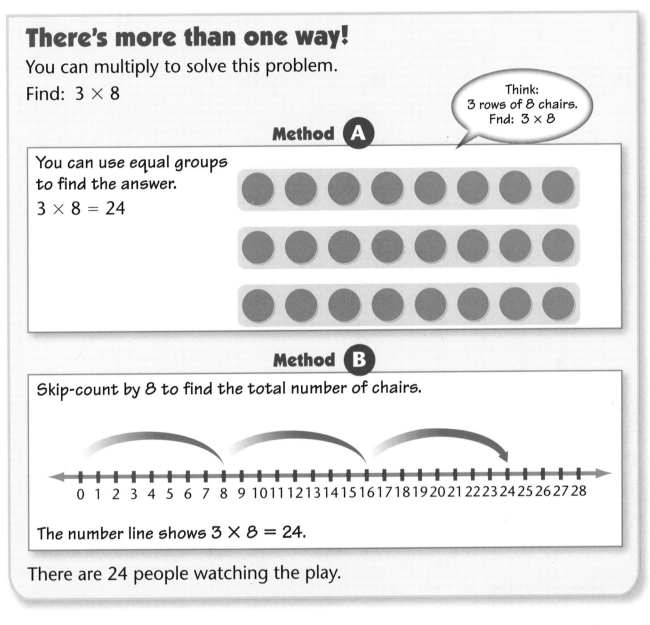

There's more than one way!

You can multiply to solve this problem.

Find: 3×8

Think:
3 rows of 8 chairs.
Fnd: 3×8

Method **A**

You can use equal groups to find the answer.
$3 \times 8 = 24$

Method **B**

Skip-count by 8 to find the total number of chairs.

0 1 2 3 4 5 6 7 8 9 10 11 12 13 14 15 16 17 18 19 20 21 22 23 24 25 26 27 28

The number line shows $3 \times 8 = 24$.

There are 24 people watching the play.

Try It   **Find each product.**

1.	4 ×5	2.	4 ×7	3.	4 ×2	4.	4 ×6	5.	4 ×4
6.	3 ×5	7.	3 ×3	8.	3 ×2	9.	6 ×3	10.	7 ×3

 Which facts can you use when using doubling to find facts for 4?

Multiply.

11.	4	12.	7	13.	4	14.	3	15.	5
	×2		×4		×4		×4		×4

16.	6	17.	9	18.	4	19.	4	20.	4
	×4		×4		×8		×1		×7

21. 1×3 **22.** 3×3 **23.** 3×2 **24.** 6×3 **25.** 7×3

26. 3×9 **27.** 3×5 **28.** 3×8 **29.** 4×3 **30.** 2×3

31. 2×9 **32.** 4×6 **33.** 2×4 **34.** 3×1 **35.** 4×5

Algebra & functions **Copy and complete.**

36.

Number of Boxes	Number of Snacks
1	4
4	▓
▓	20
▓	36

37.

Number Packs	Number of Juice Boxes
1	3
3	▓
▓	21
8	▓

Describe and complete the skip-counting pattern.

38. 42, 45, 48, ▓, ▓, 57, 60

39. 72, ▓, 80, 84, ▓, 92, ▓, ▓

Solve.

★**40.** $4 \times (3 - 1)$ ★**41.** $4 \times (2 - 1)$ ★**42.** $4 \times (5 - 2)$ ★**43.** $4 \times (5 - 3)$

44.

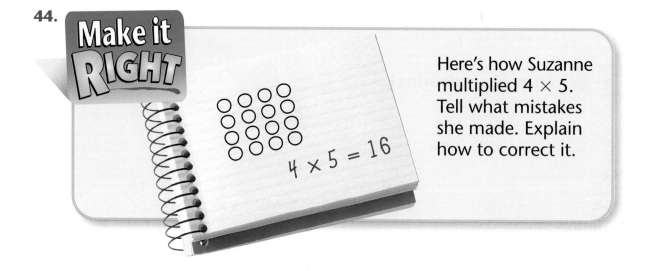

Make it RIGHT

$4 \times 5 = 16$

Here's how Suzanne multiplied 4×5. Tell what mistakes she made. Explain how to correct it.

Problem Solving

Use data from the chart for problems 45–47.

45. Each actor in the play needs 4 scarves. If there are 8 actors in the play, will they use all the scarves? Why or why not?

46. **Measurement:** An actor ties 3 scarves together. Each scarf is 36 inches long. He uses 3 inches from the scarves to make the knots. How long are the knotted scarves?

47. **Create a problem** using the data from the chart. Solve your problem. Challenge another student to solve your problem.

Props Available for the Play

Item	Number
Colored scarves	35
Hats	112
Gold wands	26

Use data from *Did You Know?* for problem 48.

48. 160,000 people participated in the 1937 choral contest. How many people did not participate in the finale?

49. **Explain** how you use doubling of a fact you know to find new facts for 4. Give an example to show your method.

Did You KNOW?

In 1937 the largest choir was made up of 60,000 people who sang together as a finale of a choral contest in Germany.

Spiral Review and Test Prep

50. 56 + 78   **51.** 1,433 − 375   **52.** 775 + 420   **53.** 79 − 39

Choose the correct answer.

54. What is the median of this set of numbers? 2, 5, 6, 2, 5
   - A. 2
   - B. 4
   - C. 5
   - D. 22

55. Kyle buys face paint for $4.09. He pays with a five-dollar bill. How much change does he get?
   - F. $9.09
   - G. $1.09
   - H. $0.91
   - J. Not Here

5·7 Problem Solving: Strategy
Find a Pattern

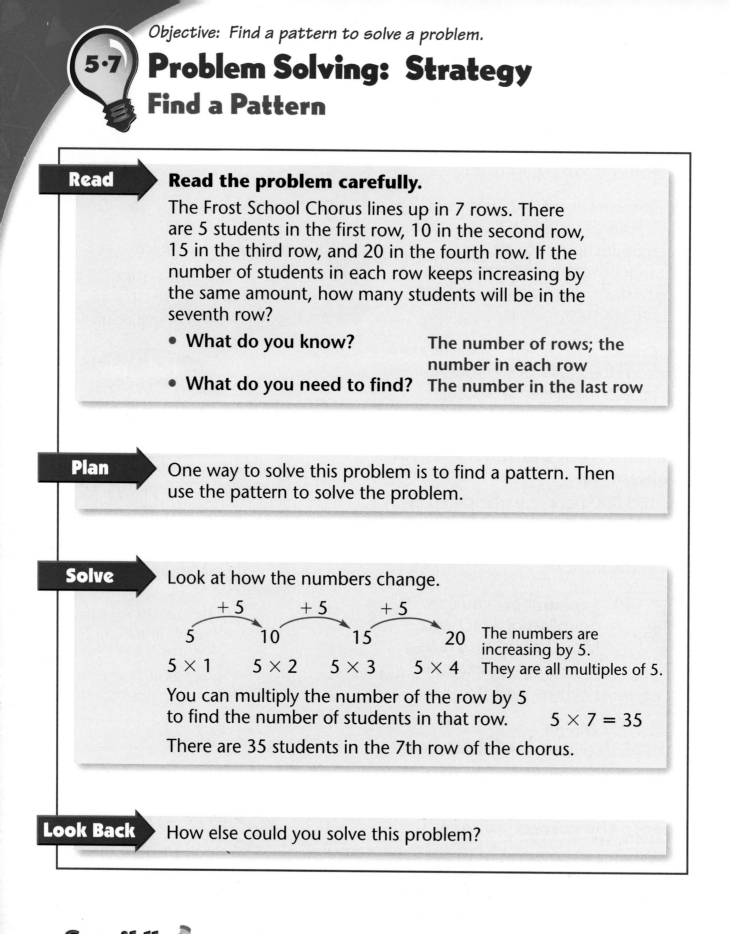

Read ▶ **Read the problem carefully.**

The Frost School Chorus lines up in 7 rows. There are 5 students in the first row, 10 in the second row, 15 in the third row, and 20 in the fourth row. If the number of students in each row keeps increasing by the same amount, how many students will be in the seventh row?

- **What do you know?** The number of rows; the number in each row
- **What do you need to find?** The number in the last row

Plan ▶ One way to solve this problem is to find a pattern. Then use the pattern to solve the problem.

Solve ▶ Look at how the numbers change.

$$+5 \qquad +5 \qquad +5$$

5   10   15   20   The numbers are increasing by 5.

5×1 5×2 5×3 5×4 They are all multiples of 5.

You can multiply the number of the row by 5 to find the number of students in that row. $5 \times 7 = 35$

There are 35 students in the 7th row of the chorus.

Look Back ▶ How else could you solve this problem?

Sum It Up!   How does finding a pattern help you solve problems?

Practice   Find a pattern to solve.

1. The 24 dancers in a show dance in one long chorus line on stage. Every third dancer wears a red costume. All of the others wear blue. Kitty is the 14th dancer on stage. What color costume does she wear?

2. During August there is a concert in the park each week. So far the concerts have been on August 1st, 8th, and 15th. On what date will the fifth concert most likely be?

3. On Monday a theater gives a free ticket to the 10th person in line, on Tuesday to the 20th person, on Wednesday to the 30th, and on Thursday to the 40th. If the position of the person chosen keeps increasing in the same way, who will get the free ticket on Friday?

4. The All-School Band lines up in 8 rows for each performance. The first row has 4 students, the second row has 8 students, and the third row has 12 students. If the number of students in each row continues to increase in the same way, how many students will be in the 8th row?

Mixed Strategy Review

★5. Miguel wants to learn to play the flute. He learns that a new flute costs $475. He can save $280 if he buys a used flute. Miguel decides to buy the used flute and a $29 carrying case. How much does he spend?

6. **Career:** Tanya plays the violin in an orchestra. She will perform on stage 5 nights a week for the next 4 weeks. How many times will she perform during these weeks?

7. Look at the picture of the chairs. There is one more row of chairs that will be set up in the back. If the pattern continues, how many more chairs are needed? How many more music stands?

8. **Create a problem** that can be solved by finding a pattern. Solve it. Ask another student to solve it.

CHOOSE A STRATEGY
- Logical Reasoning
- Draw a Picture
- Make a Graph
- Act It Out
- Make a Table or List
- Find a Pattern
- Guess and Check
- Write a Number Sentence
- Work Backward
- Solve a Simpler Problem

5·8

Multiply by 0 and 1

Algebra & functions **Learn**

Sometimes only 1 row of 4 players is needed to play a song. How many players is this?

Math Words

Properties of Multiplication

Identity The product of any number times one is that number.

Zero The product of any number times zero is zero.

Example 1

You can use the **Identity Property of Multiplication** to solve this problem.

The product is a factor if the other factor is 1.

$1 \times 4 = 4$

There are 4 players.

When the players are finished, there are 0 rows of 4 players. How many players is this?

Example 2

You can use the **Zero Property of Multiplication** to solve this problem.

The product is 0 if 0 is a factor.

$0 \times 4 = 0$

There are 0 players.

 Find each product. Write the property you used.

1. 2×0 2. 8×1 3. 7×0 4. 6×1 5. 3×0

Sum it Up Sam says it is easy to solve $6,789,342 \times 0$. Why?

Practice Find each product.

6. 4
   ×0

7. 1
   ×7

8. 0
   ×3

9. 5
   ×1

10. 8
    ×0

11. 6×0 12. 0×5 13. 1×2 14. 1×9 15. 1×7

16. 0×9 17. 1×3 18. 8×1 19. 1×6 20. 0×7

Find each missing number.

21. $\blacksquare \times 5 = 0$

22. $4 \times \blacksquare = 4$

23. $1 \times 5 = \blacksquare$

24. $6 \times 3 = 3 \times \blacksquare$

25. $8 \times \blacksquare = 0$

26. $24 \times \blacksquare = 24$

27. $\blacksquare \times 13 = 13 \times 9$

28. $1{,}236 \times \blacksquare = 0$

29. $\blacksquare \times 287 = 287$

Problem Solving

30. **Science:** The sound of a musical instrument can travel through the air at 1,125 feet each second. How far does the sound travel in 1 second? How can you tell?

31. Sometimes the drum players in the band march in 2 rows with 4 players in each row. Sometimes they march in 4 rows. How many players are in each of the 4 rows? How can you tell?

32. A trumpet music book costs $9.95. The band leader bought 2 trumpet music books. How much did they cost altogether?

Journal

33. **Explain:** Show two different methods you can use to find 6×4.

Spiral Review and Test Prep

34. $6.75
    + 6.75

35. $2.46
    − 0.97

36. $8.42
    + 6.99

37.   427
    +540

38.   362
    −129

Choose the correct answer.

39. Which shows numbers in order from least to greatest?

   A. 1,110; 1,091; 1,121; 1,099
   B. 2,020; 2,220; 2,202; 2,222
   C. 3,111; 3,131; 3,113; 3,099
   D. 4,040; 4,104; 4,400; 4,440

40. Which data set has a range of 4?

   F. 1, 3, 5, 6, 7, 9
   G. 5, 3, 4, 5, 6, 7
   H. 5, 5, 6, 7, 8, 8
   J. Not Here

5·9 Multiplication Table

 Algebra & functions **Learn**

Each part of the music below is called a measure. Each measure has 4 beats.

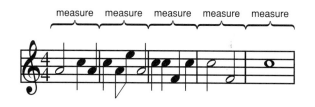

×	0	1	2	3	4	5
0	0	0	0	0	0	0
1	0	1	2	3	4	5
2	0	2	4	6	8	10
3	0	3	6	9	12	15
4	0	4	8	12	16	20
5	0	5	10	15	20	25
6	0	6	12	18	24	30
7	0	7	14	21	28	35
8	0	8	16	24	32	40
9	0	9	18	27	36	45

How many beats are in the first 5 measures of the song?

Example

You can use the multiplication table to recall facts.

> Find 5 × 4 to solve the problem.
>
> **Think:** To find the product of 5 × 4, look where the 5s row and the 4s column meet, or where the 4s row and the 5s column meet.

There are 20 beats in the first 5 measures.

Try It **Copy and complete the table. Look for patterns in your multiplication table.**

1. When you multiply by ____ , the product is always 0.

2. Look at the 2s column and the 4s column. What patterns do you see?

 **Sum it Up** What pattern do you see whenever you find the row and column or column and row for any two factors?

Use the multiplication table to solve.

3. Which columns have only even numbers?

4. Which rows have only even numbers?

Compare. Write >, <, or =.

5. $2 \times 4 \bullet 2 \times 5$

6. $6 \times 3 \bullet 3 \times 6$

7. $1 \times 1 \bullet 9 \times 0$

★8. $4 \times 6 \bullet 3 \times 2$

★9. $3 \times 4 \bullet 6 - 3$

★10. $5 + 2 \bullet 5 \times 2$

Describe and complete each skip-counting pattern.

11. 30, 35, 40, 45, ▮, ▮, ▮

12. 68, 72, 76, ▮, ▮, ▮

Problem Solving

Use data from the chart for problem 13.

13. How many Grammys were won in all by the artists listed in the table? How can you use the multiplication table to find out?

14. **Create a problem** using the table that's solved using the multiplication table. Challenge another student to solve your problem.

Music Grammy Awards Won

Artist	Year	Grammys
Roger Miller	1965	5
Stevie Wonder	1977	5
Chris Cross	1981	5
Quincy Jones	1982	5
Toto	1983	5

Spiral Review and Test Prep

15.
$$\begin{array}{r} 352 \\ +247 \\ \hline \end{array}$$

16.
$$\begin{array}{r} 664 \\ -200 \\ \hline \end{array}$$

17.
$$\begin{array}{r} 841 \\ -384 \\ \hline \end{array}$$

18.
$$\begin{array}{r} 627 \\ +362 \\ \hline \end{array}$$

19.
$$\begin{array}{r} 691 \\ -254 \\ \hline \end{array}$$

Choose the correct answer.

20. How much time has passed between 3:45 P.M. and 4:50 P.M.?

   A. 55 minutes   C. 1 hour

   B. 65 minutes   D. Not Here

21. A play has been running at a theater for about 2 years. About how long is that?

   F. 12 months   H. 24 months

   G. 400 days   J. Not Here

Facts Practice – Multiplication

Multiply. You must be able to recall these facts quickly.

1. 4×4
2. 4×1
3. 5×2
4. 6×3
5. 2×2
6. 9×3
7. 1×2
8. 6×4
9. 9×5
10. 8×3
11. 5×0
12. 3×3
13. 5×1
14. 6×5
15. 2×4
16. 9×4
17. 7×2
18. 6×3
19. 4×5
20. 0×8
21. 5×7
22. 2×5
23. 3×9
24. 8×2
25. 5×6
26. 4×4
27. 2×3
28. 4×7

29. $\begin{array}{r} 7 \\ \times 3 \\ \hline \end{array}$
30. $\begin{array}{r} 5 \\ \times 5 \\ \hline \end{array}$
31. $\begin{array}{r} 4 \\ \times 9 \\ \hline \end{array}$
32. $\begin{array}{r} 6 \\ \times 1 \\ \hline \end{array}$

33. $\begin{array}{r} 2 \\ \times 6 \\ \hline \end{array}$
34. $\begin{array}{r} 3 \\ \times 4 \\ \hline \end{array}$
35. $\begin{array}{r} 9 \\ \times 2 \\ \hline \end{array}$
36. $\begin{array}{r} 7 \\ \times 4 \\ \hline \end{array}$

37. $\begin{array}{r} 7 \\ \times 5 \\ \hline \end{array}$
38. $\begin{array}{r} 3 \\ \times 8 \\ \hline \end{array}$
39. $\begin{array}{r} 4 \\ \times 4 \\ \hline \end{array}$
40. $\begin{array}{r} 1 \\ \times 3 \\ \hline \end{array}$

41. $\begin{array}{r} 1 \\ \times 1 \\ \hline \end{array}$
42. $\begin{array}{r} 5 \\ \times 8 \\ \hline \end{array}$
43. $\begin{array}{r} 6 \\ \times 0 \\ \hline \end{array}$
44. $\begin{array}{r} 4 \\ \times 2 \\ \hline \end{array}$

45. $\begin{array}{r} 6 \\ \times 5 \\ \hline \end{array}$
46. $\begin{array}{r} 2 \\ \times 2 \\ \hline \end{array}$
47. $\begin{array}{r} 3 \\ \times 9 \\ \hline \end{array}$
48. $\begin{array}{r} 6 \\ \times 2 \\ \hline \end{array}$

49. $\begin{array}{r} 7 \\ \times 0 \\ \hline \end{array}$
50. $\begin{array}{r} 6 \\ \times 3 \\ \hline \end{array}$
51. $\begin{array}{r} 1 \\ \times 9 \\ \hline \end{array}$
52. $\begin{array}{r} 5 \\ \times 1 \\ \hline \end{array}$

53. $\begin{array}{r} 2 \\ \times 2 \\ \hline \end{array}$
54. $\begin{array}{r} 0 \\ \times 3 \\ \hline \end{array}$
55. $\begin{array}{r} 3 \\ \times 9 \\ \hline \end{array}$
56. $\begin{array}{r} 4 \\ \times 6 \\ \hline \end{array}$

57. $\begin{array}{r} 1 \\ \times 7 \\ \hline \end{array}$
58. $\begin{array}{r} 5 \\ \times 8 \\ \hline \end{array}$
59. $\begin{array}{r} 2 \\ \times 1 \\ \hline \end{array}$
60. $\begin{array}{r} 4 \\ \times 4 \\ \hline \end{array}$

PICK A FACT GAME

Each pair of students makes two cards for each of eight facts. One card has the problem; the second card has the answer.

You Will Need
• index cards

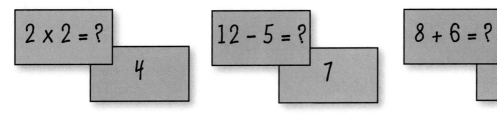

$2 \times 2 = ?$ 4

$12 - 5 = ?$ 7

$8 + 6 = ?$ 14

Pair 1 makes 8 different multiplication facts. $2 \times 2 = 4$
Pair 2 makes 8 different subtraction facts. $12 - 5 = 7$
Pair 3 makes 8 different addition facts. $8 + 6 = 14$

Play the Game

1. Each pair mixes up their cards and lays them face down in four rows of four cards.

2. The first player turns over two cards.

If the cards make a true sentence, the player keeps the cards and chooses again.

If the two cards do not make a true sentence, the player turns the cards face down. Then it is the other player's turn.

3. The first round of the game is over when all the pairs of cards have been matched.

4. Keep score by recording the number of cards each player got to keep.

5. Trade cards with another team and play again for round 2.

6. Repeat and play round 3.

7. The player with the most cards after 3 rounds wins.

Objective: Analyze data and make decisions.

5·10 A Problem Solving: Application
Decision Making

You Decide!

Which show do you want?

Lights! Camera! Action! You are the student director of the spring theater presentation, which will be in 5 weeks. You must decide whether to have a puppet show, a musical, or a dance show.

Puppet Show

Practice time:
4 times a week after school

Practice length:
1 hour

Performers:
3 students

Backstage help:
0 students

Puppet makers:
4 students

Musical

Practice time:
3 times a week after school

Practice length:
2 hours

Performers:
7 students

Backstage help:
2 students

Dance Show

Practice time:
5 times a week after school

Practice length:
1 hour

Performers:
5 students

Backstage help:
3 students

Read for Understanding

1. How long would the practice for each show be for 1 week?

2. How long would the practice for each show be for 5 weeks?

3. How many students would be involved in each show?

4. Which show does not need any help backstage?

5. Which show needs more than 6 performers?

6. Which show needs the most backstage help?

Make Decisions

7. Each performer and backstage helper can invite 2 people to the show. Which show would have the fewest number of guests in the audience? Which show would have the greatest number of guests?

8. If all the people who were invited came to the show, how many people would be in the audience for each kind of show?

9. Each performer in the musical changes costumes 3 times during the show. How many costumes are needed for the show?

10. Each dancer wears 4 different pairs of shoes during the dance show. How many pairs of shoes are needed altogether?

11. It takes 4 hours to make each puppet. The show needs 4 puppets. How many hours would it take to make all of the puppets?

12. Some students cannot practice on Tuesdays and Thursdays. Which show can these students work on? Why?

13. One student cannot practice more than 90 minutes on a school day. Which shows can he work on? Why?

14. What would be some advantages to directing the puppet show? What would be some disadvantages?

15. What would be some advantages to directing the dance show? What would be some disadvantages?

16. What would be some advantages to directing the musical? What would be some disadvantages?

Which show will you direct? Explain.

Objective: *Apply multiplication to investigate science concepts.*

Problem Solving: Math and Science
Does it help to cooperate?

If you were cleaning up your room, would it go faster if you worked alone or with a friend?

In this activity, you will move connecting cubes by yourself and with partners. You will decide if working with others makes a job go faster.

You Will Need
- 2 boxes
- 50 connecting cubes

Hypothesize

If you can move 7 cubes in 30 seconds, estimate how many cubes you and a partner could move together in 30 seconds. What if you have 2 partners?

Procedure

1. Work in a team of 5.

2. You will move cubes, one at a time, from one box to the other.

3. Your teacher will tell you when to start and stop.

4. In the first race, only 1 person will move the cubes.

5. In the second race, 2 people will move cubes.

6. In the third race, 3 people will move cubes, and so on up to 5 people.

9. A theater club is putting on a play. They are making a background for one of the scenes. The background can be no wider than 108 inches. Which of these is *not* a possible measurement for the background?

   A. 104 inches   C. 98 inches

   B. 180 inches   D. 89 inches

Use the graph for problems 13–16.

Theater Club Attendance						
Week	Number of Students					
1	☆	☆	☆	☆	☆	☆
2	☆	☆	☆	☆	☆	
3	☆	☆	☆	☆		
4	☆	☆	☆	☆	☆	

Each ☆ = 2 students

10. Joshua decides to measure the background to see if it will fit. Which would be the best tool to use?

    F. scale

    G. measuring cup

    H. tape measure

    J. centimeter ruler

13. How many students attended the club in week 1?

    A. 6   C. 12

    B. 8   D. 18

14. At the meeting for week 3, Cara brought cookies for a snack. Each member gets 1 cookie. How many cookies did they have altogether?

    F. 4   H. 16

    G. 8   J. 12

11. A recipe states that there are 4 servings in a quart of punch. How many servings are there in 4 quarts of punch?

    A. 4   C. 12

    B. 8   D. 16

15. How many more members attended in week 1 than week 3?

    A. 2   C. 4

    B. 3   D. 6

12. The school band performs a concert. Which is a reasonable length of time for the concert?

    F. 50 minutes   H. 50 seconds

    G. 50 hours   J. 5 days

16. Once you count the number of symbols to solve problem 15, which operations could you use in order to solve?

    F. subtract, then multiply

    G. subtraction only

    H. addition, then subtraction

    J. Not Here

Theme: Here, There, and Everywhere

Use the Data

Oregon Hiking Trails

Elk Lake
Creek Trail .... about 10 miles

Twin Lakes
Trail .... about 2 miles

Clackamas River
Trail #715 .... about 8 miles

Source: Bryan Kinnamon, Oregon's Best Internet Services, Inc. 1999

- Jenny and her family hiked on the Elk Lake Creek Trail 6 times last year. How many miles did they hike last year?

- How can you use multiplication to help you solve the problem?

What You Will Learn

In this chapter you will learn how to
- multiply facts through 12.
- multiply with 3 numbers.
- use strategies to solve problems.

Additional activities at
www.mhschool.com/math

6·1 Explore Square Numbers

Algebra & functions

Learn

You can use grids to explore square numbers. How many small squares are there in a grid 3 squares long and 3 squares wide?

Math Words

factor number that is multiplied to give a product

product the answer in multiplication

square number the product of multiplying a number by itself

Work Together

▶ Draw a square on graph paper that is 3 small squares wide and 3 small squares long.

Note: A square has the same number of □ on each side.

• How many rows did you draw in your square?

• How many □ are in each row?

• How many □ in all?

• Record your work in a table like the one shown. Show each **factor** and the **product**.

▶ Draw other squares.

• How will you decide how many rows?

• How will you decide how many □ to draw in each row?

• Record your work in your table.

• What patterns do you see in the table?

You Will Need
• **graph paper**
• **crayons or markers**

Number of Rows	×	Number in Each Row	=	Total
3 factor	×	3 factor	=	9 product

Make Connections

Here is how to find **square numbers**.

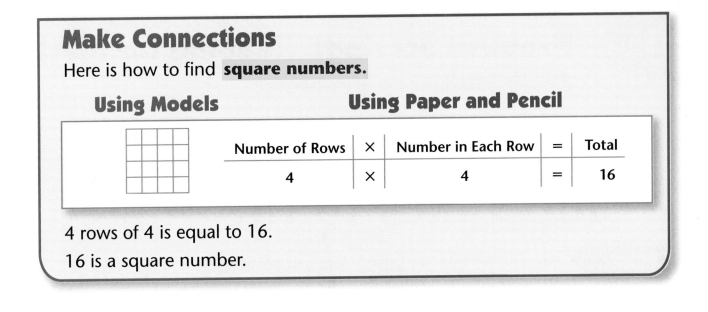

Using Models   **Using Paper and Pencil**

	Number of Rows	×	Number in Each Row	=	Total
	4	×	4	=	16

4 rows of 4 is equal to 16.

16 is a square number.

Try It **Write a multiplication sentence.**

1. ☐

2.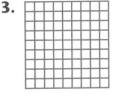

3.

4.

Draw the model and find the product.

5. 2×2 6. 8×8 7. 5×5 8. 7×7

Sum it Up!  What multiplication sentence is shown by a square 4 small squares wide and 4 small squares long?

Practice **Write a multiplication sentence.**

9.   10.   11. 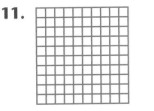   12.

Draw the model and find the product.

13. 3×3 14. 6×6 15. 9×9 16. 1×1

17. **Analyze:** Is 3×4 a square number? Explain.

6·2 Problem Solving: Reading for Math
Solve Multistep Problems

Club Takes to the Stage!

Read ▶ Mr. and Mrs. Li are taking 5 members of the drama club on a bus trip to tour theaters. How much will the bus ride cost?

Bus Tickets
Adults $8
Students $3

READING SKILL ▶ **Make an Inference**
You make inferences based on things you know, or that are hinted at. Sometimes there is a "hidden question" that you have to infer to solve the problem.

- **What do you know?** Number of tickets needed; cost of each ticket.
- **What do you need to find?** Total cost of the tickets
- **What do you need to infer?** Totals for 2 adult tickets and for 5 student tickets

MATH SKILL ▶ **Solve Multistep Problems**
Some problems take more than one step to solve. You must decide how to solve each step and in what order.

Plan ▶ You can multiply to find the cost of each type of ticket. Then, add the products to find the total cost of the tickets.

Solve ▶ They need 2 adult tickets. $2 \times 8 = 16$
They need 5 student tickets. $5 \times 3 = 15$
$16 + 15 = 31$
The tickets cost $31.

Look Back ▶ Is your answer reasonable?

Sum it Up! What hidden question did you have to infer to solve the problem?

Solve. Tell what hidden questions you inferred.

1. Two families go on a boat tour. There are 3 children and 4 adults. Children's tickets are $4 and adult tickets are $7. How much will the boat ride cost?

2. The science club goes on a trip to a museum. There are 3 cars of 5 people each and 4 vans of 7 people each. How many people go on the trip?

3. Amy walked 1 block to the bus stop. Then she rode a bus 4 blocks to the theater. After the theater, she went home the same way. How many blocks did Amy travel on her entire trip?

4. John and Tina are eating lunch. Drinks cost $2 each and salads cost $4. John has 1 drink and 2 salads. Tina has 1 drink and 1 salad. How much does their lunch cost?

Problem Solving

Use data from the map for problems 5–6.

5. May walked from the post office to the bank then to the police station. Sue walked from the library to the post office then to the bank. Who walked farther?

6. Starting at the Bank, describe the shortest route you can to visit all five buildings.

Map showing: Post Office, Bank, Library, School, Police Station

Spiral Review and Test Prep

Choose the correct answer.

Pete rides a subway for 3 blocks each morning. After school, he rides the same distance home. How many blocks does he ride in a 5-day school week?

7. Which of the following statements is true?
   A. Pete lives 5 blocks away.
   B. Pete lives 6 blocks away.
   C. Pete rides for 3 blocks each way.

8. The "hidden question" you must solve first is: How many
   F. blocks does he ride each trip?
   G. blocks does he ride each day?
   H. days does he ride the subway?

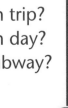

6·3 Multiply by 6 and 8

Learn

What a view! You can see a lot riding burros down the Grand Canyon. Suppose there are 6 groups on the trail. Each group has 4 riders. How many people are on the trail ride?

Memorizing facts will help you in multiplying greater numbers. These strategies will help you recall facts.

There's more than one way!

You can multiply 6 × 4 to solve this problem.

Method A

You can double a known fact to find a new fact.

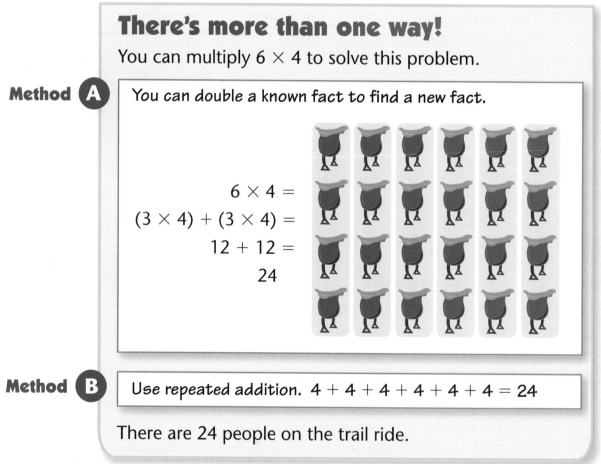

$$6 \times 4 =$$
$$(3 \times 4) + (3 \times 4) =$$
$$12 + 12 =$$
$$24$$

Method B   Use repeated addition. $4 + 4 + 4 + 4 + 4 + 4 = 24$

There are 24 people on the trail ride.

A family of tourists is traveling through the Sahara desert in Africa with 8 camels. Each camel carries 9 sacks of supplies. How many sacks are the camels carrying in all?

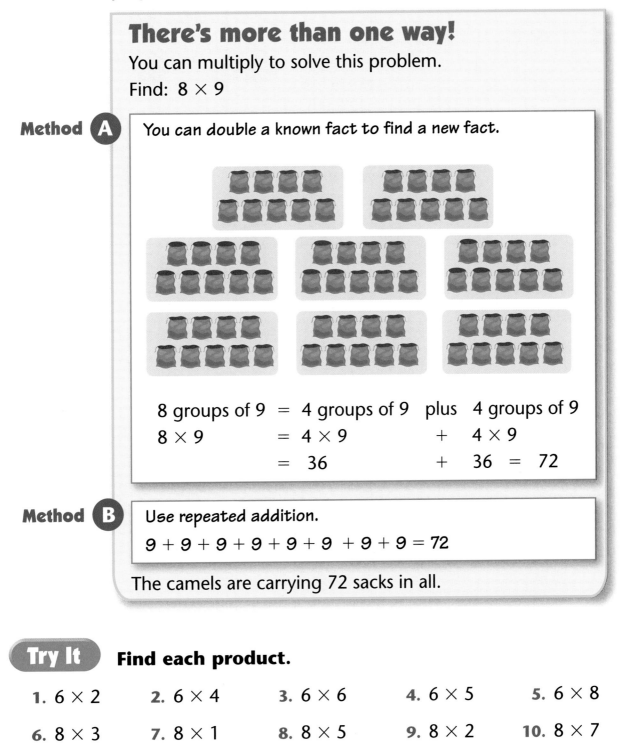

There's more than one way!

You can multiply to solve this problem.

Find: 8×9

Method A

You can double a known fact to find a new fact.

8 groups of 9 = 4 groups of 9 plus 4 groups of 9

8×9 $= 4 \times 9$ $+$ 4×9

           $=$ 36 $+$ 36 $=$ 72

Method B

Use repeated addition.

$9 + 9 + 9 + 9 + 9 + 9 + 9 + 9 = 72$

The camels are carrying 72 sacks in all.

Try It   **Find each product.**

1. 6×2 2. 6×4 3. 6×6 4. 6×5 5. 6×8

6. 8×3 7. 8×1 8. 8×5 9. 8×2 10. 8×7

Sum it Up!   How can knowing facts for 3 help you find facts for 6?
How can knowing facts for 4 help you find facts for 8?

Write a multiplication sentence for each picture.

11.

12.

13.

Find each product.

14.	5	**15.**	7	**16.**	2	**17.**	8	**18.**	6	**19.**	6	**20.**	9
	$\times 6$		$\times 8$		$\times 6$		$\times 8$		$\times 8$		$\times 3$		$\times 6$

21. 1×8 **22.** 0×6 **23.** 4×8 **24.** 5×8 **25.** 0×8

26. 9×8 **27.** 3×5 **28.** 5×5 **29.** 4×9 **30.** 3×8

★**31.** $(3 + 1) \times 6$ ★**32.** $(2 + 1) \times 6$ ★**33.** $(3 + 3) \times 6$

Algebra & functions **Complete the table.**

34. Rule: Multiply by 6.

Number of Planes	1	2	4	5	8
Number of People					

35. Rule: Multiply by 8.

Input	3			
Output	24	32	8	16

36. **Make it RIGHT**

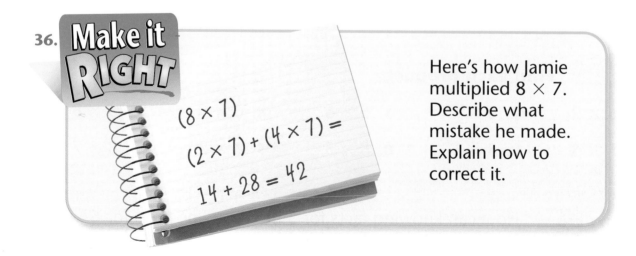

Here's how Jamie multiplied 8×7. Describe what mistake he made. Explain how to correct it.

(8×7)

$(2 \times 7) + (4 \times 7) =$

$14 + 28 = 42$

Problem Solving

37. Tour buses often travel to the Grand Canyon. On one bus tour the tour guide had 7 boxes of lunches. Each box had 8 lunches. How many lunches were on this bus?

38. Explain how to use adding to help find multiplication facts. Give an example.

39. Tourists can go camel riding in the Sahara desert. One tour group takes 6 riders at a time. If they take 5 different groups in 1 day, how many riders is this?

40. Time: Suppose it takes 45 minutes to drive from home to a friend's house. How many hours does it take to drive there and back home?

Use data from the table for problem 41.

★**41. Logical Reasoning:** Phil went on vacation. He wants to do a different activity on Monday, Wednesday, and Friday. He wants to spend as little money as possible. What should his schedule be?

Activity	Cost
Horseback Riding Monday–Thursday Friday–Sunday	$15.50 $18.50
Museum	$5.00 (Wednesday free)
Hike	free

42. Collect data from students in your classroom. Ask where they have gone on vacation. Make a table or graph to show the results.

43. Create a problem that can be solved using a fact for 8. Solve it. Ask others to solve it.

Spiral Review and Test Prep

44. 342 + 113   **45.** 686 − 259   **46.** 492 + 173   **47.** 278 − 196

Choose the correct answer.

48. A road map costs $1.75. How much change should you get back if you pay with a five-dollar bill?

   A. $3.25   **C.** $4.25

   B. $3.75   **D.** Not Here

49. Which is the same as a half hour?

   F. 30 minutes **H.** 15 minutes

   G. 45 minutes **J.** 60 minutes

6·4 Multiply by 7

Learn

The National Toy Train Museum in Strasburg, Pennsylvania, has many toy trains on display. If 6 toy trains are on display and each train has the number of cars in the picture below, how many cars are there altogether?

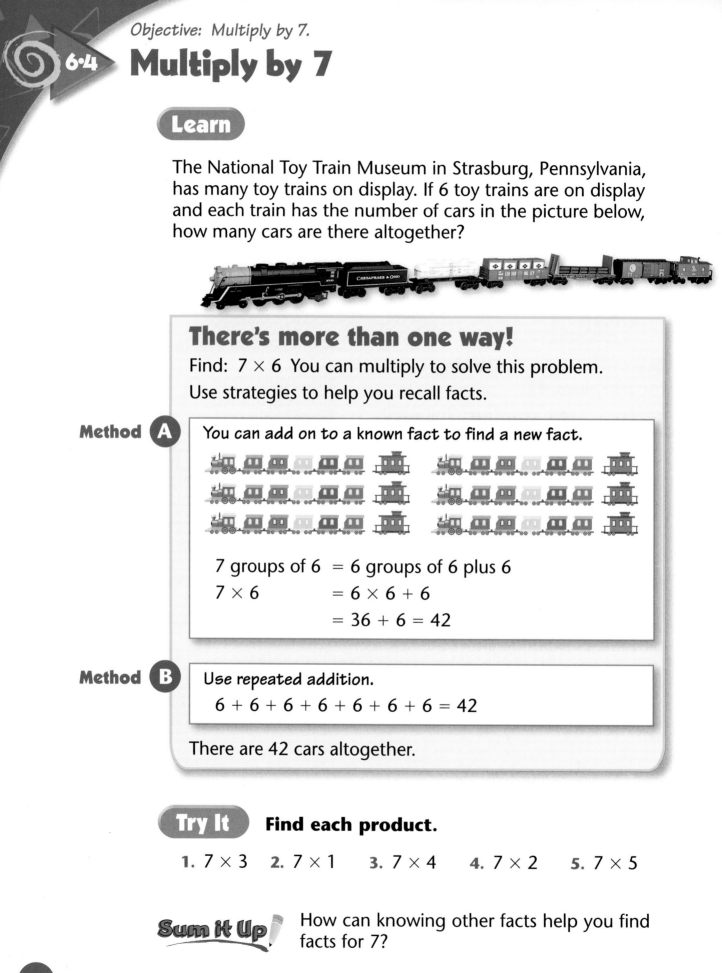

There's more than one way!

Find: 7 × 6 You can multiply to solve this problem.
Use strategies to help you recall facts.

Method A

You can add on to a known fact to find a new fact.

7 groups of 6 = 6 groups of 6 plus 6
7 × 6   = 6 × 6 + 6
            = 36 + 6 = 42

Method B

Use repeated addition.
6 + 6 + 6 + 6 + 6 + 6 + 6 = 42

There are 42 cars altogether.

Try It **Find each product.**

1. 7 × 3   **2.** 7 × 1   **3.** 7 × 4   **4.** 7 × 2   **5.** 7 × 5

Sum it Up How can knowing other facts help you find facts for 7?

Write a multiplication sentence for each picture.

6.

7.

Find each product.

8. $\begin{array}{r} 5 \\ \times 7 \\ \hline \end{array}$ 9. $\begin{array}{r} 7 \\ \times 8 \\ \hline \end{array}$ 10. $\begin{array}{r} 2 \\ \times 7 \\ \hline \end{array}$ 11. $\begin{array}{r} 7 \\ \times 7 \\ \hline \end{array}$ 12. $\begin{array}{r} 7 \\ \times 1 \\ \hline \end{array}$ 13. $\begin{array}{r} 6 \\ \times 7 \\ \hline \end{array}$ 14. $\begin{array}{r} 4 \\ \times 7 \\ \hline \end{array}$

15. 6×8 16. 4×9 17. 3×8 18. 6×5 19. 5×8

★20. $(1 + 1) \times 7$ ★21. $(2 + 2) \times 7$ ★22. $(3 + 3) \times 7$

Algebra & functions **Complete the table.**

23.

Rule: ▓			
Input	2	3	5
Output	14	21	35

24.

Rule: Multiply by 7.				
Number of Trains	1	3	▓	8
Number of cars	7	▓	42	▓

Problem Solving

Use data from *Did You Know?* for problem 25.

25. How many miles can a train in the TGV Atlantique and Nord system travel in 7 minutes?

26. **Analyze:** To find 4×8, Cary thinks "5×8 subtract 8; so $40 - 8 = 32$." Explain why this works.

Did You KNOW?

In France, the TGV Atlantique and the TGV Nord trains run up to about 3 miles in one minute.

Spiral Review and Test Prep

27. $22 + 45 + 476$ 28. $3,419 - 326$ 29. $209 + 775 + 98$

Choose the correct answer.

30. There are 3 passengers in each of 8 seats on a train car. How many passengers are there altogether?

A. 11   B. 24   C. 16   D. 21

31. Which comes next in this skip-counting pattern? 20, 24, 28, ▓

F. 29   G. 30   H. 32

Algebra & functions **Write a multiplication sentence.** (pages 224–225)

1.

2.

Draw the model and find the product. (pages 224–225)

3. 2 × 2   **4.** 5 × 5   **5.** 8 × 8   **6.** 3 × 3

Find each product. (pages 228–233)

7. 6 × 4   **8.** 7 × 6   **9.** 8 × 3   **10.** 6 × 6

11. 8 × 5   **12.** 6 × 1   **13.** 7 × 0   **14.** 3 × 8

15. 7
×4

16. 8
×7

17. 6
×8

18. 4
×8

19. 9
×7

20. 8
×9

21. 6
×9

Solve. (pages 224–233)

22. Janell drove 8 hours each day for 4 days. How long did she travel in all?

23. If 6 people each have 4 pieces of luggage, how many pieces of luggage do they have altogether?

24. A conductor on a train works 7 hours each day. One week she worked 4 weekdays and 1 day on the weekend. The next week she worked only 3 weekdays. How many more hours did she work the first week?

 25. Analyze: What method do you prefer to use to remember facts?

Additional activities at
www.mhschool.com/math

Use the Internet

Ramón is looking for recipes to make for his party. He is inviting a lot of people and will need to make more than one batch of each recipe. How can he use the Internet to find recipes he can use?

Name of Recipe	Number of Servings	Number of Servings * 6	Number of Servings * 7	Number of Servings * 8

- Go to www.mhschool.com/math.
- Find the list of sites that provide recipes.
- Click on a link.
- Find the recipes. Choose two recipes.
- Copy the table. Write the names of the recipes in your table. Be sure to include the number of servings.

- Multiply the number of servings for each recipe by 6. Record the products in the third column.
- Multiply the number of servings for each recipe by 7. Record the products in the fourth column.
- Multiply the number of servings for each recipe by 8. Record the products in the fifth column.

1. Which recipe do you think Ramón should use if he is inviting 60 people to his party? Why?

2. **Analyze:** Why does using the Internet make more sense than using another reference source to find the recipes?

For more practice, use Math Traveler™.

6·5 Multiply by 10

 Where would you like to go on vacation? The pictograph shows the top choices of 160 third grade students. How many chose an amusement park?

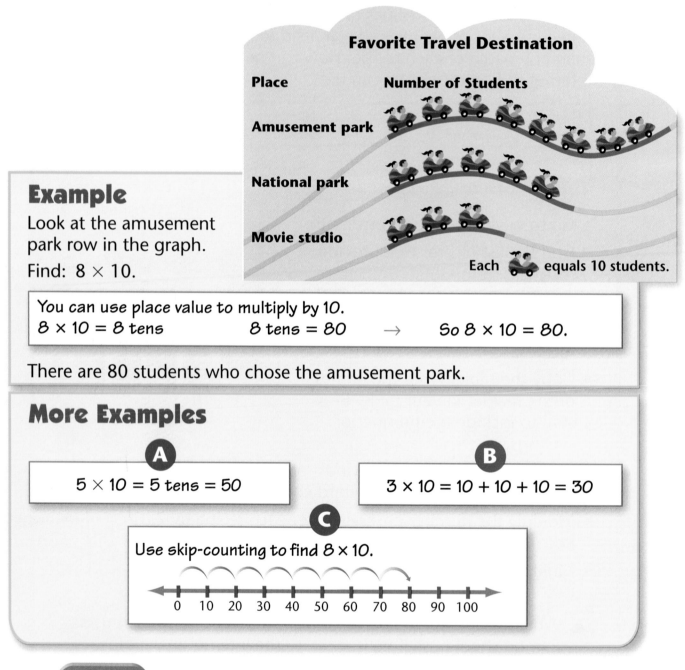

Favorite Travel Destination

Place	Number of Students
Amusement park	
National park	
Movie studio	

Each 🚗 equals 10 students.

Example

Look at the amusement park row in the graph.

Find: 8×10.

You can use place value to multiply by 10.

$8 \times 10 = 8$ tens   8 tens = 80   →   So $8 \times 10 = 80$.

There are 80 students who chose the amusement park.

More Examples

A

$5 \times 10 = 5$ tens $= 50$

B

$3 \times 10 = 10 + 10 + 10 = 30$

C

Use skip-counting to find 8×10.

0 10 20 30 40 50 60 70 80 90 100

Try It **Find each product. Explain the method you used.**

1. 7×10 **2.** 4×10 **3.** 10×2 **4.** 6×10 **5.** 10×5

Sum It Up! Compare the product and the other factor when you multiply by 10. What do you notice?

Practice **Find each product.**

6. 10
×7

7. 10
×8

8. 10
×0

9. 10
×4

10. 10
×10

11. 10
×9

12. 10
×3

13. 1 × 10   14. 10 × 2   15. 0 × 10   16. 10 × 9   17. 10 × 3

18. 8 × 6   19. 8 × 7   20. 7 × 7   21. 5 × 9   22. 4 × 7

★23. 12 × 10   ★24. 21 × 10   ★25. 32 × 10

Algebra & functions **Describe and complete the skip-counting pattern.**

26. 20, 30, 40, ▪, 60, 70, 80, ▪, 100, ▪, 120, 130, 140, 150

Problem Solving

Use data from the pictograph for problems 27–29.

27. How many more people can ride on the tram than on the super coaster?

28. **Language Arts:** Write a paragraph about the number of people that can fit on the rides.

29. On one ride of the skywalk, there are 20 empty seats. How many people are on the ride?

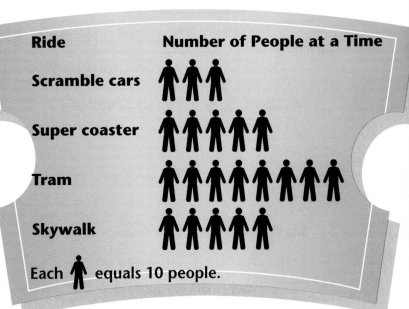

Number of People on Rides

Spiral Review and Test Prep

30. 104 − 86   31. 501 + 321   32. 1,743 − 276   33. 2,307 + 456

Choose the correct answer.

34. Six bicycles need all new tires. How many tires is this?

   A. 10   C. 6
   B. 12   D. 8

35. What is the missing number in this skip-counting pattern?
    5, 10, 15, 20, 25, ▪

   F. 26   H. 31
   G. 30   J. Not Here

Objective: Multiply by 9.

6·6 **Multiply by 9**

Math in ACTION

Learn

If Patrick Hong test drives 7 cars a day, how many cars will he have test driven in 9 days?

Patrick Hong of Newport Beach, California, road tests cars for *Road & Track* magazine.

There's more than one way!

You can multiply 9 × 7 to solve this problem.

Method A

You can multiply by 10 and subtract to find facts for 9.

$$9 \times 7 = (10 \times 7) - 7$$
$$= \quad 70 \quad - 7 = 63$$

So 9 × 7 = 63.

Think: 7 cars each day × 9 days

Method B

Use skip-counting.

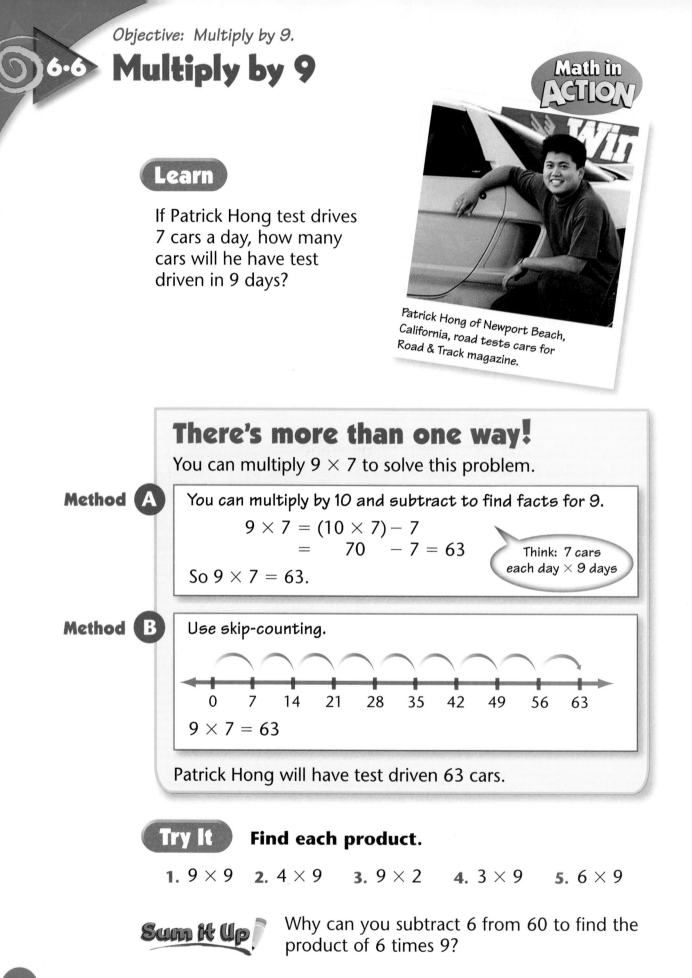

| 0 | 7 | 14 | 21 | 28 | 35 | 42 | 49 | 56 | 63 |

9 × 7 = 63

Patrick Hong will have test driven 63 cars.

Try It Find each product.

1. 9 × 9 **2.** 4 × 9 **3.** 9 × 2 **4.** 3 × 9 **5.** 6 × 9

Sum it Up! Why can you subtract 6 from 60 to find the product of 6 times 9?

Division Concepts

Theme: Outer Space

Use the Data
Space Camps in Alabama and California

Alabama Bay	Number of Counselors	Number of Trainees
A	2	20
B	4	40
C	6	60

California Bay	Number of Counselors	Number of Trainees
A	4	16
B	8	32
C	12	48

Source: U.S. Space Camp Foundation

- In California Bay A, how many trainees are in a group with each counselor?

- How can division help you solve problems involving equal groups?

What You Will Learn
In this chapter you will learn how to
- divide, using facts through 5.
- relate multiplication and division.
- use strategies to solve problems.

Additional activities at
www.mhschool.com/math

Chapter 7 Division Concepts **267**

7·1 Explore the Meaning of Division

Algebra & functions **Learn**

Math Word

division an operation on two numbers that tells how many groups or how many are in each group

You can use counters to explore division. What is 15 ÷ 3?

Work Together

▶ Use counters to model the problem.
- Count out 15 counters.
- Share them with your partner to make 3 equal groups.
- How many counters are in each group?
- Record your work in a table.

You Will Need
- **two-color counters**

Original Number	Number of Groups	Number in Each Group
15	3	5

What if you want to divide 18 by 6?

▶ Use counters.

- How many counters do you need?
- How many counters will you put in each group?
- How many groups did you make? Record your work in a table.
- How is this problem different from the one above?

Make Connections

Here is how to find the number of equal groups and the number in each group.

You can use models or write a **division** sentence.

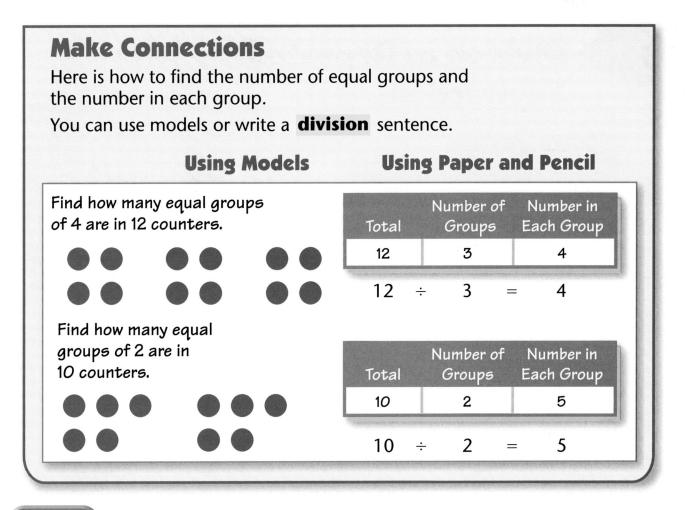

Using Models

Find how many equal groups of 4 are in 12 counters.

Find how many equal groups of 2 are in 10 counters.

Using Paper and Pencil

Total	Number of Groups	Number in Each Group
12	3	4

$$12 \div 3 = 4$$

Total	Number of Groups	Number in Each Group
10	2	5

$$10 \div 2 = 5$$

Try It Use counters to complete.

	Total	Number of Groups	Number in Each Group
1.	8	4	▮
2.	14	▮	7

Sum it Up! What are two questions you can answer by using division?

Practice Use counters to complete.

	Total	Number of Groups	Number in Each Group
3.	20	5	▮
4.	15	▮	3
5.	12	▮	2

6. **Analyze:** Start with 16 counters. Can you share them equally betweem 2 people? 3 people? 4 people? Tell why or why not.

7·2 Division as Repeated Subtraction

Math in ACTION

Algebra & functions **Learn**

An astrophysicist takes 12 photographs of 3 regions of space. He takes the same number of photographs for each region. How many photographs of each region does he take?

Dr. Neil Tyson is an astrophysicist. Astrophysicists are scientists who study space.

Example

You can use division to solve this problem.

Find: $12 \div 3$

You can use repeated subtraction.
Keep subtracting until there is nothing left.
Then count how many times you subtracted.

$$12 - 3 = 9 \qquad 9 - 3 = 6 \qquad 6 - 3 = 3 \qquad 3 - 3 = 0$$

You subtracted 4 times.
So $12 \div 3 = 4$.

He took 4 photographs of each region.

Try It **Divide.**

1. $24 \div 4$ **2.** $18 \div 3$ **3.** $32 \div 8$ **4.** $20 \div 5$ **5.** $27 \div 3$

6. $36 \div 4$ **7.** $35 \div 7$ **8.** $28 \div 4$ **9.** $12 \div 3$ **10.** $25 \div 5$

Sum it Up Which number do you subtract when you divide using repeated subtraction?

Write the division sentence.

11. $8 - 4 = 4, 4 - 4 = 0$ **12.** $6 - 3 = 3, 3 - 3 = 0$

Divide.

13. $20 \div 4$ **14.** $10 \div 2$ **15.** $9 \div 3$ **16.** $15 \div 5$ **17.** $21 \div 7$

18. $24 \div 6$ **19.** $18 \div 6$ **20.** $30 \div 5$ **21.** $24 \div 4$ **22.** $16 \div 4$

23. $18 \div 9$ **24.** $5 \div 5$ **25.** $32 \div 8$ **26.** $12 \div 3$ **27.** $8 \div 4$

Compare. Write >, <, or =.

28. $12 \div 6 \bullet 3$ **29.** $28 \div 4 \bullet 7$ **30.** $35 \div 7 \bullet 4$

★**31.** $(40 + 2) \div 7 \bullet 8$ ★**32.** $(30 - 5) \div 5 \bullet 4$ ★**33.** $(21 + 7) \div 4 \bullet 7$

Problem Solving

Use data from _Did You Know?_ for problem 34.

34. If a line of the smallest neutron stars measure a total of 18 miles across, how many neutron stars are there?

35. Science: The revolving of Earth around the sun causes the four seasons we have each year. If each season is about the same number of months, about how many months long is each season? How can you tell?

36. Analyze: How can you use counters to find $28 \div 4$?

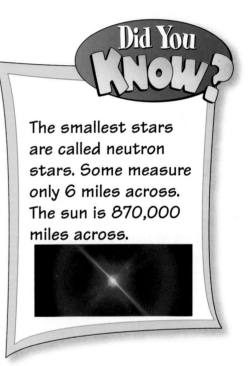

Did You Know?

The smallest stars are called neutron stars. Some measure only 6 miles across. The sun is 870,000 miles across.

Spiral Review and Test Prep

37. 8×7 **38.** $543 + 1,007$ **39.** 7×5 **40.** 9×0 **41.** $604 - 26$

Choose the correct answer.

42. Rita read 3 articles about Mars in each of 5 different magazines. How many articles did she read?

   A. 8   **C.** 16

   B. 12   **D.** Not Here

43. Chris paid $5.00 for a model ship. Eric bought the same model for $1.45 less. How much did Eric pay?

   F. $4.45   **H.** $3.55

   G. $4.65   **J.** $4.55

Objective: Relate multiplication and division.

7·3 Relate Multiplication to Division

 Algebra & functions **Learn**

In Antarctica, scientists collect meteors in order to study where they come from.

Math Words

dividend a number to be divided

divisor the number by which the dividend is divided

quotient the answer in division

One week the scientists collected 24 meteors. They packed the same number of meteors in 3 boxes. How many meteors went in each box?

> Multiplication and division are inverse operations. Using your multiplication facts can help you quickly recall division facts.

Example 1

You can divide to solve this problem. Find: $24 \div 3$

Use multiplication to help you divide. Separate 24 objects into 3 equal groups to stand for the 3 boxes.

Think: You know the number of groups and the number in all. Write a multiplication sentence to show this.

Number of groups		Number in each group		Number in all
3	×	8	=	24

You can also write a division sentence about this picture.

Number in all		Number of groups		Number in each group
24	÷	3	=	8
dividend		**divisor**		**quotient**

There are 8 meteors in each box.

The scientists have to store 40 smaller meteors in boxes that each hold the same number of meteors. How many boxes do they need?

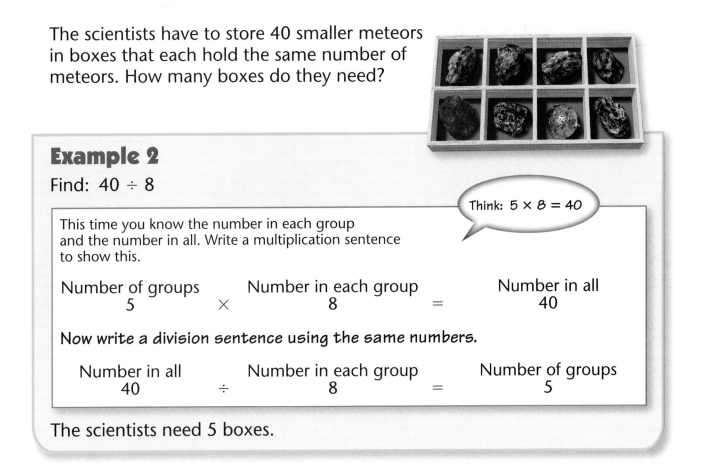

Example 2

Find: 40 ÷ 8

Think: 5 × 8 = 40

This time you know the number in each group and the number in all. Write a multiplication sentence to show this.

Number of groups		Number in each group		Number in all
5	×	8	=	40

Now write a division sentence using the same numbers.

Number in all		Number in each group		Number of groups
40	÷	8	=	5

The scientists need 5 boxes.

Try It Write related multiplication and division sentences for each picture.

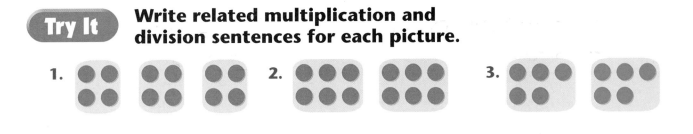

1. 2. 3.

Write related multiplication and division sentences for each group of numbers.

4. 2, 6, 12   5. 7, 3, 21   6. 5, 8, 40   7. 1, 9, 9   8. 2, 4, 8

Sum it Up Which multiplication sentence would help you find 28 ÷ 7?

Write related multiplication and division sentences for each picture.

9.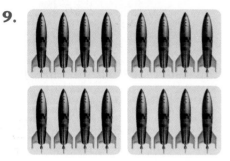

10.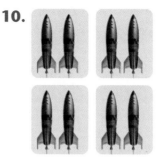

Write related multiplication and division sentences for each group of numbers.

11. 2, 7, 14   **12.** 1, 2, 2   **13.** 3, 5, 15   **14.** 4, 5, 20   **15.** 5, 6, 30

16. 6, 3, 18   **17.** 4, 3, 12   **18.** 5, 5, 25   **19.** 2, 9, 18   **20.** 7, 4, 28

Write × or ÷ to make each sentence true.

21. 72 ● 9 = 8   **22.** 8 ● 8 = 64   **23.** 12 ● 6 = 2   **24.** 7 ● 6 = 42

★**25.** (18 + 2) ● 4 = 5   ★**26.** (27 ● 3) ÷ 9 = 1   ★**27.** (8 ● 3) ÷ 4 = 6

28.

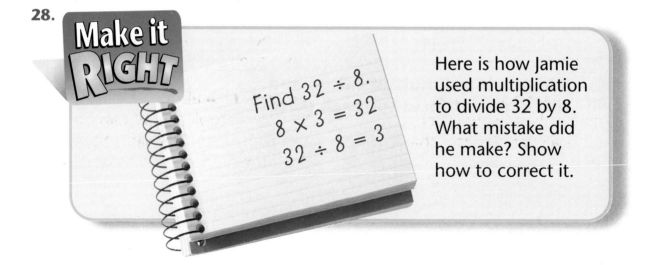

Find 32 ÷ 8.
8 × 3 = 32
32 ÷ 8 = 3

Here is how Jamie used multiplication to divide 32 by 8. What mistake did he make? Show how to correct it.

Problem Solving

29. In 1969 the Apollo 11 and Apollo 12 missions sent a total of 6 astronauts to the moon. Each Apollo mission carried the same number of astronauts. How many astronauts went on each mission?

30. Science: John Glenn is the oldest American to travel in space. He was born in 1921. How old was he when he went into space in 1998?

Use data from the table for problems 31–32.

31. Literature: All of the science fiction books were written by either Isaac Asimov or William Gibson. There is an equal number of books by each author. How many books are there by Isaac Asimov?

★ **32.** There are 6 students in Mrs. Talbot's class who are giving a group report on outer space. They borrowed all of the books the school library had on the subject. If each student reads the same number of books, how many books does each read?

School Library Book Count

Books on Outer Space	Number of Books
Science fiction	6
Moons	4
Astronaut biographies	8

33. Science: The Tempel 1 comet can be seen about 3 times in 18 years. The number of years between each sighting is the same. About how often can the Tempel 1 comet be seen?

34. Gina wants to buy a book about moons. The book costs $9.24 on sale. She has 1 five-dollar bill, 3 one-dollar bills, 3 quarters, and 2 dimes. How much more money does she need?

35. Time: A year on Mars lasts 687 Earth days. How much longer is a year on Mars than a year on Earth?

36. Collect data about a comet. Create a problem that can be solved by using division. Solve it. Ask other students to solve it.

Spiral Review and Test Prep

Find each missing number.

37. $n \times 4 = 8$ **38.** $4 \times y = 4$ **39.** $z \times 8 = 16$ **40.** $3 \times t = 9$

Choose the correct answer.

41. Ray can read 9 pages of his book about rockets in 1 hour. How many pages can he read in 3 hours?

    A. 12 pages   **C.** 27 pages

    B. 15 pages   **D.** 18 pages

42. Ellen is 3 years younger than Stan. Joe is 4 years older than Stan. If Joe is 10 years old, how old is Ellen?

    F. 3 years old   **H.** 7 years old

    G. 14 years old   **J.** 6 years old

7·4 Problem Solving: Reading for Math
Choose an Operation

Space Fair Blasts Off

Read

Leon is making a model of the solar system. He has 18 pieces of clay. Leon will divide the clay evenly to form 9 planets. How many pieces of clay will he use to make each planet?

READING ▶ SKILL

Make a Judgment

When you make a judgment, it is based on what you know.

- **What do you know?** — How much clay Leon has; How many planets he will make

- **What do you need to find?** — How much clay used for each planet

- **What judgment is called for?** — Which operation to use

MATH ▶ SKILL

Choose the Operation

Understanding what the problem is asking you to find can help you decide which operation to use.

Plan — Divide the total into equal groups.

Solve — There are 18 pieces of clay divided into 9 groups.

Write a division sentence. 18 ÷ 9 = 2

Look Back — • Does your answer make sense?

 **Sum it Up!** How do you decide which way to divide to solve a problem?

Solve. Tell how you choose the operation.

1. Rico's project is on the constellations. He used 18 stars to make the constellation Orion. Then he used 7 stars to make the Little Dipper (Ursa Minor). How many more stars did Rico use in Orion?

2. Beth is making a model of Earth's 3 layers. She has 12 pieces of wire. She will use an equal number of wire pieces for each layer. How many wire pieces will each layer of her model have?

Use data from the Supply List for problems 3–8.

3. How many more moon stickers are there than sun stickers?

4. The white paper is divided evenly among 3 students. How many sheets did each student get?

Supply List for Space Poster	
White Paper	15 sheets
Moon Stickers	14 stickers
Sun Stickers	8 stickers
Black Paper	10 sheets
Blue Paper	12 sheets

5. The black paper is divided evenly among 5 students. How many sheets of paper did each student get?

6. How many fewer sheets of black paper are there than white paper?

7. **What if** all the stickers were divided evenly between 2 students? How many stickers would each student get?

8. Emily wants to use 3 sheets of blue paper to make posters. How many blue sheets will be left over for other students?

Spiral Review and Test Prep

Choose the correct answer.

Mia has 27 labels for her project. She used the same number of labels on each of the 9 planets. How many labels did she put on Mars?

9. Which of these statements is true?
   A. Mia labeled only 3 planets.
   B. Mia has 27 labels.
   C. Mia used only 9 labels.

10. Which number sentence can you use to solve this problem?
   F. $27 - 9 = 18$
   G. $27 \div 9 = 3$
   H. $27 + 9 = 33$

Problem Solving

7.5 Divide by 2

Learn

The pull of the moon's gravity causes oceans to have high and low tides. If there are 14 high tides, how many days have passed?

The gravitational pull of the moon produces 2 high tides every day.

There's more than one way!

Here are strategies you can use to help you remember how to divide by 2. Find $14 \div 2$ to solve this problem.

Method A

You can skip-count backward.

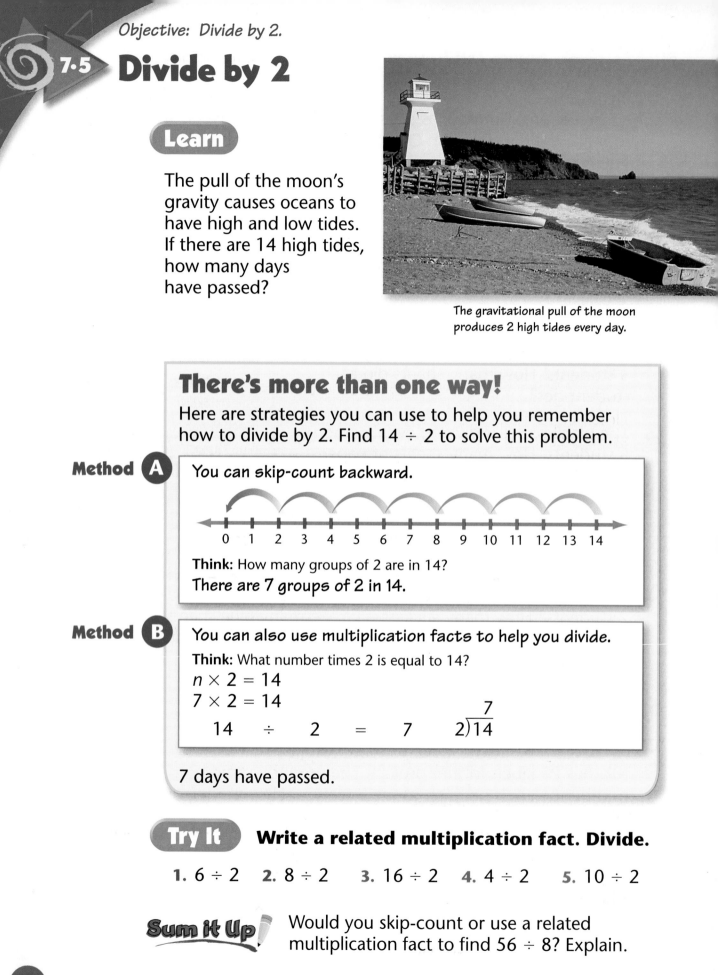

0 1 2 3 4 5 6 7 8 9 10 11 12 13 14

Think: How many groups of 2 are in 14?
There are 7 groups of 2 in 14.

Method B

You can also use multiplication facts to help you divide.

Think: What number times 2 is equal to 14?
$n \times 2 = 14$
$7 \times 2 = 14$

$14 \div 2 = 7$ $\qquad 2\overline{)14}^{\,7}$

7 days have passed.

Try It **Write a related multiplication fact. Divide.**

1. $6 \div 2$ **2.** $8 \div 2$ **3.** $16 \div 2$ **4.** $4 \div 2$ **5.** $10 \div 2$

Sum it Up Would you skip-count or use a related multiplication fact to find $56 \div 8$? Explain.

Practice Write a related multiplication fact. Divide.

6. 12 ÷ 2

7. 10 ÷ 2

8. 18 ÷ 2

9. 4 ÷ 2

10. 6 ÷ 2

11. 2)‾2‾

12. 2)‾16‾

13. 2)‾8‾

14. 2)‾14‾

15. 2)‾18‾

Algebra & functions Describe and complete the skip-counting patterns.

16. 18, 16, ▮, 12

17. 10, 8, 6, ▮

18. 990, ▮, 986, 984

★**19.** Create your own pattern with more than 1 missing number. Ask other students to describe it.

Problem Solving

Use data from the journal for problem 20.

20. Flora keeps track of the tides while on vacation at the beach. There are two low tides each day. How many days has she been at the beach?

21. Flora and Carmen decide to share a telescope an equal number of months each year. How many months will Flora use the telescope this year?

22. **Analyze:** Can Flora and Carmen share the telescope the same number of days each week? Explain.

23. **Create a problem** that can be solved using the division sentence 12 ÷ 2 = 6. Solve it. Then ask other students to solve it.

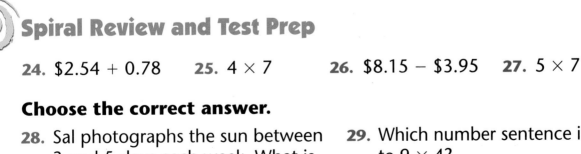

July 8, 2001

I recorded 18 low tides on my vacation.

Spiral Review and Test Prep

24. $2.54 + 0.78

25. 4 × 7

26. $8.15 − $3.95

27. 5 × 7

Choose the correct answer.

28. Sal photographs the sun between 3 and 5 days each week. What is the least number of times he photographs the sun in 8 weeks?

A. 15

B. 24

C. 40

D. Not Here

29. Which number sentence is equal to 9 × 4?

F. 3 × 2 × 4

H. 3 × 3 × 4

G. 6 × 3 × 4

J. 3 × 6 × 2

7·6 Divide by 5

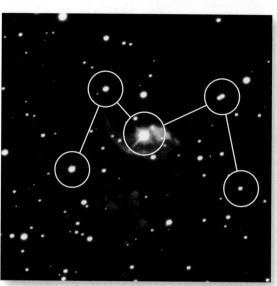

Cassiopeia with its 5 major stars shown

Learn

Aidan sees 30 stars in his favorite constellations. Each constellation has the same number of stars as the constellation Cassiopeia. How many favorite constellations does Aidan have?

There's more than one way!

You can find $30 \div 5$ to solve this problem.

Method A

You can skip-count backward.

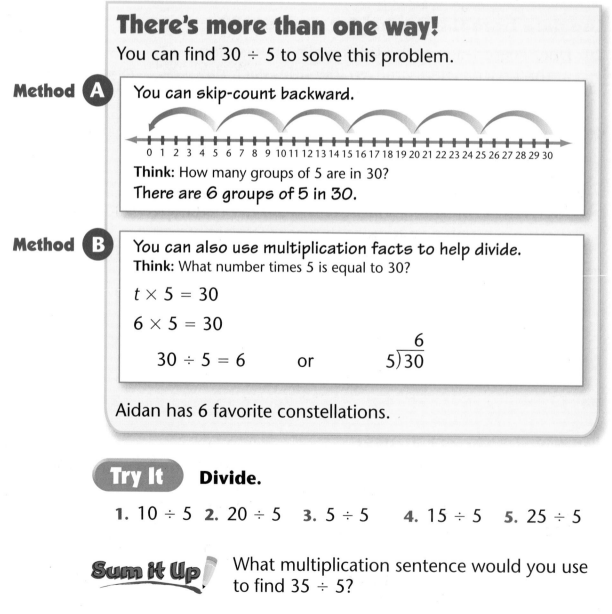

0 1 2 3 4 5 6 7 8 9 10 11 12 13 14 15 16 17 18 19 20 21 22 23 24 25 26 27 28 29 30

Think: How many groups of 5 are in 30?
There are 6 groups of 5 in 30.

Method B

You can also use multiplication facts to help divide.
Think: What number times 5 is equal to 30?

$t \times 5 = 30$

$6 \times 5 = 30$

$30 \div 5 = 6$ or $5\overline{)30}$ (= 6)

Aidan has 6 favorite constellations.

Try It   Divide.

1. $10 \div 5$ **2.** $20 \div 5$ **3.** $5 \div 5$ **4.** $15 \div 5$ **5.** $25 \div 5$

Sum it Up What multiplication sentence would you use to find $35 \div 5$?

Divide.

6. $35 \div 5$ **7.** $25 \div 5$ **8.** $45 \div 5$ **9.** $15 \div 5$ **10.** $5 \div 5$

11. $5\overline{)40}$ **12.** $5\overline{)30}$ **13.** $5\overline{)20}$ **14.** $5\overline{)10}$ **15.** $2\overline{)8}$

Algebra & functions **Solve. Find each missing number.**

16. $5 \times d = 15$ **17.** $h + 5 = 20$ **18.** $12 - s = 7$ **19.** $4 \times r = 16$

20. $25 \div a = 5$ ★**21.** $(6 + b) \div 5 = 2$ ★**22.** $(8 - 3) \div p = 1$ ★**23.** $(8 + 4) \div c = 6$

Problem Solving

Use data from the table for problems 24–25.

24. Allan spent $15.00 to buy each of his sisters a Challenger key chain. How many sisters does Allan have?

★**25.** Beth spent a total of $30.00. She bought 1 model of Apollo 12 and some key chains. How many key chains did she buy?

Souvenir	Price
Challenger key chain	$5.00
Model of Apollo 12	$10.00
Astronaut figures	$3.00

26. **Career:** Jesse is training to be an astronaut. Part of her exercise routine is to jog 8 miles each weekday. If Jesse jogs 5 days each week for 2 weeks, how many miles does she jog altogether?

27. **Create a problem** that can be solved using division. Include data from the table in your problem. Solve it. Ask other students to solve it.

Spiral Review and Test Prep

28. 9×8 **29.** $7 + 8$ **30.** $18 - 9$ **31.** 9×7 **32.** 6×3

Choose the correct answer.

33. The average distance between Earth and the moon is 238,857 miles. Which digit is in the ten thousands place in this number?

A. 2   **C.** 3

B. 8   **D.** Not Here

34. Jupiter has 8 times as many moons as Mars. Mars has 2 moons. How many moons does Jupiter have?

F. 10   **H.** 6

G. 4   **J.** 16

Complete. (pages 268–271)

	Total	Number of Groups	Number in Each Group
1.	45	5	y
2.	18	a	3
3.	16	p	2
4.	18	9	d

Write related multiplication and division sentences for each group of numbers. (pages 272–275)

5. 3, 7, 21   6. 2, 4, 8   7. 4, 4, 16   8. 5, 7, 35   9. 2, 6, 12

Divide. (pages 278–281)

10. $12 \div 2$ 11. $15 \div 5$ 12. $8 \div 2$ 13. $40 \div 5$ 14. $12 \div 3$

15. $2\overline{)10}$ 16. $5\overline{)25}$ 17. $5\overline{)15}$ 18. $5\overline{)20}$ 19. $2\overline{)18}$

Solve. Find each missing number. (pages 278–281)

20. $3 \times h = 6$

21. $d \times 4 = 24$

Solve. (pages 268–281)

22. There are 25 students in Mr. Martell's class. They will work in groups of 5 on their outer space projects. How many groups are there?

23. You separate 16 counters into 2 equal groups. How many counters are in each group? Explain how you chose the operation.

24. Kevin spends $15.00 on 5 packs of space food. Each pack costs the same amount. How much does each pack cost?

25. **Analyze:** Which method do you prefer to use to find $20 \div 5$? Why?

Additional activities at www.mhschool.com/math

Model Division

Mrs. Jansen is planning a birthday party for her son. There are 7 children coming to the party. She wants to put the children in teams of 2 to play a game. How many teams will be formed?

You can use counters to stamp out a model of the problem.

Each party hat represents one child.

- Choose division for the mat type.

- At the bottom of the screen, choose 2 and "In a Group." This means you are putting the 8 hats in groups of 2.

The number boxes show that you are finding 8 ÷ 2.

How many teams will be formed?

Use the computer to model each fact. Then write the quotient.

1. 14 ÷ 2   2. 15 ÷ 5   3. 12 ÷ 3   4. 20 ÷ 4

Solve.

5. Joel has 10 oatmeal cookies. He wants to give each of 5 friends the same number of cookies. How many cookies will he give each friend?

6. Belinda and her sister together have 18 beads. They want to divide the beads into 2 equal groups. How many beads will be in each group?

7. **Analyze:** How does using the model help you divide?

For more practice, use Math Traveler™.

Objective: Choose a strategy to solve a problem.

7·7 Problem Solving: Strategy
Choose a Strategy

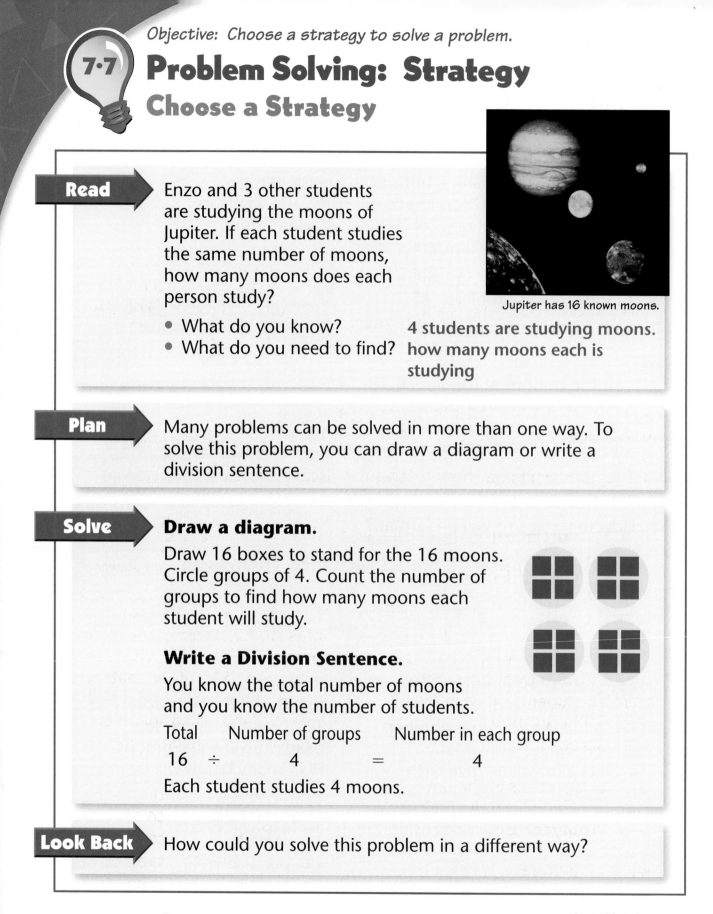

Read

Enzo and 3 other students are studying the moons of Jupiter. If each student studies the same number of moons, how many moons does each person study?

Jupiter has 16 known moons.

- What do you know?
- What do you need to find?

4 students are studying moons.
how many moons each is studying

Plan

Many problems can be solved in more than one way. To solve this problem, you can draw a diagram or write a division sentence.

Solve

Draw a diagram.

Draw 16 boxes to stand for the 16 moons. Circle groups of 4. Count the number of groups to find how many moons each student will study.

Write a Division Sentence.

You know the total number of moons and you know the number of students.

Total		Number of groups		Number in each group
16	÷	4	=	4

Each student studies 4 moons.

Look Back

How could you solve this problem in a different way?

Sum it Up! How are drawing a diagram and writing a division sentence alike? How are they different?

Solve. Tell which strategy you used.

1. Enzo has collected many pictures of Jupiter. Enzo shares 10 of his pictures equally between 2 friends. How many pictures does each friend get?

2. For his birthday, Enzo gets 6 packs of Solar System trading cards. Each pack has 4 cards in it. How many cards does he receive altogether?

3. Enzo arrives at the Air and Space Museum at 9:45 A.M. He spends 1 hour looking at airplanes. Then he takes 30 minutes to have a snack. How much time is left until noon?

4. **Music:** Eliot can play the song "Fly Me to the Moon" on the piano in 5 minutes. He must practice this song for a half hour. How many times can Eliot play the song during practice?

Mixed Strategy Review

5. **Art:** The Hill Street School is making murals to honor our astronauts. Each mural will be painted on 5 wall tiles in the hallway. There are 15 tiles in all, that the students can use. How many murals will they paint?

CHOOSE A STRATEGY
- Logical Reasoning
- Draw a Picture
- Make a Graph
- Act It Out
- Make a Table or List
- Find a Pattern
- Guess and Check
- Write a Number Sentence
- Work Backward

6. **Create a problem** that can be solved using more than one strategy. Solve it at least two different ways. Ask others to solve it. Compare strategies.

7. **Mental Math:** The 7th Street School students went on a bus trip to the Smithsonian. There were 40 students on each of 4 school buses. How many students went on the trip?

8. Three students were participating in the science fair. If each student could spend $15.50 on materials, what is the greatest amount all three students could spend on their science fair projects?

★9. Look at the prices in the table. Suppose you have 2 five-dollar bills, 3 quarters, 2 dimes, and 7 nickels. How much will you have left if you buy a ticket for yourself and an adult on a Saturday?

Space Museum Ticket Prices	
Adult (weekends)	$6.00
(weekdays)	$5.00
Children (weekends)	$3.50
(weekdays)	$2.50

7·8

Divide by 3

Learn

Mr. Michaels wants to know how many times the comet Encke has orbited the sun in his life so far. If Mr. Michaels is 24 years old, how many times has Encke orbited?

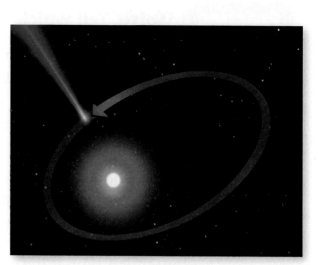

1 orbit takes 3 years.

Example

You can use division to solve this problem.

Find: 24 ÷ 3

> You can use a related multiplication fact to help you recall the division fact.
>
> **Think:** 3 times what number is 24?
>
> $$3 \times n = 24$$
>
> $$3 \times 8 = 24$$
>
> So 24 ÷ 3 = 8.

Encke has orbited the sun 8 times so far.

Try It **Divide.**

1. 9 ÷ 3   **2.** 18 ÷ 3   **3.** 3 ÷ 3   **4.** 27 ÷ 3   **5.** 12 ÷ 3

6. 6 ÷ 3   **7.** 15 ÷ 3   **8.** 21 ÷ 3   **9.** 24 ÷ 3   **10.** 9 ÷ 3

Sum It Up! Draw a picture to show how many groups of 3 are in 15. Explain your drawing.

Divide.

11. $15 \div 3$ **12.** $21 \div 3$ **13.** $6 \div 3$ **14.** $24 \div 3$ **15.** $3 \div 3$

16. $3\overline{)9}$ **17.** $3\overline{)18}$ **18.** $3\overline{)3}$ **19.** $3\overline{)12}$ **20.** $3\overline{)27}$ **21.** $3\overline{)15}$ **22.** $5\overline{)10}$

23. $2\overline{)18}$ **24.** $3\overline{)6}$ **25.** $3\overline{)21}$ **26.** $5\overline{)20}$ **27.** $3\overline{)24}$ **28.** $3\overline{)30}$ **29.** $3\overline{)18}$

★**30.** $(8 + 7) \div 3$ ★**31.** $(12 - 9) \div 3$ ★**32.** $(3 + 3) \div 3$

Algebra & functions **Copy and complete.**

33.

Rule: Divide by 3	
Input	Output
24	
15	
27	

34.

Rule: Subtract 3	
Input	Output
15	
21	
9	

Problem Solving

Use data from *Did You Know?* for problem 35.

35. Ms. Wallace teaches her class about 3 planets each day. How many days will it take to teach all of the planets?

 36. **Compare:** Use two strategies to find $18 \div 3$. Which do you prefer to use and why?

Did You KNOW?

There are 9 planets in our solar system.

Spiral Review and Test Prep

Find each missing number.

37. $9 \times n = 72$ **38.** $7 + r = 15$ **39.** $t \times 6 = 54$ **40.** $14 - 7 = s$

Choose the correct answer.

41. Earth turns on its axis one time each day. How many times does it turn in one week?

A. 7 times   **C.** 24 times

B. 30 times   **D.** 365 times

42. Which number is missing?
17, 14, 11, ▪, 5

F. 10   **H.** 12

G. 9   **J.** 8

7·9 Divide by 4

Learn

A total of 20 students are writing reports on Pluto. How can this be shown on the pictograph? You can use a related multiplication fact to help you quickly recall division facts.

Planet Reports

Planet	Number of Students
Mars	🪐🪐
Venus	🪐
Pluto	?

Each 🪐 = 4 students

Example

You can use division to find 20 ÷ 4.

Think: What number times 4 equals 20?

$d \times 4 = 20$
$5 \times 4 = 20$

So $20 \div 4 = 5$.

There are 5 groups of 4 in 20.

You need to show 5 🪐 in the pictograph.

Try It   Divide.

1. $8 \div 4$ 2. $16 \div 4$ 3. $12 \div 4$ 4. $24 \div 4$ 5. $4 \div 4$

6. $20 \div 4$ 7. $36 \div 4$ 8. $32 \div 4$ 9. $8 \div 4$ 10. $28 \div 4$

Sum It Up!   Draw a picture to show how many groups of 4 are in 24. Explain your drawing.

Divide.

11. $36 \div 4$ **12.** $28 \div 4$ **13.** $32 \div 4$ **14.** $24 \div 4$ **15.** $4 \div 4$

16. $2\overline{)12}$ **17.** $5\overline{)15}$ **18.** $2\overline{)16}$ **19.** $5\overline{)10}$ **20.** $3\overline{)21}$ **21.** $5\overline{)30}$ **22.** $4\overline{)28}$

★**23.** $(8 + 8) \div 4$ ★**24.** $(12 - 4) \div 4$ ★**25.** $(7 + 5) \div 4$

Algebra & functions   **Copy and complete.**

26.

Rule: Divide by 4	
Input	Output
24	
16	
32	

27.

Rule: Add 4	
Input	Output
16	
24	
12	

Problem Solving

Use data from the pictograph for problems 28–29.

28. There are 32 students who will ride on Bus 3. How many figures do you need to show in the pictograph?

29. How many more students will ride on Bus 3 than on Bus 1?

Journal **30. Generalize:** How can you use skip-counting backward to find $24 \div 4$?

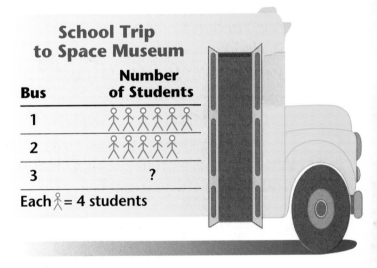

School Trip to Space Museum

Bus	Number of Students
1	👤👤👤👤👤👤
2	👤👤👤👤👤
3	?

Each 👤 = 4 students

Spiral Review and Test Prep

31. $325 - 39$ **32.** 9×9 **33.** $812 - 576$ **34.** $4,007 + 168$

Choose the correct answer.

35. Mel read 4 books about outer space. Jill read 12 more books than Mel. Which number sentence shows how many books Jill read?

A. $12 - 4 = 8$ **C.** $12 + 4 = 16$

B. $12 \div 4 = 3$ **D.** $4 \times 3 = 12$

36. There are 6 books about outer space on each of 8 shelves in the library. How many books are there altogether?

F. 14   **H.** 24

G. 48   **J.** 46

7·10 Divide with 0 and 1

Algebra & functions **Learn**

Mrs. Rourke has 4 model rockets. She gives the same number of rockets to each of 4 students. How many rockets does each student get?

Example 1

You can find 4 ÷ 4 to solve the problem.

You can use a related multiplication fact.

Think: 4 times what number equals 4?

$4 \times n = 4 \rightarrow 4 \times 1 = 4$ So $4 \div 4 = 1$.

> When you divide any number (except 0) by itself, the quotient is 1.

You can find a related division fact.

Think: 1 times what number equals 4?

$1 \times n = 4 \rightarrow 1 \times 4 = 4$ So $4 \div 1 = 4$.

> When you divide any number by 1, the quotient is the original number.

Mrs. Rourke gives each student 1 rocket.

What if there are 0 rockets? How many rockets would each student get?

Example 2

Find: $0 \div 4$

> When you divide 0 by any other number (except 0), the quotient is 0.

Think: 4 times what number equals 0?

$4 \times n = 0 \rightarrow 4 \times 0 = 0 \rightarrow$ So $0 \div 4 = 0$.

Can you find 4 ÷ 0? **Think:** 0 times what number equals 4?

$0 \times n = 4$ No number can complete the number sentence.

> You cannot divide any number by zero.

Each student would get 0 rockets.

Try It **Divide.**

1. $5 \div 5$ **2.** $0 \div 3$ **3.** $2 \div 1$ **4.** $0 \div 9$ **5.** $7 \div 7$

Sum it Up Explain how you can find $327 \div 327$.

Copy and complete the table to record your observation.

Sequence	Number of Digits	Accurate (Yes or No) ?
1		
2		
3		
4		
5		
6		
7		
8		
9		
10		
11		
12		
13		
14		
15		

Problem Solving

Conclude and Apply

- What is the maximum number of digits you can memorize? How do you know?

- Explain how division can make memorization easier.

- Describe the strategies you used to memorize the lists.

Did You KNOW?

Psychologists say that people can usually memorize no more than 5 to 9 numbers at a time. How does the number of digits you can memorize compare with the average?

Going Further

1. Repeat the activity with people older and younger than you. How does age affect the maximum number of digits you can memorize?

Divide. (pages 278–286)

1. $36 \div 4$
2. $18 \div 3$
3. $24 \div 3$
4. $35 \div 5$
5. $12 \div 4$

6. $5\overline{)20}$
7. $4\overline{)24}$
8. $4\overline{)16}$
9. $2\overline{)16}$
10. $3\overline{)12}$

11. $20 \div 4$
12. $27 \div 3$
13. $15 \div 3$
14. $25 \div 5$
15. $8 \div 4$

16. $5\overline{)40}$
17. $4\overline{)32}$
18. $2\overline{)18}$
19. $2\overline{)6}$
20. $3\overline{)9}$

Find each missing number. (pages 290–291)

21. $7 \div 7 = z$
22. $n \div 6 = 0$
23. $4 \div t = 4$
24. $y \div 3 = 1$

25. $14 \div 14 = m$
26. $s \div 8 = 0$
27. $0 \div 9 = z$

Solve. (pages 284–297)

28. There are 35 people on a Space Mountain roller coaster ride. Each car holds 5 people. How many cars are there?

29. Bob tapes 24 large space collector's cards on sheets of paper. He puts 3 on each sheet. How many sheets does he use?

30. You have 3 friends. How can you find how to share equally 12 packs of space food with them? How many packs will each of you get?

31. The 21 third-grade students will divide into equal groups and present skits about the planets to the second-grade class. There will be 7 students in each group. How many groups will present skits?

32. There are 24 books about our solar system in the library. Ms. Hernandez is dividing them evenly among 6 groups of students. How many books does each group get?

Journal

33. **Explain** which strategy you would use to find $27 \div 3$.

Additional activities at
www.mhschool.com/math

Relate multiplication and division. (pages 268–275)

Example
5, 6, 30
Solution
$5 \times 6 = 30$ or $6 \times 5 = 30$
$30 \div 5 = 6$ $30 \div 6 = 5$

Write related multiplication and division sentences for each group of numbers.

17. 3, 5, 15

18. 4, 6, 24

19. 3, 9, 27

20. 2, 7, 14

21. 5, 5, 25

22. 5, 8, 40

Use strategies to solve problems. (pages 276–277, 284–285)

Example
Use more than one strategy to solve.
Suppose you want to hang 9 pictures of astronauts on a wall. You want 3 pictures in each row. How many rows of pictures will you hang?

Solution

Strategy 1: Draw a diagram. You will show 3 rows.

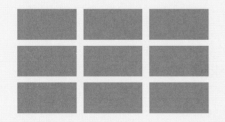

Strategy 2: Write a division number sentence.

$9 \div 3 = 3$ **Think:** $3 \times r = 9$

You will show 3 rows.

Use more than one strategy to solve.

23. A ticket to the new outer space movie costs $5.00. Is $16.00 enough to buy 3 tickets? How can you tell?

24. Tom decorates the walls in his room with stick-ons of the 9 planets. Each of his 4 walls has 1 stick-on of each planet. How many stick-ons did Tom use?

25. Nina has 32 galaxy pictures. She will divide them evenly among herself and 7 friends. How many pictures will each person get?

Chapter Test

Divide.

1. $4\overline{)16}$ 2. $3\overline{)24}$ 3. $5\overline{)20}$ 4. $4\overline{)12}$ 5. $2\overline{)14}$

6. $15 \div 3$ 7. $36 \div 4$ 8. $40 \div 5$ 9. $8 \div 2$ 10. $28 \div 4$

11. $5 \div 5$ 12. $4 \div 1$ 13. $0 \div 2$ 14. $3 \div 3$ 15. $2 \div 1$

Write related multiplication and division sentences for each picture or group of numbers.

16.   17.

18. 5, 7, 35   19. 5, 9, 45

20. 3, 6, 18   21. 8, 4, 32

Solve.

22. Mr. Malson spent 14 hours over 2 days visiting the Air and Space Museum. If he spent the same amount of time each day, how long did he visit the museum each day?

23. Connie is arranging her drawings of the 9 planets in rows of 3. How many rows does she need to make? Tell how you choose which operation to use.

24. Len spent $24.00 for 3 spaceship models. Jerry spent $28.00 for 4 of the same models. Who spent more on each model? how much more?

25. There are 24 students in Mr. Ortez's third-grade class. The class is divided into 4 groups for a gravity experiment. How many students are in each group?

Performance Assessment

You and your friends can save money by buying space figures by the box. Then you can divide the figures evenly among your friends.

Make a chart like the one below to help you.

- Find the number of figures each person will get.
- Find numbers that divide evenly.
- Find the number that each friend gets.
- Explain how you made your decisions.

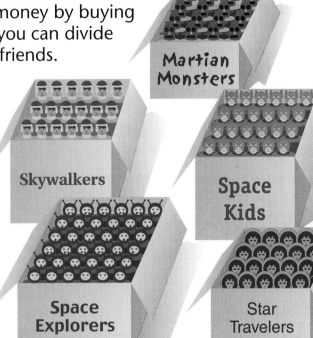

Action Figure	Number in Box	Number of Friends (include yourself)	Number Each Gets
Space Kids			
Skywalkers			
Star Travelers			
Martian Monsters			
Space Explorers			

Journal

A Good Answer

- has a completely-filled-in chart.
- shows that you used numbers that divide evenly.
- shows your division examples.
- has a clear explanation of how you decided which numbers to use.

Portfolio

You may want to save this work in your portfolio.

Enrichment

Odd or Even Products and Quotients

When you multiply or divide even and odd numbers, can you predict what the result will be? Will you get an odd number? Will you get an even number?

1. Make a table like the one below to find products. Choose numbers to test.

Numbers	Example	Product	Odd or Even?
odd × odd	3 × 5		
odd × odd	1 × 7		
even × even	2 × 6		
even × even	4 × 6		
odd × even	3 × 4		
even × odd	6 × 5		

2. Make a table like the one below to find quotients. Choose numbers to test.

Numbers	Example	Quotient	Odd or Even?
odd ÷ odd	15 ÷ 3		
odd ÷ odd	25 ÷ 5		
even ÷ even	6 ÷ 2		
even ÷ even	16 ÷ 4		
even ÷ odd	14 ÷ 7		
even ÷ odd	12 ÷ 3		

3. **Analyze:** What happens when you try to divide an odd number by an even number?

4. **Generalize:** What patterns did you see? Compare your conclusions to those of other students.

5. How can you use these generalizations to check the reasonableness of a product or quotient?

Test-Taking Tips

S.O.S.

You may have taken tests where one of the answer choices was "Not Here." Sometimes, that actually is the correct answer!

Yoshi and Carol are going to share a collection of 18 stickers equally. How many stickers will each of them get?

A. 6   **C.** 16
B. 8   **D.** Not Here

You can divide to solve the problem:
$18 \div 2 = 9$

They would each get 9 stickers.

Check the answer choices: 9 is not one of the answers. Double-check your work. The correct choice is D, "Not Here."

Choose the correct answer. Check your work before you choose.

1. Find the missing number.
   $24 \div x = 12$
   A. 0   **C.** 6
   B. 1   **D.** Not Here

2. Which is more than twice as great as 12?
   F. 2   **H.** 22
   G. 20   **J.** Not Here

Jeff bought these items.

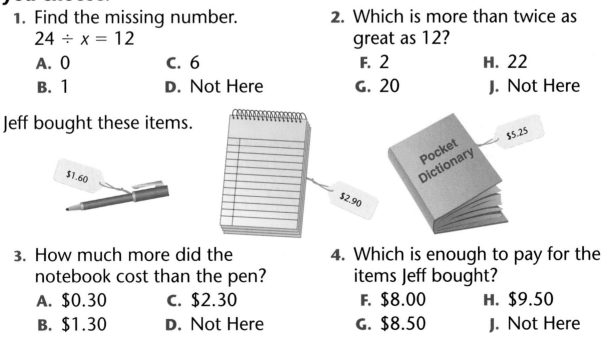

$1.60

$2.90

Pocket Dictionary $5.25

3. How much more did the notebook cost than the pen?
   A. $0.30   **C.** $2.30
   B. $1.30   **D.** Not Here

4. Which is enough to pay for the items Jeff bought?
   F. $8.00   **H.** $9.50
   G. $8.50   **J.** Not Here

Test Prep

Test-Taking Tips

Spiral Review and Test Prep
Chapters 1-7

Choose the correct answer.

Number Sense

1. Which multiplication fact makes the sentence true?

   $7 \times 6 < t$

   A. 9×4 C. 6×6

   B. 4×8 D. 5×9

2. Which difference is about 200?

   F. $587 - 135$ H. $1,304 - 691$

   G. $703 - 598$ J. $2,439 - 2,210$

3. Chris needs to save $435.00 to buy a bicycle. He has $290.00. How much more must he save?

   A. $145.00   C. $265.00

   B. $245.00   D. Not Here

4. There are 28 students in the third grade. They are working in groups of 4 on planet reports. Each group will do one report. How many reports will there be?

   F. 32   H. 8

   G. 28   J. 7

Measurement and Geometry

5. Chim practices the piano for 45 minutes each day. If he starts at 4:30 P.M., what time does he finish?

   A. 3:15 P.M.   C. 5:00 P.M.

   B. 4:45 P.M.   D. 5:15 P.M.

6. Today's date is March 20. What was the date one week ago?

   F. March 27   H. March 10

   G. March 13   J. March 7

7. Which is true?

   A. A square has exactly 3 equal sides.

   B. A circle has exactly 2 equal sides.

   C. A square is a rectangle.

   D. Not Here

8. A tiled floor has 36 tiles in all. There are the same number of rows and columns of tiles. How many rows of tiles are there?

   F. 4   H. 6

   G. 5   J. 9

Algebra and Functions

9. Find the rule.

Rule: ▪
Input: 3, 9, 12
Output: 6, 18, 24

A. Add 3   **C.** Multiply by 2
B. Multiply by 3 **D.** Add 6

10. Which number makes the sentence true?

$(3 + 12) + 35 = 3 + (a + 35)$

F. 12   **H.** 35
G. 15   **J.** Not Here

11. Which belongs in the ●?

$12 ● 8 = 4$

A. +   **C.** −
B. ×   **D.** ÷

12. Harry began with $35.00 on Monday. He spends $5.00 each day for lunch. On which day does he have $15.00 left?

F. Thursday   **H.** Saturday
G. Friday   **J.** Sunday

Statistics, Data Analysis, and Probability

Use the bar graph for exercises 13–16.

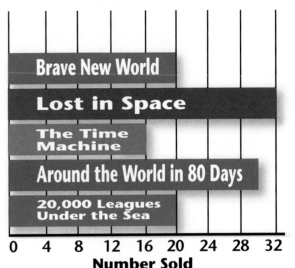

Summer Book Sales

13. How many more copies of *Lost in Space* were sold than copies of *Brave New World*?

A. 8   **C.** 16
B. 12   **D.** 56

14. Which book sold 2 times as many copies as *The Time Machine*?

F. *Brave New World*
G. *Lost in Space*
H. *Around the World in 80 Days*
J. *20,000 Leagues Under the Sea*

15. How many books were sold in all?

A. 116   **C.** 122
B. 118   **D.** 244

16. How many more books of *Lost in Space* were sold than *The Time Machine*? Explain how you found your answer.

CHAPTER 8

Division Facts

Theme: Our Earth

Use the Data

How Water Is Used

Activity	Amount of Water (per Activity)
Take a shower	between 15 and 30 gallons
Run a dishwasher	between 10 and 25 gallons
Wash dishes by hand	about 20 gallons

Source: World Almanac and Book of Facts

- Running a dishwasher with the least amount of water uses about 5 times as much water as brushing your teeth with the greatest amount of water. How can division help you find the number of gallons someone would use when brushing their teeth with the greatest amount of water?

What You Will Learn

In this chapter you will learn how to

- divide, using facts through 12.
- identify fact families and find missing factors.
- use strategies to solve problems.

Additional activities at
www.mhschool.com/math

8·1 Divide by 6 and 7

Learn

A park ranger reintroduces plants, like the wildflower golden alexanders, back into the environment.

If June plants 24 wildflowers in groups of 6, how many wildflowers are in each group?

You need to be able to recall facts quickly. You can use different strategies to help you remember.

Math in ACTION

June Yoo is an urban park ranger.

There's more than one way!

Find: 24 ÷ 6

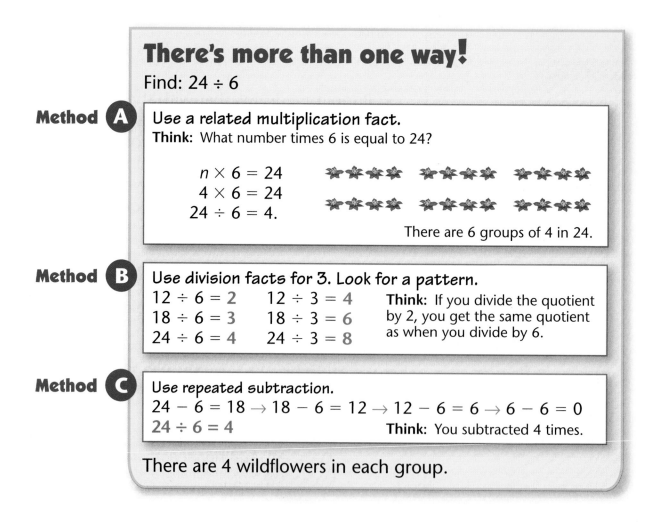

Method A

Use a related multiplication fact.
Think: What number times 6 is equal to 24?

$n \times 6 = 24$
$4 \times 6 = 24$
$24 \div 6 = 4.$

There are 6 groups of 4 in 24.

Method B

Use division facts for 3. Look for a pattern.

$12 \div 6 = 2$	$12 \div 3 = 4$
$18 \div 6 = 3$	$18 \div 3 = 6$
$24 \div 6 = 4$	$24 \div 3 = 8$

Think: If you divide the quotient by 2, you get the same quotient as when you divide by 6.

Method C

Use repeated subtraction.
$24 - 6 = 18 \rightarrow 18 - 6 = 12 \rightarrow 12 - 6 = 6 \rightarrow 6 - 6 = 0$
$24 \div 6 = 4$

Think: You subtracted 4 times.

There are 4 wildflowers in each group.

A park ranger also guides groups of people through trails. If a group of 42 people separate into groups of 7, how many people are in each group?

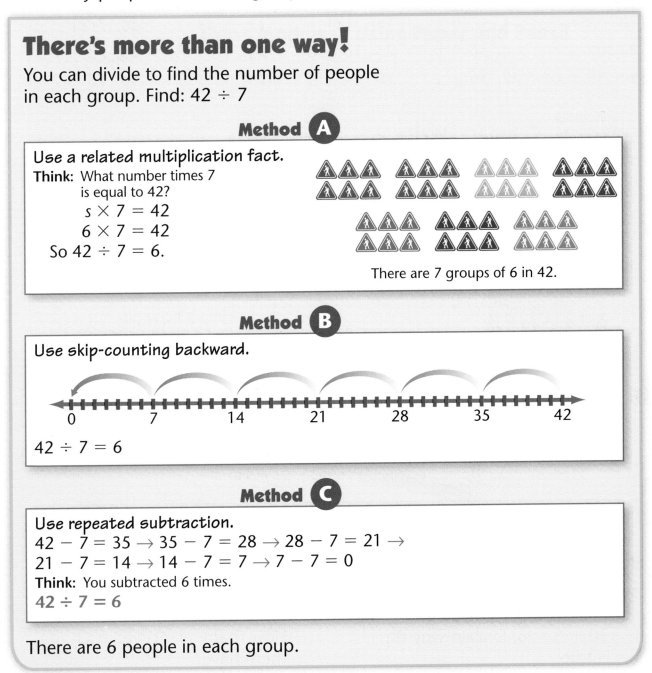

There's more than one way!

You can divide to find the number of people in each group. Find: $42 \div 7$

Method A

Use a related multiplication fact.

Think: What number times 7 is equal to 42?

$$s \times 7 = 42$$
$$6 \times 7 = 42$$
So $42 \div 7 = 6$.

There are 7 groups of 6 in 42.

Method B

Use skip-counting backward.

$$42 \div 7 = 6$$

Method C

Use repeated subtraction.

$42 - 7 = 35 \rightarrow 35 - 7 = 28 \rightarrow 28 - 7 = 21 \rightarrow$
$21 - 7 = 14 \rightarrow 14 - 7 = 7 \rightarrow 7 - 7 = 0$

Think: You subtracted 6 times.

$$42 \div 7 = 6$$

There are 6 people in each group.

Try It **Divide.**

1. $6\overline{)54}$
2. $7\overline{)56}$
3. $6\overline{)18}$
4. $7\overline{)28}$
5. $6\overline{)36}$
6. $49 \div 7$
7. $12 \div 6$
8. $35 \div 7$
9. $48 \div 6$
10. $7 \div 7$

Sum It Up! Which strategy do you prefer to use to find facts for 7? for 6? Why?

Practice Divide.

11. $6\overline{)6}$	**12.** $4\overline{)32}$	**13.** $3\overline{)15}$	**14.** $7\overline{)14}$	**15.** $6\overline{)30}$
16. $6\overline{)42}$	**17.** $4\overline{)36}$	**18.** $3\overline{)21}$	**19.** $6\overline{)54}$	**20.** $7\overline{)21}$
21. $63 \div 7$	**22.** $36 \div 6$	**23.** $18 \div 6$	**24.** $49 \div 7$	**25.** $28 \div 7$
26. $48 \div 6$	**27.** $56 \div 7$	**28.** $24 \div 4$	**29.** $45 \div 5$	**30.** $16 \div 2$

Algebra & functions Compare. Write >, <, or =.

31. $48 \div 6 \bullet 8$ **32.** $49 \div 7 \bullet 9$ **33.** $30 \div 6 \bullet 4$ **34.** $63 \div 7 \bullet 8$

★**35.** $35 \div 7 \bullet 24 \div 6$ ★**36.** $36 \div 4 \bullet 56 \div 7$ ★**37.** $28 \div 7 \bullet 36 \div 9$

38.

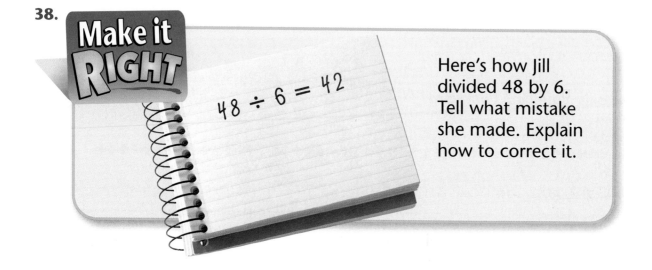

Make it RIGHT

$$48 \div 6 = 42$$

Here's how Jill divided 48 by 6. Tell what mistake she made. Explain how to correct it.

Problem Solving

39. Analyze: When you know that $30 \div 6 = 5$, you also know $30 \div 5 = 6$. Explain why this is true.

40. Lia has 14 plants. She wants to share them equally with Matt. How many plants will each of them have?

41. Mariposa gives away some baseball cards. She gives 5 to Anna, 4 to Apu, 7 to Jodi, and 4 to Joe. Do you add or multiply to find how many cards she gave away? Why?

42. Social Studies: The deepest freshwater lake in the United States is Crater Lake in Oregon. It is 88 meters deeper than Lake Tahoe in California and Nevada. If Lake Tahoe is 501 meters deep, how deep is Crater Lake?

Use data from the table for problems 43–45.

43. There are 56 club members hiking these mountains. The club members broke into equal teams to hike the mountains. How many hikers are on Mt. Davis?

44. Mt. Everest is 29,028 feet high. What is the difference in height between it and the highest mountain shown here?

45. **Create a problem** using the data from the table. Solve it. Ask others to solve it.

★46. Two farmers each have 18 acres of land. They combine their land and then divide it into 6 equal sections. How many acres are in each section?

Use data from *Did You Know?* for problem 47.

47. James visited Maine on his United States tour. The temperature recorded in Death Valley is about 10 times as high as the temperature in Maine when James was there. What was the temperature in Maine?

Mountain	State	Height (in Feet)
Sassafras	SC	3,560
Woodall	MS	806
Brasstown Bald	GA	4,784
Mt. Marcy	NY	5,344
Mt. Davis	PA	3,213
Mt. Mitchell	NC	6,684
Mt. Sunflower	KS	4,039

Source: World Almanac and Book of Facts

Did You KNOW?

Temperatures greater than 120°F were recorded for 43 days in a row in 1917 in Death Valley, California.

Death Valley, California

Spiral Review and Test Prep

48. $18 \div 3$ 49. 6×9 50. $4\overline{)36}$ 51. 7×5 52. $5\overline{)35}$

Choose the correct answer.

53. Sid wants to make 8 earthworm boxes with 6 worms in each box. How many worms does he need?

   A. 2   C. 48
   B. 14   D. 56

54. Lake Tahoe is 1,645 feet deep. What is this number rounded to the nearest thousand?

   F. 1,000   H. 1,700
   G. 1,600   J. 2,000

8·2 Problem Solving: Reading for Math
Solve Multistep Problems

Cans for Cash

Read ▶ Jamie raises $9.00 recycling cans. He raises twice as much recycling bottles. He plans to split the money equally among 3 groups. How much will each group receive?

READING ▶ **Make an Inference**
SKILL
You make inferences based on things you know or that are hinted at. Sometimes, there is a "hidden question" that you have to infer.

- **What do you know?** How much he raised; number of groups

- **What do you need to find?** How much money each group will receive.

- **What can you infer?** How much he raised recycling bottles; how much he raised in all.

MATH ▶ **Solve Multistep Problems**
SKILL
Some problems take more than one step to solve. You must decide how to solve each step and in what order.

Plan ▶ Multiply to find the amount raised recycling bottles. Add to find the total amount raised. Divide to find the amount each group will receive.

Solve ▶ $2 \times 9 = 18$ $\qquad$ $9 + 18 = 27$ $\qquad$ $27 \div 3 = 9$
Jamie will give each group $9.00.

Look Back ▶ • Is your answer reasonable?

Sum It Up! What hidden question did you have to infer to solve the problem?

Practice **Solve. Tell what hidden question you inferred.**

1. Tala collected 37 cans. Her sister collected 7 fewer cans. How many cans did the girls collect altogether?

2. For 5 days in a row, Kyle bundled 9 bags and Jeff bundled 3 bags. How many bags had the boys bundled after the fifth day?

Use data from the chart for problems 3–6.

3. Which grade gathered the greatest number of cans in week 1? How much greater was this total than that of each other grade?

4. During week 3, which grade collected the greatest number of cans? How much greater was this total than that of each other grade?

Can Collection Totals

Grade	Week 1	Week 2	Week 3
1	117	89	53
2	72	113	134
3	109	255	216

5. What is the difference between the least number of cans collected by a grade in a week and the greatest number of cans collected by a grade in a week?

6. Sam collected 6 cans each day for 5 days. Hank collected half as many cans as Sam. At the end of the fifth day, how many cans did the two boys collect?

Spiral Review and Test Prep

Choose the correct answer.

May fills 12 bags with cans. Seth fills twice as many bags as May. They put an equal number of bags in each of 6 large recycling bins. How many bags do they put in each bin?

7. Which is true?
   A. May filled more bags than Seth.
   B. They put 9 bags in each bin.
   C. May filled 12 bags.

8. The "hidden question" you must solve first is: How many
   F. bags did May fill?
   G. bags did they fill in all?
   H. bins are there?

8·3 Divide by 8 and 9

Learn

A group of 8 people are picking up litter along the beach. They share 16 trash bags equally. How many trash bags does each person get?

Here are strategies you can use to help you remember how to divide by 8 and 9.

There's more than one way!

Find: $16 \div 8$

Method A Use a related multiplication fact.
Think: 8 times what number is equal to 16?

$$8 \times n = 16$$
$$8 \times 2 = 16$$
So $16 \div 8 = 2$.

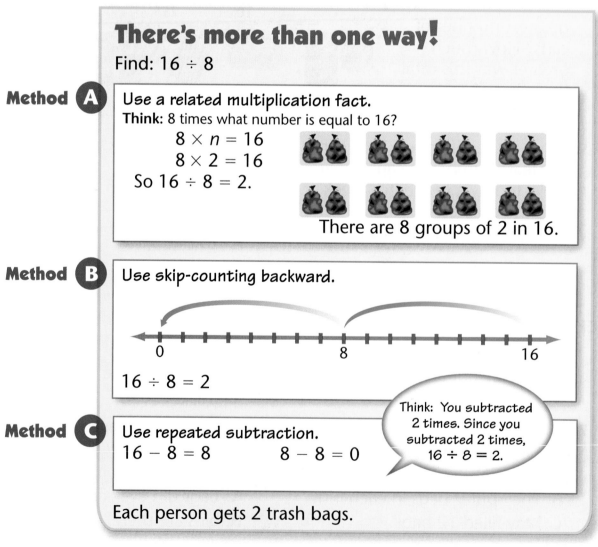

There are 8 groups of 2 in 16.

Method B Use skip-counting backward.

0   8   16

$16 \div 8 = 2$

Think: You subtracted 2 times. Since you subtracted 2 times, $16 \div 8 = 2$.

Method C Use repeated subtraction.
$16 - 8 = 8$ $8 - 8 = 0$

Each person gets 2 trash bags.

Mr. Olson surveyed his class to find which bodies of water students have seen. He drew this pictograph to show the results. There are 27 students who have seen the Pacific Ocean. How many symbols should he show in the pictograph?

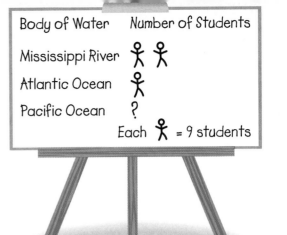

Body of Water	Number of Students
Mississippi River	👤 👤
Atlantic Ocean	👤
Pacific Ocean	?

Each 👤 = 9 students

There's more than one way!

Find: 27 ÷ 9

Method A

Use a related multiplication fact.

Think: What number times 9 is equal to 27?

$n \times 9 = 27$
$3 \times 9 = 27$
So $27 \div 9 = 3$

Method B

Use skip-counting backward.

0   9   18   27

$27 \div 9 = 3$

Method C

Use repeated subtraction.

$27 - 9 = 18$ $18 - 9 = 9$ $9 - 9 = 0$

He should show 3 👤s in the pictograph.

Think: You subtracted 3 times. Since you subtracted 3 times, $27 \div 9 = 3$.

Try It Divide.

1. $8\overline{)8}$ 2. $9\overline{)36}$ 3. $8\overline{)40}$ 4. $9\overline{)54}$ 5. $8\overline{)56}$

6. $24 \div 8$ 7. $27 \div 9$ 8. $45 \div 9$ 9. $48 \div 8$ 10. $18 \div 9$

Sum It Up When you know $36 \div 9 = 4$, you also know that $36 \div 4 = 9$. Explain why this is true.

Divide.

11. 8)16   **12.** 9)9   **13.** 8)32   **14.** 9)63   **15.** 8)56

16. 8)64   **17.** 9)72   **18.** 3)27   **19.** 5)30   **20.** 6)48

21. 40 ÷ 8   **22.** 45 ÷ 9   **23.** 64 ÷ 8   **24.** 72 ÷ 8   **25.** 28 ÷ 7

26. 42 ÷ 6   **27.** 81 ÷ 9   **28.** 32 ÷ 4   **29.** 40 ÷ 5   **30.** 12 ÷ 2

★**31.** (4 + 4) ÷ 8   ★**32.** (8 + 8) ÷ 8   ★**33.** (12 + 12) ÷ 8

Algebra & functions   Solve.

34.

Rule: ÷ 8				
Input:	24	▓	56	▓
Output:	▓	5	▓	9

35.

Rule: ▓			
Input:	3	5	7
Output:	27	45	63

36.

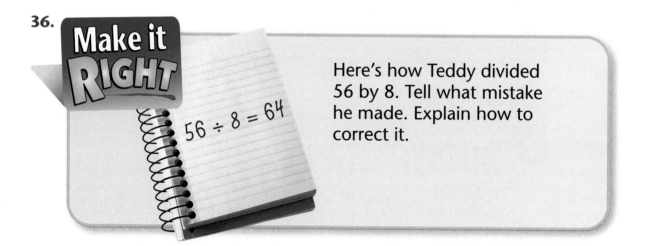

Make it RIGHT

$56 ÷ 8 = 64$

Here's how Teddy divided 56 by 8. Tell what mistake he made. Explain how to correct it.

Problem Solving

37. Social Studies: Ireland is an island with an area of about 32,000 square miles. Jamaica is also an island. Ireland has about 8 times more area than Jamaica. About how many thousand square miles is Jamaica?

38. Science: The shorelines of the world's oceans are being worn away. About 24 feet of the Pacific Ocean shoreline has worn away in 8 years. About how much shoreline is lost each year?

Use data from the table for problems 39–40.

39. You travel a total of 63 miles along the Minnesota River in 9 days. You travel the same number of miles each day. How many miles did you travel each day? How many miles of the river have you not traveled?

★ 40. Max wants to travel the length of the Trinity River. He has traveled 306 miles so far. If he travels 9 miles each day for the rest of the trip, how many days will he have left to travel?

Some Rivers in North America

River	Length in Miles
Yukon	1,979
Missouri	2,315
Red	1,290
Mississippi	2,340
Minnesota	332
Trinity	360

Sources: World Almanac and Book of Facts

41. Collect data from other students about the oceans or rivers they have visited. Make a pictograph to show your data.

42. Create a problem that can be solved by dividing by 9. Solve it. Ask others to solve it.

Journal

43. Compare: Divide the same number by 2, 4, and 8. What pattern do you see?

Spiral Review and Test Prep

44. $547 + 12 + 689$

45. $4,307 - 768$

46. $\$4.89 + \$9.09$

47.
$$\begin{array}{r} 9,432 \\ 753 \\ +1,435 \\ \hline \end{array}$$

48. $5 \times 3 \times 4$

49.
$$\begin{array}{r} 3,467 \\ -\ 905 \\ \hline \end{array}$$

50.
$$\begin{array}{r} \$7.31 \\ -\ 5.67 \\ \hline \end{array}$$

Choose the correct answer.

51. Rico bought a sandwich and a drink that cost $6.35. He paid with a ten-dollar bill. How much change will he get?

   A. $4.35   **C.** $3.75

   B. $4.65   **D.** $3.65

52. Canoe rentals cost $8.75 per hour in the fall. In the summer they cost $0.85 more per hour. How much are canoe rentals in the summer?

   F. $7.90   **H.** $7.60

   G. $9.60   **J.** $9.90

Divide. (pages 312–321)

1. $7\overline{)63}$ 2. $6\overline{)42}$ 3. $8\overline{)32}$ 4. $7\overline{)21}$ 5. $7\overline{)42}$

6. $9\overline{)81}$ 7. $6\overline{)54}$ 8. $7\overline{)49}$ 9. $8\overline{)40}$ 10. $8\overline{)64}$

11. $18 \div 6$ 12. $35 \div 7$ 13. $56 \div 8$ 14. $36 \div 9$ 15. $36 \div 6$

16. $27 \div 9$ 17. $54 \div 6$ 18. $45 \div 9$ 19. $72 \div 8$ 20. $63 \div 9$

21. $32 \div 8$ 22. $54 \div 9$ 23. $24 \div 8$ 24. $72 \div 9$

25. $14 \div 7$ 26. $12 \div 6$ 27. $64 \div 8$ 28. $18 \div 9$

Solve. (pages 312–321)

29. The science group plants 54 tree seedlings in 9 different parks. They plant the same number in each park. How many seedlings are planted in each park?

30. You spend $72 on 8 tickets for a river raft ride. How much is each ticket?

31. You want to put pictures of your canoe ride in an album. You have 2 packages of pictures. One package has 12 pictures. The other has 24 pictures. Each page of the album holds 6 pictures. How many pages of the album will you fill?

32. There are 28 people signed up for a nature canoe ride. There are 7 canoes for the trip. How many people will ride in each canoe?

33. **Analyze:** How can you use skip-counting to find $30 \div 6$?

Additional activities at
www.mhschool.com/math

Use Tables to Divide

Students must sign up if they want to help plan the carnival. Each planning group will have 6 students. How many groups will there be if 36 students sign up? if 42 students sign up? if 48 students sign up? if 54 students sign up?

You can use a spreadsheet table to divide.

- Click on the table key ⊞
- Label the columns *Total Students*, *Students in Each Group*, and *Number of Groups*.
- In the column labeled *Total students*, enter the number of students who signed up.
- In the column labeled *Students in Each Group*, enter 6.
- In the column labeled *Number of Groups*, enter a formula to divide Total Students by Students in Each Group.

How many groups will there be if 36 students sign up? if 42 students sign up? if 48 students sign up? if 54 students sign up?

Use the computer to find each set of quotients. Then complete each number sentence.

1. $18 \div 6 = \blacksquare$
   $24 \div 6 = \blacksquare$
   $36 \div 6 = \blacksquare$

2. $27 \div 9 = \blacksquare$
   $36 \div 9 = \blacksquare$
   $45 \div 9 = \blacksquare$

3. $56 \div 8 = \blacksquare$
   $64 \div 8 = \blacksquare$
   $72 \div 8 = \blacksquare$

4. $35 \div 7 = \blacksquare$
   $42 \div 7 = \blacksquare$
   $49 \div 7 = \blacksquare$

5. **Analyze:** How does using the table help when you have to divide several times?

For more practice, use Math Traveler™.

Objective: Use guess and check to solve a problem.

8·4 Problem Solving: Strategy
Guess and Check

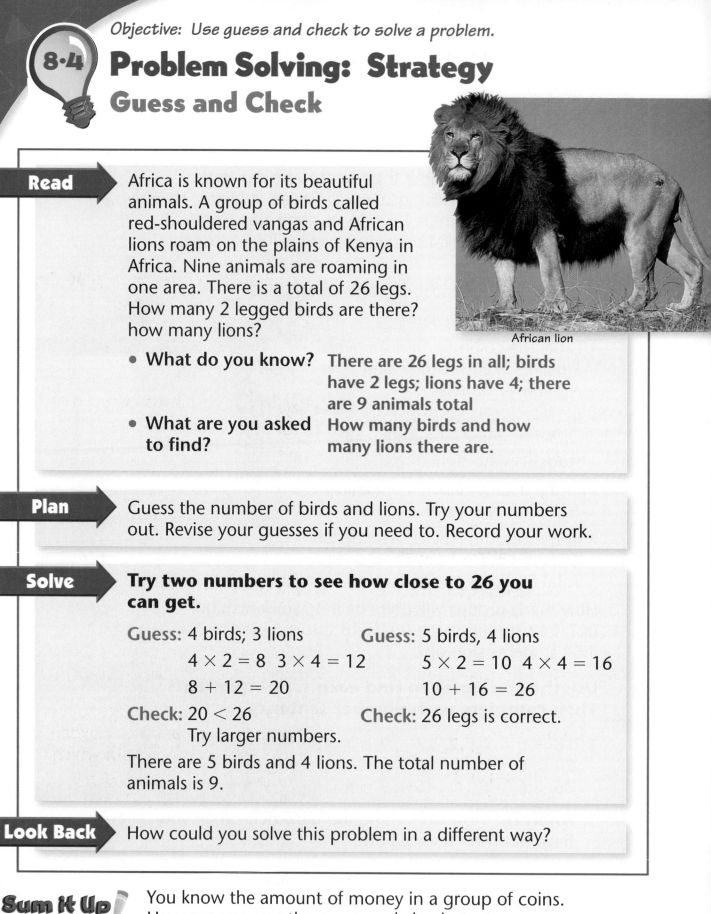

African lion

Read

Africa is known for its beautiful animals. A group of birds called red-shouldered vangas and African lions roam on the plains of Kenya in Africa. Nine animals are roaming in one area. There is a total of 26 legs. How many 2 legged birds are there? how many lions?

- **What do you know?**   There are 26 legs in all; birds have 2 legs; lions have 4; there are 9 animals total

- **What are you asked to find?**   How many birds and how many lions there are.

Plan

Guess the number of birds and lions. Try your numbers out. Revise your guesses if you need to. Record your work.

Solve

Try two numbers to see how close to 26 you can get.

Guess: 4 birds; 3 lions
$4 \times 2 = 8$ $3 \times 4 = 12$
$8 + 12 = 20$
Check: $20 < 26$
     Try larger numbers.

Guess: 5 birds, 4 lions
$5 \times 2 = 10$ $4 \times 4 = 16$
$10 + 16 = 26$
Check: 26 legs is correct.

There are 5 birds and 4 lions. The total number of animals is 9.

Look Back

How could you solve this problem in a different way?

Sum It Up

You know the amount of money in a group of coins. How can you use the guess and check strategy to decide what coins are in the group?

Use the guess and check strategy to solve.

1. **Music:** Justin's string band has banjo players and guitar players. The band has 7 members. Each banjo has 5 strings. Each guitar has 6 strings. Justin bought 38 new strings for the banjos and guitars. How many banjos will get new strings? How many guitars?

2. **Language Arts:** Frank writes his spelling word *environment* over and over on a sheet of paper. When he is finished he has written a total of 45 *e*s and *n*s. How many times has he written this spelling word?

3. There are two numbers whose sum is 8 and quotient is 3. What are the two numbers?

4. You have 5 coins that total $0.75. What coins do you have?

Mixed Strategy Review

5. A charter boat took 5 fishers out for the day. They caught a total of 45 fish. If they each caught the same number of fish, how many did each catch?

CHOOSE A STRATEGY
- Logical Reasoning
- Draw a Picture
- Make a Graph
- Act It Out
- Make a Table or List
- Find a Pattern
- Guess and Check
- Write a Number Sentence
- Work Backward
- Solve a Simpler Problem

6. The Bird Watchers Club has recorded a total of 24 kinds of birds for 6 weeks. They recorded the same number each week. How many kinds of birds did they see in 1 week?

7. Ana's science group plants tree seedlings to help save forests. There are 9 people in her group. Each planted 7 tree seedlings. How many did they plant?

8. Lila spends $54.00 on a backpack and a canteen. The backpack costs twice as much as the canteen. How much does the backpack cost? the canteen cost?

9. A small box holds 5 books. A large box holds 9 books. A bookstore gets a shipment of 7 small boxes and 8 large boxes. How many books are in the shipment?

★10. Yellowstone National Park is home to many animals. Builders have 36 fence posts with which to make a square fence in the park. A post will be on each corner. How many posts will be on each side?

11. **Create a problem** that can be solved using the guess-and-check strategy. Solve it. Ask others to solve it.

8·5 Explore: **Dividing by 10**

Learn

You can use place value models to explore dividing by 10.

What is 90 ÷ 10?

Work Together

▶ Use place value models to find 90 ÷ 10.

You Will Need
- place value models

- Show the number 90 using tens place value models.

- Divide the models into groups of 10.

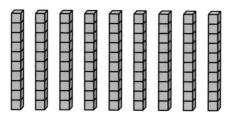

- How many groups of 10 are in 90? Record your work. Solve the problem.

▶ Use tens models to divide. Record your work.

▶ Try some more problems.

50 ÷ 10	70 ÷ 10
60 ÷ 10	40 ÷ 10
20 ÷ 10	10 ÷ 10
90 ÷ 1	30 ÷ 10
80 ÷ 10	40 ÷ 1

Make Connections

Here is how to divide by 10.

Find: 30 ÷ 10

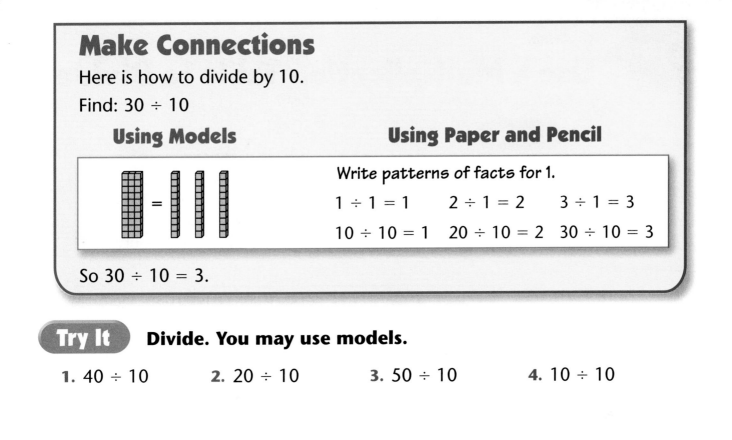

Using Models

Using Paper and Pencil

Write patterns of facts for 1.

$1 \div 1 = 1$	$2 \div 1 = 2$	$3 \div 1 = 3$
$10 \div 10 = 1$	$20 \div 10 = 2$	$30 \div 10 = 3$

So 30 ÷ 10 = 3.

Try It **Divide. You may use models.**

1. 40 ÷ 10   **2.** 20 ÷ 10   **3.** 50 ÷ 10   **4.** 10 ÷ 10

Sum it Up! Compare the quotient and the divisor when you divide by 10. What do you notice?

Practice **Divide.**

5. 10)‾40   **6.** 10)‾70   **7.** 1)‾50   **8.** 10)‾60   **9.** 10)‾70

10. 30 ÷ 1   **11.** 80 ÷ 10   **12.** 30 ÷ 10   **13.** 50 ÷ 10   **14.** 90 ÷ 10

Find the missing number.

15.

Rule: Divide by 10				
Input:	40	20	90	50
Output:	▓	▓	▓	▓

16.

Rule: Divide by 10				
Input:	▓	▓	▓	▓
Output:	7	9	1	6

17. Generalize: Write the related multiplication sentences for these division sentences:

12 ÷ 4 = 3

12 ÷ 3 = 4

Objective: Use the multiplication table that names facts to 12 to divide.

Use a Multiplication Table to Divide

Learn

Margo will travel around the world. She will visit 12 countries. Margo plans to spend a total of 36 months on her world tour, staying the same amount of time in each country. How many months will she stay in each country?

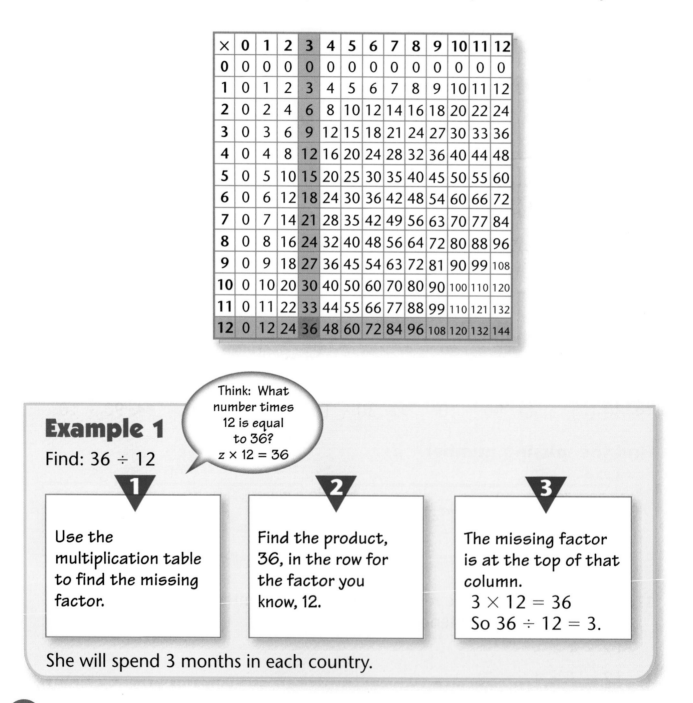

×	0	1	2	3	4	5	6	7	8	9	10	11	12
0	0	0	0	0	0	0	0	0	0	0	0	0	0
1	0	1	2	3	4	5	6	7	8	9	10	11	12
2	0	2	4	6	8	10	12	14	16	18	20	22	24
3	0	3	6	9	12	15	18	21	24	27	30	33	36
4	0	4	8	12	16	20	24	28	32	36	40	44	48
5	0	5	10	15	20	25	30	35	40	45	50	55	60
6	0	6	12	18	24	30	36	42	48	54	60	66	72
7	0	7	14	21	28	35	42	49	56	63	70	77	84
8	0	8	16	24	32	40	48	56	64	72	80	88	96
9	0	9	18	27	36	45	54	63	72	81	90	99	108
10	0	10	20	30	40	50	60	70	80	90	100	110	120
11	0	11	22	33	44	55	66	77	88	99	110	121	132
12	0	12	24	36	48	60	72	84	96	108	120	132	144

Example 1

Find: $36 \div 12$

> Think: What number times 12 is equal to 36?
> $z \times 12 = 36$

1

Use the multiplication table to find the missing factor.

2

Find the product, 36, in the row for the factor you know, 12.

3

The missing factor is at the top of that column.
$3 \times 12 = 36$
So $36 \div 12 = 3$.

She will spend 3 months in each country.

During her travels Margo sends out a total of 88 postcards to 11 friends. Each friend receives the same number of postcards. How many postcards does each friend receive?

Example 2

Find $88 \div 11$. You can use patterns in a multiplication table to divide.

1 ▶ Find the pattern that the numbers follow in each row. For example, in row 1, each column increases by 1; in row 2 they increase by 2. Continue the pattern in row 11.

2 ▶ Find the product, 88, in row 11.

3 ▶ The number at the top of the column is the missing factor.

$8 \times 11 = 88$

So $88 \div 11 = 8$.

Each of Margo's friends receives 8 postcards.

Try It Find each missing number. Use the multiplication table to help you find patterns.

1. $33 \div 11 = n$
   $11 \times n = 33$

2. $66 \div 11 = y$
   $11 \times y = 66$

3. $48 \div 12 = z$
   $12 \times z = 48$

4. $60 \div 12 = m$
   $12 \times m = 60$

5. $84 \div 12 = w$
   $12 \times w = 84$

6. $88 \div 11 = x$
   $11 \times x = 88$

7. $24 \div 12 = p$
   $12 \times p = 24$

8. $55 \div 11 = q$
   $11 \times q = 55$

9. $96 \div 12 = k$
   $12 \times k = 96$

10. $22 \div 11 = w$
    $11 \times w = 22$

11. $99 \div 11 = v$
    $11 \times v = 99$

12. $12 \div 12 = p$
    $12 \times p = 12$

Sum it Up! Explain how to use the multiplication table to find $60 \div 12$.

Find each missing number.

13. $72 \div 12 = t$ **14.** $64 \div 8 = s$ **15.** $56 \div 7 = c$ **16.** $63 \div 9 = d$
     $12 \times t = 72$ $8 \times s = 64$ $7 \times c = 56$ $9 \times d = 63$

Divide.

17. $18 \div 6$ **18.** $45 \div 5$ **19.** $32 \div 8$ **20.** $72 \div 9$ **21.** $77 \div 11$

22. $7\overline{)49}$ **23.** $3\overline{)27}$ **24.** $10\overline{)70}$ **25.** $12\overline{)84}$ **26.** $11\overline{)44}$

★**27.** $(5 \times 9) \div 9$ ★**28.** $(6 \times 7) \div 7$ ★**29.** $(8 \times 4) \div 4$ ★**30.** $(9 \times 10) \div 10$

Algebra
& functions   **Write $+$, $-$, $\times$, or $\div$.**

31. $30 \bullet 5 = 6$ **32.** $7 \bullet 7 = 14$ **33.** $12 \bullet 6 = 72$ **34.** $55 \bullet 11 = 5$

35.

Make it RIGHT

To find $48 \div 12$, I went to row 12 and found 48. Then I went to the number at the top of the column. That is 3. So $48 \div 12 = 3$.

David explained how he used the multiplication table to find $48 \div 12$. What was his mistake? Show how to correct it.

Problem Solving

36. Art: Students are painting pictures of grassy meadows. They need to mix equal amounts of blue and yellow paint to make green. They want to make 12 cups of green paint. How many cups each of yellow and blue paint do they need?

★**37.** There are 5 days in a week of school. The students in Mr. Marsh's class will spend a total of 7 school weeks learning about the 7 continents of the world. They will study each continent for the same number of days. For how many days will they study Asia?

38. Jada brings 4 packs of juice to a party. Each pack has 6 cans in it. How many cans of juice does Jada bring?

39. Mindy buys 6 boxes of cat food. Each box holds six cans. How many cans does she buy?

40. Donna walked 28 miles in 7 days. She walked the same amount each day. How many miles did she walk each day?

41. Linda gives 30 oatmeal cookies to 5 friends. If each person gets the same amount, how many oatmeal cookies does each person get?

42. Logical Reasoning: Kim, Vic, and Tia live at the shore, city, or farm. Kim and Vic do not live at the shore. Kim does not live in the city. Vic does not live on a farm. Who lives on the farm?

43. Number Sense: Masud lived in Africa for 12 years. His parents lived there even longer. Is it more likely that they lived there 2 times as long or 12 times as long? How can you tell?

44. Create a problem that you can solve by using the multiplication table. Solve your problem. Tell how you used the multiplication table to solve it. Ask others to solve your problem.

Journal **45. Compare:** How is using the multiplication table the same for finding multiplication facts and division facts? How is it different?

Spiral Review and Test Prep

46. $15 \div 5$

47. $8\overline{)32}$

48. 9×3

49. $7\overline{)56}$

50.
$$\begin{array}{r} 1,523 \\ -876 \end{array}$$

51.
$$\begin{array}{r} 4,968 \\ +2,420 \end{array}$$

52.
$$\begin{array}{r} 1,568 \\ -949 \end{array}$$

53.
$$\begin{array}{r} 8 \\ \times 3 \end{array}$$

54.
$$\begin{array}{r} 9 \\ \times 6 \end{array}$$

55.
$$\begin{array}{r} \$7.96 \\ -3.07 \end{array}$$

56.
$$\begin{array}{r} 6,854 \\ +693 \end{array}$$

57.
$$\begin{array}{r} 5 \\ \times 7 \end{array}$$

Choose the correct answer.

58. Adam hiked in the mountains for 2 hours 45 minutes. He began at 4:30 P.M. What time did he finish?
   A. 6:15 P.M. **C.** 7:15 P.M.
   B. 6:45 P.M. **D.** 7:45 P.M.

59. Which number is missing in the skip-counting pattern?
   242, 342, _____, 542
   F. 352 **H.** 424
   G. 362 **J.** 442

Objective: Develop fact families and use them to find missing factors.

Use Properties and Related Facts

Algebra & functions

Learn

Daily Temperatures for January
(Rounded to the Nearest Degree °F)

City	High	Low
Minneapolis, MN	21°	
Omaha, NE	31°	11°
Milwaukee, WI	26°	12°

Source: The Wall Street Journal Almanac

Math Words

factors numbers that are multiplied to give a product.

fact family a group of related facts using the same numbers.

Ruben wants to finish recording the data in this table. The high temperature for Minneapolis is 7 times its low temperature. What temperature should he record in the low column for Minneapolis?

Example 1

You can find a missing **factor** to solve this problem.

Find: $7 \times n = 21$

> Use a related division fact.
> **Think:** Divide 21 by 7 to find the missing factor.
> $$21 \div 3 = 7 \text{ or } 21 \div 7 = 3$$
> So the missing factor in $7 \times n = 21$ is 3.

The low temperature in Minneapolis for January is 3°F.

More Examples

A You can also write other related sentences using these numbers:

$21 \div 7 = 3 \qquad 3 \times 7 = 21 \qquad 21 \div 3 = 7 \qquad 7 \times 3 = 21$

Together, these four related facts are called a **fact family**.

B $\quad 48 \div 6 = 8 \qquad\qquad 6 \times 8 = 48 \qquad\qquad 48 \div 8 = 6 \qquad\qquad 8 \times 6 = 48$

C $\qquad\qquad 9 \times 9 = 81 \qquad\qquad\qquad\qquad\qquad 81 \div 9 = 9$

D $\quad 8 \div 1 = 8 \qquad\qquad 1 \times 8 = 8 \qquad\qquad 8 \div 8 = 1 \qquad\qquad 8 \times 1 = 8$

Ruben is adding Toledo, Ohio, to his chart. The low is 15°F and the high is 10 times Minneapolis' low temperature. What is Toledo's high temperature for January?

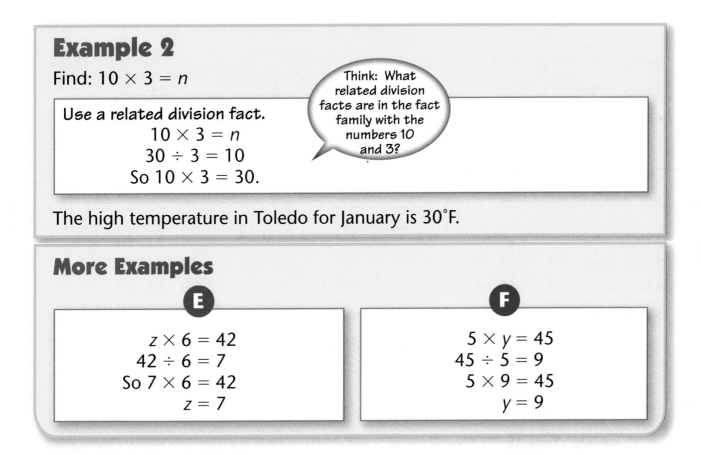

Example 2

Find: $10 \times 3 = n$

Think: What related division facts are in the fact family with the numbers 10 and 3?

Use a related division fact.
$$10 \times 3 = n$$
$$30 \div 3 = 10$$
So $10 \times 3 = 30$.

The high temperature in Toledo for January is 30°F.

More Examples

E

$$z \times 6 = 42$$
$$42 \div 6 = 7$$
So $7 \times 6 = 42$
$$z = 7$$

F

$$5 \times y = 45$$
$$45 \div 5 = 9$$
$$5 \times 9 = 45$$
$$y = 9$$

 **Write a fact family for each group of numbers.**

1. 6, 8, 48
2. 7, 9, 63
3. 5, 8, 40
4. 4, 9, 36
5. 5, 4, 20
6. 7, 7, 49
7. 3, 9, 27
8. 8, 7, 56

Find each missing factor.

9. $8 \times n = 24$
10. $y \times 7 = 28$
11. $t \times 9 = 72$
12. $6 \times r = 18$
13. $5 \times d = 35$
14. $f \times 3 = 15$
15. $s \times 8 = 16$
16. $4 \times k = 36$

Sum It Up How can you solve $n \times 12 = 48$ using related multiplication facts?

Write a fact family for each group of numbers.

17. 4, 6, 24   **18.** 8, 9, 72   **19.** 7, 8, 56   **20.** 6, 6, 36

21. 3, 7, 21   **22.** 8, 8, 64   **23.** 4, 8, 32   **24.** 2, 9, 18

Solve. Write a related fact.

25. 5×4 **26.** 6×7 **27.** 7×4 **28.** 9×9 **29.** 8×2

30. $35 \div 7$ **31.** $54 \div 9$ **32.** $25 \div 5$ **33.** $21 \div 7$ **34.** $63 \div 9$

Find each number.

35. $3 \times y = 24$ **36.** $z \times 5 = 20$ **37.** $s \times 7 = 49$ **38.** $3 \times t = 27$

39. $8 \times r = 64$ **40.** $p \times 10 = 80$ **41.** $y \times 6 = 42$ **42.** $9 \times z = 54$

43. $6 \times f = 36$ **44.** $d \times 7 = 35$ **45.** $n \times 8 = 32$ **46.** $6 \times p = 12$

47. $56 \div s = 8$ **48.** $y \div 4 = 7$ **49.** $t \div 9 = 7$ **50.** $16 \div l = 4$

51. $8 \times p = 16$ **52.** $d \times 10 = 30$ **53.** $g \div 6 = 3$ **54.** $7 \times 6 = r$

55. $3 \times t = 24$ **56.** $90 \div f = 9$ **57.** $n \div 7 = 4$ **58.** $2 \times 7 = z$

59.

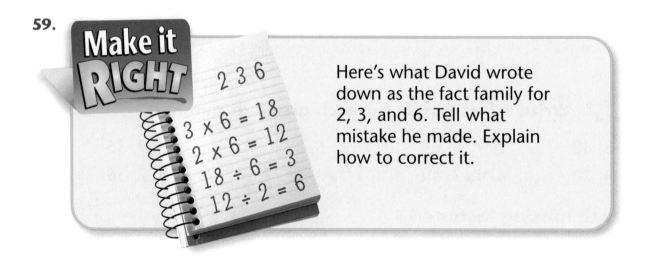

Here's what David wrote down as the fact family for 2, 3, and 6. Tell what mistake he made. Explain how to correct it.

Problem Solving

60. Mental Math: Suppose 800 people go camping during one week, and only 700 go the next week. How many people went camping in all?

★**61.** A group of campers hikes part of the Appalachian Trail. The hike covers 84 miles. The campers must hike another 8 miles each day for 4 more days. How many miles have they hiked so far?

Use data from *Did You Know?* for problems 62–63.

62. **Health:** Humans need fresh water to live. We get fresh water from the ground. We also get water from foods. How much water do humans need each day?

63. How much water do humans need in a 4-week period?

Use data from the table for problem 64.

64. Luisa knows that Chicago's high temperature is 7 times greater than 12. What multiplication sentence can she use to find Chicago's high temperature? What temperature will she record in the table?

65. **Generalize:** How can you create a fact family given 2 factors?

Did You KNOW?

Humans need about 35 pints of water each week.

Daily Temperatures for July (Rounded to the Nearest Degree °F)

City	High	Low
Chicago, IL		63°
Tucson, AZ	99°	74°
Miami, FL	89°	

Source: The Wall Street Journal Almanac

Spiral Review and Test Prep

66. $7\overline{)56}$ 67. $201 + 37$ 68. $4\overline{)28}$ 69. $829 - 13$ 70. 5×9

71. $\begin{array}{r} 7 \\ \times 4 \end{array}$ 72. $\begin{array}{r} 856 \\ -597 \end{array}$ 73. $\begin{array}{r} 4{,}376 \\ +\ 845 \end{array}$ 74. $\begin{array}{r} 5 \\ \times 6 \end{array}$ 75. $\begin{array}{r} 198 \\ +928 \end{array}$

Choose the correct answer.

76. Each section of a canoe can fit 2 people. There are 3 sections in each canoe. If 4 full canoes are taken down the river, how many people are in them altogether?
   A. 9   C. 24
   B. 12   D. 30

77. Marco starts work at 8:15 A.M. He finishes at 4:00 P.M. How long does he work?
   F. 8 hours 45 minutes   H. 7 hours 15 minutes
   G. 8 hours 15 minutes   J. 7 hours 45 minutes

Facts Practice: Division

Divide. You must be able to recall these facts quickly.

1. $6\overline{)12}$ 2. $7\overline{)49}$ 3. $9\overline{)45}$ 4. $12\overline{)84}$ 5. $8\overline{)64}$

6. $9\overline{)9}$ 7. $11\overline{)110}$ 8. $12\overline{)48}$ 9. $10\overline{)90}$ 10. $8\overline{)0}$

11. $9\overline{)72}$ 12. $7\overline{)42}$ 13. $9\overline{)81}$ 14. $5\overline{)45}$ 15. $6\overline{)54}$

16. $8\overline{)48}$ 17. $12\overline{)96}$ 18. $11\overline{)77}$ 19. $10\overline{)100}$ 20. $12\overline{)12}$

21. $8\overline{)72}$ 22. $11\overline{)99}$ 23. $12\overline{)60}$ 24. $7\overline{)63}$ 25. $6\overline{)36}$

26. $7\overline{)56}$ 27. $9\overline{)27}$ 28. $12\overline{)60}$ 29. $8\overline{)72}$ 30. $7\overline{)7}$

31. $6\overline{)54}$ 32. $11\overline{)99}$ 33. $12\overline{)24}$ 34. $10\overline{)40}$ 35. $30 \div 6$

36. $56 \div 8$ 37. $14 \div 7$ 38. $36 \div 9$ 39. $36 \div 12$ 40. $50 \div 10$

41. $42 \div 6$ 42. $45 \div 9$ 43. $121 \div 11$ 44. $16 \div 8$ 45. $21 \div 7$

46. $32 \div 8$ 47. $60 \div 12$ 48. $72 \div 9$ 49. $10 \div 10$ 50. $18 \div 6$

51. $35 \div 7$ 52. $20 \div 10$ 53. $54 \div 9$ 54. $66 \div 11$ 55. $6 \div 6$

56. $28 \div 7$ 57. $24 \div 8$ 58. $27 \div 9$ 59. $27 \div 3$ 60. $24 \div 6$

61. $42 \div 7$ 62. $60 \div 10$ 63. $63 \div 9$ 64. $88 \div 11$ 65. $3 \div 3$

66. $48 \div 12$ 67. $49 \div 7$ 68. $72 \div 8$ 69. $36 \div 3$ 70. $60 \div 5$

71. $66 \div 6$ 72. $20 \div 10$ 73. $4 \div 4$ 74. $45 \div 5$ 75. $81 \div 9$

SPIN A FACT

Play the Game

Make a spinner with 4 equal sections. Place the symbols +, −, ×, and ÷ one in each section. Make another spinner with 12 numbers between 1 and 12.

You Will Need
- **2 spinners**
- **a stopwatch**

1. Play the game with 2 players and a timer.

2. Player 1 spins one spinner. Player 2 spins the other.

3. Timer starts the stopwatch. Both players write as many facts as they can that include the number and the operation shown on the spinners.

4. After 1 minute the timer says "Stop."

5. Players check their facts and score 1 point for each correct fact.

6. Repeat until one player reaches 20 points and wins the game.

For additional practice, see Fact Dash.

Objective: *Analyze data and make decisions.*

8·8 A Problem Solving: Application
Decision Making

Which project will you choose?

The Earth Care Club uses volunteers for its projects. The members choose from 3 different projects.

Earth Care Club
Volunteer Program
Which project will you choose?

RECYCLE PROJECT	CLEAN-UP PROJECT	POSTER PROJECT
What to do: 1) Donate $2.00 to help raise $18 for tubs that hold bottles and cans 2) Collect and sort bottles and cans into separate tubs. **When:** 1 hour after school each week during the school year (36 weeks)	**What to do:** 1) Donate 5 hours or $5.00 to help raise $50.00 for supplies. 2) Choose a street each month. Pick up trash and litter on that street. **When:** 1 hour each month of the year	**What to do:** 1) Donate $3.50 for art supplies 2) Make posters about recycling bottles and cans. 3) Hang posters in the neighborhood and at school. **When:** 2 hours next Friday

Read for Understanding

1. How much more do you have to donate to work on the Poster Project than the Recycle Project?

2. How many hours will you work altogether on the Recycle Project?

3. Which project requires the least amount of time? how much time?

4. How many people need to donate $5.00 to buy the supplies for the Clean-Up Project?

5. If there are 4 weeks in each month of the school year, how many months will the Recycle Project last?

6. How many streets will one person clean each year in the Clean-Up Project?

7. How many hours will you work together on the Poster Project?

8. How many people need to donate $2.00 to buy 1 tub to hold bottles?

Make Decisions

9. Suppose you decide to donate $5.00 and work on the Clean-Up Project. How much time will you work in all? How much time will you work on this project if you decide to donate 5 hours instead of $5.00?

10. You decide to work on the Recycle Project. Your friend decides to donate 5 hours and work on the Clean-Up Project. Who will volunteer more hours? how many more hours?

11. Which project would you choose if you want to volunteer for a year, but you cannot work after school? Why?

12. How does division help you find how many people are needed to donate a total of $18.00 for the Recycle Project?

13. Write a list of other things you would think about to help you decide on a project.

14. Think of another project the Earth Care Club could do. Describe it.

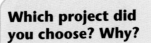
Which project did you choose? Why?

Your Decision!

8·8 B

Problem Solving: Math and Science
Can you move faster on 2 legs or 4 legs?

You Will Need
• **timer or clock**

You see a dog running and begin to chase after it. Can you catch the dog? People run on two legs, but most animals run very fast on four legs.

In this activity you will find out if you can run faster on 2 legs or 4 legs.

Hypothesize

Can you run faster on 2 legs or 4?

Safety

Be careful when running.

Procedure

1. Work with a partner.
2. Set up a clear, straight track.
3. Time how many seconds it takes for you to run on 2 legs.
4. Time how long it takes for you to run on 2 legs and 2 arms.

Data

Copy and complete a chart to record your data.

	Time (in Seconds)
2 legs	
4 legs (2 legs and 2 arms)	

Conclude and Apply

- Did you run faster on 2 legs or 4? How do you know?

- Divide to find how many times more it took you to run the longer race than the shorter race.

- Collect the data from your class.
  - How many people ran faster on 2 legs?
  - How many people ran faster on 4 legs?
  - Did more people run faster on 2 or 4 legs? how many more?

- Explain how having 5 limbs makes it easier for a monkey to climb a tree.

Going Further

1. Design and complete an activity to determine whether you can run for a longer time on 2 legs or 4.

2. Design and complete an activity to compare speedwalking, hopping, and skipping.

Did You KNOW?

Monkeys have 5 limbs that they use for walking and climbing. They have 2 arms, 2 legs, and a tail.

Divide. (pages 326–331)

1. 55 ÷ 11
2. 24 ÷ 12
3. 60 ÷ 10
4. 56 ÷ 8
5. 84 ÷ 12
6. 72 ÷ 9
7. 66 ÷ 11
8. 36 ÷ 12
9. 63 ÷ 7
10. 45 ÷ 9
11. 80 ÷ 10
12. 24 ÷ 6

Write a fact family for each group of numbers. (pages 332–335)

13. 3, 9, 27
14. 7, 5, 35
15. 8, 6, 48
16. 7, 7, 49
17. 6, 9, 54

Find each missing number. (pages 332–335)

18. $48 ÷ t = 12$
19. $72 ÷ d = 8$
20. $36 ÷ r = 6$
21. $v ÷ 4 = 3$
22. $32 ÷ a = 4$
23. $8 × n = 64$
24. $36 ÷ y = 4$
25. $z × 7 = 21$
26. $45 ÷ x = 9$
27. $48 ÷ c = 6$
28. $3 × m = 3$
29. $s × 4 = 20$

Solve. (pages 324–341)

30. A group of children and dogs is standing on the shore. There are 14 footprints left in the sand. How many children are there? how many dogs?

31. Grant is thinking of 2 numbers. When you multiply the numbers, the product is 32. When you divide the numbers, the quotient is 2. What are the 2 numbers?

32. Tara spent a total of 24 hours over 6 days rowing a canoe on the river. If she rowed the same number of hours each day, how many hours each day did she row?

Journal 33. **Analyze:** How can you use a fact family to find the missing factor in $9 × n = 36$?

Additional activities at www.mhschool.com/math

Extra Practice

Divide by 6 and 7 (pages 312–315)

Divide.

1. $42 \div 6$
2. $28 \div 7$
3. $7\overline{)42}$
4. $18 \div 6$
5. $24 \div 6$

6. $7\overline{)7}$
7. $6\overline{)30}$
8. $6\overline{)48}$
9. $7\overline{)63}$
10. $6\overline{)0}$

11. $49 \div 7$
12. $36 \div 6$
13. $14 \div 7$
14. $0 \div 7$
15. $21 \div 7$

16. $6\overline{)12}$
17. $7\overline{)35}$
18. $6 \div 6$
19. $6\overline{)54}$
20. $7\overline{)56}$

Find each missing number.

21.

Rule: Divide by 6.								
Input:	6	18	▊	36	▊	54	▊	▊
Output:	▊	▊	4	▊	7	▊	8	2

22. Samantha is paid $7.00 each hour that she shovels snow at the trailhead parking lot. She has earned $14.00 so far. How many hours has she worked?

23. The scouts clean the trailhead parking lot each spring. There are 28 scouts who have signed up for the clean-up. If the scouts are evenly divided among 7 groups, how many are in each group?

Problem Solving: Reading for Math
Solve Multistep Problems (pages 316–317)

1. There are 31 people on the bus. At the first stop, 9 people get off and 4 people get on. How many people are now on the bus?

2. Lily walked 4 blocks east, 4 blocks south, 4 blocks west, and 4 blocks north. How many blocks did she walk in all? How far is she from her starting point?

3. Elizabeth is on a train traveling 60 miles an hour. The train is 193 miles from Elizabeth's stop. Will Elizabeth be there in 3 hours? Why or why not?

Extra Practice

Divide.

1. $9\overline{)63}$
2. $54 \div 9$
3. $27 \div 9$
4. $16 \div 8$
5. $72 \div 8$

6. $8\overline{)64}$
7. $8\overline{)32}$
8. $8\overline{)8}$
9. $9\overline{)81}$
10. $8\overline{)56}$

11. $24 \div 8$
12. $9 \div 9$
13. $48 \div 8$
14. $0 \div 9$
15. $72 \div 9$

16. $40 \div 8$
17. $9\overline{)18}$
18. $9\overline{)36}$
19. $8\overline{)0}$
20. $9\overline{)45}$

Find each missing number.

21.

Number of hot dog buns:	32	▮	24	16	▮	40	▮	8
Number of packages:	4	6	▮	▮	9	▮	8	▮

Problem Solving: Strategy Guess and Check (pages 324–325)

Use the guess-and-check strategy to solve.

1. Paul is learning to count. He counts tires on cars and motorcycles sitting in the parking lot. If he counts 20 tires, how many motorcycles and cars are parked?

2. Tom and Carol have lived near the shore for a total of 9 years. Tom has lived there 3 years longer than Carol. How many years has each person lived at the shore?

Use a Multiplication Table to Divide (pages 328–331)

Divide. Use the Multiplication Table on page 328.

1. $50 \div 10$
2. $66 \div 11$
3. $45 \div 9$
4. $24 \div 12$
5. $72 \div 8$

6. $9\overline{)18}$
7. $10\overline{)100}$
8. $12\overline{)36}$
9. $11\overline{)110}$
10. $6\overline{)48}$

11. $72 \div 6$
12. $12 \div 12$
13. $77 \div 11$
14. $96 \div 8$
15. $121 \div 11$

16. $10\overline{)20}$
17. $8\overline{)64}$
18. $11\overline{)88}$
19. $9\overline{)36}$
20. $12\overline{)120}$

Extra Practice

Use Properties and Related Facts (pages 332–335)

Write a fact family for each group of numbers.

1. 6, 7, 42
2. 3, 9, 27
3. 5, 8, 40
4. 7, 7, 49
5. 6, 8, 48
6. 4, 7, 28
7. 2, 7, 14
8. 5, 9, 45

Solve. Write a related fact.

9. 6×9
10. 8×4
11. 7×3
12. 9×8
13. 10×8
14. $36 \div 6$
15. $45 \div 9$
16. $81 \div 9$
17. $42 \div 7$
18. $48 \div 8$

Find each missing factor.

19. $8 \times a = 16$
20. $c \times 7 = 21$
21. $f \times 7 = 56$
22. $3 \times k = 24$
23. $8 \times m = 40$
24. $p \times 10 = 70$
25. $n \times 6 = 36$
26. $9 \times b = 81$
27. $4 \times z = 40$
28. $t \times 7 = 63$
29. $l \times 8 = 64$
30. $6 \times g = 54$
31. $7 \times d = 49$
32. $v \times 5 = 30$
33. $h \times 9 = 72$
34. $4 \times s = 24$

Find each missing number.

35. $32 \div d = 8$
36. $m \div 4 = 3$
37. $v \div 9 = 8$
38. $25 \div c = 5$
39. $8 \times p = 72$
40. $y \times 10 = 80$
41. $30 \div x = 3$
42. $7 \times 4 = z$
43. $18 \div g = 3$
44. $n \div 7 = 3$
45. $r \times 8 = 32$
46. $64 \div a = 8$
47. $7 \times s = 56$
48. $k \times 6 = 60$
49. $b \times 4 = 44$
50. $12 \times f = 48$

Chapter Study Guide

Language and Math

Complete. Use a word from the list.

1. If you want to find what number times 8 is equal to 56, then you are finding a ____.

2. The numbers 5, 6, and 30 all belong to the same ____.

Skills and Applications

Divide, using facts through 12. (pages 312–315, 318–321, 326–331)

Example
Find the quotient.
$48 \div 8$

Solution
Use a related multiplication sentence.
$$n \times 8 = 48$$
$$6 \times 8 = 48$$
So $48 \div 8 = 6$.

Find each quotient.

3. $7\overline{)35}$

4. $8\overline{)72}$

5. $6\overline{)48}$

6. $12\overline{)72}$

7. $88 \div 11$

8. $54 \div 6$

9. $64 \div 8$

10. $60 \div 10$

11. $24 \div 6$

12. $72 \div 9$

13. $60 \div 12$

14. $63 \div 9$

15. $42 \div 7$

16. $24 \div 6$

17. $40 \div 8$

Identify fact families and find missing factors.
(pages 332–335)

Example
Find the missing number.
$b \times 7 = 28$

Solution
Use the related division fact in the fact family.
$$28 \div 7 = 4$$
$$4 \times 7 = 28$$
So $b = 4$.

Find each missing number.

18. $8 \times s = 32$

19. $5 \times m = 45$

20. $54 \div y = 9$

21. $g \times 7 = 49$

22. $60 \div t = 6$

23. $k \div 7 = 9$

24. $z \times 6 = 24$

25. $8 \times c = 56$

26. $a \div 8 = 7$

27. $p \times 3 = 30$

Example
Solve.
A group of motorcycles and trucks are inspecting mountain roads for possible rock slides. There are 7 vehicles in all. They need new tires to make the trip. They need 22 tires in all. How many motorcycles are there? how many trucks?

Solution
Use the guess and check strategy:

Guess 1: 2 tires × 3 = 6 tires
4 tires × 3 = 12 tires
12 + 6 = 18 tires

Check: 18 < 22

Guess 2: 2 tires × 3 = 6 tires
4 tires × 4 = 16 tires
6 + 16 = 22 tires

Check: 22 tires is correct. There are 3 motorcycles and 4 trucks. The total number of vehicles is 7.

Solve.

28. What two numbers have a product of 27 and a quotient of 3?

29. Suppose a group of bicycles and wagons needs a total of 16 new tires. There are 6 vehicles in total. How many bicycles are there? how many wagons?

30. Judy is counting the birds and squirrels she sees out the window. She sees a total of 32 legs and 10 animals. How many birds does she spot? how many squirrels?

31. At a garage sale, hardcover books cost $0.75, and paperback books cost $0.50. If Samantha spent $2.50 and bought both kinds, how many of each did she buy?

32. John went to a horse farm on vacation. If he shared 8 apples equally among 8 horses, how many apples did each horse get?

33. Madeleine pays $16.75 for 4 rolls of film. She gives the clerk a twenty-dollar bill. How much is her change?

Chapter Test

Divide.

1. $9\overline{)18}$ 2. $6\overline{)24}$ 3. $10\overline{)20}$ 4. $12\overline{)12}$ 5. $8\overline{)48}$

6. $32 \div 8$ 7. $55 \div 11$ 8. $40 \div 10$ 9. $63 \div 7$ 10. $36 \div 9$

11. $45 \div 5$ 12. $24 \div 8$ 13. $56 \div 7$ 14. $60 \div 12$ 15. $42 \div 6$

Write a fact family for each group of numbers.

16. 6, 7, 42   17. 8, 8, 64   18. 2, 9, 18   19. 7, 8, 56

Find each missing factor.

20. $4 \times c = 16$ 21. $g \times 8 = 48$ 22. $7 \times k = 35$ 23. $m \times 6 = 54$

Find each missing number.

24. $s \div 4 = 7$ 25. $56 \div y = 8$ 26. $50 \div z = 5$

27. $n \div 9 = 4$ 28. $44 \div t = 4$ 29. $21 \div f = 3$

Solve.

30. In 6 days Zuri saw 42 birds in the rain forest. If she saw the same number of birds each day, how many did she see in 1 day?

31. Ella is moving to the country. She is packing her books in boxes. In some boxes she packs 3 books. In other boxes she packs 4 books. She packs 24 books in all. How many boxes have 3 books? how many have 4?

32. Mr. Fung is buying a copy of a book about the White Mountains National Forest for each of his 7 grandchildren. He spends a total of $63.00. How much does each book cost?

33. There are 32 members in the Earth Club. They travel with 4 members in each car. How many cars did they use?

Performance Assessment

For Earth Day last year, the schools in one town raised money to plant new trees.

Leewood School—42 trees
Horizon School—18 trees
Crossroads School—63 trees
Pine Road School—54 trees
Clark School—36 trees

Each school can plant their trees in groups of 6, 7, 8, or 9. The groups have to be equal and no trees can be left.

Make a chart like the one below.
Use it to show

- how the trees for each school can be grouped.

- a number sentence that shows how each school divided the trees they planted.

School	Number of Trees	Number of Groups	Number Sentences

Journal

A Good Answer
- shows a completed chart.
- shows that you chose divisors that would result in equal groups with nothing left.
- shows the correct number sentence for each grouping.

Portfolio You may want to save this work in your portfolio.

Enrichment

Egyptian Doubling

Ancient Egyptians used multiplication and addition to divide. Their method is called **Egyptian Doubling.**

Here is how to use this method to find 32 ÷ 4.

Start with one group of 4	1	4
Continue doubling each column until you reach 32. The number in the left column is the quotient.	2	8
	4	16
	8	32

Sometimes the method requires using addition as well as doubling.

Here is how to use this method to find 96 ÷ 8.

Start with one group of 8	1	8
Continue doubling each column. Look for numbers that add up to 96. Then find the sum of the corresponding numbers in the left column. This sum is the quotient.	2	16
	4	32
	8	64
	Think: 4 + 8 = 12	Think: 32 + 64 = 96

Now you try! Use Egyptian Doubling to complete.

1.	Find 24 ÷ 3		2.	Find 54 ÷9	
	1	3		1	9
	2	▢		2	18
	4	▢		4	36
	8	▢		x + y = ▢	z + w = ▢

Find the quotient.

3. 48 ÷ 8   **4.** 35 ÷ 7   **5.** 42 ÷ 7   **6.** 36 ÷ 3

7. Summarize: Describe how to use Egyptian Doubling to find 108 ÷ 12.

Test-Taking Tips

S.O.S.

For some tests you need to give a written answer. These questions are often worth more than multiple-choice questions. Plan your time accordingly.

Always show your work. If you make a small mistake, you may get some points if you show you understand how to solve the problem.

Estimate the number of dots in the box.

Show the mathematics you used to make your estimate.

Since an estimate is asked for, you do not need to count every dot in the box.

You can divide the box into smaller, equally sized parts and estimate the total.

Estimate: about 16 dots.

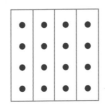

Check for Success

Before turning in a test, go back one last time to check.
- ☑ I understood and answered the questions asked.
- ☑ I checked my work for errors.
- ☑ My answers make sense.

Solve. Show your work.

1. Carl saw 5 people riding bicycles or tricycles. He saw a total of 12 wheels. How many bicycles and tricycles did he see?

2. Lena wants to buy nuts from a vending machine. She must use exact change. The nuts cost $0.85. List 3 different combinations of coins she could use.

3. Write a problem that uses multiplication. The answer must be "64 animals."

Spiral Review and Test Prep
Chapters 1–8

Choose the correct answer.

Number Sense

1. Find $6{,}743 + 68 + 846$.
   - A. 6,895
   - B. 7,657
   - C. 8,269
   - D. 22,003

2. Find $6 \times 4 \times 2$.
   - F. 24
   - G. 36
   - H. 48
   - J. 56

3. A road atlas costs $7.39. Aaron pays for it with a ten-dollar bill. How much change does he get?
   - A. $3.71
   - B. $3.61
   - C. $2.71
   - D. $2.61

4. Estimate the difference between 912 and 377. Round to the nearest hundred.
   - F. 400
   - G. 500
   - H. 1,200
   - J. 1,300

Algebra and Functions

5. Find the missing number.
   $r \times 8 = 8$
   - A. 0
   - B. 1
   - C. 8
   - D. 64

6. Which number makes the sentence true?
   $(3 \times 4) \times 8 = 3 \times (g \times 8)$
   - F. 4
   - G. 8
   - H. 12
   - J. 32

7. Which belongs in the ●?
   $16 \; ● \; 8 = 2$
   - A. $+$
   - B. $\times$
   - C. $-$
   - D. $\div$

8. Morgan saves $2.00 the first week. Each week after that she saves twice as much money as the week before. How much money did she save the fourth week?
   - F. $8.00
   - G. $16.00
   - H. $20.00
   - J. $24.00

Statistics, Data Analysis, and Probability

Use data from the pictograph for problems 9–12.

Third-Grade Students Vote on Favorite Summer Activity

Activity	Number of Votes
Swimming	☺ ☺ ☺ ☺ ☺ ☺ ☺ ☺
Camping	☺ ☺ ☺ ☺ ☺
Hiking	☺ ☺
Canoeing	☺ ☺ ☺ ☺
Fishing	☺ ☺ ☺

Each ☺ equals 4 votes.

9. How many votes did the activity with the least number of votes get?

   A. 2   C. 6
   B. 4   D. 8

10. Which activity got 4 times as many votes as hiking?

    F. Canoeing   H. Fishing
    G. Camping   J. Swimming

11. One activity got 12 more votes than hiking. Which activity is this?

    A. Canoeing   C. Fishing
    B. Camping   D. Swimming

12. Suppose 8 students changed their votes from swimming to fishing. How would this change the pictograph?

Mathematical Reasoning

Solve.

13. Rico walked along a nature trail for 4 miles a day for 3 days. This is 5 miles more than Felix walked. How many miles did Felix walk?

    A. 2 miles   C. 7 miles
    B. 5 miles   D. 12 miles

14. Alan works from 8:15 A.M. to 12:30 P.M. Jesse works from 12:30 P.M. to 4:30 P.M. How much longer does Alan work than Jesse?

    F. 1 hour 15   H. 30 minutes
       minutes
    G. 1 hour   J. 15 minutes

15. Carl, Gary, Haley, and Li are in a bicycle race. Carl is ahead of Gary. Haley is right behind Carl. Li is ahead of Carl. Who is first in the race?

    A. Li   C. Carl
    B. Gary   D. Haley

16. Ian puts 5 trading cards on some album pages. He puts 4 cards on some other pages. He has filled the pages with 31 cards. On how many album pages did he put 5 cards?

    F. 3   H. 5
    G. 4   J. 6

CHAPTER 9

Multiply by 1-Digit Numbers

Theme: Cool Collections

Use the Data

Values of 1999 Mint Condition Baseball Cards

Baseball Cards	
Player	Current Price
Cal Ripken	$3.50
Chipper Jones	$5.00
Mark McGwire	$3.00
Sammy Sosa	$1.25
Nomar Garciaparra	$4.00
Mo Vaughn	$0.60
Derek Jeter	$1.00

- A collector has 5 Chipper Jones cards. How can she find out how much her collection is worth?

- What other information could you find out using the data and multiplication?

What You Will Learn

In this chapter you will learn how to
- multiply multiples of 10, 100, and 1,000.
- multiply a multi-digit number.
- estimate products.
- use strategies to solve problems.

Additional activities at
www.mhschool.com/math

9·1 Explore Multiplying Multiples of 10

Learn

Math Word

multiple the product of a number and any whole number.

You can use place value models to explore multiplying multiples of 10.

Find: 4 × 30

Work Together

▶ Use models to find 4 × 30.

- Use place value models to show 4 groups of 3.
- Count by tens.
- Record your answer to the problem.

You Will Need
- **place value models**

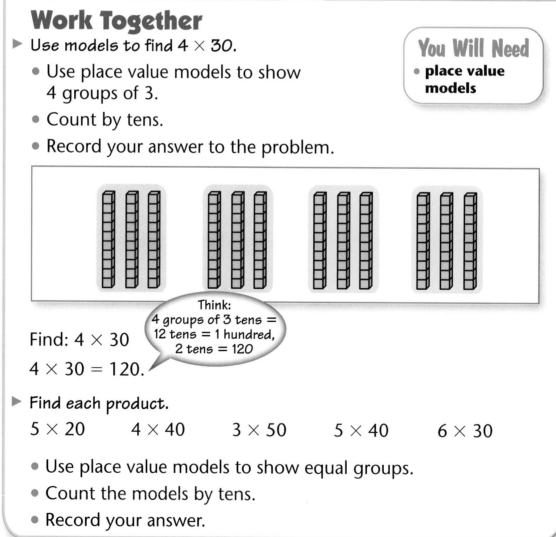

Find: 4 × 30

4 × 30 = 120.

Think:
4 groups of 3 tens =
12 tens = 1 hundred,
2 tens = 120

▶ Find each product.

5 × 20   4 × 40   3 × 50   5 × 40   6 × 30

- Use place value models to show equal groups.
- Count the models by tens.
- Record your answer.

Make Connections

Here is how to find products of **multiples** of 10.

Find: 2 × 40

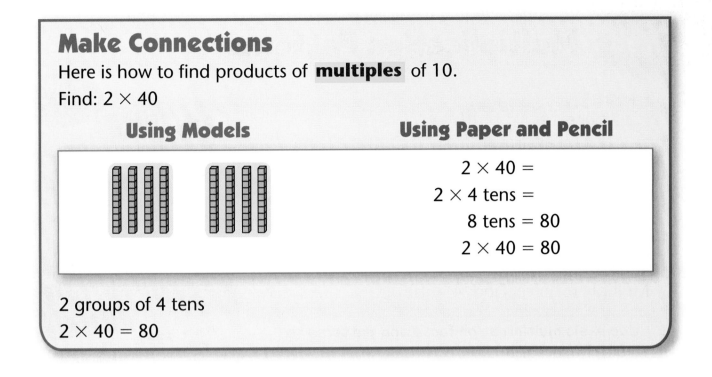

Using Models

Using Paper and Pencil

2 × 40 =
2 × 4 tens =
8 tens = 80
2 × 40 = 80

2 groups of 4 tens
2 × 40 = 80

Try It **Multiply. You may use models.**

1. 4 × 40
2. 2 × 60
3. 7 × 30
4. 3 × 60
5. 3 × 20

Sum it Up! What pattern do you see in all of the products when you multiply a multiple of 10?

Practice **Multiply. Write the multiplication sentence.**

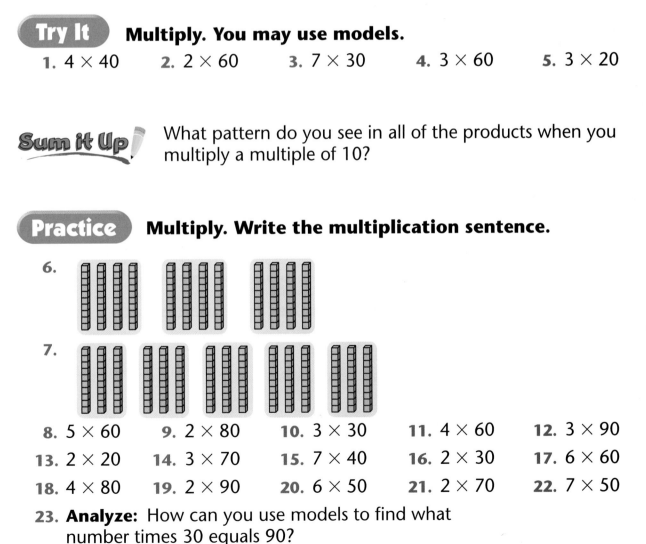

6.

7.

8. 5 × 60
9. 2 × 80
10. 3 × 30
11. 4 × 60
12. 3 × 90
13. 2 × 20
14. 3 × 70
15. 7 × 40
16. 2 × 30
17. 6 × 60
18. 4 × 80
19. 2 × 90
20. 6 × 50
21. 2 × 70
22. 7 × 50

23. **Analyze:** How can you use models to find what number times 30 equals 90?

9·2 Multiplication Patterns

Algebra & functions

Learn

Many people collect valuable books. A collector has 4 books worth $100 each. How much would it cost to buy this collector's set of books?

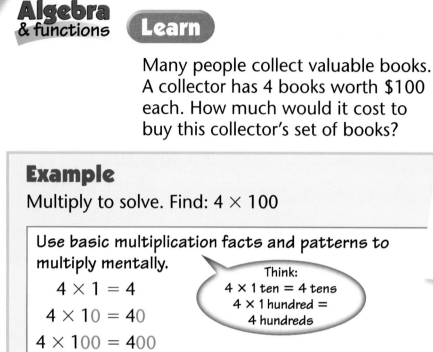

James Stevenson writes many children's books, including What's Under My Bed?

Math in ACTION

Example

Multiply to solve. Find: 4×100

Use basic multiplication facts and patterns to multiply mentally.

$4 \times 1 = 4$

$4 \times 10 = 40$

$4 \times 100 = 400$

Think:
4×1 ten = 4 tens
4×1 hundred = 4 hundreds

The collection is worth $400.

More Examples

A

$6 \times 5 = 30$

$6 \times 50 = 300$

$6 \times 500 = 3,000$

B

$9 \times 7 = 63$

$9 \times 70 = 630$

$9 \times 700 = 6,300$

Try It **Write the number that makes each sentence true.**

1. $2 \times 3 = n$
   $2 \times 30 = m$
   $2 \times 300 = p$

2. $3 \times 6 = y$
   $t \times 60 = 180$
   $3 \times w = 1,800$

Multiply. Use mental math.

3. 40×8 4. 300×7 5. 7×600 6. $3 \times 3,000$

 Explain how to find 7×200.

Write the number that makes each sentence true.

7.
$4 \times 5 = n$
$4 \times m = 200$
$p \times 500 = 2,000$
$4 \times 5,000 = q$

8.
$8 \times 4 = a$
$8 \times b = 320$
$8 \times 400 = c$
$8 \times d = 32,000$

9.
$7 \times r = 49$
$7 \times 70 = s$
$7 \times t = 4,900$
$7 \times 7,000 = v$

★ **10.** $8 \times (y \times 100) = 3,200$ ★ **11.** $3 \times (w \times 1,000) = 18,000$

Multiply. Use mental math.

12. 3×80 **13.** 8×40 **14.** 70×7 **15.** 9×30 **16.** 2×400

17. 500×8 **18.** 500×7 **19.** $7 \times 1,000$ **20.** $5,000 \times 4$ **21.** $3,000 \times 2$

Problem Solving

22. A bookstore wants to buy new collectible nursery rhyme books. They will buy 60 books for the price shown here. How much will the store pay for the books?

★ **23. Art:** The library owns 30 books on Greek artifacts and 20 books on Roman artifacts. Half of the books in each collection cannot be removed from the library. How many books is this in all?

24. Create a problem multiplying multiples of 10. Solve it. Ask others to solve it.

25. Analyze: Which basic fact will you use to multiply $8 \times 5,000$ mentally?

26. Collect Data: Find out what kinds of collections other students have. Record the results in a graph. Share the results with your class.

Spiral Review and Test Prep

27. $63 \div 7$ **28.** 7×4 **29.** $64 \div 8$ **30.** 9×8 **31.** $144 \div 12$

Choose the correct answer.

32. Jenna has 8 more mystery books than animal books. She has 12 mystery books. How many animal books does she have?
A. 20 **B.** 4 **C.** 2 **D.** 40

33. Last month a bookstore sold 1,432 books. What is this number rounded to the nearest thousand?
F. 2,000 **H.** 1,000
G. 1,400 **J.** Not Here

9·3 Explore Multiplying 2-Digit Numbers by 1-Digit Numbers

Learn

You can use place value models to explore multiplying 2-digit numbers by 1-digit numbers. Find: 3 × 14

Work Together

▶ Use place value models to find 3 × 14.

- Show 3 groups of 14.
- Use models to find the total.

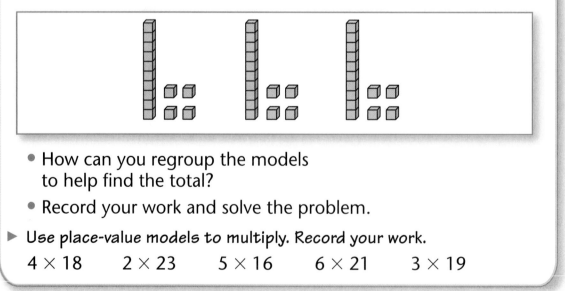

- How can you regroup the models to help find the total?
- Record your work and solve the problem.

▶ Use place-value models to multiply. Record your work.

| 4 × 18 | 2 × 23 | 5 × 16 | 6 × 21 | 3 × 19 |

Make Connections

Here is how to multiply by 1-digit numbers.

Find: 3×26

Using Models

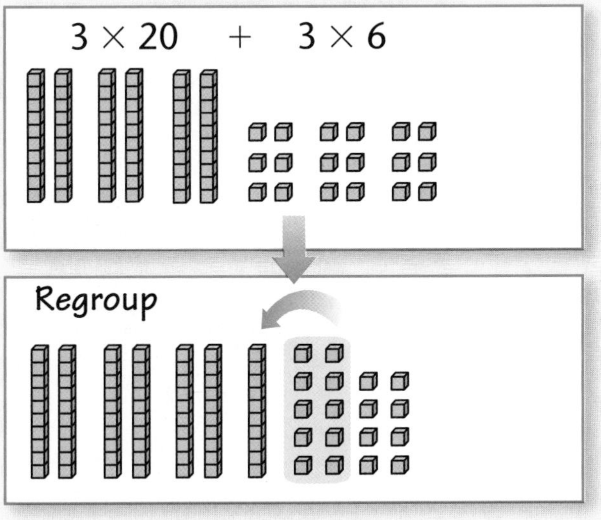

$3 \times 20 \quad + \quad 3 \times 6$

Regroup

$3 \times 26 = 78$

Using Paper and Pencil

$$
\begin{array}{r}
26 \\
\times\ 3 \\
\hline
18 \quad \leftarrow 3 \times 6 \\
+60 \quad \leftarrow 3 \times 20 \\
\hline
78
\end{array}
$$

Try It **Write a number sentence and then solve.**

1. 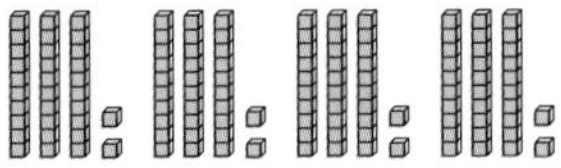 2. 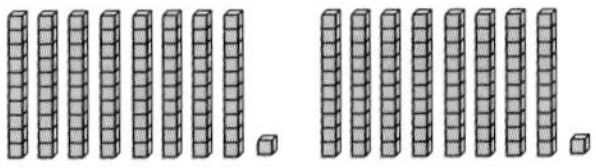 3.

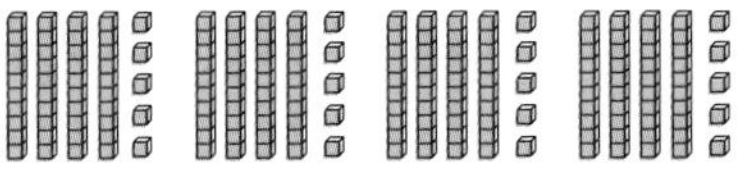

Multiply. You may wish to use models.

4. 2×19 5. 3×24 6. 4×13 7. 5×19 8. 3×17

Sum It Up! Explain a method you can use to multiply a 2-digit number by a 1-digit number.

Practice **Write a number sentence and then solve.**

9. 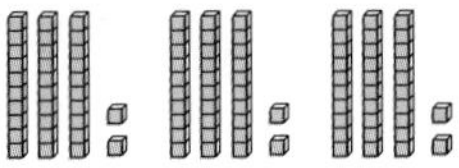 10. 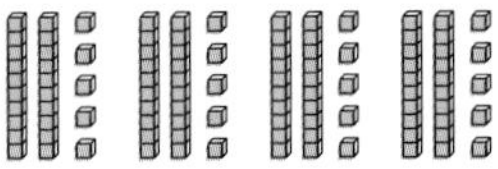 11.

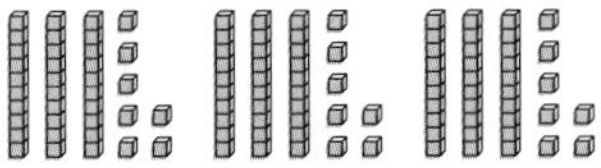

Multiply.

12. 2×14 13. 5×21 14. 4×21 15. 6×23 16. 2×27

17. 3×28 18. 2×17 19. 6×11 20. 5×14 21. 3×16

22. **Generalize:** How do you know to regroup when you multiply by 1-digit numbers?

9·4 Multiply 2-Digit Numbers by 1-Digit Numbers

Learn

Math Word

regroup to name a number in a different way

Yosemite National Park is a great place to collect rocks. Each collector in your 12-person team needs a kit with 6 tools to uncover the best rocks. How many tools are needed for the entire team?

These are the tools each rock collector needs.

Example 1

Find: 6 × 12

1 Multiply the ones. **Regroup** if necessary.

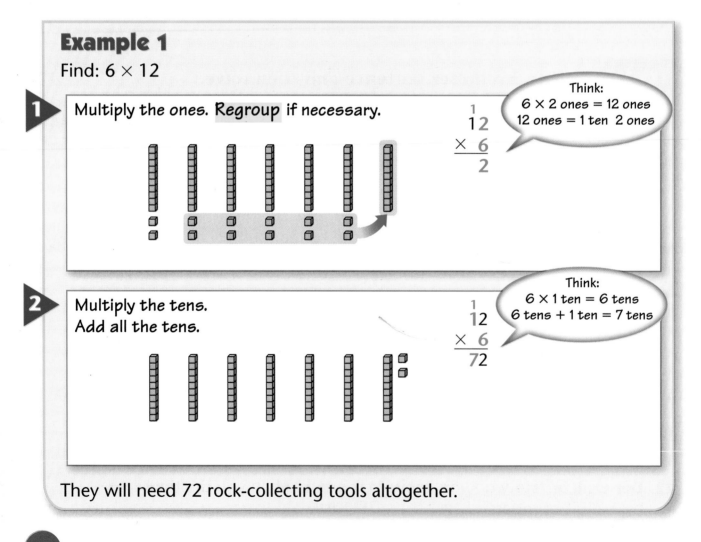

$$\begin{array}{r} \overset{1}{1}2 \\ \times\ 6 \\ \hline 2 \end{array}$$

Think:
6 × 2 ones = 12 ones
12 ones = 1 ten 2 ones

2 Multiply the tens.
Add all the tens.

$$\begin{array}{r} \overset{1}{1}2 \\ \times\ 6 \\ \hline 72 \end{array}$$

Think:
6 × 1 ten = 6 tens
6 tens + 1 ten = 7 tens

They will need 72 rock-collecting tools altogether.

The rock collectors club meets 3 times a week for 45 minutes each time. How many minutes do they meet each week?

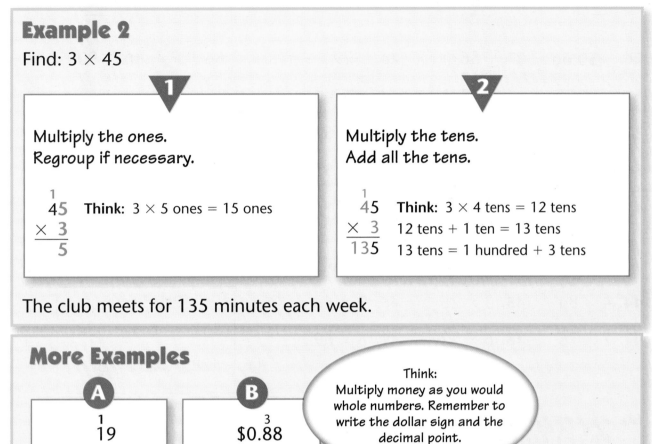

Example 2

Find: 3 × 45

1

Multiply the ones.
Regroup if necessary.

$$\begin{array}{r} \overset{1}{45} \\ \times\ 3 \\ \hline 5 \end{array}$$

Think: 3 × 5 ones = 15 ones

2

Multiply the tens.
Add all the tens.

$$\begin{array}{r} \overset{1}{45} \\ \times\ 3 \\ \hline 135 \end{array}$$

Think: 3 × 4 tens = 12 tens
12 tens + 1 ten = 13 tens
13 tens = 1 hundred + 3 tens

The club meets for 135 minutes each week.

More Examples

A

$$\begin{array}{r} \overset{1}{19} \\ \times\ 2 \\ \hline 38 \end{array}$$

B

$$\begin{array}{r} \overset{3}{\$0.88} \\ \times\ 4 \\ \hline \$3.52 \end{array}$$

Think:
Multiply money as you would whole numbers. Remember to write the dollar sign and the decimal point.

Try It **Multiply.**

1. $\begin{array}{r} 25 \\ \times\ 4 \end{array}$

2. $\begin{array}{r} \$0.37 \\ \times\ 2 \end{array}$

3. $\begin{array}{r} 16 \\ \times\ 7 \end{array}$

4. $\begin{array}{r} 22 \\ \times\ 8 \end{array}$

5. $\begin{array}{r} 63 \\ \times\ 3 \end{array}$

6. $\begin{array}{r} \$50 \\ \times\ 9 \end{array}$

7. $\begin{array}{r} 54 \\ \times\ 6 \end{array}$

8. $\begin{array}{r} \$0.72 \\ \times\ 4 \end{array}$

9. $\begin{array}{r} \$0.58 \\ \times\ 6 \end{array}$

10. $\begin{array}{r} 34 \\ \times\ 9 \end{array}$

11. 3 × 39

12. 62 × 4

13. 27 × 6

14. 42 × 5

15. 51 × 4

16. 5 × 48

17. 28 × 7

18. 56 × 8

19. 73 × 4

20. 37 × 6

Sum it Up! How many times did you need to regroup the tens into hundreds in problem 20? How did you show the regrouping?

Multiply.

21. 28
    × 4

22. $0.42
    ×   2

23. 26
    × 7

24. $0.71
    ×   8

25. 58
    × 3

26. $0.66
    ×   7

27. 56
    × 3

28. 29
    × 9

29. 86
    × 8

30. 90
    × 7

31. $0.77 × 4 32. 5 × 49 33. 7 × 63 34. 6 × $27 35. 9 × 32

36. 8 × $49 37. 6 × 32 38. 4 × 55 39. $0.57 × 3 40. 5 × 98

★41. (6 × 7) × 4   ★42. (9 × 9) × 8   ★43. (9 × 6) × 5

Algebra & functions **Match the multiplication with a product in the box.**

44. 4 × 84   45. 3 × 26   46. 9 × 68

47. 7 × 76   48. 6 × 42   49. 8 × 69

Products		
552	612	532
78	252	336

50.

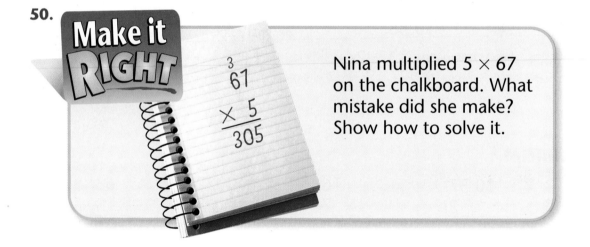

Nina multiplied 5 × 67 on the chalkboard. What mistake did she make? Show how to solve it.

Problem Solving

51. **Measurement:** Each rock in Paul's rock collection weighs about 3 ounces. If he has 48 rocks in his collection, about how many ounces do all of the rocks weigh?

52. There are 16 ounces in a pound. John is sending his friend 148 ounces of rocks. Will he be able to use a box that can hold 9 pounds?

Use data from the table for problems 53–54.

53. **Science:** One way scientists identify rocks is to rate their hardness. This table shows the hardness of different minerals in rocks from softest to hardest. Hank has 3 boxes of 36 samples of gypsum. He also has 4 boxes of 24 samples of quartz. Does he have more hard rocks or soft rocks? how many more?

54. **Logical Reasoning:** A mineral with a higher number can scratch any mineral that has a lower number. Sal has a mineral that can scratch fluorite and gypsum. It cannot scratch orthoclase. Which mineral does Sal have?

Mohs' Scale of Hardness
1. talc
2. gypsum
3. calcite
4. fluorite
5. apatite
6. orthoclase
7. quartz
8. topaz
9. corundum
10. diamond

Source: Compton's Encyclopedia

55. **Compare:** Explain two ways you can multiply 3×23. Show how to use the method you prefer.

56. Jane has 56 rocks in her collection. She has them in display boxes. Each box holds 8 rocks. How many boxes does she have filled?

57. **Create a problem** multiplying a 2-digit number by a 1-digit number. Solve it. Ask others to solve it.

Spiral Review and Test Prep

Find each missing number.

58. $8 \times n = 40$ 59. $p \times 6 = 42$ 60. $9 \times b = 27$ 61. $72 \div c = 9$

62. $15 - t = 6$ 63. $m + 5 = 12$ 64. $r - 7 = 14$ 65. $8 + g = 17$

Choose the correct answer.

66. Bert keeps his 28 rocks in small boxes. One kind of box holds 4 rocks, another kind holds 8. How many boxes does he have that hold 8 rocks?

 A. 2   C. 6

 B. 4   D. Not Here

67. Steve starts with 32 rocks in his collection. He finds 8 more rocks. Which number sentence shows how many rocks Steve has now?

 F. $32 - 8 = 24$ H. $32 \div 8 = 4$

 G. $32 + 8 = 40$ J. $32 \times 8 = 256$

9·5 Estimate Products

Learn

Every year 42 basketball cards are made for every team. If Abdul collects all the cards from his 9 favorite teams, about how many basketball cards are in Abdul's collection?

Math Words

estimate to find an answer that is close to the exact answer

round to find the value of a number based on a given place value.

Example

Estimate 9 × 42 to solve this problem.

Round the factor that is greater than 10. Then multiply mentally.

$$9 \times 42$$
$$\downarrow \qquad \downarrow$$
$$9 \times 40 = 360$$

Think: Round to the nearest ten.

Abdul has about 360 basketball cards.

More Examples

A

Estimate: 3 × 431

$$3 \times 431$$ **Think:** Round to the nearest hundred.
$$\downarrow \qquad \downarrow$$
$$3 \times 400 = 1,200$$

B

Estimate: 8 × 5,623

$$8 \times 5,623$$ **Think:** Round to the nearest thousand.
$$\downarrow \qquad \downarrow$$
$$8 \times 6,000 = 48,000$$

Try It   Estimate each product.

1. 7 × 32   **2.** 8 × 16   **3.** 9 × 123   **4.** 3 × 921   **5.** 8 × 7,040

Sum It Up   Explain how you would estimate 7 × 329.

Estimate each product.

6. 475
   × 9

7. 5,673
   × 7

8. 8,765
   × 6

9. 8,982
   × 7

10. 6 × 421   11. 8 × 5,322   12. 4 × 210   13. 9 × 675   14. 7 × 169

15. 8 × $78   16. 6 × $395   17. 3 × $988   18. 9 × $641   19. 4 × $897

Algebra & functions **Estimate. Write > or < to make a true sentence.**

20. 3 × 57 ● 210

21. 7 × 84 ● 560

22. 5 × 32 ● 200

★23. 7 × 908 ● 9 × 778

★24. 8 × 712 ● 6 × 829

Problem Solving

Use data from _Did You Know?_ for problems 25–26.

25. Ove Nordstrom of Sweden has about 12 times more piggy banks than Lotta Sjolin has parking meters. About how many piggy banks does Ove have?

26. **What if** Lotta collects another 12 meters during the next year? How many meters does she have now?

27. **Create a problem** that can be solved by estimating 6 × 432. Solve it. Ask others to solve it.

28. **Generalize:** How do you use basic facts to help you estimate products?

Did You KNOW?

Lotta Sjolin of Sweden has the largest collection of parking meters. She has collected 292 meters since 1989.

Spiral Review and Test Prep

29. $5.98 + $0.87   30. $7.21 − $2.34   31. 72 ÷ 8   32. 6 × 12

Choose the correct answer.

33. Greg has 72 baseball cards. He has 9 cards for each of his favorite players. How many favorite players does Greg have?

   A. 6   B. 7   C. 8   D. 9

34. Which is equal to 6 × 6?
   F. 36 ÷ 6   H. 6 + 6
   G. 12 × 3   J. 8 × 4

Objective: Form conclusions to decide if an estimate or exact answer is needed.

Problem Solving: Reading for Math
Find an Estimate or Exact Answer

A Penny for Your Thoughts

Read ▶ Matt collects pennies. His uncle gives him 6 bags of pennies. Each bag has 24 coins. Did Matt's uncle give him more than 100 coins?

READING SKILL ▶ **Form a Conclusion**

You form a conclusion when you make a decision. You use what you already know and the information given in a problem.

- **What do you know?**
- **What do you need to find?**

Matt has 6 bags of coins; each bag has 24 coins

About how many pennies are in all 6 bags.

MATH SKILL ▶ **Estimate or Exact Answer**

Sometimes you need to find an exact answer to solve problems. Other times an estimate is enough.

Plan ▶ You need to know if the product is greater than a given number. You can try an estimate.

Solve ▶ You can round to estimate the product.

24 rounds to 20 $20 \times 6 = 120$ $120 > 100$

Matt's uncle gave him more than 100 coins.

Look Back ▶ • Is your answer reasonable? Explain.

Sum It Up! Explain why an estimate was all that was needed to solve this problem.

Practice Solve.

1. Cora has 3 bags of pennies. Each bag holds 98 coins. Does she have over 300 coins in the bags?

2. Trey has 6 jars of coins. Each jar has 32 coins. How many coins are in the jars?

3. Alicia bought 2 piggy banks. Each bank can hold 90 coins. How many coins can the two banks hold?

4. Kevin has 200 foreign coins. He bought 7 albums to store his coins. Each can hold 32 coins. Did he buy enough albums? Explain.

5. Erin is counting her collection of Susan B. Anthony coins. She has 24 piles of 5 coins each. Does she have more than 125 coins?

6. Maria is organizing her coin collection. She has 8 groups of coins. Each group has 56 coins. How many coins does she have?

Use data from the list for problems 7–12.

7. Are there more than 350 coins in Cody's albums?

8. All of Scott's albums hold pennies. How many pennies does Scott have?

9. About how many coins are in all of Pauline's albums?

10. What is the total number of coins in Mavis's collection?

11. Erin says that James has fewer than 180 coins. Is she correct? Why?

12. Which club member has the greatest number of coins?

Coin Collectors Club

Member	Number of Albums	Coins in Each Album
Cody	7	52
Mavis	8	32
Pauline	5	75
Scott	9	24
James	6	34

Spiral Review and Test Prep

Choose the correct answer.

Ula has 4 jars of pennies. Each jar holds 92 pennies. Does she have over 400 pennies?

13. Which statement is true?
   A. Ula has 54 pennies in all.
   B. Ula has 92 pennies in all.
   C. Each jar has 92 pennies.

14. An estimate is enough because the exact product ____.
   F. must be greater than 400.
   G. must be less than 400.
   H. is 400.

Write the number that makes each sentence true. (pages 358–359)

1. $8 \times 6 = a$
    $8 \times 60 = b$
    $8 \times 600 = c$
    $8 \times 6{,}000 = d$

2. $6 \times e = 36$
    $g \times 60 = 360$
    $6 \times 600 = h$
    $6 \times j = 36{,}000$

3. $m \times 5 = 20$
    $4 \times n = 200$
    $4 \times 500 = p$
    $r \times 5{,}000 = 20{,}000$

Multiply. Use mental math. (pages 358–359)

4. 7×40

5. 6×80

6. $5 \times 4{,}000$

7. 7×900

Multiply. (pages 362–365)

8. $\begin{array}{r} 47 \\ \times\ 8 \\ \hline \end{array}$

9. $\begin{array}{r} \$54 \\ \times\ 3 \\ \hline \end{array}$

10. $\begin{array}{r} 91 \\ \times\ 6 \\ \hline \end{array}$

11. $\begin{array}{r} \$99 \\ \times\ 9 \\ \hline \end{array}$

12. 3×72

13. 9×94

14. 2×57

15. 4×87

Estimate each product. (pages 366–367)

16. 4×54

17. 7×287

18. 8×489

19. 3×679

20. $9 \times 4{,}391$

21. $6 \times 4{,}234$

22. You have saved $120 to buy gems for your collection. The gems you want are $42 each. Can you buy 3 of them? Why or why not?

23. It takes Mrs. Marlton 32 minutes to clean her plate collection. She cleans it 3 times each month. About how much time does she spend cleaning her plates each month?

Journal 24. **Analyze:** How can you use estimation to decide if 7×78 is greater than or less than 560?

25. Grant and Suni each have a collection of 60 baseball cards. How many do they have in all?

Additional activities at
www.mhschool.com/math

Use Place-Value Models to Multiply

Mr. Whitney's class is collecting phone books to recycle. They have filled each of 6 boxes with 12 phone books. How many phone books have they collected so far?

You can build a model of 6 groups of 12 phone books using place-value or base-ten models.

- Choose multiplication as the mat type.
- Stamp out 1 ten and 2 ones in each of the 6 sections at the top of the mat.

The number boxes keep count as you stamp.

How many phone books have they collected so far?

Use the computer to model each multiplication. Then write the product.

1. 4×16 2. 6×22 3. 7×43 4. 3×65

Solve.

5. Raphael is collecting cans to recycle. He has collected 8 bags of 36 cans. How many cans has he collected?

6. Laurel is buying 7 packages of pencils. Each package contains 12 pencils. How many pencils is she buying?

7. **Analyze:** How does modeling the problem help you multiply?

For more practice, use Math Traveler™.

9·7

Problem Solving: Strategy
Make a Graph

Collection	Number of Collectors
Stamps	66
Coins	132
Comics	144
Glass Figures	42
Rocks	120
Dolls	132

Read **Read the problem carefully.**

The magazine *Collectors' Monthly* recently asked its readers what they like to collect. How can the editor display the data to show what type of collecting is most popular?

- **What do you know?** How many people have each type of collection.

- **What do you need to find?** What kind of display will help compare the data.

Plan You want a display that allows you to compare data quickly. You can make a pictograph.

Solve Make the pictograph. Then compare the number of symbols for each type of collection.

Comics have the most symbols, so they are the most popular items to collect.

Most Popular Collections

Stamps
Coins
Comics
Glass Figures
Rocks
Dolls

Key: Each ♞ represents 12 collectors.

Look Back Can you compare the data another way?

Sum It Up Why is it easier to compare the data by looking at a graph than a table?

Use data from the table to solve problems 1–6.

1. Make a graph to show the data in the table.

2. Which collection is largest? smallest?

3. How many more items are in the largest collection than are in the next largest collection?

4. **What if** the student with the comic collection got 225 more comics at a yard sale? How would the graph change?

Largest Collection in our School

Collection	Number of Items
Records	225
Toy Robots	75
Comics	175
Game Cards	350
Dolls	150

5. Find the range. Determine how many more items are in the largest collection than in the smallest collection.

6. **Create a problem** using the data from the graph. Solve it. Ask others to solve it.

Mixed Strategy Review

7. Dan and Niko have collected 120 bean bag toys. Dan has twice as many as Niko. How many toys does each have?

8. Isaac wants to be at the collector convention when it opens at 9:00. It takes him 5 minutes to walk to the train. The train ride takes 45 minutes. What is the latest Isaac should leave his house?

★9. **Spatial Reasoning:** How many triangles are in this figure?

10. Valerie's two most valuable baseball cards are worth $25.50 and $18.50. How much are her two cards worth?

11. At a collectors' convention, Carl buys three sets of baseball cards. The first set has 3 cards, the second has 5 cards, and the third has 7. How many cards does he buy?

12. **Collect data** about collections. Organize it into a table. Create a problem based on the data. Solve it. Ask others to solve it.

CHOOSE A STRATEGY
- Logical Reasoning
- Draw a Picture
- Make a Graph
- Act It Out
- Make a Table or List
- Find a Pattern
- Guess and Check
- Write a Number Sentence
- Work Backward

Problem Solving

9·8 Multiply Greater Numbers

Learn

Richfield's is having a big art auction! How many paintings are for sale altogether?

Richfield's Art Auction
Largest Oil Painting Collection in the Area
2 floors of paintings
172 paintings on each floor
Tomorrow only.
Hayward Hotel
4:00 pm to 9:00 pm

Example 1

Find: 2 × 172

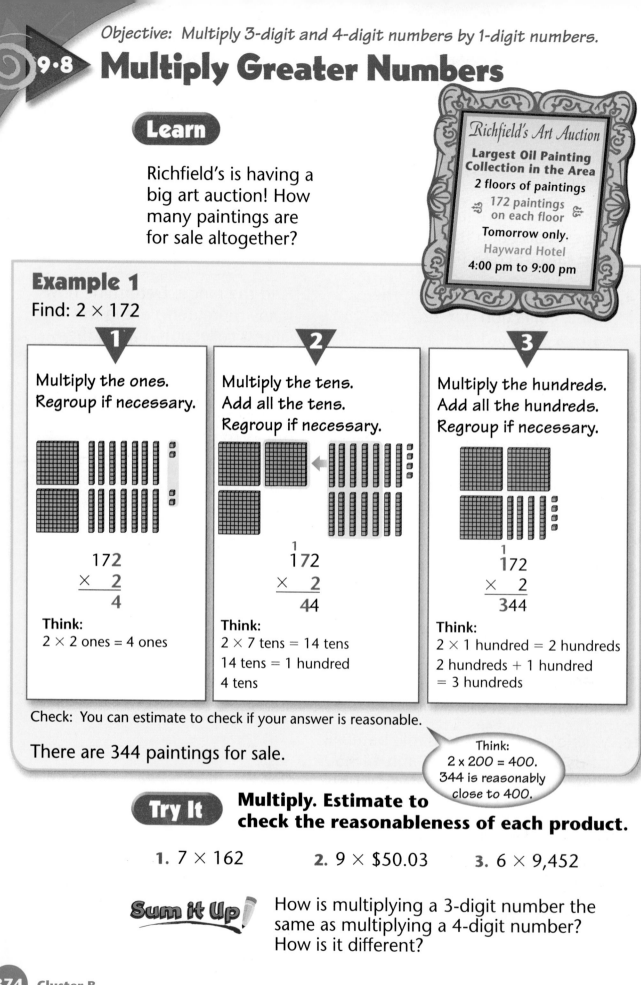

1

Multiply the ones. Regroup if necessary.

172
× 2
───
4

Think:
2 × 2 ones = 4 ones

2

Multiply the tens. Add all the tens. Regroup if necessary.

1
172
× 2
───
44

Think:
2 × 7 tens = 14 tens
14 tens = 1 hundred
4 tens

3

Multiply the hundreds. Add all the hundreds. Regroup if necessary.

1
172
× 2
───
344

Think:
2 × 1 hundred = 2 hundreds
2 hundreds + 1 hundred
= 3 hundreds

Check: You can estimate to check if your answer is reasonable.

There are 344 paintings for sale.

Think:
2 × 200 = 400.
344 is reasonably close to 400.

Try It **Multiply. Estimate to check the reasonableness of each product.**

1. 7 × 162   **2.** 9 × $50.03   **3.** 6 × 9,452

Sum it Up! How is multiplying a 3-digit number the same as multiplying a 4-digit number? How is it different?

Practice Multiply.

4. 285
   × 4

5. $5.12
   × 3

6. 5,087
   × 5

7. $97.80
   × 2

8. 8,445
   × 7

9. 6 × 236

10. 9 × $6.57

11. 5 × 7,950

12. 3 × $9,876

Find each product that is greater than 1,500 and less than 50,000. Use estimation to decide.

13. 7 × 197

14. 6 × 319

15. 4 × 9,876

16. 7 × 8,006

Algebra & functions Compare. Write > or <.

17. 7 × 197 ● 418 + 52

18. 672 + 480 ● 5 × 120

19. 4 × 329 ● 800 + 49

Problem Solving

Use data from *Did You Know?* for problem 20.

20. *David Copperfield* was printed in 19 installments. What month and year was the final installment published?

21. **Compare:** How is multiplying money like multiplying whole numbers? How is it different?

22. There are 1,245 items on each of 3 floors of an auction house. How many items are there?

★23. What is the mystery number? It is an even number. The number is greater than the product of 4 × 136 but less than the sum of 287 + 261.

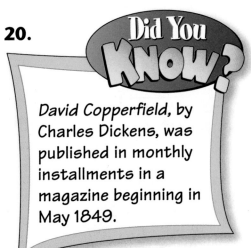

Did You Know?

David Copperfield, by Charles Dickens, was published in monthly installments in a magazine beginning in May 1849.

Spiral Review and Test Prep

24. 5 × 14

25. 6 × 23

26. 72 ÷ 8

27. 72 − 14

28. 8,356 + 789

Choose the correct answer.

29. Mika went to the Museum of Art at 10:25 A.M. She stayed for $\frac{1}{2}$ hour. What time did she leave?
    A. 10:40 A.M.
    B. 10:55 A.M.
    C. 11:05 A.M.
    D. 11:35 A.M.

30. Which sign makes the number sentence true? 12 ● 2 = 24
    F. ÷
    G. ×
    H. +
    J. −

9·9 A Problem Solving: Application
Decision Making

You Decide!

Which comic books should he buy?

"Wow!" Ben thought as he arrived at the Comic Book Trading Show. "I have $25 to spend. What should I buy?"

Option 1 **Super Hero Comics**

$1.25 each or
3 comics for $3.50

Option 2 **Sci-Fi Comic Adventures**

Bag-o-comics
5 comics in a bag
2 bags in a package
$15.50 for a package

Option 3 **Outer Space Stories**

$1.55 a comic
Buy 6, pay for 5
Buy 9, pay for 8

Read for Understanding

1. If you want to buy only 1 comic book, which kind can you not buy? Why?

2. How much more does 1 Outer Space comic book cost than 1 Super Hero comic book?

3. How many comic books do you get in a package of Sci-Fi Adventures?

4. How much do 9 Outer Space comic books cost?

5. How much do 6 Outer Space comic books cost?

6. How much do 6 Super Hero Comics cost?

Make Decisions

7. How much would you pay for 10 Outer Space comic books?

8. How much more do 6 Outer Space comics cost than 6 Super Hero Comics?

9. Write a list of things Ben should know before he decides which comic books to buy.

10. Which comic books should Ben buy if he wants to spend only five dollars of his money? Why?

11. **What if** Ben decides to buy a package of Sci-Fi comic books. He pays with a twenty-dollar bill. How much change does he get?

12. How many sets of 3 comic books will Ben buy if he decides to buy 9 Super Hero Comic books? How much will it cost him? How can you tell?

13. For what reason would you choose to buy your comic books here?

14. What else do you need to consider when making choices of which comic books to buy?

Your Decision!

Which comic books should Ben buy? How many of each? How much money will he have left?

Problem Solving

Objective: Apply multiplying a 1-digit number to investigate science concepts.

Problem Solving: Math and Science
How many servings of fruits and vegetables do you eat each week?

A healthful diet has at least 35 servings of fruits and vegetables each week. A serving could be an apple, a bunch of grapes, a carrot, or a cup of green vegetables.

In this activity you will discover whether you are eating the recommended amount of fruits and vegetables.

Hypothesize

Estimate how many times you eat a serving of fruits or vegetables each week.

Procedure

1. Think about what you ate yesterday.

2. Write down how many times you ate a serving of fruits or vegetables yesterday.

3. Multiply by 7 to find the number of servings you might eat in a week.

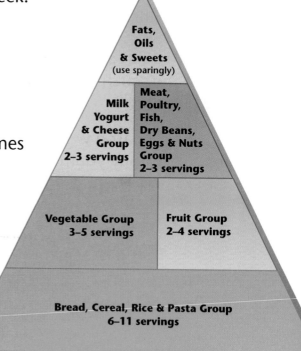

Fats, Oils & Sweets (use sparingly)

Milk Yogurt & Cheese Group 2–3 servings

Meat, Poultry, Fish, Dry Beans, Eggs & Nuts Group 2–3 servings

Vegetable Group 3–5 servings

Fruit Group 2–4 servings

Bread, Cereal, Rice & Pasta Group 6–11 servings

Food Guide Pyramid:
A Guide to Daily Food Choices

Copy and complete each box to record your data.

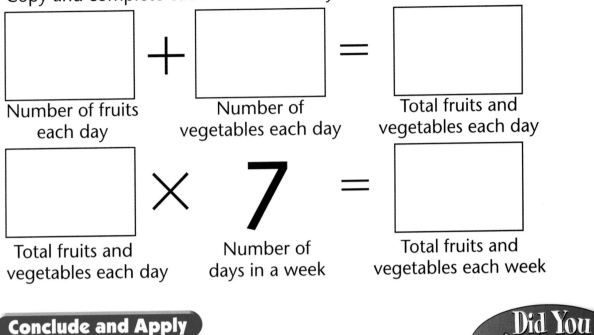

Number of fruits each day $+$ Number of vegetables each day $=$ Total fruits and vegetables each day

Total fruits and vegetables each day $\times$ **7** Number of days in a week $=$ Total fruits and vegetables each week

Conclude and Apply

Problem Solving

- Do you eat the recommended number of servings of fruits and vegetables each week? How do you know?

- Carmen eats 2 apples, a carrot, and a serving of peas on Monday. Multiply to find the number of servings of fruits and vegetables she will probably eat this week.

- Max usually eats 6 servings of fruits and vegetables each day. On Tuesday, he is sick with a stomachache and eats only toast. What would happen if Max used Tuesday to make his estimate for the week? Explain why he may calculate a misleading answer.

- Explain how eating the proper number of servings of fruits and vegetables contributes to your good health.

Did You KNOW?

It is usually best to eat fruits and vegetables as uncooked as possible. This way they give your body the most vitamins and minerals.

Going Further

Use a food pyramid to decide whether you are eating the recommended amount of breads/grains and fat in your diet.

Multiply. (pages 374–375)

1. 421
   × 9

2. $653
   × 5

3. 809
   × 2

4. 417
   × 4

5. 274
   × 3

6. 4,169
   × 6

7. 6,204
   × 8

8. 1,740
   × 7

9. 3,009
   × 4

10. $8,798
    × 5

11. $4.78
    × 9

12. $0.27
    × 5

13. $9.05
    × 8

14. $83.19
    × 6

15. 4 × 317

16. 6 × $4.69

17. 7 × 4,863

18. 3 × 5,735

19. 5 × 426

20. $51.36 × 4

Use data from the table to solve problems 21–22. (pages 372–375)

Ryan's Marble Collection	
Color	Number of Items
Blue	15
Green	12
Silver	14
Black	21
Yellow	7
Red	18

21. Make a graph to show the data in the table.

22. Which color of marbles does Ryan have the most of? the least?

23. Lita paid $15.75 for each of 2 dolls she wanted for her collection. How much did both dolls cost altogether?

24. Jim has 368 marbles in each of 8 boxes. What number sentence can you use to find out how many marbles Jim has in all? How many does he have?

25. **Analyze:** How can estimation help you decide if the exact product for 7 × $74.65 is greater than or less than $600?

Additional activities at
www.mhschool.com/math

Extra Practice

Multiplication Patterns (pages 358–359)

Write the number that makes each sentence true.

1. $8 \times 5 = a$
   $8 \times 50 = b$
   $8 \times 500 = c$
   $8 \times 5,000 = d$

2. $6 \times 7 = f$
   $6 \times 70 = g$
   $6 \times h = 4,200$
   $6 \times 7,000 = j$

3. $4 \times 2 = m$
   $4 \times 20 = n$
   $4 \times 200 = p$
   $r \times 2,000 = 8,000$

Multiply. Use mental math.

4. 2×40
5. 4×60
6. 7×30
7. 5×20
8. 6×90
9. 8×70
10. 4×50
11. 3×200
12. 6×500
13. 8×900
14. 7×100
15. 9×700
16. 6×300
17. $5 \times 8,000$
18. $9 \times 6,000$
19. $2 \times 7,000$
20. $8 \times 8,000$
21. $3 \times 9,000$
22. $7 \times 4,000$
23. $9 \times 9,000$

24. Len wants to buy 20 more books for his book collection at a book fair. If each book he buys is $4, how much will the books cost?

Multiply 2-Digit Numbers by 1-Digit Numbers (pages 362–365)

Multiply.

1. $\begin{array}{r} 41 \\ \times\ 5 \\ \hline \end{array}$

2. $\begin{array}{r} \$0.38 \\ \times\quad 2 \\ \hline \end{array}$

3. $\begin{array}{r} 67 \\ \times\ 7 \\ \hline \end{array}$

4. $\begin{array}{r} \$0.54 \\ \times\quad 9 \\ \hline \end{array}$

5. $\begin{array}{r} 83 \\ \times\ 4 \\ \hline \end{array}$

6. $\begin{array}{r} \$99 \\ \times\ 9 \\ \hline \end{array}$

7. $\begin{array}{r} 44 \\ \times\ 6 \\ \hline \end{array}$

8. $\begin{array}{r} 25 \\ \times\ 4 \\ \hline \end{array}$

9. $\begin{array}{r} 94 \\ \times\ 7 \\ \hline \end{array}$

10. $\begin{array}{r} 76 \\ \times\ 3 \\ \hline \end{array}$

11. $\begin{array}{r} \$0.55 \\ \times\quad 9 \\ \hline \end{array}$

12. $\begin{array}{r} 32 \\ \times\ 6 \\ \hline \end{array}$

13. $\begin{array}{r} 43 \\ \times\ 5 \\ \hline \end{array}$

14. $\begin{array}{r} \$68 \\ \times\ 7 \\ \hline \end{array}$

15. $\begin{array}{r} 97 \\ \times\ 8 \\ \hline \end{array}$

16. $\begin{array}{r} \$0.38 \\ \times\quad 4 \\ \hline \end{array}$

17. $\begin{array}{r} 57 \\ \times\ 2 \\ \hline \end{array}$

18. $\begin{array}{r} 74 \\ \times\ 6 \\ \hline \end{array}$

19. $\begin{array}{r} 29 \\ \times\ 3 \\ \hline \end{array}$

20. $\begin{array}{r} 86 \\ \times\ 7 \\ \hline \end{array}$

21. Ella has 6 boxes of mineral rocks in her collection. If she has 34 rocks in each box, how many mineral rocks does she have?

Extra Practice

Estimate each product.

1. $852
   × 3

2. 42
   × 6

3. 679
   × 8

4. 39
   × 4

5. 405
   × 7

6. 513
   × 2

7. 24
   × 9

8. 19
   × 6

9. 602
   × 5

10. 58
    × 4

11. 5 × 91   12. 3 × 12   13. 6 × 49   14. 7 × 69   15. 8 × 46

16. 3 × 38   17. 8 × 59   18. 2 × $88   19. 4 × 156   20. 6 × 572

21. 9 × 363   22. 7 × $412 23. 5 × 255   24. 7 × $902 25. 3 × 265

Write > or < to make a true sentence.

26. 5 × 82 ▮ 400

27. 3 × 29 ▮ 60

28. 9 × 71 ▮ 720

29. 8 × 426 ▮ 3,200

30. 6 × 672 ▮ 4,200

31. 7 × 354 ▮ 2,100

32. Jessica collects 4 new baseball cards each week. She has collected for 17 weeks. About how many baseball cards does Jessica have?

Problem Solving: Reading for Math
Find an Estimate or Exact Answer (pages 368–369)

Solve.

1. Cindy has 5 bags of pennies. Each bag holds 87 coins. Does she have over 500 coins in the bags?

2. Roberto has 8 jars of coins. Each jar has 41 coins. How many coins does Roberto have?

3. Rebecca has 3 bags of nickels. Each bag holds 45 coins. Does she have over 150 coins in the bags?

4. Jonathan has 6 jars of coins. Each jar has 56 coins. How many coins does Jonathan have?

Extra Practice

Problem Solving: Strategy
Make a Graph (pages 372–373)

Use data from the table for problems 1–3.

1. Make a graph to show the data in the table.

2. How many more items are in the largest group of autographs than in the next largest group of autographs?

3. **What if** Jenny got 5 more men writers' autographs at a book fair? How would the graph change?

Jenny's Autograph Collection	
Type of Autographs	Number of Autographs
Women writers	5
Men writers	16
Women actors	11
Men actors	20
Women athletes	9
Men athletes	13

Multiply Greater Numbers (pages 374–375)

Multiply.

1. 143
   × 2

2. $507
   × 3

3. 346
   × 9

4. $4.25
   × 4

5. 287
   × 8

6. $3.12
   × 5

7. 807
   × 7

8. $978
   × 2

9. 645
   × 6

10. $750
   × 8

11. 2,481
   × 4

12. $5,469
   × 3

13. $66.65
   × 9

14. 3,406
   × 8

15. 7,008
   × 2

16. 1,886
   × 5

17. 8,944
   × 6

18. 4,751
   × 4

19. $39.90
   × 9

20. $6,736
   × 8

21. Jessica and 4 of her friends make decorations for the gym. They each make 24 paper flowers. How many paper flowers do they make in all?

Chapter Study Guide

Language and Math

Complete. Use a word from the list.

1. If you do not need an exact answer, you can round to find an ____.

2. If you have more than 9 ones you can ____ the ones as tens.

3. You can ____ 456 to 500 or 460.

Math Words

estimate
multiple
regroup
round

Skills and Applications

Multiply multiples of 10, 100, and 1,000 by a 1-digit number. (pages 356–359)

Example

Multiply: 6×700
Use mental math.

Solution

Use basic multiplication facts and patterns.

$6 \times 7 = 42$
$6 \times 70 = 420$
$6 \times 700 = 4,200$
$6 \times 7000 = 42,000$

Think:
6×7 tens $= 42$ tens
6×7 hundreds $=$
42 hundreds

Multiply. Use mental math.

4. 5×80
5. 4×200
6. $3 \times 4,000$
7. $7 \times 5,000$
8. 6×900
9. $9 \times 8,000$
10. 8×600
11. $5 \times 3,000$

Multiply a multi-digit number by a 1-digit number. (pages 360–365, 374–375)

Example

Multiply: $3 \times 1,568$

Solution

Multiply each place.
Regroup and add if necessary.

$$\begin{array}{r} \overset{1\,2\,2}{1568} \\ \times \quad 3 \\ \hline 4,704 \end{array}$$

Multiply.

12. $4 \times 5,307$
13. $7 \times 2,786$
14. $9 \times 6,094$
15. $3 \times \$52.69$
16. $8 \times \$66.82$
17. $6 \times \$91.75$
18. $5 \times \$36.43$
19. $7 \times 4,372$

Example

Estimate the product.

9 × 78

Solution

Round the factor that is greater than 10. Then multiply mentally.

Think: Round to the nearest ten.

9 × 78

↓ ↓

9 × 80 = 720

So 9 × 78 is about 720.

Estimate each product.

20. 4 × 36

21. 7 × 91

22. 5 × 432

23. 8 × 497

24. 3 × $569

25. 9 × $712

26. 6 × $2,149

27. 2 × $7,832

28. 6 × $726

29. 3 × 921

Example

Make a graph to show the data in the table. Which collection is the largest?

Collections	Number of Items
Stickers	300
Stuffed Animals	50
Stamps	250
Compact Disc	150
Dolls	100

Solution

Make a pictograph.

Most Popular Collections

Collection	Number of Items
Stickers	
Stuffed Animals	
Stamps	
Compact Disc	
Dolls	

Each ☺ equals 50 items.

Stickers is the largest collection.

Use data from the table to solve problems 30–32.

Club	Number of Students
Art	33
Chess	12
Collections	17
Computer	24
Music	26
Sports	36

30. Make a graph to show the data in the table.

31. Which club is the largest? smallest?

32. **What if** the Art Club got 5 more members? How would the graph change?

33. Janine has 300 stamps. She bought 4 stamp-collecting albums to display her stamps. Each can hold 68 stamps. Did she buy enough albums? Explain.

Chapter Test

Multiply. Use mental math.

1. 6×20

2. 2×500

3. $5 \times 3,000$

4. $8 \times 5,000$

5. 9×400

6. $7 \times 4,000$

Multiply.

7.
$$\begin{array}{r} \$6.13 \\ \times \quad 5 \\ \hline \end{array}$$

8.
$$\begin{array}{r} \$4.88 \\ \times \quad 8 \\ \hline \end{array}$$

9.
$$\begin{array}{r} \$29.78 \\ \times \quad 3 \\ \hline \end{array}$$

10.
$$\begin{array}{r} \$44.32 \\ \times \quad 7 \\ \hline \end{array}$$

11. $3 \times 7,044$

12. $7 \times \$71.09$

13. $6 \times \$44.55$

14. $4 \times \$89.40$

15. $5 \times 3,976$

16. $8 \times 7,007$

17. $9 \times \$76.55$

18. $2 \times \$88.96$

Estimate each product.

19. 3×27

20. $9 \times 5,876$

21. 6×494

22. 4×875

Solve.

23. Tanya has her book collection displayed on a large bookcase. There are 74 books on each of 7 shelves. How many books are in Tanya's collection?

24. Han-su wants to buy 6 new model airplanes for his collection. Each plane costs $17.95. So far he has saved $100. Does he have enough money for the airplane models? How can you tell? Will you find an exact answer or an estimate?

25. Make a graph given the following data about Katie's coin collection: 52 dimes, 132 pennies, 67 nickels, 12 half-dollars, 43 quarters. Draw a conclusion based on the information in the graph.

Performance Assessment

Your family loves to collect things! But you have to pack some of your collections away because you have too many to keep out. You need to use a number of each type of box listed below.

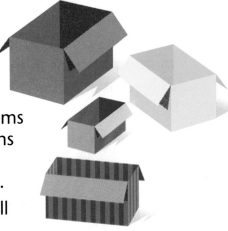

Red boxes–hold between 1,000 and 2,000 items
Yellow boxes–hold between 500 and 999 items
Blue boxes–hold between 100 and 499 items
Striped boxes–hold between 50 and 99 items.

- pick the number of each type of box you will need to store away some of your collection.
- decide how many items fit into each box.
- find out how many items you will store away altogether in each type of box.

Use a chart like the one below to organize and show your work.

Color of Box	Number of Boxes	Number in Each Box	Total Number of Items

A Good Answer

- shows a completed chart.
- includes the steps you followed to find the total for each type of box.
- shows the correct total for each type of box.

You may want to save this work for your portfolio.

Enrichment

Hindu Lattice

Here is another way to multiply. Long ago, the Hindu mathematicians in India used this method to multiply large numbers. You can use grid paper to try Hindu Lattice Multiplication.

Find: 17 × 32

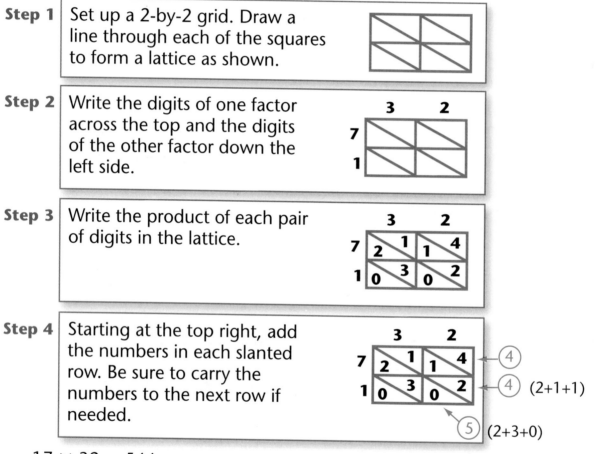

Step 1	Set up a 2-by-2 grid. Draw a line through each of the squares to form a lattice as shown.

| Step 2 | Write the digits of one factor across the top and the digits of the other factor down the left side. |

| Step 3 | Write the product of each pair of digits in the lattice. |

| Step 4 | Starting at the top right, add the numbers in each slanted row. Be sure to carry the numbers to the next row if needed. |

17 × 32 = 544

Use lattice multiplication to find the product. Show your work.

1. 14 × 48

2. 15 × 51

3. 12 × 62

4. 25 × 387

5. Analyze: Describe how you would use the lattice method to find 74 × 1,245.

Test-Taking Tips

S.O.S.

The problems you find on tests sometimes contain extra information that you do not need to use to solve the problem.

It is important to read the problem carefully, decide on the facts you need to use, and **cross out any extra information** that may confuse you.

The Hat Hut has 195 boxes of hats. Forty-five of the hats are green. Each box holds 3 hats. How many hats are in the boxes?

A. 35   **C.** 375

B. 55   **D.** 585

To find the total number of hats in the boxes, you need to know the number of boxes and the number of hats in each box. You do not need to the know the color of any of them.

Find: 195 × 3

195 × 3 = 585

D is the correct choice.

> **Check for Success**
>
> Before turning in a test, go back one last time to check.
>
> ☑ I understood and answered the questions asked.
>
> ☑ I checked my work for errors.
>
> ☑ My answers make sense.

Read the problem. Cross out the extra information. Then choose the correct answer.

1. Gary bought 2 pens for $1.95 and a notebook for $2.25. How much did he pay for the pens?

    A. $1.95   **C.** $4.20

    B. $3.90   **D.** $6.15

2. Cara practices piano 3 times a week. Her class starts as 3:45 and ends at 5:15. How long is the class?

    F. $2\frac{1}{2}$ hours   **H.** $1\frac{1}{2}$ hours

    G. 2 hours   **J.** 1 hour

3. Each bookcase holds books on one subject. There are 14 bookcases with 8 shelves in each bookcase. How many shelves are there in all?

    A. 6 **B.** 22 **C.** 84 **D.** 112

4. Mrs. Fenway has 18 fewer students in her class this year than last year. Five of them moved to the next town. If she had 32 students last year, how many are there this year?

    F. 14 **G.** 26 **H.** 42 **J.** 50

Spiral Review and Test Prep
Chapters 1–9

Choose the correct answer.

Number Sense

1. Find: 6,008 − 1,549
   - **A.** 4,451
   - **B.** 4,459
   - **C.** 5,451
   - **D.** Not Here

2. Kim buys 2 boxes of film on sale. Each box holds 5 rolls of film. How many rolls of film does Kim buy?
   - **F.** 3
   - **G.** 7
   - **H.** 10
   - **J.** 15

3. Selma has 432 coins in her collection. She buys 9 more on Saturday and 7 more on Sunday. How many coins does she have now?
   - **A.** 448
   - **B.** 456
   - **C.** 3,024
   - **D.** 3,888

4. Round 9,827 to the nearest thousand.
   - **F.** 9,900
   - **G.** 9,800
   - **H.** 10,000
   - **J.** 9,000

Measurement and Geometry

5. Which is true?
   - **A.** Some rectangles do not have 4 sides.
   - **B.** All triangles have more than 3 sides.
   - **C.** All squares have 4 sides.
   - **D.** All rectangles have only 3 sides.

6. What time is on the clock?
   - **F.** 5:33
   - **H.** 6:33
   - **G.** 5:38
   - **J.** 6:38

7. Which names the figure?

   - **A.** Cylinder
   - **B.** Triangle
   - **C.** Cone
   - **D.** Cube

8. Len has 6 model boats that are each 12 inches long. He puts them end-to-end on a shelf that is 80 inches long. How many inches are empty on the shelf?
   - **F.** 72
   - **G.** 68
   - **H.** 12
   - **J.** 8

Statistics, Data Analysis, and Probability

Use data from the table for problems 9–12.

Boxes of Trading Cards		
Kind	Number in Box	Price
Basketball	25	$22.75
Baseball	125	$75.99
Football	180	$95.00

9. If you buy 3 boxes of football cards, how many cards will you have in all?

   A. 360   **C.** 630

   B. 540   **D.** 680

10. Jeremy pays for the least expensive cards with $25. How much change should he get?

    F. $1.75   **H.** $2.25

    G. $2.00   **J.** $3.25

11. How many more football cards are in a box than in a box of baseball cards?

    A. 45   **C.** 65

    B. 55   **D.** Not Here

12. How much do 2 boxes of basketball cards cost?

    F. $45.50   **H.** $44.50

    G. $45.25   **J.** $44.25

Mathematical Reasoning

13. Pearl buys 6 postcards from each city she visits. She visited 18 cities over the last 3 years. How many postcards did she buy?

    A. 21   **C.** 108

    B. 54   **D.** 162

14. Tisa sat at her booth at the Coin Collectors' Show from 9:15 A.M. to 2:00 P.M. How long did she sit at the booth?

    F. 5 hr 45 min   **H.** 4 hr 15 min

    G. 5 hr 15 min   **J.** 4 hr 45 min

15. Erin displays her stuffed animals on shelves in her room. She has 4 animals on some shelves and 5 on others. Erin has 26 stuffed animals in all. How many shelves does she have with 5 stuffed animals?

    A. 2   **C.** 4

    B. 3   **D.** 5

16. Kaitlin has these shirts and skirts for her favorite doll: red shirt, blue shirt, white shirt; black skirt, red skirt, blue skirt. How many different outfits can she put on the doll? What are they? Explain how you found your answer.

CHAPTER 10

Divide by 1-Digit Numbers

Theme: Work Together

Use the Data

Number of Community Helpers in Atlanta Organizations for a Month

Arts for All	20
Zoo Atlanta	50
Big Trees Forest Preserve	80
Nexus Art Center	120

Source: data provided by each organization.

- **What if** you make a pictograph from the data and each 😊 stands for 5 children? How many 😊 do you draw for Zoo Atlanta? How can you use division to find out?

What You Will Learn
In this chapter you will learn how to
- divide multiples of 10 by a 1-digit number.
- divide 1-digit numbers.
- estimate quotients.
- use strategies to solve problems.

Additional activities at
www.mhschool.com/math

Objective: Use models to divide tens by 1-digit numbers.

Explore Dividing Multiples of 10

Learn

You can use place value models to explore dividing multiples of 10.
Find: 80 ÷ 4

Work Together

▶ Use place value models to find 80 ÷ 4.

- Show 80 as 8 tens using place value models.

- Divide the models into 4 equal groups.

You Will Need
- place value models

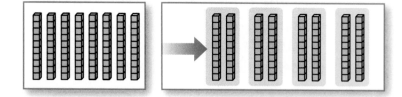

- Record your work. What is 80 ÷ 4?

▶ Use place value models to divide. Record your work.

| 90 ÷ 9 | 60 ÷ 2 | 120 ÷ 4 | 160 ÷ 8 |

Make Connections

Here are two ways to find the quotient when dividing tens.

Find: 280 ÷ 7

Using Models	**Using Paper and Pencil**

Divide the tens into 7 equal groups.

Think: 280 = 28 tens
Divide the tens.
28 tens ÷ 7 = 4 tens
4 tens = 40

Each group has 4 tens.

$280 \div 7 = 40$

Try It Divide. You may use place value models.

1. $2\overline{)40}$
2. $7\overline{)70}$
3. $5\overline{)150}$
4. $200 \div 4$
5. $720 \div 9$

Write and solve a division sentence.

6.

7.

8.

Sum it Up Explain how to use place value models to find 120 ÷ 6.

Practice Divide.

9. $2\overline{)80}$
10. $3\overline{)90}$
11. $7\overline{)210}$
12. $9\overline{)180}$
13. $6\overline{)300}$

14. $420 \div 6$
15. $810 \div 9$
16. $240 \div 3$
17. $630 \div 7$
18. $500 \div 5$

19. **Analyze:** How would you find the quotient of 2,000 ÷ 5 using paper and pencil?

Objective: Use mental math strategies to divide multiples of 10 and 100 mentally.

Division Patterns

 Algebra & functions **Learn**

Math Words

dividend A number to be divided

quotient the answer in division

Maria makes oatmeal cookies for the school bake sale. She puts the same number of cookies into plastic bags. She has 300 cookies. How many bags does she need?

3 cookies

Example

You can use basic facts to divide mentally.
Look for division patterns.

$3 \div 3 = 1$	**Think:** 3 ones $\div$ 3 = 1 one
$30 \div 3 = 10$	3 tens $\div$ 3 = 1 ten
$300 \div 3 = 100$	3 hundreds $\div$ 3 = 1 hundred

Maria needs 100 bags.

More Examples

A

$40 \div 5 = 8$
$400 \div 5 = 80$

B

$36 \div 9 = 4$
$360 \div 9 = 40$

C

$6 \div 2 = 3$
$60 \div 2 = 30$

Try It **Write the number that makes each sentence true.**

1. $20 \div 5 = r$
   $200 \div 5 = s$

2. $45 \div 9 = b$
   $c \div 9 = 50$

3. $4 \div 2 = n$
   $40 \div 2 = t$
   $400 \div 2 = p$

Divide. Use mental math.

4. $50 \div 5$ 5. $90 \div 3$ 6. $120 \div 2$ 7. $200 \div 4$ 8. $480 \div 6$

Sum it Up  How does the **quotient** change when the number of zeros in the **dividend** increases?

Write the number that makes each sentence true.

9. $18 \div 3 = x$
$180 \div 3 = w$

10. $30 \div 6 = y$
$s \div 6 = 50$

11. $8 \div 2 = q$
$80 \div 2 = r$
$800 \div 2 = t$

Divide.

12. $7\overline{)420}$
13. $4\overline{)\$280}$
14. $7\overline{)140}$
15. $8\overline{)320}$
16. $9\overline{)540}$

17. $20 \div 2$
18. $70 \div 7$
19. $\$150 \div 5$
20. $350 \div 7$
21. $560 \div 8$

Describe and complete these skip-counting patterns.

22. 30, 60, 90, ____, 150

23. 70, ____, 50, 40

24. 40, 60, ____, 100, 120

25. ____, 80, 120, 160

Problem Solving

Use data from the pictograph for problems 26–27.

26. How many more blueberry muffins were sold than corn muffins?

27. **If** each 🧁 stands for 100 muffins, how many 🧁 will represent lemon muffins now? bran muffins?

Number of Muffins

Bran 🧁🧁🧁🧁🧁🧁🧁

Corn 🧁🧁🧁

Blueberry 🧁🧁🧁🧁🧁🧁🧁

Lemon 🧁🧁🧁🧁🧁🧁🧁

Each 🧁 stands for 50.

Journal 28. **Compare:** How is dividing 21 by 7 like dividing 210 by 7? How is it different?

Spiral Review and Test Prep

29. 658×3
30. $\$24.05 \times 8$
31. $315 + 136$
32. $833 - 49$

Choose the correct answer.

33. Which number does not round to 70?

A. 74
C. 66
B. 64
D. 72

34. What is the value of the 9 in 42,936?

F. 9,000
H. 90
G. 900
J. Not Here

Objective: *Use models to divide 2-digit numbers by 1-digit numbers.*

Explore Division

Learn

Math Word

remainder the number left over after dividing

You can use place value models to explore dividing 2-digit numbers by 1-digit numbers. Find: 75 ÷ 5

Work Together

▶ Use place value models to find 75 ÷ 5.

You Will Need
- **place value models**

- Show 75 as 7 tens and 5 ones using place value models.

- Divide the tens into 5 equal groups.

- Regroup the extra tens. Divide the ones into 5 equal groups.

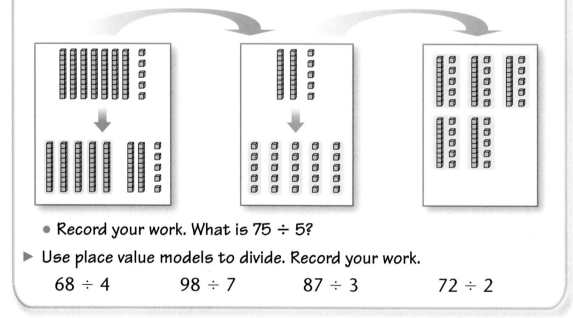

- Record your work. What is 75 ÷ 5?

▶ Use place value models to divide. Record your work.

68 ÷ 4   98 ÷ 7   87 ÷ 3   72 ÷ 2

Make Connections

Sometimes there is a **remainder** when you divide.

Find: 62 ÷ 4

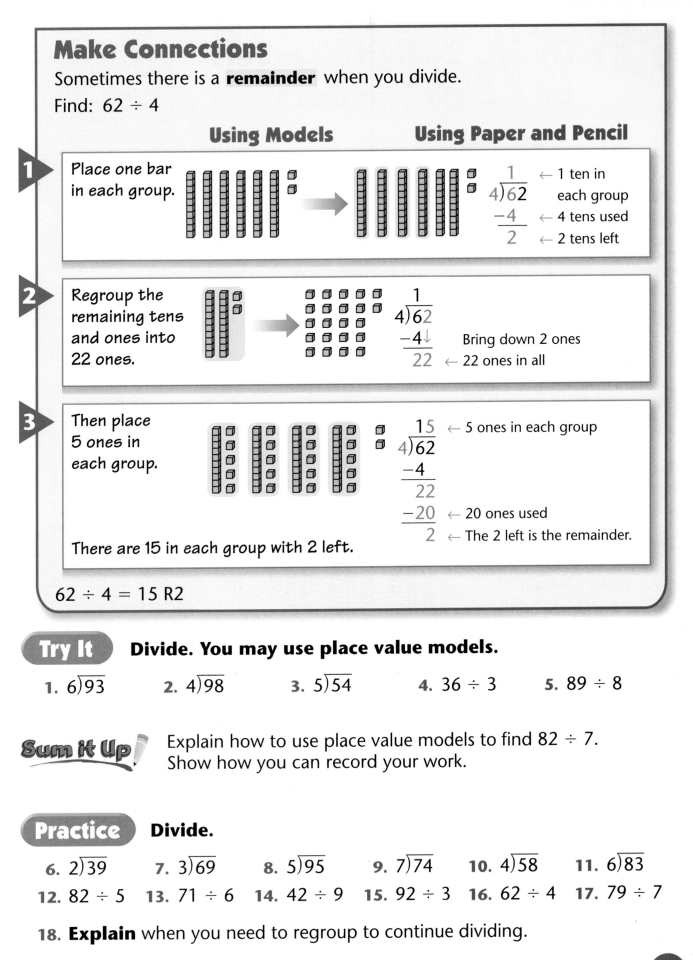

| | **Using Models** | **Using Paper and Pencil** |

1 Place one bar in each group.

$$\begin{array}{r} 1 \\ 4\overline{)62} \\ -4 \\ \hline 2 \end{array}$$

← 1 ten in each group
← 4 tens used
← 2 tens left

2 Regroup the remaining tens and ones into 22 ones.

$$\begin{array}{r} 1 \\ 4\overline{)62} \\ -4\downarrow \\ \hline 22 \end{array}$$

Bring down 2 ones
← 22 ones in all

3 Then place 5 ones in each group.

$$\begin{array}{r} 15 \\ 4\overline{)62} \\ -4 \\ \hline 22 \\ -20 \\ \hline 2 \end{array}$$

← 5 ones in each group
← 20 ones used
← The 2 left is the remainder.

There are 15 in each group with 2 left.

62 ÷ 4 = 15 R2

Try It **Divide. You may use place value models.**

1. 6)93   2. 4)98   3. 5)54   4. 36 ÷ 3   5. 89 ÷ 8

Sum it Up Explain how to use place value models to find 82 ÷ 7. Show how you can record your work.

Practice **Divide.**

6. 2)39   7. 3)69   8. 5)95   9. 7)74   10. 4)58   11. 6)83

12. 82 ÷ 5   13. 71 ÷ 6   14. 42 ÷ 9   15. 92 ÷ 3   16. 62 ÷ 4   17. 79 ÷ 7

18. **Explain** when you need to regroup to continue dividing.

10·4 Divide 2-Digit Numbers by 1-Digit Numbers

Learn

Math Word

divisor the number by which the dividend is divided

Rosa plants 73 seedlings in her garden. She plants the same number of seedlings in 3 rows. How many does she plant in each row? How many are left over?

Example

You can divide to solve the problem. Find: 73 ÷ 3

1 Place the first digit in the quotient. How many tens can be put in each of 3 groups?

$$\begin{array}{r} 2 \\ 3\overline{)73} \\ -6 \\ \hline 1 \end{array}$$

Enough tens. The first digit is in the tens place.
Multiply: 2 × 3 = 6
Subtract: 7 − 6 = 1
Compare: 1 < 3

2 Regroup the tens. How many ones can be put in each of 3 groups?

$$\begin{array}{r} 24 \text{ R1} \\ 3\overline{)73} \\ -6\downarrow \\ \hline 13 \\ -12 \\ \hline 1 \end{array}$$

Multiply: 4 × 3 = 12
Subtract: 13 − 12 = 1
Compare: 1 < 3

3 Check. Use the inverse relationship between division and multiplication.

$$\begin{array}{r} 24 \leftarrow \text{quotient} \\ \text{divisor} \rightarrow 3\overline{)73} \leftarrow \text{dividend} \end{array}$$

$$\begin{array}{r} 24 \leftarrow \text{quotient} \\ \times\ 3 \leftarrow \text{divisor} \\ \hline 72 \end{array}$$

$$\begin{array}{r} 72 \\ +\ 1 \leftarrow \text{remainder} \\ \hline 73 \leftarrow \text{dividend} \end{array}$$

Rosa put 24 seedlings in each row. She has 1 seedling left over.

Try It   Divide. Check your answer.

1. 5)74   **2.** 3)98   **3.** 7)80   **4.** 65 ÷ 4   **5.** 84 ÷ 3   **6.** 58 ÷ 6

Sum it Up!   Explain how you would divide 78 ÷ 4.

Divide. Check your answer.

7. $4\overline{)72}$ **8.** $2\overline{)32}$ **9.** $3\overline{)96}$ **10.** $6\overline{)75}$ **11.** $5\overline{)86}$ **12.** $7\overline{)83}$

13. $6\overline{)93}$ **14.** $8\overline{)90}$ **15.** $2\overline{)77}$ **16.** $4\overline{)88}$ **17.** $3\overline{)67}$ **18.** $5\overline{)62}$

19. $55 \div 4$ **20.** $38 \div 8$ **21.** $78 \div 7$ **22.** $34 \div 4$

23. $67 \div 8$ **24.** $49 \div 5$ **25.** $51 \div 6$ **26.** $82 \div 3$

Algebra & functions **Copy and complete the table. Describe the pattern.**

27.

Rule: Divide by 6.								
Input	78	79	80	81	82	83	84	85
Output	13	13 R1	▨	▨	▨	▨	▨	▨

Problem Solving

Use data from *Did You Know?* for problems 28–29.

28. How many minutes did it take to plant the trees?

★**29.** It takes 2 volunteers to plant one tree. About how many trees did each pair of volunteers plant altogether?

30. What remainders are possible when the divisor is 6? when the divisor is 9?

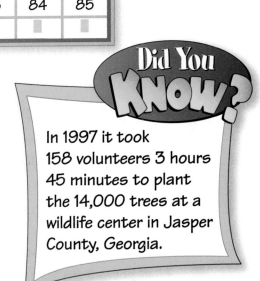

Did You KNOW?

In 1997 it took 158 volunteers 3 hours 45 minutes to plant the 14,000 trees at a wildlife center in Jasper County, Georgia.

31. Create a problem involving division with an answer of 12 R3. Ask others to solve it.

Spiral Review and Test Prep

32. 722×5 **33.** $(293 - 47) \times 9$ **34.** $8 \times 9 \times 3 \times 2$

Choose the correct answer.

35. Which shows the Commutative Property for addition?
  A. $3 + 5 = 5 + 3$
  B. $3 \times 5 = 5 \times 3$
  C. $2 + (3 + 5) = (2 + 3) + 5$
  D. Not Here

36. What is the value of the three in 2<u>3</u>4,048
  F. 3 hundred thousands
  G. 3 thousands
  H. 3 ten thousands
  J. 3 hundreds

Objective: Make an inference to interpret remainders and solve problems.

Problem Solving: Reading for Math
Interpret the Remainder

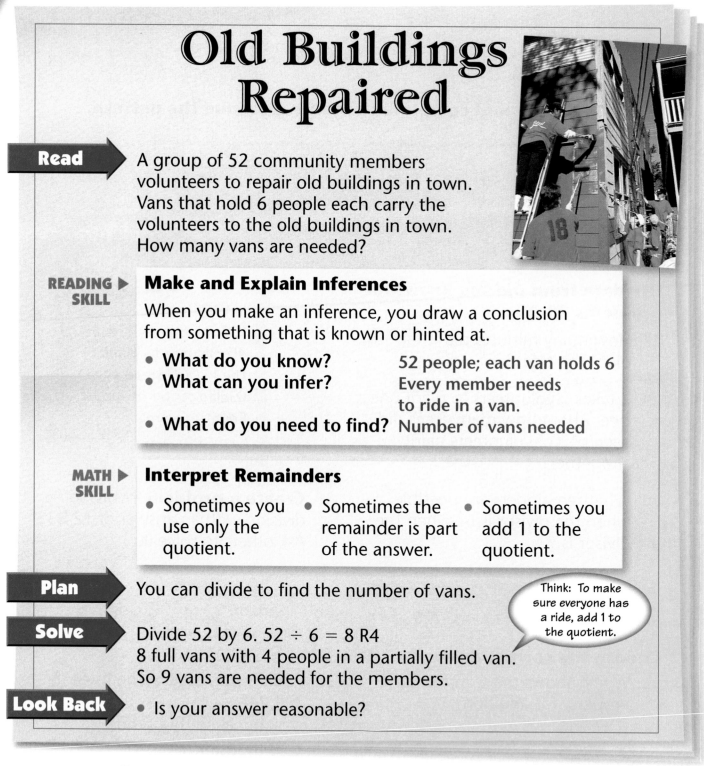

Old Buildings Repaired

Read ▶

A group of 52 community members volunteers to repair old buildings in town. Vans that hold 6 people each carry the volunteers to the old buildings in town. How many vans are needed?

READING SKILL ▶

Make and Explain Inferences

When you make an inference, you draw a conclusion from something that is known or hinted at.

- **What do you know?** — 52 people; each van holds 6
- **What can you infer?** — Every member needs to ride in a van.
- **What do you need to find?** — Number of vans needed

MATH SKILL ▶

Interpret Remainders

- Sometimes you use only the quotient.
- Sometimes the remainder is part of the answer.
- Sometimes you add 1 to the quotient.

Plan ▶

You can divide to find the number of vans.

Think: To make sure everyone has a ride, add 1 to the quotient.

Solve ▶

Divide 52 by 6. $52 \div 6 = 8$ R4
8 full vans with 4 people in a partially filled van.
So 9 vans are needed for the members.

Look Back ▶

- Is your answer reasonable?

Sum it Up! How did you use an inference to help you decide how to interpret the remainder?

Solve. Tell how you interpreted the remainder.

1. There are 3 paintbrushes in a bag. The committee needs 11 paintbrushes. How many bags should they buy?

2. If you have 46 nails and it takes 7 nails for each board, how many boards can you use?

3. The committee has $36 for paint. Each can costs $5. How many cans can the committee buy?

4. Timmy and his father are making 55 sandwiches for the community members. People sit 6 to a table. How many sandwiches are placed at each table?

Use data from the Supply List for problems 5–7.

5. The buckets will be shared equally by 36 community members. How many members will share each bucket?

6. A total of 16 members need to use the ladders. If the ladders are divided evenly among this group, how many members will share each ladder?

7. A total of 18 members need to use the hammers. How many members will share each one?

SUPPLY LIST
4 ladders
9 buckets
6 hammers
5 boxes of nails

8. Name two ways that a group of 24 town members could be divided evenly into groups of more than 3 people.

Spiral Review and Test Prep

Choose the correct answer.

A group of 42 town members is going to work on a house in the next community. They will drive to the house in cars holding 5 people. How many cars are needed?

9. Which of the following statements is true?
   A. Each car holds 9 people.
   B. There are 42 people in the group.
   C. Each car will be full.

10. How did you interpret the remainder to solve this problem?
   F. The answer lacked a remainder.
   G. Add 1 to the quotient.
   H. Use only the quotient.

Problem Solving

Divide. Use mental math. (pages 394–395)

1. $2\overline{)60}$ 2. $7\overline{)490}$ 3. $5\overline{)300}$ 4. $\$360 \div 4$ 5. $300 \div 3$

Write the number that makes each sentence true. (pages 396–397)

6. $27 \div 3 = r$
    $270 \div 3 = s$

7. $40 \div 5 = x$
   $y \div 5 = 80$

8. $6 \div 2 = o$
    $60 \div 2 = p$
    $600 \div 2 = q$

Divide. (pages 398–401)

9. $4\overline{)76}$ 10. $3\overline{)77}$ 11. $9\overline{)59}$ 12. $8\overline{)68}$

13. $68 \div 6$ 14. $7\overline{)55}$ 15. $40 \div 3$

16. $96 \div 3$ 17. $5\overline{)85}$ 18. $84 \div 6$

19. $90 \div 5$ 20. $9\overline{)97}$ 21. $87 \div 7$

Solve. (pages 402–403)

22. The 91 members of Kelly's youth group want to plant trees in their neighborhood. If it takes 4 members to plant 1 tree, what is the greatest number of trees they can plant at one time?

23. James earned $364 selling used books. If he wants to give the same amount to 3 different groups, about how much will he give to each group?

24. All 53 members of the Historical Society are driving to the town hall celebration. Each car holds 5 people. How many cars do they need?

 Journal

25. **Analyze:** The quotient in a division problem is 11 and the remainder is 2. If the divisor is 4, what is the dividend? Explain how you got your answer.

Additional activities at
www.mhschool.com/math

Use Place Value Models to Divide

Melissa baked 92 muffins. She plans to place an equal number of them in each of 5 boxes. How many muffins will be in each box?

You can build a model using place-value or base-ten models that shows how Melissa divides the bran muffins.

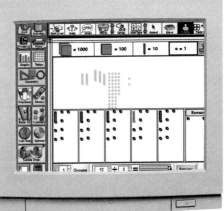

- Choose division as the type of mat.
- Stamp out the number of muffins.
- Group them into 5 equal groups.
- Regroup the models if necessary.

The number boxes keep count as you stamp and group.

How many muffins will be in each box? Are any muffins left over?

Use the computer to model each division. Then write the quotient.

1. $80 \div 5$ 2. $72 \div 3$ 3. $86 \div 7$ 4. $95 \div 4$

Solve.

5. Mona needs to buy 96 party hats for a party. The party hats come in packages of 12. How many packages does she need to buy?

6. There are 44 students on a bus. Each seat on the bus holds 3 students. How many seats on the bus can be filled completely? How many students will be in an unfilled seat?

7. **Analyze:** How does modeling the problem help you divide?

For more practice, use Math Traveler™.

Objective: Estimate quotients using compatible numbers.

Estimate Quotients

Learn

Math Word

compatible numbers

Numbers that are close to the original numbers in a problem and easy to divide mentally.

Tony makes birdhouses to raise money for his youth group. His goal this year is to raise $175. About how many birdhouses does he need to sell?

There's more than one way!

You can use **compatible numbers** to estimate 175 ÷ 4.
What number close to 175 is easy to divide by 4 mentally?

Method A

Think: 16 ÷ 4 = 4

160 is close to 175
160 ÷ 4 = 40

Method B

Think: 20 ÷ 4 = 5

200 is close to 175
200 ÷ 4 = 50

Tony needs to sell about 40 birdhouses.

More Examples

A

Think: 40 and 60 are close to 57.

57 ÷ 2
40 ÷ 2 = 20
60 ÷ 2 = 30

B

Think: 450 and 500 are close to 495.

495 ÷ 5
450 ÷ 5 = 90
500 ÷ 5 = 100

Try It — Estimate. Use compatible numbers.

1. 4)‾337   2. 8)‾85   3. 3)‾165   4. 682 ÷ 9   5. 234 ÷ 8

Sum it Up Which estimate should Tony use to make sure he has enough money for the youth group? Explain.

Practice **Estimate. Use compatible numbers.**

6. $3\overline{)260}$ 7. $4\overline{)115}$ 8. $5\overline{)127}$ 9. $7\overline{)502}$ 10. $9\overline{)5{,}183}$

11. $533 \div 7$ 12. $170 \div 9$ 13. $400 \div 6$ 14. $329 \div 8$ 15. $220 \div 6$

16. $527 \div 5$ ★17. $5{,}627 \div 8$ ★18. $8{,}742 \div 9$ ★19. $1{,}300 \div 2$

Algebra & functions **Compare. Write > or <.**

20. $126 \div 4$ ● 30   21. $490 \div 7$ ● 60   22. $510 \div 8$ ● 60   23. $400 \div 8$ ● 60

★24. $(27 \times 2) \div 9$ ● 5   ★25. $(128 - 4) \div 4$ ● 31

★26. $(100 - 51) \div 7$ ● 50   ★27. $(300 - 20) \div 7$ ● 60

Problem Solving

28. Mary Sue earned \$210 selling birdhouses. She wants to give the same amount of money to 4 different groups. About how much will she give each group?

29. **Analyze:** Why is there more than one good estimate for $328 \div 9$?

30. **Spatial Reasoning:** How many different triangles are in this design?

31. Kite string costs \$4 for each spool. Edwina has \$30. Can she buy 7 spools of string? Why or why not?

32. **Create a problem** using compatible numbers to estimate $500 \div 7$. Solve it. Ask others to solve it.

Spiral Review and Test Prep

33. $8{,}910 - 5{,}289$ 34. 5×623 35. $4{,}753 + 609$ 36. 573×3

Choose the correct answer.

37. Which square number is missing?
    1, 4, 9, ■, 25, 36, 49, 38
    A. 10   C. 12
    B. 16   D. 20

38. Which number is 9 thousands 3 hundreds 6 ones in standard form?
    F. 9,360   H. 9,036
    G. 936   J. Not Here

10·7

Divide 3-Digit Numbers by 1-Digit Numbers

Learn

Math Words

unit price a price given as the cost for a single unit

per for each

Alina prepares 557 cans to deliver to people in need. Alina packs 4 cans in each carton. How many cartons does she fill?

Example 1

You can divide to solve the problem. Find: 557 ÷ 4

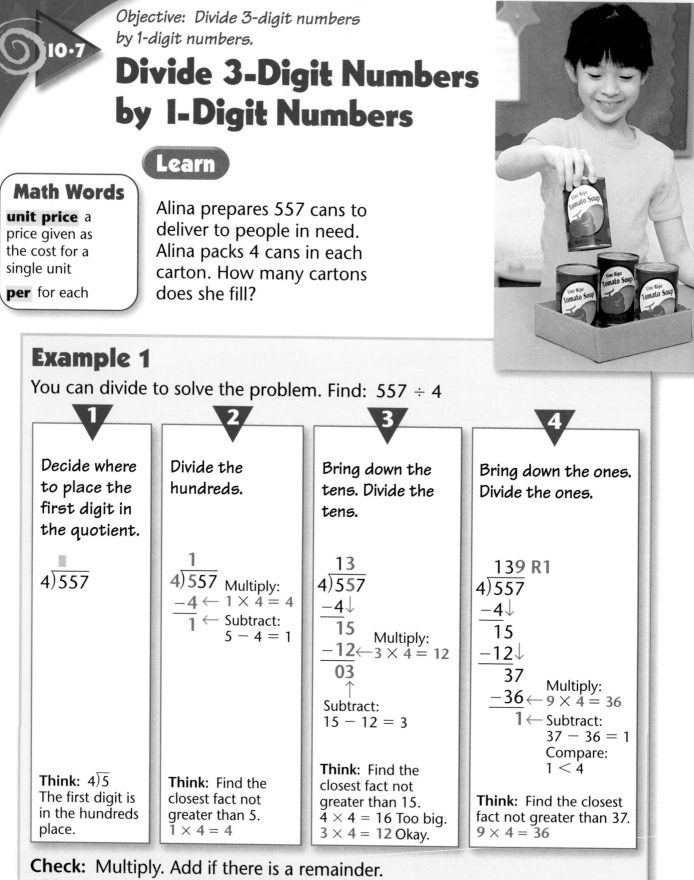

1

Decide where to place the first digit in the quotient.

$4\overline{)557}$

Think: $4\overline{)5}$
The first digit is in the hundreds place.

2

Divide the hundreds.

$$\begin{array}{r} 1 \\ 4\overline{)557} \\ -4 \\ \hline 1 \end{array}$$ Multiply:
← 1 × 4 = 4
← Subtract:
5 − 4 = 1

Think: Find the closest fact not greater than 5.
1 × 4 = 4

3

Bring down the tens. Divide the tens.

$$\begin{array}{r} 13 \\ 4\overline{)557} \\ -4\downarrow \\ \hline 15 \\ -12 \\ \hline 03 \end{array}$$ Multiply:
← 3 × 4 = 12
↑
Subtract:
15 − 12 = 3

Think: Find the closest fact not greater than 15.
4 × 4 = 16 Too big.
3 × 4 = 12 Okay.

4

Bring down the ones. Divide the ones.

$$\begin{array}{r} 139\ \text{R1} \\ 4\overline{)557} \\ -4\downarrow \\ \hline 15 \\ -12\downarrow \\ \hline 37 \\ -36 \\ \hline 1 \end{array}$$ Multiply:
← 9 × 4 = 36
← Subtract:
37 − 36 = 1
Compare:
1 < 4

Think: Find the closest fact not greater than 37.
9 × 4 = 36

Check: Multiply. Add if there is a remainder.
139 × 4 = 556; 556 + 1 = 557

She fills 139 cartons. There is one soup can left.

Alina buys some canned vegetables on sale,
3 for $6.99. What is the unit price?

Example 2

To find the unit price of each can of vegetables, you can
divide $6.99 by 3.

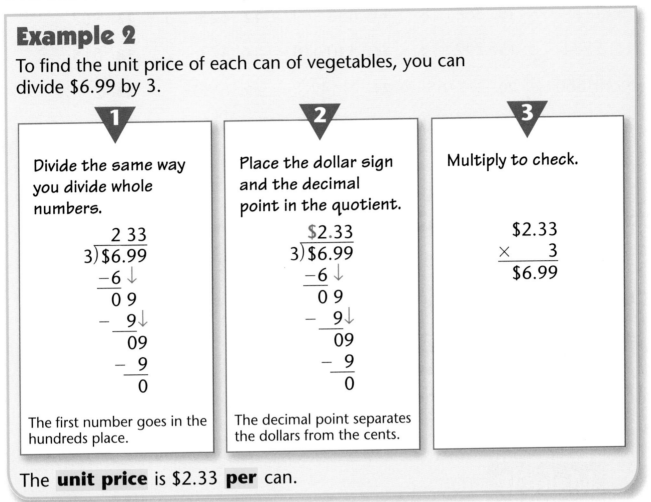

1

Divide the same way you divide whole numbers.

```
    2 33
3)$6.99
   −6 ↓
    0 9
  −  9↓
     09
   −  9
      0
```

The first number goes in the hundreds place.

2

Place the dollar sign and the decimal point in the quotient.

```
   $2.33
3)$6.99
   −6 ↓
    0 9
  −  9↓
     09
   −  9
      0
```

The decimal point separates the dollars from the cents.

3

Multiply to check.

```
   $2.33
 ×     3
  $6.99
```

The **unit price** is $2.33 **per** can.

Try It **Copy and complete.**

1.
```
   ▮58
3)474
  −3
  17
 −15
  24
 −▮▮
   ▮
```

2.
```
  1▮1 R▮
5)557
  −5
  0▮
 − 5
  07
 − 5
   ▮
```

3.
```
  ▮▮
4)372
 −36
  ▮▮
 −12
   0
```

4.
```
  ▮8 R1
6)409
 −▮▮
  4▮
 −▮▮
   1
```

Divide. Check your answer.

5. 652 ÷ 4

6. 284 ÷ 3

7. 5)740

8. 7)400

 How do you know where to place the first number in the quotient?

Divide. Check your answer.

9. $116 \div 2$ 10. $368 \div 8$ 11. $888 \div 9$ 12. $625 \div 5$ 13. $362 \div 7$

14. $\$984 \div 4$ 15. $792 \div 5$ 16. $440 \div 8$ 17. $473 \div 2$ 18. $518 \div 3$

19. $5\overline{)680}$ 20. $3\overline{)\$765}$ 21. $4\overline{)447}$ 22. $6\overline{)868}$ 23. $2\overline{)939}$

24. $6\overline{)479}$ 25. $7\overline{)288}$ 26. $3\overline{)649}$ 27. $9\overline{)555}$ 28. $8\overline{)904}$

29. $4\overline{)127}$ 30. $3\overline{)298}$ 31. $2\overline{)1,244}$ 32. $4\overline{)4,568}$ 33. $5\overline{)2,749}$

Algebra & functions **Write the number that makes each sentence true.**

34. $480 \div 5 = n$ 35. $600 \div 8 = q$ 36. $p \div 4 = 218$ 37. $649 \div r = 81$ R1

Copy and complete the chart.

38.

Items	Total Price	Unit Price
4 pounds grapes	$5.12	
9 markers	$8.28	
8 ounces juice	$2.24	

39.

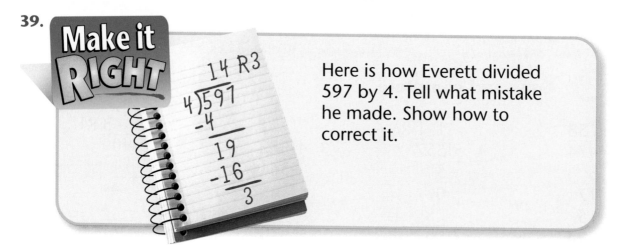

Here is how Everett divided 597 by 4. Tell what mistake he made. Show how to correct it.

Problem Solving

40. Mr. Garcia's family took Owen out to dinner. The bill was $57.31 and with the tip totaled $69.74. If three people divide the total cost evenly, about how much do they each pay?

41. **Collect Data:** Use ads and store flyers to make a chart of items that are sold in groups and their prices. Complete your chart by finding the unit cost of each kind of item.

Use data from *Did You Know?* for problems 42–43.

42. How many free meals were provided altogether in South Carolina?

43. How many people other than children received food from food pantries?

44. **Explain** how you can tell that the quotient of 321 ÷ 7 is a 2-digit number without dividing.

45. **Health:** Alina's brother gave blood at the Blood Drive. He was told he had to wait 56 days before he could give blood again. How many weeks does he have to wait? How many times a year can he give blood?

★46. A neighborhood food pantry has 115 boxes of cereal to give to 9 families. If each family is to get the same number of boxes, with no boxes left over, how many more boxes of cereal are needed?

47. Suppose you have 96 carrot seeds to plant in 8 rows. If each row has the same number of seeds, how many holes do you make in each row?

48. **Science:** The oldest living tree is a bristlecone pine tree named Methuselah. It is 4,765 years old. How much older is Methuselah than you? your parents? your grandparents?

> **Did You KNOW?**
>
> The Golden Harvest Food Bank agencies provided free meals for 316,227 children and 36,522 seniors in South Carolina in 1998. In Georgia and South Carolina, 145,139 people, 57,160 of which were children, received free food from pantries supplied by Golden Harvest.

Spiral Review and Test Prep

49. $6\overline{)79}$

50. $\begin{array}{r} \$2.27 \\ 5.95 \\ + \ 3.09 \\ \hline \end{array}$

51. $\begin{array}{r} \$45.22 \\ - \ \ 4.39 \\ \hline \end{array}$

52. 70×8

Choose the correct answer.

53. Which are compatible numbers for estimating 292 ÷ 4?
    - **A.** 300 ÷ 4
    - **B.** 280 ÷ 4
    - **C.** 290 ÷ 4
    - **D.** 210 ÷ 4

54. The quotient for 487 ÷ 7 is closest to
    - **F.** 6
    - **G.** 7
    - **H.** 60
    - **J.** 70

10·8 Problem Solving: Strategy
Choose a Strategy

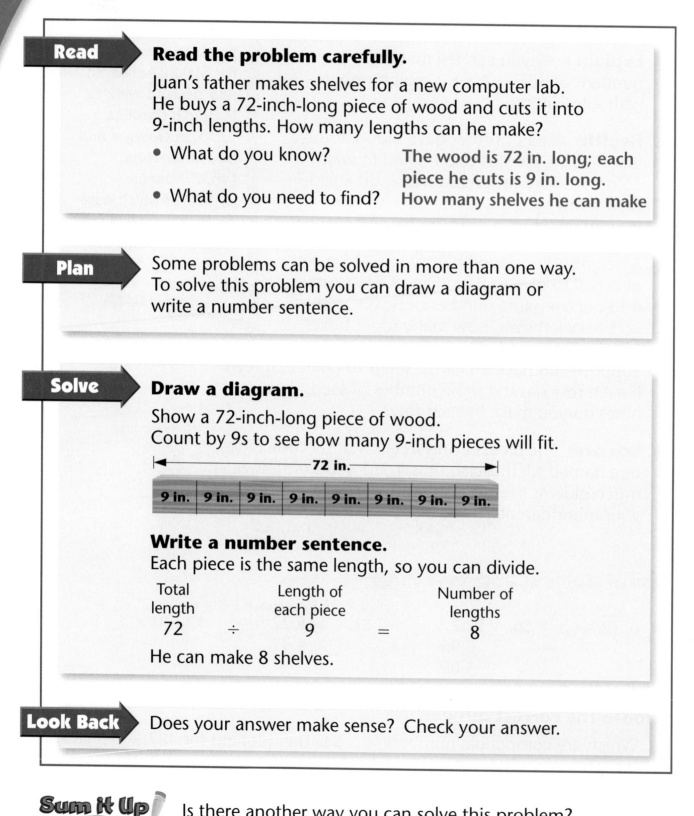

Read → **Read the problem carefully.**

Juan's father makes shelves for a new computer lab. He buys a 72-inch-long piece of wood and cuts it into 9-inch lengths. How many lengths can he make?

- What do you know?   The wood is 72 in. long; each piece he cuts is 9 in. long.

- What do you need to find?   How many shelves he can make

Plan → Some problems can be solved in more than one way. To solve this problem you can draw a diagram or write a number sentence.

Solve → **Draw a diagram.**

Show a 72-inch-long piece of wood.
Count by 9s to see how many 9-inch pieces will fit.

|←————————————— 72 in. —————————————→|

| 9 in. | 9 in. | 9 in. | 9 in. | 9 in. | 9 in. | 9 in. | 9 in. |

Write a number sentence.
Each piece is the same length, so you can divide.

Total length		Length of each piece		Number of lengths
72	÷	9	=	8

He can make 8 shelves.

Look Back → Does your answer make sense? Check your answer.

Sum it Up Is there another way you can solve this problem?

Solve. Tell which strategy you choose.

1. If Juan cuts a 144-inch-long piece of wood into 8-inch pieces, how many pieces will he have?

2. The round tables in the library will seat 8 children or 6 adults. How many children can sit at 8 tables? how many adults?

3. One part of the library will have 36 bookcases in 2 equal-sized sections. How many rows of 3 bookcases are in each section?

4. **Measurement:** Juan makes a square picture frame for his art project. Each side is 15-inches long. How many inches around is the picture frame?

Mixed Strategy Review

5. Mia has 3 times as many nickels as dimes. Altogether she has $1.75. How many nickels and dimes does she have?

6. **What if** Mia has 25 nickels in her collection of nickels and dimes that totals $1.75? How many more nickels than dimes does she have?

7. **Social Studies:** The Washington Monument in Washington, D.C., opened to the public 4 years after the construction was completed. If it took 36 years to build the monument, when did the construction begin?

8. **Language Arts:** Shaun has to write a 150-word composition about his community for homework. How can he estimate the number of words he has written without counting each word?

9. **Create a problem** that can be solved by drawing a diagram or writing a number sentence. Solve it. Ask others to solve it.

★10. **Art:** Keesha wants to put flower stickers around a picture frame that is 3 inches wide and 6 inches long. How many stickers does she need?

CHOOSE A STRATEGY
- Find a Pattern
- Work-Backwards
- Use Logical Reasoning
- Write a Number Sentence
- Make a Table or List
- Guess and Check
- Make a Graph
- Solve Simpler Problem

The Washington Monument opened in 1888.

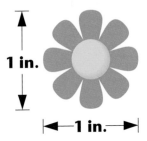

1 in.

1 in.

Problem Solving

10·9 Quotients with Zeros

Math in ACTION

Learn

The students are rehearsing together for a production of Swan Lake. If there were 429 dancers in the production, and they were divided into 4 lines for rehearsal, how many were in each line?

Students at Pontecorvo Ballet Studio in Dayton, Ohio

Example

Find $4\overline{)429}$ to solve the problem.

1

Decide where to place the first digit in the quotient.

$$4\overline{)429}$$

Think: $4\overline{)4}$ The first digit is in the hundreds place.

2

Divide the hundreds.

$$\begin{array}{r} 1 \\ 4\overline{)429} \\ -4 \\ \hline 0 \end{array}$$
← $1 \times 4 = 4$ Multiply:
← Subtract: $4 - 4 = 0$
Compare: $0 < 4$

Think: Find the closest fact not greater than 4.
$1 \times 4 = 4$

3

Bring down the tens. Divide the tens.

$$\begin{array}{r} 10 \\ 4\overline{)429} \\ -4\downarrow \\ \hline 02 \\ -0 \\ \hline 2 \end{array}$$
Compare: $2 < 4$

Think: There are not enough tens. Write 0 in the quotient.

4

Bring down the ones. Divide the ones.

$$\begin{array}{r} 107 \text{ R1} \\ 4\overline{)429} \\ -4 \\ \hline 2 \\ -0 \\ \hline 29 \\ -28 \\ \hline 1 \end{array}$$
Multiply: $4 \times 7 = 28$
Subtract: $29 - 28 = 1$
Compare: $1 < 4$

Think: Find the closest fact not greater than 29.
$4 \times 7 = 28$

Check: $4 \times 107 = 428$; $428 + 1 = 429$
Each line had 107 dancers. There was 1 dancer left.

Try It Divide. Check your answer.

1. $7\overline{)752}$ **2.** $9\overline{)\$9.09}$ **3.** $437 \div 4$

Sum it Up Where is the zero in the quotient when you divide 552 by 5?

Divide. Check your answer.

4. $6\overline{)65}$ **5.** $9\overline{)724}$ **6.** $2\overline{)803}$ **7.** $6\overline{)668}$ **8.** $3\overline{)927}$

9. $5\overline{)\$5.95}$ **10.** $4\overline{)808}$ **11.** $2\overline{)\$7.00}$ **12.** $8\overline{)187}$ **13.** $3\overline{)912}$

14. $864 \div 8$ **15.** $\$2.10 \div 7$ **16.** $531 \div 5$ **17.** $91 \div 3$ **18.** $442 \div 4$

★ **19.** $3,200 \div 4$ ★ **20.** $7,700 \div 7$ ★ **21.** $2,500 \div 5$

Algebra & functions **Find each missing operation.**

22. $27 \bullet 9 = 18$ **23.** $15 \bullet 3 = 45$ **24.** $56 \bullet 8 = 7$ **25.** $36 \bullet 6 = 30$

★ **26.** $(4 \bullet 4) \div 8 = 1$ ★ **27.** $(21 \bullet 3) \div 6 = 3$ ★ **28.** $(17 \bullet 3) \times 5 = 100$

Problem Solving

29. Create a problem whose quotient has 2 digits with a zero in the ones place. Solve it. Ask others to solve it.

 30. Generalize: When do you get a zero in the tens place of a quotient? the ones place? Give examples.

Use data from the flyer for problems 31–33.

31. If you buy 3 tickets, how much does each cost? How much do you save altogether?

32. There are 7 people in Mary's family. How much do they pay for tickets?

33. Number Sense: If 300 tickets are sold for the dance, what is the greatest amount of money raised for charity? What is the least amount?

CHARITY DANCE

Date: March 10
Time: 1:30 P.M.
Place: School

TICKETS
$6 each or 3 for $15

Spiral Review and Test Prep

34. $6\overline{)81}$ **35.** 62×7 **36.** $\$21.30 + \$11.70$ **37.** $4\overline{)444}$

Choose the correct answer.

38. Which means the same as $81 \div 9$?

   A. $9 \div 81$ **C.** $9\overline{)81}$
   B. $81\overline{)9}$ **D.** 9×81

39. Which is 2 hours earlier than 1:30 P.M.?

   F. 11:00 A.M.   **H.** 11:30 A.M.
   G. 3:30 P.M.   **J.** 11:30 P.M.

Problem Solving: Application
Decision Making

You Decide!

Which items should they buy at the store?

"How would you like to go on a picnic?" said Mr. Stokes to his extended family. "Yes!" shouted the family. "Great," said Mr. Stokes. "There will be 25 of us. Let's find the best way to buy the things we need."

Grocery List

dinner plates
napkins
paper cups
lemonade
ground beef
hamburger buns
watermelon

GROCERYLAND
Savings Galore!

Let's Party brand Dinner Plates
8 plates $1.39

Party Planner brand Cups
20 cups $1.79

Napkins Kids R Fun brand
25 napkins Sale!
4 for $4

Splash brand Dinner Plates
50 plates
Sale! 2 for $5

Specials

EVERFRESH
Hamburger Buns
Count 8 buns   Price $1.49

Enjoy! brand
200 napkins
$5.75

Celebrate! brand
50 cups
$2.29

Specials

GROCERIES
GROUND BEEF
Net Weight 3 lb   Price $3.87

DOUGHY BRAND
Hamburger Buns
Count 6 buns   Price $1.29

PRODUCE
CUT WATERMELON
Price 39¢ per pound

GROCERIES
GROUND BEEF
Net Weight 2 lb   Price $4.58

TART TWIST
LEMONADE MIX
Makes 2 gallons
Price $3.29

PRODUCE
WHOLE WATERMELON
Price 18¢ per pound

PARTY ADE
LEMONADE MIX
Makes 1 quart
4 for $1.49

Read for Understanding

1. What size packages of ground beef can they buy?

2. What is the cost of 8 hamburger buns?

3. What items are on sale?

4. How many brands of dinner plates can they choose?

5. What is the greatest number of paper cups in a package?

6. Which costs more, a pound of cut watermelon or a whole watermelon weighing one pound?

7. How much does a package of each brand of lemonade cost?

8. What is the least number of plates in a package?

Make Decisions

9. Suppose each person will use 3 dinner plates. How many dinner plates will they need?

10. How much would they spend on plates if they buy Let's Party! brand plates? Splash brand?

11. Which brand of cups is a better buy? Why?

12. Would buying Kids R Fun brand napkins on sale be the better buy? Explain why or why not.

13. What are some advantages and disadvantages of buying more napkins than they need?

14. What is the cost of a pound of ground beef if they buy a 2-pound package? a 3-pound package?

15. A pound of ground beef makes 4 hamburgers. Suppose each adult will eat 2 hamburgers and each child will eat 1 hamburger. There are 11 adults and 14 children at the picnic. How many pounds of beef do they need?

16. How many packages of each brand of hamburger buns should they buy? at what cost?

17. Does buying the largest size always save the most money? Give an example.

18. What else should they think about besides the cost of the items?

Which items do you suggest they buy? Explain.

Your Decision!

Objective: Apply dividing by 1-digit numbers to investigate science concepts.

Problem Solving: Math and Science
Which paper plane flies farthest?

Airplanes often look different. Some are small and pointed, while others are large and rounded.

A plane's shape will affect how fast or far it can fly. In this activity, you will compare the flights of three paper planes to see which one can fly the farthest.

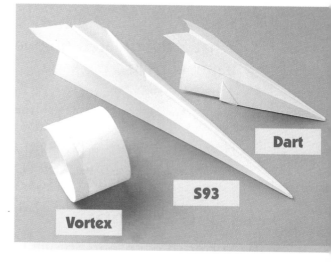

Dart

S93

Vortex

You Will Need
- **paper plane instruction sheets**
- **scissors**
- **tape**
- **meterstick or tape measure**

Safety

Be careful when working with scissors.

Hypothesize

Look at the picture of the three paper planes. Which plane do you think will fly the farthest?

Procedure

1. Work in a group. Build the three paper plane models.

2. Go to a long hallway or gym. Practice throwing the planes until you master each one.

3. Throw the S93. Measure how far it traveled.

4. Throw the Dart. Measure how far it traveled.

5. Throw the Vortex. Measure how far it traveled.

6. Round all measurements to the nearest centimeter.

418 Cluster B

Copy and complete the chart to record the distance that each plane traveled.

Plane	Distance
S93	
Dart	
Vortex	

Conclude and Apply

- Which paper plane flew the farthest? How do you know? Was your hypothesis correct?

- Divide to find how many times farther the first-place plane traveled than the second- and third-place planes. Round your answers to the nearest whole number.

- *Journal* If you could build only one plane model, which would you choose? Think about the length of the flight, the overall look of the plane, how flat or straight the flight was, and the purpose of the plane. Justify your choice.

- Use the idea of lift to explain why the S93 is able to fly.

Going Further

1. Design your own paper plane. How does its flight distance compare to that of the other planes?

2. Work with your classmates to make a giant S93 and the original one. How does size affect the flight and distance? Make your measurements in meters instead of feet.

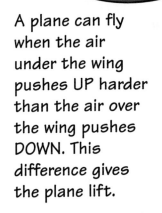

Did You KNOW?

A plane can fly when the air under the wing pushes UP harder than the air over the wing pushes DOWN. This difference gives the plane lift.

Problem Solving

Check Your Progress B

Divide. Check your answer. (pages 408–415)

1. 8)376
2. 3)$705
3. 4)419
4. 5)54

5. $7.76 ÷ 2
6. 868 ÷ 6
7. 808 ÷ 9
8. $6.25 ÷ 5

9. 967 ÷ 3
10. $574 ÷ 7
11. $5.34 ÷ 6
12. 307 ÷ 3

13. 6)$0.24
14. 9)427
15. 5)800
16. 4)668

Estimate. Use compatible numbers. (pages 406–407)

17. 8)503
18. 7)418
19. 500 ÷ 6

20. 189 ÷ 7
21. 83 ÷ 9
22. 375 ÷ 5

Solve. (pages 406–415)

23. The Food Pantry has 144 cans of soup to put into 3 cases. Each case can hold 2 layers of cans. How many cans will go in each layer?

24. Large plants are priced at 3 for $8.97. Small plants cost 3 for $3.99. If Lee buys one large and one small plant, how much does she spend?

Journal 25. Explain how you can use unit cost to compare items to find the better value.

Additional activities at
www.mhschool.com/math

Extra Practice

Division Patterns (pages 396–397)

Complete each pattern.

1. $32 \div 8 = n$
   $320 \div 8 = k$

2. $27 \div 9 = t$
   $270 \div 9 = r$

3. $60 \div 6 = g$
   $600 \div 6 = m$

4. $x \div 5 = 11$
   $y \div 5 = 110$

Solve.

5. Chen sold 250 bran muffins at the bake sale. If there were 5 bran muffins in a pack, how many packs were sold?

Divide 2-Digit Numbers by 1-Digit Numbers (pages 400–401)

Divide. Check your answer.

1. $3\overline{)38}$

2. $6\overline{)78}$

3. $69 \div 5$

4. $44 \div 7$

Divide. Use mental math.

5. $280 \div 4$

6. $420 \div 7$

7. $350 \div 5$

8. $300 \div 3$

Solve.

9. Suppose you plant 96 sunflower seeds into 8 equal rows. How many seeds do you plant in each row?

Problem Solving: Reading for Math
Interpret the Remainder (pages 402–403)

Solve. Interpret any remainder.

1. A group of 29 clean-up volunteers are separated into crews of 5. How many complete crews are there?

2. A committee has $26 to buy signs. Each sign costs $4. How many signs can be purchased?

3. There are 37 students going to a musical. Each car takes 4 students. How many cars are needed?

4. Lenny buys plants for $4 each. He has $25 to spend. How many plants can Lenny buy?

Extra Practice

Estimate Quotients (pages 406–407)

Estimate. Use compatible numbers.

1. $2\overline{)59}$ 2. $7\overline{)187}$ 3. $9\overline{)639}$ 4. $5\overline{)295}$

5. $3\overline{)124}$ 6. $5\overline{)153}$ 7. $4\overline{)358}$ 8. $6\overline{)421}$

Solve.

9. Skye wants to raise $175 for her youth group by selling pencil boxes. If she sells each box for $6, about how many boxes does she need to sell?

10. So far the youth group has raised $492 selling the pencil boxes for $6. About how many boxes have been sold?

11. Marisa wants to raise $165 for her youth group by selling granola bars. If she sells each box of granola bars for $4, about how many boxes does she need to sell?

Divide 3-Digit Numbers by 1-Digit Numbers (pages 408–411)

Divide. Check your answer.

1. $8\overline{)138}$ 2. $7\overline{)871}$ 3. $3\overline{)\$6.93}$ 4. $5\overline{)582}$

5. $352 \div 6$ 6. $\$9.72 \div 3$ 7. $489 \div 4$ 8. $135 \div 2$

9. $745 \div 9$ 10. $202 \div 8$ 11. $\$6.15 \div 5$ 12. $123 \div 3$

Solve.

13. A shelter can fit 8 beds in a row. They have 104 beds. How many rows of beds are there?

14. The Food Pantry packs 6 boxes of pasta into one carton. They have 507 boxes of pasta to pack. How many cartons do they need?

15. Duane brought 3 roses to Mrs. Jackson at the senior center. The sign at the florist said 6 roses for $12.25. About how much did each rose cost?

Extra Practice

Problem Solving: Strategy
Choose a Strategy (pages 412–413)

Solve.

1. A carpenter is making 4-foot shelves for the library. She has 3 boards. Each board is 10 feet long. How many shelves can she make?

2. A carpenter has 3 pieces of board. Each is 2 feet long. Can she make a shelf that is 4 feet long?

3. The children's librarian has 75 books about birds, 671 books about mammals, 128 books about fish, and 209 books about other animals. How many books are there in all?

Solve. Explain your answer.

4. The music store has 473 rock CDs, 452 classical CDs, and 475 rap CDs. For which type of music does the store have the most CDs?

5. Harry wants to pack 5 soup cans in each box. There are 108 soup cans. How many boxes does he need?

Quotients with Zeros (pages 414–415)

Divide. Check your answer.

1. $2\overline{)407}$ 2. $5\overline{)510}$ 3. $4\overline{)83}$ 4. $6\overline{)542}$

5. $314 \div 3$ 6. $831 \div 8$ 7. $721 \div 7$ 8. $975 \div 9$

9. $426 \div 4$ 10. $620 \div 6$ 11. $322 \div 3$ 12. $816 \div 8$

Solve.

13. There are 54 concert posters to put in store windows. Each volunteer can take 5 posters. Are 10 volunteers enough? Why or why not?

14. Last year the dance committee collected $606. All tickets were $3 each. How many tickets did they sell?

Chapter Study Guide

Language and Math

Complete. Use a word from the list.

1. In 40 ÷ 5, 5 is the ____.

2. You divide the total cost by the number of items to find the ____.

3. When you divide compatible numbers there is no ____.

4. Changing numbers to other numbers that form a basic fact to estimate an answer is using ____.

5. When you divide 24 by 4, the ____ is 6.

> **Math Words**
> compatible numbers
> dividend
> divisor
> quotient
> remainder
> unit cost

Skills and Applications

Divide multiples of 10 and 100 mentally. (pages 394–397)

Example
Find: 810 ÷ 9
Solution
Use patterns.
81 ÷ 9 = 9
810 ÷ 9 = 90

Divide. Use mental math.

6. 600 ÷ 3   7. 360 ÷ 6

8. 250 ÷ 5   9. 210 ÷ 7

10. 640 ÷ 8   11. 400 ÷ 4

12. 360 ÷ 9   13. 100 ÷ 2

Divide up to 3-digit numbers by 1-digit numbers. (pages 408–411)

Example
Find: $3\overline{)595}$
Solution
Place first digit. Divide each place.

$$
\begin{array}{r}
198 \text{ R}1 \\
3\overline{)595} \\
-3\downarrow \\
\overline{29} \\
-27\downarrow \\
\overline{25} \\
-24 \\
\overline{1}
\end{array}
$$

Divide. Check your answers.

14. $6\overline{)79}$ 15. $7\overline{)\$3.15}$

16. $6\overline{)\$9.78}$ 17. $9\overline{)\$8.01}$

18. $8\overline{)453}$ 19. $4\overline{)726}$

20. 53 ÷ 7   21. 533 ÷ 5

22. $0.54 ÷ 9   23. $8.64 ÷ 8

24. If 616 cans are packed 8 in a carton, how many cartons are needed?

Estimate quotients. (pages 406–407)

Example

Estimate: 435 ÷ 6

Solution

Use compatible numbers.

435 ÷ 6

↓   ↓   435 is about 420.

420 ÷ 6 = 70

435 ÷ 6 is about 70.

Estimate.
Use compatible numbers.

25. 627 ÷ 9   **26.** 281 ÷ 3

27. 345 ÷ 7   **28.** 218 ÷ 5

29. Carla wants to divide $552 equally among 6 charities. About how much should she give to each?

30. There are 247 jelly beans to be shared by 4 people equally. About how many will each person get?

Use strategies to solve problems. (pages 412–413)

Example

A piece of wood 36 inches long is cut into 6-inch pieces. How many pieces will there be?

Solution

Draw a diagram or write a number sentence.

Diagram

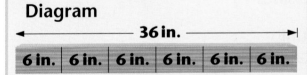

| ← | 36 in. | → |

| 6 in. | 6 in. | 6 in. | 6 in. | 6 in. | 6 in. |

Number sentence

36 ÷ 6 = 6

There will be 6 pieces.

Solve.

31. The Sewing Club sells blankets made of square pieces of cloth. Each blanket has 200 squares with 8 squares in each row. How many rows of squares are there?

32. Another blanket has 6 squares in each row. There are 480 squares made. How many rows are there?

33. Manny and Dee are sewing a blanket using 12 squares in each row. They have 604 squares of cloth to use. How many rows can they make?

Chapter Test

Divide. Use mental math.

1. $80 \div 2$ **2.** $180 \div 9$ **3.** $540 \div 6$ **4.** $440 \div 4$

Divide.

5. $5\overline{)92}$ **6.** $8\overline{)59}$ **7.** $4\overline{)85}$ **8.** $9\overline{)\$198}$

9. $5\overline{)\$0.55}$ **10.** $6\overline{)493}$ **11.** $8\overline{)604}$ **12.** $3\overline{)902}$

13. $79 \div 7$ **14.** $678 \div 3$ **15.** $\$7.56 \div 2$ **16.** $429 \div 4$

Estimate. Use compatible numbers.

17. $5\overline{)392}$ **18.** $6\overline{)588}$ **19.** $7\overline{)475}$ **20.** $3\overline{)319}$

Solve.

21. A 6-pack of juice costs $2.39. About how much are you paying for each can?

22. How many 6-packs of juice do you need for 125 people?

23. Suppose you buy eight 6-packs of juice for $2.16 each. How much are you paying for each can?

24. A table is 6 feet long and 4 feet wide. Each person seated needs 2 feet of space along a side of the table. How many people can be seated on the sides?

25. There are 60 people invited to a community celebration. If 8 people can sit at each table, how many tables will be needed?

Performance Assessment

Volunteers from your town are making baskets. They will give them to places like the Senior Citizens Home.

The baskets are packed in boxes of 4, 5, 7, or 9.

Make a chart like the one below to help you:

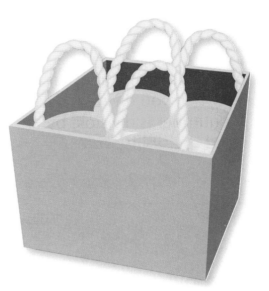

- find how many boxes you will need.

- decide which kind of box to use.

Copy and complete the chart to record your observations.

Number of Baskets	Number in Box	Number of Boxes Needed
254		
175		
196		
218		

A Good Answer

- shows a completed chart.
- shows that you tried different sized boxes to find the best one to use.
- shows the steps you used to divide.

 You may want to save this work in your portfolio.

Enrichment

Divisibility Rules for 2, 5, and 10

One number is **divisible** by another number if there is no remainder when you divide. There are rules to help you know if a number is divisible by another number. These are called **divisibility rules**.

A number is divisible by 2 if the ones digit is 0, 2, 4, 6, or 8.

Divisible by 2:	Not divisible by 2:
34　　80　　118　574　546	21　　57　　93　　189　777
The ones digit is 0, 2, 4, 6 or 8.	The ones digit is **not** 0, 2, 4, 6, or 8.

A number is divisible by 5 if the ones digit is 0 or 5.

Divisible by 5:	Not divisible by 5:
55 15　　110　405　900	23　　59　　276　847 1,362
The ones digit is 0 or 5.	The ones digit is **not** 0 or 5.

A number is divisible by 10 if the ones digit is 0.

Divisible by 10:	Not divisible by 10:
40　　90　550　200　620	65　　99　　111　208　714
The ones digit is 0.	The ones digit is **not** 0.

List if each number is divisible by 2, 5, or 10.

1. 75　　　　2. 125　　　　3. 100　　　　4. 42　　　　5. 83

6. 112　　　7. 86　　　　8. 807　　　　9. 6,330　　　10. 7,154

11. 31,790　12. 76,538　13. 1,000,000　14. 1,543,265　15. 2,500,003

16. **Analyze:** What do you notice about numbers that are divisible by both 2 and 5?

Test-Taking Tips

One way you can be a better test taker is to try and use **mental math** to help you find the answer.

Dawn drove 400 miles in 2 days. How many miles did she drive each day?

- **A.** 100 miles
- **C.** 300 miles
- **B.** 200 miles
- **D.** 500 miles

She could not have driven 500 miles. It is more than the 400 total miles she drove.

Using mental math, think:

$$4 \div 2 = 2$$
$$40 \div 2 = 20$$
$$400 \div 2 = 200$$

Check that 200 is one of the choices. It is.

The correct answer is B.

Check for Success

Before turning in a test, go back one last time to check.

- ✓ I understood and answered the questions asked.
- ✓ I checked my work for errors.
- ✓ My answers make sense.

**Choose the correct answer.
Use mental math if possible.**

1. A store has 120 bags of marbles. Each bag has 8 marbles. How many marbles are there altogether?
   - **A.** 96
   - **C.** 800
   - **B.** 480
   - **D.** 960

2. There are 5 bags of marbles, each holding the same amount. Altogether there are 75 marbles. How many marbles are in each bag?
   - **F.** 15
   - **H.** 35
   - **G.** 25
   - **J.** 40

3. Matt has $19.75. He buys 2 items for $5.75 each. How much does he have left?
   - **A.** $8.25
   - **C.** $14.00
   - **B.** $11.20
   - **D.** $15.25

4. You can build 4 toys using a building set with 360 pieces. If each toy has the same number pieces, how many pieces are in each toy?
   - **F.** 8
   - **H.** 80
   - **G.** 9
   - **J.** 90

Test Prep

Spiral Review and Test Prep
Chapters 1–10

Choose the correct answer.

Number Sense

1. What is the value of the underlined digit? 84,<u>8</u>98
- **A.** 8 thousands
- **C.** 8 tens
- **B.** 8 hundreds
- **D.** 8 ones

2. Which shows the numbers ordered from least to greatest?
- **F.** 281, 411, 187
- **H.** 187, 281, 411
- **G.** 411, 281, 187
- **J.** Not Here

3. $381 \div 4 = \blacksquare$
- **A.** 96 R1
- **C.** 95 R1
- **B.** 95 R2
- **D.** 95

4. Which number sentence describes 8 groups of 3?
- **F.** $8 \div 3$
- **H.** $8 \times n = 32$
- **G.** 8×3
- **J.** $8 - 3 - 3$

Measurement and Geometry

5. What two shapes make up this figure?

- **A.** Square, circle
- **C.** Square, pentagon
- **B.** Rectangle, square
- **D.** Square, triangle

6. Joe had a party on July 3. Mickela had a party on July 31. How many weeks between their parties?
- **F.** 4 weeks
- **H.** 2 weeks
- **G.** 3 weeks
- **J.** 1 week

7. The clocks show the times a train leaves Station A and arrives at Station B. How long does it take to go from one station to the other?

Station A   **Station B**

- **A.** $\frac{1}{2}$ hour
- **C.** 50 minutes
- **B.** 45 minutes
- **D.** 1 hour

8. Tanya has 1 foot of ribbon. She uses 8 inches of ribbon to wrap a present. How much ribbon does she have left?
- **F.** 4 inches
- **H.** 2 feet
- **G.** 14 inches
- **J.** Not Here

Algebra and Functions

9. What operation makes this number sentence true?

    96 ● 6 = 16

    A. +   C. ×
    B. −   D. ÷

10. What is the missing number?

    45 + 23 = 23 + ▯

    F. 22   H. 68
    G. 45   J. Not Here

11. Which rule describes this pattern?

    243, 81, 27, 9, 3, 1

    A. Multiply   C. Subtract
       by 3.   162.
    B. Divide by 3. D. Add 162.

12. Which is an example of the Associative Property?

    F. 3 + 4 = 4 + 3
    H. (3 + 4) + 2 = 3 + (4 + 2)
    G. 3 + 0 = 3
    J. 3 × 0 = 0

Statistics, Data Analysis, and Probability

Use data from the bar graph for problems 13–16.

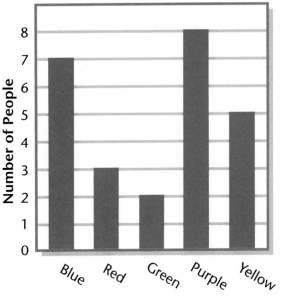

Bar Graph Showing Favorite Colors

13. Which is the most popular color?

    A. Red   C. Blue
    B. Yellow   D. Purple

14. How many people were surveyed?

    F. 20   H. 23
    G. 25   J. 30

15. How many more people like purple than green?

    A. 1   C. 5
    B. 3   D. 6

16. What are the favorite colors, in order from greatest to least? How do you know?

Theme: Sports and Fitness

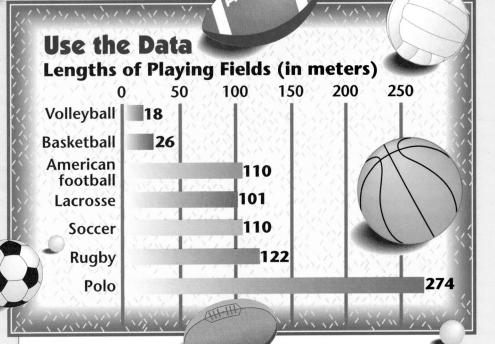

Use the Data
Lengths of Playing Fields (in meters)

Sport	Length
Volleyball	18
Basketball	26
American football	110
Lacrosse	101
Soccer	110
Rugby	122
Polo	274

- How much longer is a soccer field than a basketball court?

- Which is the longest field? How long is it?

What You Will Learn
In this chapter you will learn how to
- estimate and measure length.
- estimate and measure weight, mass, and capacity.
- estimate temperature.
- convert units of measure.
- use strategies to solve problems.

Additional activities at
www.mhschool.com/math

11·1 # Explore Customary Length

Learn

You can use a ruler to explore customary **length**.

Customary Units of Length	
yard (yd)	1 yard = 3 feet
foot (ft)	1 foot = 12 inches
inch (in.)	12 inches = 1 foot

Work Together

▶ Estimate and measure how wide your desk is.

You Will Need
- **12-inch ruler**
- **yardstick or measuring tape**
- **classroom objects**

- First estimate, then measure to the nearest inch using a ruler or yardstick.

- Record your estimate and measurement in a table.

Remember:
Line up one end of the object with the 0 mark on the ruler. Look for the closest inch mark at the other end.

Object	Estimate	Measurement

▶ Choose four other classroom objects. Estimate and record their measurements in a table. List them in order from shortest to longest.

- How do your estimates compare with your measurements?

- How can you make better estimates?

Make Connections

Use the best measuring tool to measure
different objects. All measurements are estimates.

Objects   **Measuring Tools and Units**

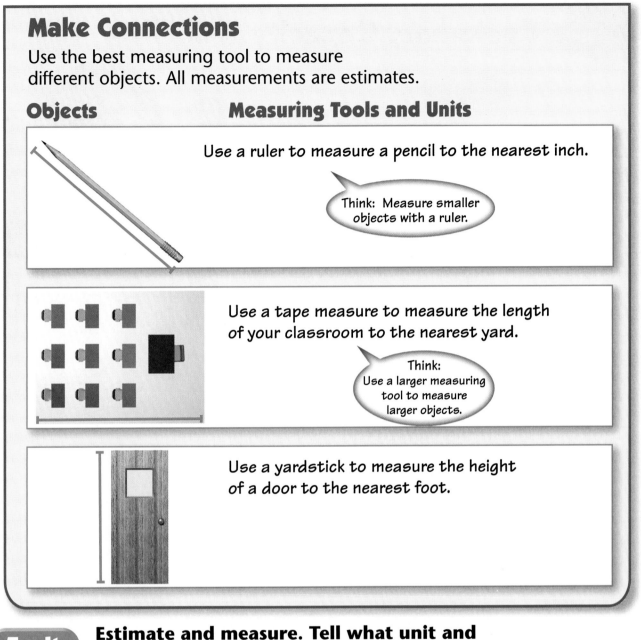

Use a ruler to measure a pencil to the nearest inch.

Think: Measure smaller objects with a ruler.

Use a tape measure to measure the length of your classroom to the nearest yard.

Think: Use a larger measuring tool to measure larger objects.

Use a yardstick to measure the height of a door to the nearest foot.

Try It **Estimate and measure. Tell what unit and tool you use and why.**

1. length of your arm   2. your height   3. width of a door

Sum it Up How do you measure to the nearest inch?

Practice **Choose the best estimate.**

4. A golf club is about 1 ___ long.
   A. inch   **B.** foot   **C.** yard

5. A football is about 6–8 ___ long.
   A. inches   **B.** feet   **C.** yards

6. **Generalize:** Why do you think a ruler rather than a person's foot is used to measure a foot?

11·2 Customary Capacity

Learn

Travis, Jerri, and Leon are at a walk-a-thon. Travis gives water to Jerri and Leon. About how much water does Travis give to the children?

Math Word

capacity
a measure of dry or liquid volume of a container

Customary Units of Capacity	
cup (c)	2 cups = 1 pint
pint (pt)	1 pint = 2 cups
quart (qt)	1 quart = 4 cups
gallon (gal)	1 gallon = 4 quarts

Example

You can estimate the **capacity** to answer this problem.
Use these containers to estimate.

| 1 cup | 1 pint | 1 quart | 1 gallon |

Travis gives about 2 cups or 1 pint of water to the children.

Try It   Choose the best estimate.

1.   A. 1 gal
                            B. 1 qt
                            C. 1 cup

2.    A. 1 gal
                            B. 1 pt
                            C. 1 c

3. 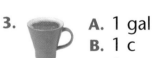   A. 1 gal
                            B. 1 c
                            C. 1 qt

Sum it Up How do you choose which unit to use to measure the capacity of a container?

Choose the best estimate.

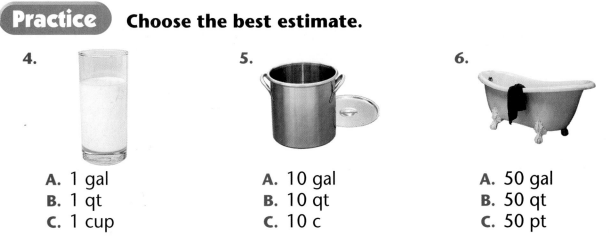

4.

A. 1 gal
B. 1 qt
C. 1 cup

5.

A. 10 gal
B. 10 qt
C. 10 c

6.

A. 50 gal
B. 50 qt
C. 50 pt

★**7.** List the numbers of the items shown in problems 4–6 in order from least to greatest capacity.

Measure the capacity of each object. Write the objects in order from least capacity to greatest.

8. cup   **9.** wastebasket   **10.** flowerpot

Name a container that makes a true sentence.

★**11.** My cup holds more than ____.   ★**12.** My bathtub holds less than ____.

★**13.** My thermos holds less than ____.   ★**14.** My sink holds more than ____.

Problem Solving

15. Jenna fills a thermos with apple juice for her lunch. Does the thermos hold 6 cups or 6 gallons of apple juice?

16. Explain why a quart of air weighs less than a quart of water.

Spiral Review and Test Prep

17. 396 ÷ 9   **18.** 280 × 7   **19.** 7,005 − 1,678   **20.** $5.78 + $9.92

Choose the correct answer.

21. What number is missing from this skip-counting pattern?
72, ▮, 56, 48
A. 60   C. 64
B. 52   D. 44

22. Jasmine practiced batting 70 minutes during the last 5 days. She practices the same number of minutes each day. How many minutes did she practice each day?
F. 75 min   H. 14 min
G. 65 min   J. 12 min

Objective: Estimate, measure, compare, and order weight in customary units.

Customary Weight

Learn

Math Word

weight
a measurement that tells how heavy an object is

Have you ever wondered how heavy something is? How can Crystal estimate and measure the weights of a golf tee and a soccer ball?

Customary Units of Weight	
ounces (oz)	16 ounces = 1 pound
pounds (lb)	1 pound = 16 ounces

Example

You can estimate the **weight** to solve the problem.
Use these objects to help estimate.

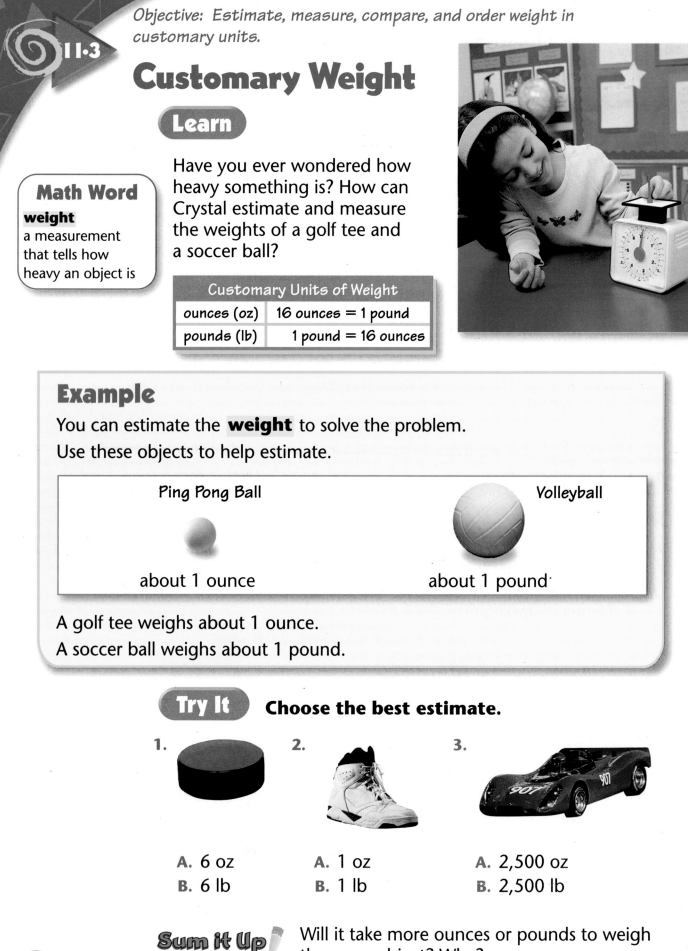

Ping Pong Ball

about 1 ounce

Volleyball

about 1 pound

A golf tee weighs about 1 ounce.
A soccer ball weighs about 1 pound.

Try It **Choose the best estimate.**

1.
A. 6 oz
B. 6 lb

2.
A. 1 oz
B. 1 lb

3.
A. 2,500 oz
B. 2,500 lb

Sum it Up Will it take more ounces or pounds to weigh the same object? Why?

Choose the better estimate.

4.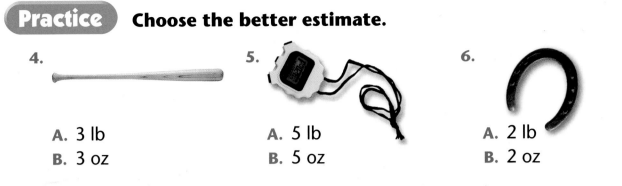

A. 3 lb
B. 3 oz

5.

A. 5 lb
B. 5 oz

6.

A. 2 lb
B. 2 oz

Measure the weight of each object. Write the objects in order from lightest to heaviest.

7. masking tape, chair, shoe

8. stapler, math book, pencil

Algebra & functions   Compare. Write >, <, or =.

9. 5 oz ● 1 lb

10. 24 oz ● 1 lb

11. 16 oz ● 1 lb

Problem Solving

Use data from *Did You Know?* for problem 12.

12. A sporting goods store has four autographed baseballs in a display case. Do the baseballs weigh more than or less than 1 pound altogether? How can you tell?

13. **Analyze:** Marcy can hold her bowling ball in her arms, but the ball will not stay on a scale. How can Marcy weigh the ball?

Did You KNOW?

A baseball weighs about 5 ounces.

Spiral Review and Test Prep

14. $4.12 ÷ 4

15. 300 − 67

16. 6 × 4,000

17. 46 + 782 + 540

Choose the correct answer.

18. A sports arena holds 19,643 people. What is this number rounded to the nearest thousand?

A. 21,000   C. 19,600
B. 20,000   D. 19,000

19. There are 250 fans at a game. They fill 5 rows in the bleachers. There are the same number of fans on each bleacher. How many fans on each bleacher?

F. 50   H. 10
G. 25   J. Not Here

11·4 Convert Customary Units

Learn

Pitcher's Plate

24 inches wide
6 inches long

Mrs. Grace measures game areas for the school's field day. She carefully measures the pitcher's plate. How many feet wide is it?

Example 1

You can divide when converting smaller units to larger units.

Change 24 inches into feet.

24 inches = ▊ feet

24 ÷ 12 = 2

24 inches = 2 feet

> **Think:**
> 1 foot = 12 inches
> Since feet are larger than inches, you need to divide to get a lesser number.

The plate is 2 feet wide.

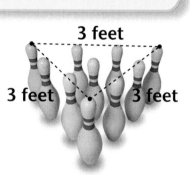

3 feet

3 feet   3 feet

The pins in bowling are set in the shape of a triangle. How many inches long is each side of the triangle?

Example 2

You can multiply when converting, or changing, larger units to smaller units

Change 3 feet into inches.

3 feet = ▊ inches

3 × 12 = 36

3 feet = 36 inches

> **Think:**
> 12 inches = 1 foot
> Since inches are smaller than feet, you need to multiply to get a greater number.

Each side of the triangle is 36 inches.

The coach brings 12 quarts of sports drink for the
players to drink. How many gallons of sports drink
does the coach bring?

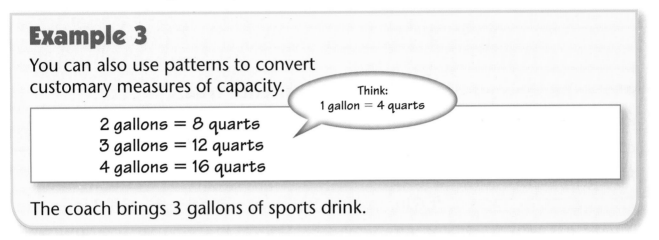

Example 3

You can also use patterns to convert
customary measures of capacity.

Think:
1 gallon = 4 quarts

2 gallons = 8 quarts
3 gallons = 12 quarts
4 gallons = 16 quarts

The coach brings 3 gallons of sports drink.

Lisa's bowling ball weighs 80 ounces.
How many pounds does it weigh?

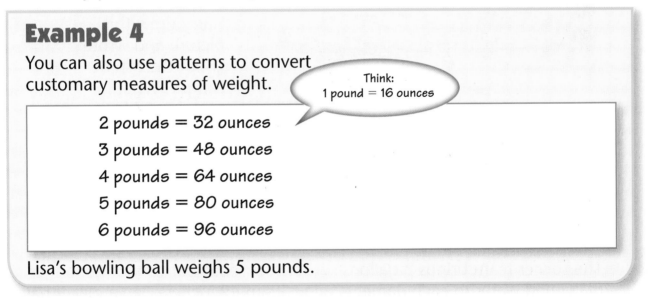

Example 4

You can also use patterns to convert
customary measures of weight.

Think:
1 pound = 16 ounces

2 pounds = 32 ounces

3 pounds = 48 ounces

4 pounds = 64 ounces

5 pounds = 80 ounces

6 pounds = 96 ounces

Lisa's bowling ball weighs 5 pounds.

Try It   **Write the number that makes each sentence true.**

1. 2 gal = ▮ qt
2. 2 ft = ▮ in.
3. 32 oz = ▮ lb
4. 4 yd = ▮ ft

5. 64 oz = ▮ lb
6. 16 qt = ▮ gal
7. 72 in. = ▮ ft
8. ▮ gal = 12 qt

Sum It Up   When do you multiply to change units?
When do you divide?

Copy and complete.

9.

Feet		2	3		5
Inches	12			48	

10.

Quarts		8		16	
Gallons	1		3		5

Write the number that makes each sentence true.

11. 7 gal = ▊ qt   12. ▊ ft = 36 in.   13. 16 oz = ▊ lb   14. 3 lb = ▊ oz

15. ▊ in. = 4 ft   16. ▊ lb = 48 oz   17. ▊ gal = 20 qt   18. 4 gal = ▊ qt

19. ▊ ft = 12 in.   20. ▊ oz = 1 lb   21. 2 gal = ▊ qt   22. 60 in. = ▊ ft

23. ▊ oz = 6 lb   ★24. 2 ft 6 in. = ▊ in. ★25. 18 qt = ▊ gal   ★26. 6 ft 7 in. = ▊ in.

Compare. Write >, <, or =.

27. 5 ft ● 48 in.   28. 5 lb ● 32 oz   29. 2 gal ● 12 qt

30. 3 ft ● 36 in.   31. 16 qt ● 4 gal   32. 48 oz ● 2 lb

33.

Harry drew this picture and wrote about the fish he caught. What mistake did he make? Write the sentence correctly.

Problem Solving

34. The soccer team brings 3 gallons of bottled water to each game. How many quarts of water is this?

35. A baseball bat cannot be longer than 42 inches. Can a player have a bat that is 4 feet long? Explain.

36. During every basketball game Sara drinks about 2 pints of water. Sara played 3 games last week. About how many pints of water did she drink in all at the 3 games? Is this more than or less than one quart?

37. Erica buys 2 pounds of granola at the store. How many ounces of granola does she buy?

Measurement and Geometry

9. July 12 is a Monday. Which day of the week is July 15?

  A. Thursday   **C.** Saturday

  B. Friday   **D.** Sunday

10. What time will it be in 15 minutes?

  F. 6:50 **H.** 6:40

  G. 7:50 **J.** 7:40

11. Which is a cone?

  A.   **C.**

  B.   **D.**

12. Beth's skates each weigh 16 ounces. How many pounds do her skates weigh altogether?

  F. 32 lb   **H.** 2 lb

  G. 16 lb   **J.** 1 lb

Statistics, Data Analysis, and Probability

Solve. Use data from the table for problems 13–16.

Favorite Sport

Each 🏀 = 4 votes

Basketball	🏀🏀🏀🏀🏀
Baseball	🏀🏀🏀🏀
Football	🏀🏀🏀
Soccer	🏀🏀🏀🏀🏀🏀🏀
Tennis	🏀🏀

13. How many more votes did baseball get than tennis?

  A. 2   **C.** 8

  B. 5   **D.** Not here

14. Which sport got 4 more votes than football?

  F. soccer   **H.** basketball

  G. baseball **J.** Not Here

15. How many people voted for baseball and tennis?

  A. 6   **C.** 18

  B. 12   **D.** 24

16. Change the pictograph to a bar graph. Explain how you did it. What conclusion can you make about the favorite sports?

Theme: Houses and Homes

- What 2-dimensional shapes can you see on the above house?
- What 3-dimensional shapes can you see on the above house?

What You Will Learn
In this chapter you will learn how to
- classify 2- and 3-dimensional figures.
- classify triangles and quadrilaterals.
- identify congruent, similar, or symmetrical figures.
- find perimeter, area, and volume.
- use strategies to solve problems.

Additional activities at
www.mhschool.com/math

12·1 3-Dimensional Figures

Learn

Graham and Naomi built this model of a house for their social studies project. Which 3-dimensional figures did they use?

Math Words

3-dimensional figure a figure in space

rectangular prism

cylinder

cube

cone

pyramid

sphere

base the flat face on which a 3-dimensional figure can rest

vertex the common point of the three or more edges of a 3-dimensional figure; plural form is **vertices**

face a flat side of a 3-dimensional figure

edge a line segment where two faces of a 3-dimensional figure meet

net a flat pattern that can be folded to make a 3-dimensional figure

Example 1

You can compare the blocks used in the house with these **3-dimensional figures** .

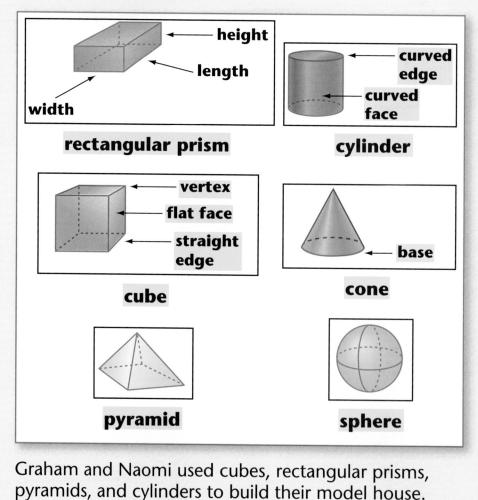

Graham and Naomi used cubes, rectangular prisms, pyramids, and cylinders to build their model house.

Graham and Naomi want to sort the blocks that they used to build their house. How can they sort them?

Example 2

You can sort the blocks by characteristics.

Figure	Name	Number of Curved Sides	Number of Flat Faces	Number of Edges	Number of Vertices
	Cube	0	6	12	8
	Rectangular prism	0	6	12	8
	Sphere	1	0	0	0

Example 3

You can make models of 3-dimensional figures out of paper.

Each **net** can be cut out and folded to make the figure shown next to it.

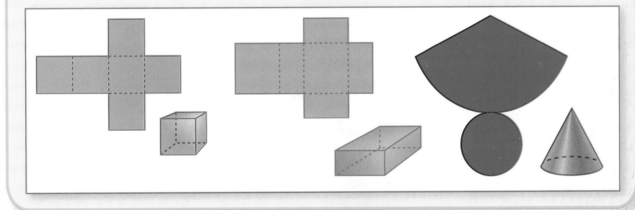

Try It   **Identify the figure for each block.**

1.   2.   3.   4.

 Why is a pyramid called 3-dimensional?

Name the 3-dimensional figure the object looks like.

5.

6.

7.

8.

Copy and fold. Identify the 3-dimensional figure.

9.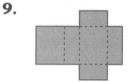

10.

Algebra & functions **What could the missing figure be? Explain.**

11.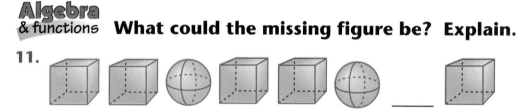

12.

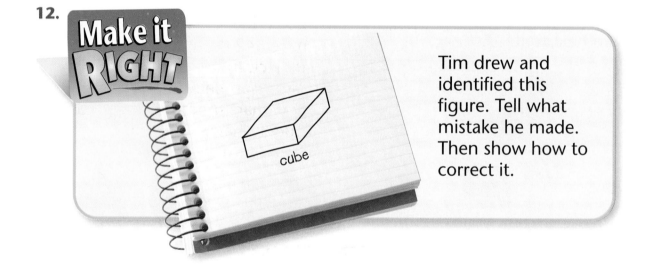

Tim drew and identified this figure. Tell what mistake he made. Then show how to correct it.

cube

Problem Solving

★**13. Art:** You have paint sponges that are shaped like these figures. Draw a picture of a house you could design by dipping 1 side of the sponges in paint and making sponge patterns on paper.

 cube

 cone

 pyramid

Use data from the table for problems 14–15.

14. How would you complete the chart for a rectangular prism?

Figure	Number of Faces	Number of Edges
Cube	6	12
Pyramid	5	8

15. **Create a problem** that can be solved using the data from the table. Solve it. Ask others to solve it.

16. Mr. Nickels is building this birdhouse. Which 2 figures has he combined to make the house?

17. **Measurement:** A doll house has a chimney that is 48 inches tall. How many feet tall is the chimney?

18. **Collect Data:** Find objects in your classroom that look like 3-dimensional figures. Make a chart that lists the objects and identifies the figures they look like.

19. **Spatial Reasoning:** Which geometric figure looks like this from the top?

20. Choose a 3-dimensional figure. Write a description of it without naming it. Show your description to other students. Have them name the figure.

21. Katharine, Cory, and Rosendo have 342 pom-poms for an art project. If they each get the same number of pom-poms, how many pom-poms will each student have?

Spiral Review and Test Prep

Write the number that makes each sentence true.

22. ▪ h = 60 min
23. ▪ d = 1 wk
24. ▪ d = 1 yr
25. 1 yr = ▪ wk

26. $\frac{1}{2}$ h = ▪ min
27. 1 m = ▪ cm
28. 1 gal = ▪ qt
29. 2 c = ▪ pt

Choose the correct answer.

30. Which weighs about 1 pound?
    - **A.** A car tire
    - **B.** A football
    - **C.** A watch
    - **D.** A lightbulb

31. Which weighs about 20 pounds?
    - **F.** A bird's nest
    - **G.** An apartment building
    - **H.** A dog house
    - **J.** A one-family house

12·2 2-Dimensional Figures

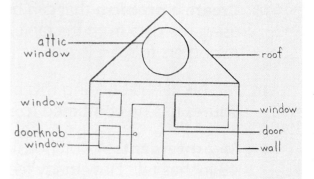

Learn

Math Word

2-dimensional figure a figure on a plane

Lester and Tyler are studying this blueprint of a house. What 2-dimensional figures were used to draw the blueprint?

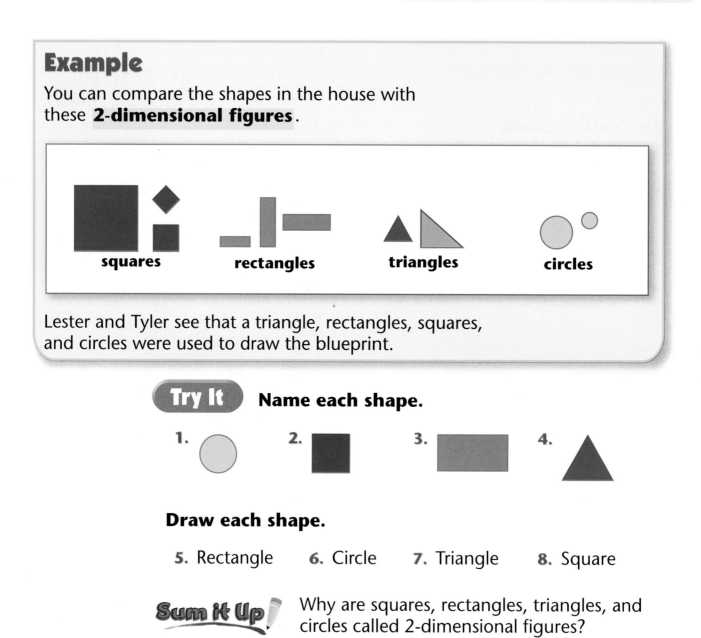

Example

You can compare the shapes in the house with these **2-dimensional figures**.

squares   **rectangles**   **triangles**   **circles**

Lester and Tyler see that a triangle, rectangles, squares, and circles were used to draw the blueprint.

Try It   Name each shape.

1.   2.   3.   4.

Draw each shape.

5. Rectangle   6. Circle   7. Triangle   8. Square

Sum it Up Why are squares, rectangles, triangles, and circles called 2-dimensional figures?

Copy and complete.

Figure	Number of sides	Number of angles
9. ▪	3	3
10. Rectangle	▪	4
11. Circle	▪	0

Identify each 2-dimensional figure.

12. **13.** **14.** **15.**

Problem Solving

Use data from *Did You Know?* for problem 16.

16. Social Studies: What 2-dimensional figures did Sir Christopher Wren include in his plan for the Sheldonian Theatre?

17. Generalize: Are all squares rectangles? Are all rectangles squares? Explain.

★18. A figure has no angles. Draw a picture of the figure and write its name.

Did You KNOW?

Christopher Wren designed the Sheldonian Theatre in Oxford, England. This was Oxford's first classical building.

Spiral Review and Test Prep

19. 567 ÷ 7   **20.** 630 × 9   **21.** 3,041 − 1,289   **22.** $3.80 + $9.44

Choose the correct answer.

23. Mr. Fox got four prices for a car. Which was the least?
  A. $17,000   **C.** $16,900
  B. $16,580   **D.** $16,200

24. Find the missing number.
  $n \times 7 = 7$
  F. 0   **H.** 2
  G. 1   **J.** 7

Lines, Line Segments, Rays, and Angles

Learn

Math Words

ray

angle a figure formed when two rays or lines meet at the same point

Parts of a line

line

line segment

endpoint the point at either end of a line segment; the beginning point of a ray

intersecting lines

parallel lines

Parts of a circle

diameter

radius

Windows come in all shapes and sizes. You can see that this window is made up of rectangles. Which other 2-dimensional figures are shown in this window?

Example 1

You can compare the figures in the window with these 2-dimensional figures.

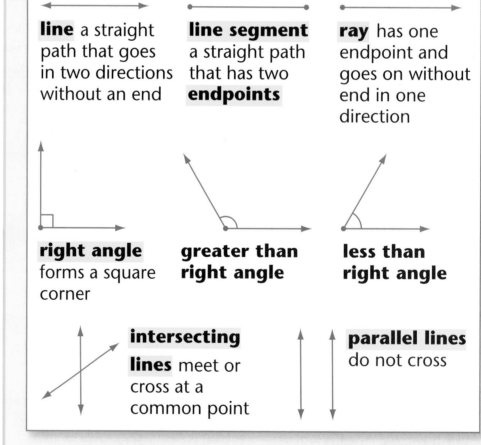

This window has right angles, parallel lines, intersecting lines, and line segments.

Some windows are round. How can you use this window to show the different parts of a circle?

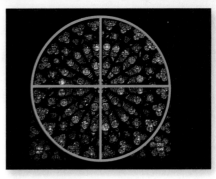

Example 2

You can draw a picture of the window and label the parts.

circle—a closed, 2-dimensional figure having all points the same distance from a given point

diameter—a line touching 2 points on a circle and passing through the center of the circle

radius—a line from the center of a circle to a point on the circle

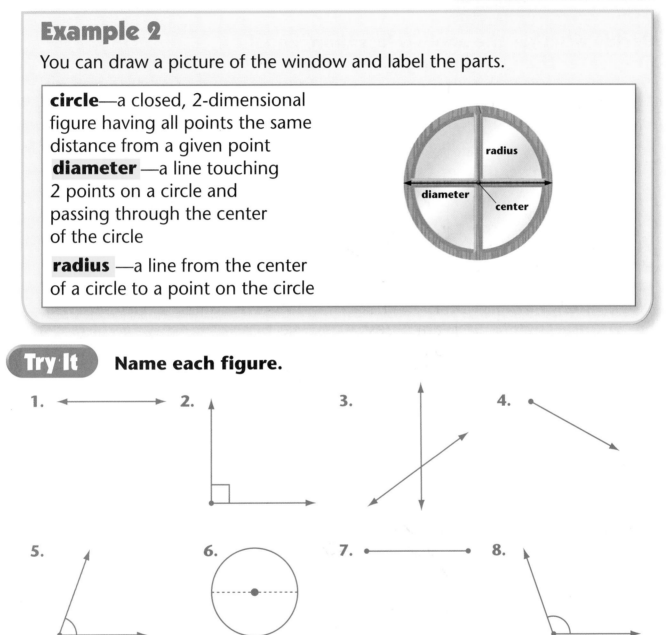

Try It   **Name each figure.**

1. ←——————→   2.   3.   4.

5.   6.   7. •——————•   8.

Sum it Up!   The rails on a straight section of railroad tracks are an example of what kind of lines?

Identify each figure.

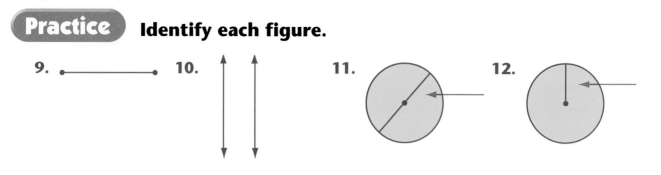

9. 10. 11. 12.

Decide whether the angle is less than, equal to, or greater than a right angle.

13. 14. 15. 16.

Algebra
& functions **Copy and complete. What pattern do you see?**

		Number of Lines	Number of Angles
17.			
18.			
19.			

20.

Make it RIGHT

Ellen drew and identified this figure. Tell what mistake she made. Then show how to correct it.

radius
center
diameter

Problem Solving

Use the picture for problem 21.

21. Science: All of the parts of a frame joined together help absorb forces that come from the outside. This is the frame of the roof for a tall building. Which figures, lines, and angles can you identify?

22. Compare: How is a line different from a line segment? How are they the same?

Journal

★**23.** Manuel's apartment building is shaped like a rectangular prism. There are 74 windows on each side of the building. If 2 window washers each wash the same number of windows, how many will each wash?

24. Logical Reasoning: Len, Harry, Alice, Charles, and Meg each drew a rectangle, a square, a circle, a triangle, or a right angle. Use the clues to decide which figure each person drew.

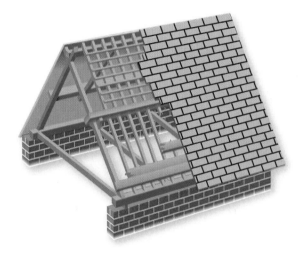

Clues:

Len drew a figure with fewer than 3 sides.

Charles drew a figure with 4 equal sides.

Meg drew a figure with no sides.

Alice drew a figure with 3 angles.

Harry drew a figure with 4 sides.

Spiral Review and Test Prep

25. $\begin{array}{r} \$23 \\ \times\ \ 4 \\ \hline \end{array}$

26. $6\overline{)708}$

27. $\begin{array}{r} 5,478 \\ +\ 767 \\ \hline \end{array}$

28. $\begin{array}{r} 600 \\ -\ 58 \\ \hline \end{array}$

29. $\begin{array}{r} 476 \\ \times\ \ 9 \\ \hline \end{array}$

Choose the correct answer.

30. What is the value of the 4 in the number 38,495?

   A. 40   **C.** 4,000

   B. 40,000   **D.** 400

31. Yori built a house for an animal with a mass of about 250 grams. Which animal did he make the house for?

   F. A flea   **H.** A dog

   G. A hamster   **J.** A horse

12·4 Polygons

Learn

Architects often use geometry in their work. The house plans they draw use different geometric figures. What polygons do you see in this plan?

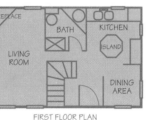

FIRST FLOOR PLAN

Raymond Ho works in New York, New York as an architect.

Math Words

open figure
a figure that does not start and end at the same point

closed figure
a figure that starts and ends at the same point

polygon
a closed figure with straight sides

pentagon

hexagon

octagon

side

Example

You can compare the figures in the plan with these.

Some figures are **open figures**.
Polygons are **closed figures**.
Not all closed figures are polygons.

side

Not Polygons

Pentagon

Hexagon

Octagon

The plan shows triangles, squares, rectangles, pentagons, and hexagons.

Try It
Write *yes* or *no* to tell if each figure is a polygon. If it is, identify the polygon.

1.

2.

3.

4.

Sum It Up
Is a circle a polygon? Explain.

 **Practice**   Write *yes* or *no* to tell if each figure is a polygon.
If it is, identify the polygon.

5.   6.   7.   8.

Draw and identify each polygon.

9. It has 3 sides.

10. It has 4 sides. All are equal.

11. It has 8 sides.

12. It has 5 sides.

Problem Solving

Use data from the picture for problem 13.

13. **Logical Reasoning:** Ray made 3 polygons using a total of 17 toothpicks. Here is one of his polygons. What other two polygons did Ray make?

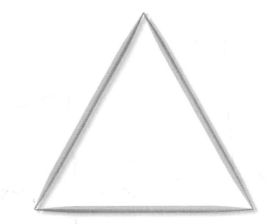

14. **Spatial Reasoning:** Suppose all of the sides of a triangle and a square are the same length. What polygon can you make by putting the triangle on top of the square? Draw a picture to show your answer.

★15. A tile designer is planning a pattern using rectangles and pentagons. He is working with 5 tiles. The tiles have a total of 23 sides. How many are pentagons?

Spiral Review and Test Prep

Write the number that makes each sentence true.

16. 3 m = ▓ cm   17. 2 wk = ▓ d   18. 32 oz = ▓ lb   19. 1 pt = ▓ c

Choose the correct answer.

20. Mr. Wallace moved into his house 3 years ago. In how many years will Mr. Wallace have lived in his house for 10 years?

    A. 7 years   C. 30 years
    B. 13 years   D. Not Here

21. A builder buys 3 stacks of lumber. Each stack weighs 125 pounds. How much does the lumber weigh in total?

    F. 128 pounds   H. 375 pounds
    G. 275 pounds   J. 3,125 pounds

Triangles

Learn

Derek made this space home with a building kit. Which kinds of triangles does it have?

Math Words

triangles

equilateral
3 sides the same length

scalene
no sides the same length

isosceles
2 sides the same length

acute all angles are less than a right angle

right contains an angle that forms a square corner

obtuse 1 angle is greater than a right angle

Example

You can compare the **triangles** in the space home with these different kinds of triangles. Triangles can be classified by their sides or by their angles.

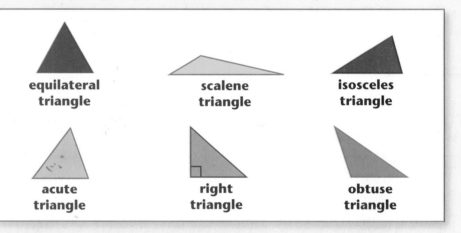

The space home has equilateral triangles. All sides are the same length.

 Identify each triangle as equilateral, isosceles, or scalene. Then identify each as acute, right, or obtuse.

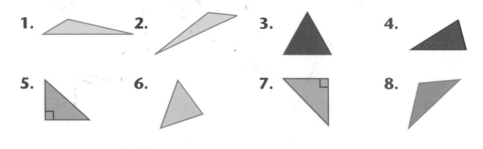

Sum It Up Can a triangle be both scalene and isosceles? Explain.

Identify each triangle as equilateral, isosceles, or scalene.

9. 10. 11. 12. 13.

Identify each triangle as acute, right, or obtuse.

14. 15. 16. 17. 18.

Problem Solving

Use the picture for problem 19.

19. The edges of the front part of the roof form a triangle. Classify the triangle in 2 different ways.

20. **Create a problem** Using classification of triangles. Solve it. Ask others to solve it.

★21. The height of a window is 4 feet. How many inches is this?

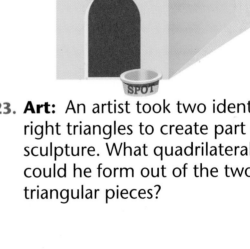

22. **Spatial Reasoning:** You have a sphere, a cylinder, and a pyramid. You slice each 3-dimensional figure straight down the middle. What 2-dimensional figures will the edges of each piece form?

23. **Art:** An artist took two identical right triangles to create part of a sculpture. What quadrilateral could he form out of the two triangular pieces?

Spiral Review and Test Prep

24. 85 − 37   25. 826 + 8,832   26. 126 ÷ 6   27. 907 × 3

Choose the correct answer.

28. Which makes the sentence true?
    4 gallons = ▮ quarts
    A. 1   C. 16
    B. 12   D. 24

29. Which number sentence is not in the same fact family as the others?
    F. 4 × 3 = 12   H. 4 + 3 = 7
    G. 12 ÷ 4 = 3   J. 3 × 4 = 12

12·6 Quadrilaterals

Learn

Frank Lloyd Wright was a famous designer who used geometric shapes in new ways. He designed this window. Are there any quadrilaterals in the window?

Math Words

quadrilaterals a polygon with 4 sides

square

rectangle

parallelogram

rhombus

trapezoid

Example

You can compare the shapes in the window to these figures. All of them are **quadrilaterals**.

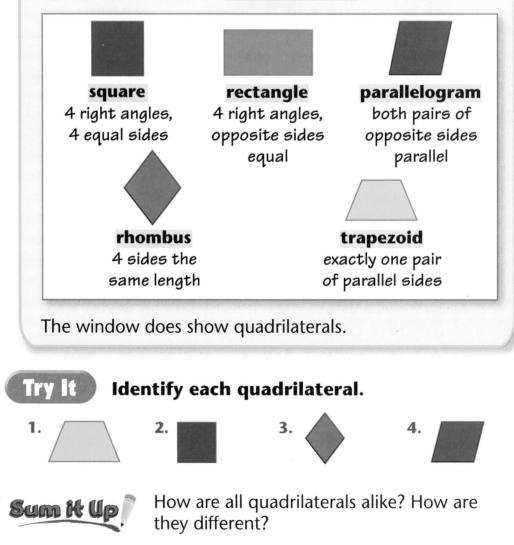

square
4 right angles, 4 equal sides

rectangle
4 right angles, opposite sides equal

parallelogram
both pairs of opposite sides parallel

rhombus
4 sides the same length

trapezoid
exactly one pair of parallel sides

The window does show quadrilaterals.

Try It   Identify each quadrilateral.

1. 　　　2. 　　　3. 　　　4.

Sum it Up!   How are all quadrilaterals alike? How are they different?

Identify each quadrilateral.

5. 　　6. 　　7. 　　8.

9. It has 4 sides of equal length with 2 angles less than right angles.

10. It has opposite sides that are parallel and no right angles.

Algebra & functions **Write the missing numbers from the table.**

11.

Number of quadrilaterals	1	2	▮	4
Number of sides	4	▮	12	▮

Problem Solving

Use data from the table for problems 12–14.

12. Choose a poster. Draw a picture to show what it might look like.

13. **Create a problem** using the table.

★14. Which poster could have squares in it?

Posters in Ms. Lorenzo's House		
Posters	Figures	Number of Figures
A	Rhombus	8
B	Trapezoid	6
C	Parallelogram	10
D	Rectangle	9

15. **Compare:** How is a square like a rhombus?

Spiral Review and Test Prep

Write the number that makes each sentence true.

16. 1 yd = ▮ in.　　17. 12 qt = ▮ gal　　18. ▮ lb = 32 oz　　19. 7 d = ▮ w

Choose the correct answer.

20. A builder uses 12,075 bricks. What is this number rounded to the nearest hundred?
   A. 12,080　　C. 12,100
   B. 12,000　　D. 12,200

21. What are the missing numbers in the table?

Rule: Subtract 9		
Input	81	63	45
Output	▮	54	▮

   F. 72; 32　　H. 9; 5
   G. 72; 36　　J. 90; 54

Problem Solving: Reading for Math

Use a Diagram

12·7

Students Design Rooms

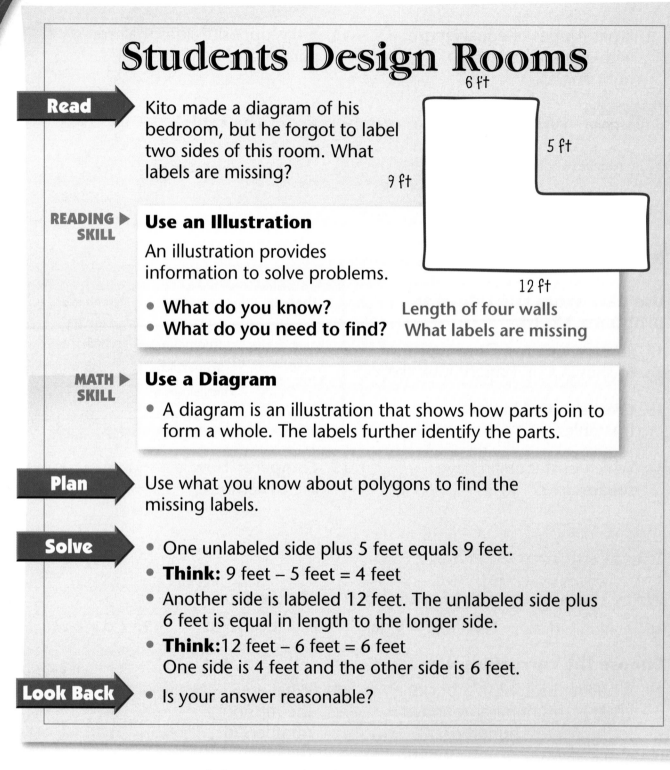

Read

Kito made a diagram of his bedroom, but he forgot to label two sides of this room. What labels are missing?

READING SKILL ▶ **Use an Illustration**

An illustration provides information to solve problems.

- **What do you know?**   Length of four walls
- **What do you need to find?**   What labels are missing

MATH SKILL ▶ **Use a Diagram**

- A diagram is an illustration that shows how parts join to form a whole. The labels further identify the parts.

Plan

Use what you know about polygons to find the missing labels.

Solve

- One unlabeled side plus 5 feet equals 9 feet.
- **Think:** 9 feet − 5 feet = 4 feet
- Another side is labeled 12 feet. The unlabeled side plus 6 feet is equal in length to the longer side.
- **Think:** 12 feet − 6 feet = 6 feet
  One side is 4 feet and the other side is 6 feet.

Look Back

- Is your answer reasonable?

Sum it Up!
How did you use the diagram to help you solve this problem?

Use data from the illustration to solve problems 1–2.

1. The diagram shows a special window Kito designed for his house. How would you classify the sides of this window?

2. What should Kito do to this window to form an equilateral triangle?

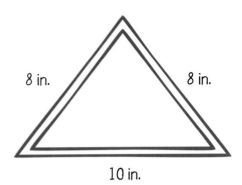

8 in.   8 in.

10 in.

Use data from the illustration for problems 3–7.

3. Alex designed this room. What two polygons make up the room?

4. What label is missing from the diagram?

5. Alex decided to change his diagram. He cut 4 feet from each 14 ft length. What two polygons make up the new design?

6. What does Alex have to do to make his room an octagon?

7. Alex also made a diagram of a triangular garden with two sides of 8 feet and a third side of 12 feet. How would you classify this garden?

8 ft

10 ft

8 ft

14 ft

Problem Solving

Spiral Review and Test Prep

Choose the correct answer.

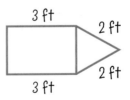

3 ft

2 ft

2 ft

3 ft

If the end of this diagram is an equilateral triangle, what are the lengths of the two unlabeled line segments?

8. Which of these statements is true?
   A. Part of the diagram is a rectangle.
   B. One side is labeled 6 feet.
   C. All sides are the same length.

9. You can find the unlabeled lengths because
   F. all sides of an equilateral triangle are equal.
   G. all sides of a rectangle are equal.
   H. a triangle is a third of a rectangle.

Identify each figure. (pages 480–489)

1.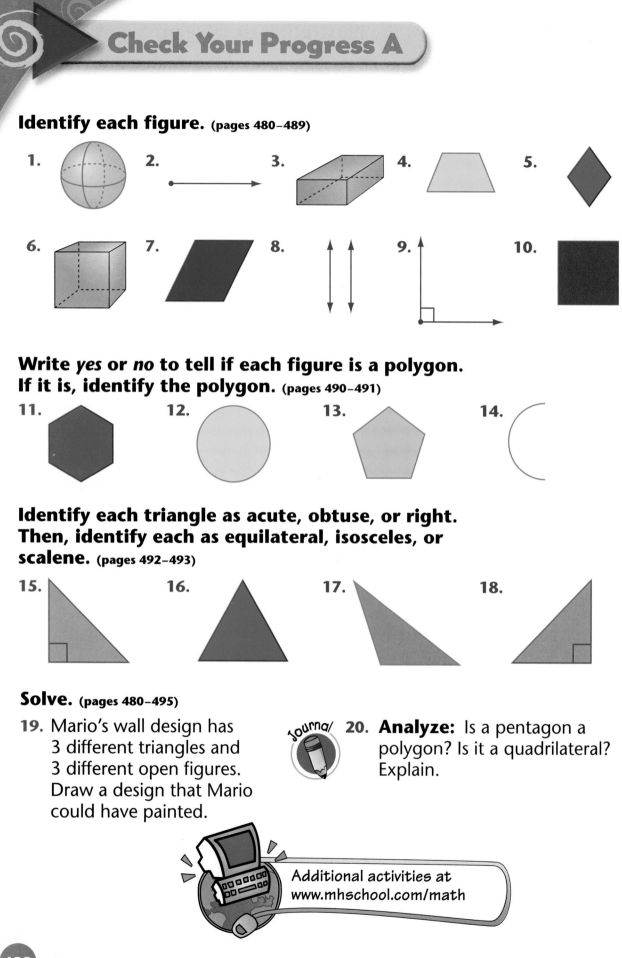

2.

3.

4.

5.

6.

7.

8.

9.

10.

Write *yes* or *no* to tell if each figure is a polygon. If it is, identify the polygon. (pages 490–491)

11.

12.

13.

14.

Identify each triangle as acute, obtuse, or right. Then, identify each as equilateral, isosceles, or scalene. (pages 492–493)

15.

16.

17.

18.

Solve. (pages 480–495)

19. Mario's wall design has 3 different triangles and 3 different open figures. Draw a design that Mario could have painted.

Journal 20. **Analyze:** Is a pentagon a polygon? Is it a quadrilateral? Explain.

Additional activities at
www.mhschool.com/math

Draw and Identify a Figure

Pablo is designing a deck. He needs to draw a regular hexagon to use in his sketch of the deck. Draw a regular hexagon. Show that the figure is a regular hexagon.

You can use a drawing program with geometry tools to draw geometric figures.

How do you know the figure is a regular hexagon?

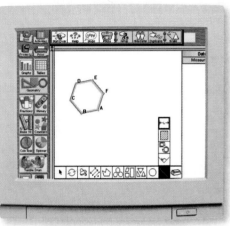

- Click on Geometry Tools.
- Choose the polygon tool. Draw a hexagon.
- Use the measurement tool to find the length of each side.

Use the computer to draw each figure. Show that the figure you have drawn is correct.

1. Equilateral triangle **2.** Regular pentagon **3.** Regular octagon

Solve.

4. Garin is drawing plans for his garden. He wants to draw a scalene triangle to show the shape of his garden. Draw a scalene triangle.

5. A square photo is to appear on a page in a book. Each side of the photo is to be 3 inches long. Draw a square to show the size of the photo. Explain how you know that your figure is correct.

6. Analyze: How do the geometry and measurement tools help you draw correct figures?

For more practice, use Math Traveler™.

12·8 Congruent and Similar Figures

Learn

Jake and his grandfather designed these two doors for the clubhouse they are building. Are the doors similar? Are they also congruent? Are the windows in the middle of the doors similar? Are they also congruent?

Math Words

similar same shape, may be different size

congruent same shape and same size

Example

You can compare the size and shape of the doors to tell if they are **similar.** You can also compare the size and shape of the doors to tell if they are also **congruent.**

> Both doors are rectangles. Both are 8 units tall and 5 units wide. They are the same size and shape.

The doors are similar and congruent.

> The windows on the doors are the same shape. The window on the first door is 4 units tall and 2 units wide. The window on the second door is 1 unit tall and 2 units wide.

The windows are similar, but not congruent.

Try It

Write whether the figures are similar. Write whether the figures are congruent.

1.

2.

3.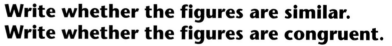

Sum it Up  All circles are similar. Explain whether you think this statement is true or false.

Measurement and Geometry

9. How many quarts equal the same amount as 3 gallons?
- **A.** 12
- **B.** 8
- **C.** 4
- **D.** 1

10. Which weighs about 8 pounds?
- **F.** An apartment building
- **G.** A bird's nest
- **H.** A birdhouse
- **J.** A tree

11. Which angle is less than a right angle?

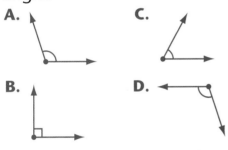

- **A.**
- **B.**
- **C.**
- **D.**

12. Which figure covers $\frac{1}{6}$ of the hexagon? Draw a picture and explain why your answer is correct.

Mathematical Reasoning

13. Haley's address is a 3-digit number. The hundreds digit is 2 times the ones digit. The sum of the hundreds digit and ones digit is 12. The tens digit is the same as the ones digit. What number is Haley's address?
- **A.** 633
- **B.** 824
- **C.** 844
- **D.** 622

14. Building 5 has 175 apartments. Building 6 has 30 more apartments than Building 5. If Building 4 has 160 apartments, how many apartments do Buildings 4, 5, and 6 have in all?
- **F.** 221
- **G.** 354
- **H.** 380
- **J.** 540

15. Jayne has a 3-gallon container and a 5-gallon container. She pours 5 gallons of water in a fish tank. Then she uses the 5-gallon container to fill the 3-gallon container. Finally she pours what is left in the 5-gallon container in the fish tank. How much water did Jayne pour into the fish tank?
- **A.** 8 gallons
- **B.** 7 gallons
- **C.** 10 gallons
- **D.** 6 gallons

16. This diagram shows the floor pattern on a newly tiled floor. What could the next column of tiles be?

- **F.** 4 squares
- **G.** 4 triangles
- **H.** 8 squares
- **J.** 8 triangles

Fractions and Probability

Theme: Let's Eat!

Use the Data

Easy Vegetable Pizza Recipe

1 pizza crust
$\frac{3}{4}$ cup pizza sauce
$\frac{1}{2}$ teaspoon olive oil
1 clove chopped garlic

2 cups mushrooms
$\frac{1}{4}$ cup chopped onion
$\frac{2}{3}$ cup mozzarella cheese
3 tablespoons grated Parmesan cheese

Spread pizza sauce, vegetables and cheeses over crust. Bake at 450° for 10 minutes. Makes 4 servings.

- Which do you use more of: pizza sauce or chopped onions? How can you tell?

- How many people does this recipe serve? How could you use this recipe to serve only 2 people?

What You Will Learn

In this chapter you will learn how to
- identify fractions and mixed numbers.
- compare, order, and find equivalent fractions.
- add and subtract fractions.
- find the probability for given situations.
- use strategies to solve problems.

Additional activities at
www.mhschool.com/math

Parts of a Whole

Learn

Louisa baked this carrot cake. She cut it into five equal parts. How much of the cake has coconut icing?

Math Words

fraction a number that names part of a whole or group

numerator the number above the bar in a fraction; it tells the number of parts

denominator the number below the bar in a fraction; tells the number of equal parts in all

Example

You can use a **fraction** to describe the part that has coconut icing.

Write the **numerator** and the **denominator** to show the correct fraction.

parts with coconut icing → **4** ← **numerator**
total number of parts → **5** ← **denominator**

Four fifths of the cake has coconut icing.

More Examples

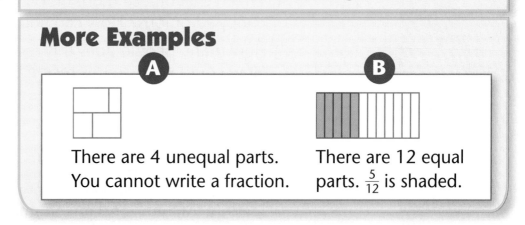

A

There are 4 unequal parts. You cannot write a fraction.

B

There are 12 equal parts. $\frac{5}{12}$ is shaded.

Try It

Tell if the figure shows equal parts. If yes, write a fraction for the part that is shaded.

1.   2. 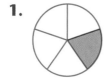   3. 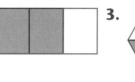   4.

 **Explain** how you write a fraction to describe the shaded parts of a whole.

Extra Practice

Parts of a Whole (pages 532–533)

Write a fraction for the part that is shaded.

1.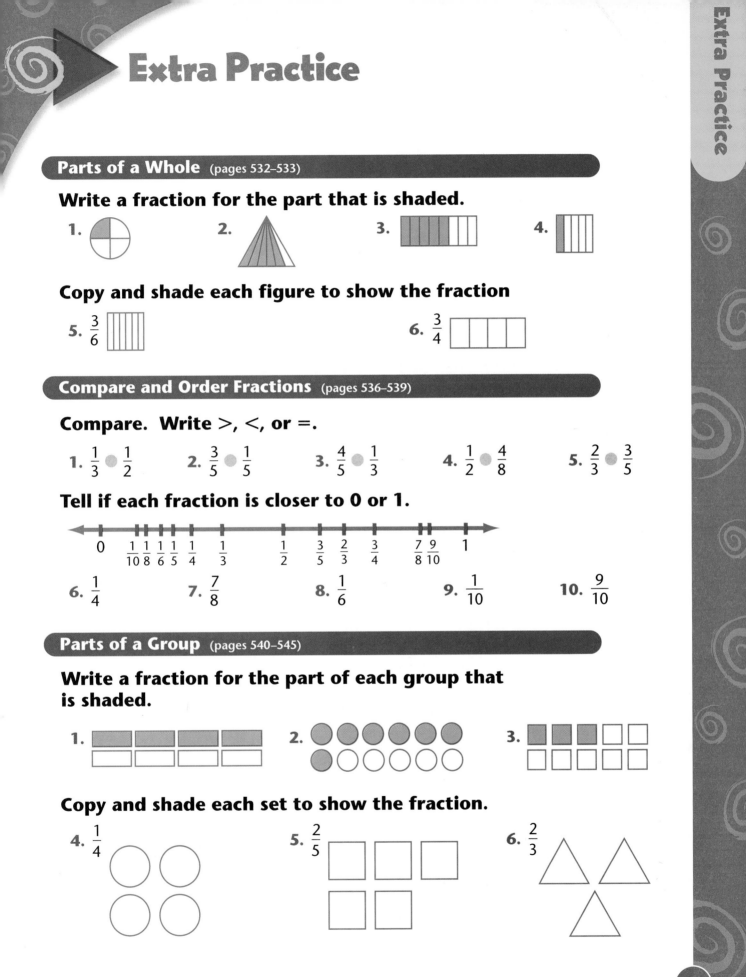
2.
3.
4.

Copy and shade each figure to show the fraction

5. $\frac{3}{6}$
6. $\frac{3}{4}$

Compare and Order Fractions (pages 536–539)

Compare. Write >, <, or =.

1. $\frac{1}{3}$ ● $\frac{1}{2}$
2. $\frac{3}{5}$ ● $\frac{1}{5}$
3. $\frac{4}{5}$ ● $\frac{1}{3}$
4. $\frac{1}{2}$ ● $\frac{4}{8}$
5. $\frac{2}{3}$ ● $\frac{3}{5}$

Tell if each fraction is closer to 0 or 1.

6. $\frac{1}{4}$
7. $\frac{7}{8}$
8. $\frac{1}{6}$
9. $\frac{1}{10}$
10. $\frac{9}{10}$

Parts of a Group (pages 540–545)

Write a fraction for the part of each group that is shaded.

1.
2.
3.

Copy and shade each set to show the fraction.

4. $\frac{1}{4}$
5. $\frac{2}{5}$
6. $\frac{2}{3}$

Extra Practice

Find Parts of a Group (pages 544–545)

Use counters to find the fraction of a number.

1. $\frac{1}{8}$ of 16
2. $\frac{1}{3}$ of 9
3. $\frac{1}{2}$ of 6
4. $\frac{1}{4}$ of 12
5. $\frac{1}{5}$ of 20
6. $\frac{1}{6}$ of 18
7. $\frac{3}{8}$ of 8
8. $\frac{5}{6}$ of 18
9. $\frac{2}{3}$ of 9
10. $\frac{3}{4}$ of 12
11. $\frac{2}{5}$ of 10
12. $\frac{5}{6}$ of 12

Problem Solving: Reading for Math
Check for Reasonableness (pages 546–547)

Solve.

1. Wanda made a dozen muffins. Her family ate $\frac{1}{3}$ of the muffins. How many muffins did her family eat?

2. Katherine has a set of twin brothers and Jace has 4 sisters. If $\frac{1}{2}$ of the students are in third grade, how many of the students are in third grade?

3. Lucy made a fruit salad out of 8 different fruits for each day of the week. How many different fruits did she use in one week?

4. During September Terrance went to cooking class $\frac{1}{3}$ of the days. How many days did Terrance have cooking class?

Mixed Numbers (pages 548–549)

Write as a mixed number.

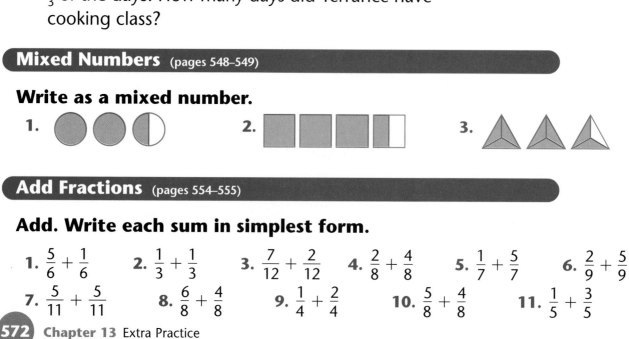

1. 2. 3.

Add Fractions (pages 554–555)

Add. Write each sum in simplest form.

1. $\frac{5}{6} + \frac{1}{6}$
2. $\frac{1}{3} + \frac{1}{3}$
3. $\frac{7}{12} + \frac{2}{12}$
4. $\frac{2}{8} + \frac{4}{8}$
5. $\frac{1}{7} + \frac{5}{7}$
6. $\frac{2}{9} + \frac{5}{9}$
7. $\frac{5}{11} + \frac{5}{11}$
8. $\frac{6}{8} + \frac{4}{8}$
9. $\frac{1}{4} + \frac{2}{4}$
10. $\frac{5}{8} + \frac{4}{8}$
11. $\frac{1}{5} + \frac{3}{5}$

Extra Practice

Subtract Fractions (pages 558–559)

Subtract. Write each difference in simplest form.

1. $\dfrac{5}{6}$
   $-\dfrac{3}{6}$

2. $\dfrac{7}{8}$
   $-\dfrac{1}{8}$

3. $\dfrac{11}{12}$
   $-\dfrac{9}{12}$

4. $\dfrac{4}{5}$
   $-\dfrac{3}{5}$

5. $\dfrac{7}{10}$
   $-\dfrac{5}{10}$

6. $\dfrac{8}{9}$
   $-\dfrac{5}{9}$

7. $\dfrac{9}{11} - \dfrac{3}{11}$

8. $\dfrac{7}{8} - \dfrac{6}{8}$

9. $\dfrac{3}{4} - \dfrac{1}{4}$

10. $\dfrac{3}{6} - \dfrac{3}{6}$

11. $\dfrac{3}{5} - \dfrac{1}{5}$

Probability (pages 560–561)

Use the words *likely, unlikely, certain,* or *impossible* to describe the probability of each event below.

1. number 7

2. an odd number

3. number 5

4. number 1

5. an even number

6. number 9

Problem Solving Strategy: Act It Out (pages 564–565)

Conduct an experiment to act it out and solve.

1. Jan said that if she tosses a coin she will get heads twice as often as tails. How can you conduct an experiment to see if she is correct? Conduct the experiment. Record your results. Do you think Jan is correct? Why or why not?

2. Steve predicts that if he spins the spinner it will land on yellow. How can you conduct an experiment to see if he made a good prediction? Conduct the experiment. Explain what the results show about Steve's prediction.

Chapter Study Guide

Language and Math

Complete. Use words from the list.

1. The number below the bar in a fraction is called the _____ .

2. You can tell that $\frac{2}{3}$ and $\frac{6}{9}$ are the same amount because they are _____ .

3. A number made up of a whole number and a fraction is called a(n) _____ .

4. If you are sure an event will occur, you can say the _____ for the event is certain.

5. The _____ for tossing a coin are heads and tails.

Math Words

denominator

equivalent fraction

fraction

mixed number

numerator

possible outcome

probability

Skills and Applications

Identify, read, and write fractions and mixed numbers. (pages 532–541, 546–549)

Example

Write a fraction for the part that is shaded.

Solution

parts shaded → $\underline{5}$ numerator

total parts → 8 denominator

So $\frac{5}{8}$ of the rectangle is shaded.

Write a fraction for the part that is shaded.

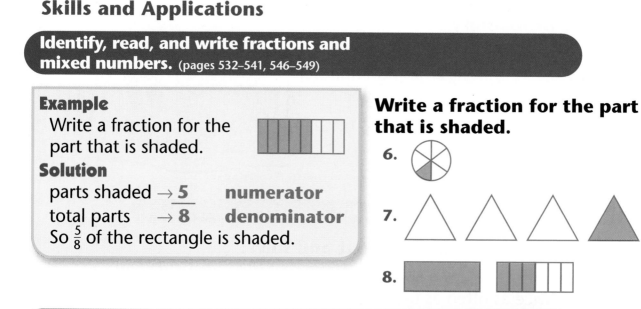

6.

7.

8.

Compare and order fractions and find equivalent fractions. (pages 534–539)

Example

Compare. $\frac{4}{5} \bullet \frac{1}{5}$

Write >, <, or =.

Solution

$\frac{4}{5} > \frac{1}{5}$

| $\frac{1}{5}$ |
| $\frac{1}{5}$ | $\frac{1}{5}$ | $\frac{1}{5}$ | $\frac{1}{5}$ |

Compare. Write >, <, or =.

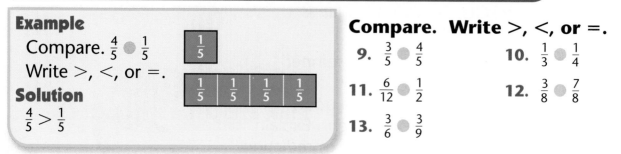

9. $\frac{3}{5} \bullet \frac{4}{5}$

10. $\frac{1}{3} \bullet \frac{1}{4}$

11. $\frac{6}{12} \bullet \frac{1}{2}$

12. $\frac{3}{8} \bullet \frac{7}{8}$

13. $\frac{3}{6} \bullet \frac{3}{9}$

Add and subtract fractions with like denominators. (pages 552–559)

Example

Find the sum in simplest form. $\frac{1}{6} + \frac{2}{6}$

Solution

Step 1

The denominators are the same, so add the numerators.

$\frac{1}{6} + \frac{2}{6} = \frac{3}{6}$

Step 2

Simplify. $\frac{3}{6} = \frac{1}{2}$

Find the sum or difference in simplest form.

14. $\frac{1}{7} + \frac{4}{7}$

15. $\frac{3}{8} + \frac{3}{8}$

16. $\frac{5}{6} + \frac{4}{6}$

17. $\frac{9}{10} - \frac{6}{10}$

18. $\frac{5}{8} - \frac{3}{8}$

19. $\frac{7}{9} - \frac{1}{9}$

Find the number of outcomes and the probability for given situations. (pages 560–563)

Example

List the possible outcomes. Which is most likely?

Solution

Think: Which numbers could the spinner possibly land on?

Possible outcomes: 1, 2, 3, 4, or 5

Most likely: 3

List the possible outcomes. Which is most likely to be picked?

20. Picking a card from six cards numbered 2 through 6 and two with number 3

21. Rolling a number cube numbered 1 through 6

22. Tossing a 2-color green and white counter

23. Picking a raisin from a mixed box of 20 yellow and 30 brown raisins

Use strategies to solve problems. (pages 546–547, 564–565)

Example

Is it **likely, unlikely, certain,** or **impossible** to spin red?

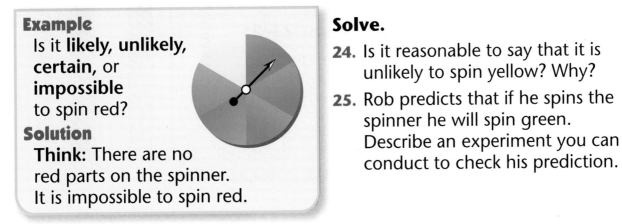

Solution

Think: There are no red parts on the spinner.

It is impossible to spin red.

Solve.

24. Is it reasonable to say that it is unlikely to spin yellow? Why?

25. Rob predicts that if he spins the spinner he will spin green. Describe an experiment you can conduct to check his prediction.

Chapter Test

Write a fraction for the part that is shaded.

1.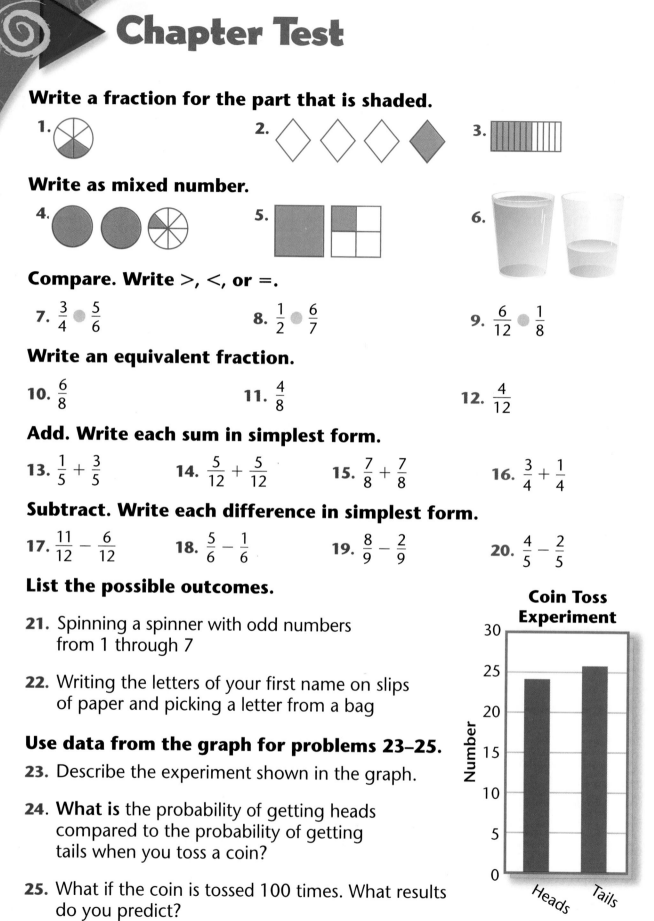

2.

3.

Write as mixed number.

4.

5.

6.

Compare. Write >, <, or =.

7. $\frac{3}{4}$ ● $\frac{5}{6}$

8. $\frac{1}{2}$ ● $\frac{6}{7}$

9. $\frac{6}{12}$ ● $\frac{1}{8}$

Write an equivalent fraction.

10. $\frac{6}{8}$

11. $\frac{4}{8}$

12. $\frac{4}{12}$

Add. Write each sum in simplest form.

13. $\frac{1}{5} + \frac{3}{5}$

14. $\frac{5}{12} + \frac{5}{12}$

15. $\frac{7}{8} + \frac{7}{8}$

16. $\frac{3}{4} + \frac{1}{4}$

Subtract. Write each difference in simplest form.

17. $\frac{11}{12} - \frac{6}{12}$

18. $\frac{5}{6} - \frac{1}{6}$

19. $\frac{8}{9} - \frac{2}{9}$

20. $\frac{4}{5} - \frac{2}{5}$

List the possible outcomes.

21. Spinning a spinner with odd numbers from 1 through 7

22. Writing the letters of your first name on slips of paper and picking a letter from a bag

Use data from the graph for problems 23–25.

23. Describe the experiment shown in the graph.

24. **What is** the probability of getting heads compared to the probability of getting tails when you toss a coin?

25. What if the coin is tossed 100 times. What results do you predict?

Coin Toss Experiment

Performance Assessment

Use different-color connecting cubes to find the probability of picking a certain fruit from a bag.

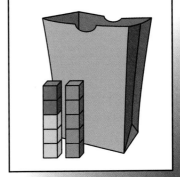

- Yellow represents banana
- Red represents apple
- Orange represents peach
- Green represents lime

Use 10 cubes: 3 yellow, 2 red, 1 orange, and 4 green.

What will the probability be that you will pick each type of fruit? Copy and complete the chart. Write a fraction to show the answer.

Write a fraction to show what part of the total number of cubes each color is.

Now put the cubes into a bag. Without looking, pick a cube. Record your results in the chart. Put the cube back in the bag. Repeat. Take 10 turns. Then fill in the probability column. Compare the two results.

Fruit	Color Cube	Number of Times Picked	Probability
Banana	Yellow		$\frac{3}{10}$
Apple	Red		
Peach	Orange		
Lime	Green		

A Good Answer

- shows a completed chart.
- shows the correct probabilities and fractions.

Journal

Portfolio

You may want to save this work for your portfolio.

Enrichment

Dependent Events

Dependent events are two events in which the result of the first affects the result of the second.

Without looking you pick a connecting cube from a bag at the right. You pick a red cube. The probability of picking a red cube is 1 out of 4, or $\frac{1}{4}$.

You do not put the red cube back in the bag. You pick another cube without looking. You pick yellow. The probability of picking yellow is 1 out of 3, or $\frac{1}{3}$.

You do not put the yellow cube back in the bag.

1. What is the probability that you will pick the purple cube?

Use the bag of cubes to the right.

2. What is the probability that you will pick a purple cube?

3. What if you pick a purple cube and do not put it back. What is the probability that you will pick purple now?

4. Design your own experiment. Choose the cubes to put in the bag. Describe the probability for each color of cube that is picked and not put back in the bag.

5. **Generalize:** How does the probability change when you do not put the cube back in the bag?

Test-Taking Tips

Sometimes you need to **use information from a chart** to answer questions on a test.

Type of Pizza	Amount Eaten
Mushroom	$\frac{5}{8}$
Sausage	$\frac{3}{8}$
Onion	$\frac{1}{8}$
Pepperoni	$\frac{6}{8}$

Check for Success

Before turning in a test, go back one last time to check.

☑ I understood and answered the questions asked.

☑ I checked my work for errors.

☑ My answers make sense.

Which kind of pizza was eaten the most?

A. Mushroom   **C.** Onion

B. Sausage   **D.** Pepperoni

Look at the column in the chart called "Amount Eaten." Each pizza was cut into 8 slices. The greater number tells you which pizza was eaten the most.

The correct choice is **D**.

Use information from the chart to choose the correct answer.

Name	Time Spent Reading
Cora	$\frac{3}{4}$ hour
Kim	$\frac{1}{3}$ hour
Sam	$\frac{2}{3}$ hour
Lou	$\frac{1}{4}$ hour
Kirk	$\frac{1}{2}$ hour

1. Who read the longest amount of time?

   A. Lou   **C.** Kirk

   B. Cora   **D.** Sam

2. Who read for the shortest amount of time?

   F. Lou   **H.** Sam

   G. Kim   **J.** Kirk

3. Who read exactly twice as long as Kim?

   A. Cora   **C.** Kirk

   B. Kirk   **D.** Sam

Test Prep

Spiral Review and Test Prep

Chapters 1–13

Choose the correct answer.

Number Sense

1. Find 6 × $11.99.
   - A. $70.94
   - B. $71.64
   - C. $71.94
   - D. $81.64

2. What is 4,595 rounded to the nearest hundred?
   - F. 4,600
   - G. 4,590
   - H. 4,500
   - J. 4,000

3. Wesley eats $\frac{1}{4}$ of a pizza. Sara eats the same amount. How much of the pizza do they eat in all?
   - A. $\frac{1}{4}$
   - B. $\frac{1}{2}$
   - C. $\frac{3}{4}$
   - D. $\frac{4}{4}$

4. Apples are 3 for $1.08. How much does each apple cost?
   - F. $0.92
   - G. $0.36
   - H. $0.33
   - J. Not Here

Algebra and Functions

5. A rectangle has a length of 5 inches and a width of 10 inches. Which number sentence shows its perimeter?
   - A. 5 + 10 = 15
   - B. 10 + 10 + 5 = 25
   - C. 5 × 10 = 50
   - D. 5 + 5 + 10 + 10 = 30

6. Which symbol makes the sentence true?

   $\frac{1}{5} + \frac{2}{5} \bullet \frac{9}{10} - \frac{3}{10}$
   - F. =
   - G. >
   - H. <
   - J. Not Here

7. Which number makes the sentence true?

   36 ÷ ▊ = 3
   - A. 6
   - B. 9
   - C. 12
   - D. 15

8. A square playground has a side that is 158 feet long. What is the perimeter of the playground?
   - F. 316 feet
   - G. 623 feet
   - H. 632 feet
   - J. 24,964 feet

Copy and complete the chart to record the data for each ball. Round to the nearest 10 centimeters.

Ball	Drop Height	Bounce Height	Bounce Height (Rounded)
Basketball	1 meter		
Baseball	1 meter		
Volleyball	1 meter		

Conclude and Apply

- Write a fraction for each ball so you can compare it to the others. Use the rounded length as the numerator and the drop height as the denominator.

- Which ball bounced the best? How do you know?

- Use the bounce height and divide to find how many times higher the first-place ball bounced than the second- and third-place balls. Round to the nearest whole number.

- Suppose you drop each ball from a different height. Could you use fractions to compare them? Explain.

- Use the idea of pressure to explain what happened in the activity.

Did You KNOW?

How high a ball bounces depends (in part) on how much pressure pushes from inside the ball. The pressure depends on how much air is squeezed inside.

Problem Solving

Going Further

1. Repeat the activity, dropping each ball from a different height. Did you get the same results as before? Use fractions to compare.

2. Design and complete an activity to compare how the same ball bounces at different pressures.

Check Your Progress B

Add. Write each sum in simplest form. (pages 552–555)

1. $\frac{2}{10} + \frac{3}{10}$ 2. $\frac{1}{6} + \frac{3}{6}$ 3. $\frac{1}{4} + \frac{2}{4}$ 4. $\frac{6}{8} + \frac{4}{8}$ 5. $\frac{7}{12} + \frac{5}{12}$

Subtract. Write each difference in simplest form. (pages 556–559)

6. $\frac{7}{11} - \frac{4}{11}$ 7. $\frac{9}{12} - \frac{3}{12}$ 8. $\frac{4}{8} - \frac{2}{8}$ 9. $\frac{9}{12} - \frac{3}{12}$ 10. $\frac{5}{7} - \frac{3}{7}$

Use the words *likely, unlikely, certain,* **or** *impossible* **to describe the probability.** (pages 560–561)

11. white   12. yellow   13. a color   14. blue

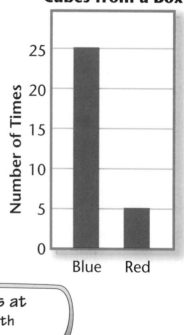

List the possible outcomes for each. (pages 562–563)

15.

16.

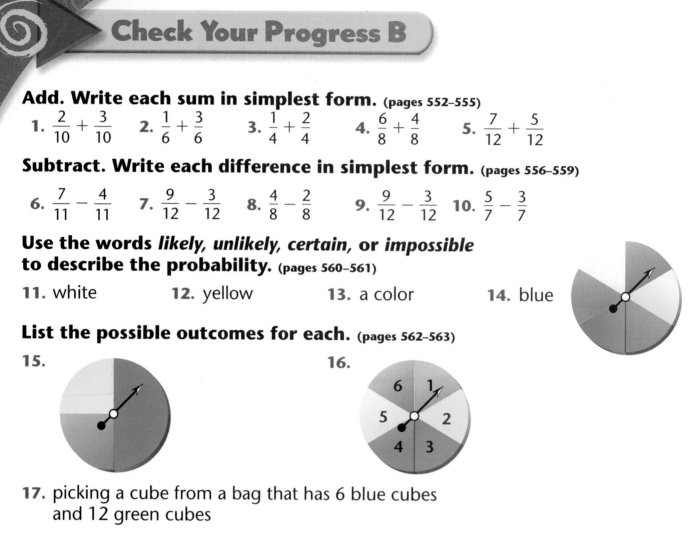

17. picking a cube from a bag that has 6 blue cubes and 12 green cubes

Use data from the graph for problems 18–20. (pages 560–563)

18. What color is there the most of in the box?

19. **What if** there are a total of 12 cubes in the box. How many of each color do you predict are in the box? Why?

20. **Explain** how to conduct an experiment to predict the number of red counters in a bag that has 30 counters in it.

Outcomes of Picking Cubes from a Box

Additional activities at
www.mhschool.com/math

Tell if the figure shows equal parts. If yes, write a fraction for the part that is shaded.

5.   6.   7.   8.

Copy and shade each figure to show the fraction.

9. $\frac{1}{4}$

10. $\frac{7}{8}$

Algebra & functions **What could the next number be? Explain.**

11. $\frac{1}{8}, \frac{2}{8}, \frac{3}{8}, \frac{4}{8},$ _____

12. $\frac{1}{2}, \frac{1}{3}, \frac{1}{4}, \frac{1}{5}, \frac{1}{6},$ _____

Problem Solving

Use data from *Did You Know?* for problems 13–14.

13. **Health:** This diagram shows the kinds of food many of us eat each day. What fraction shows the grains?

14. Which kinds of food are each $\frac{1}{10}$ of our diet?

★15. **Compare:** If you cut a square into 4 equal parts and a friend cuts the same size square into 8 equal parts, which parts are larger? Why?

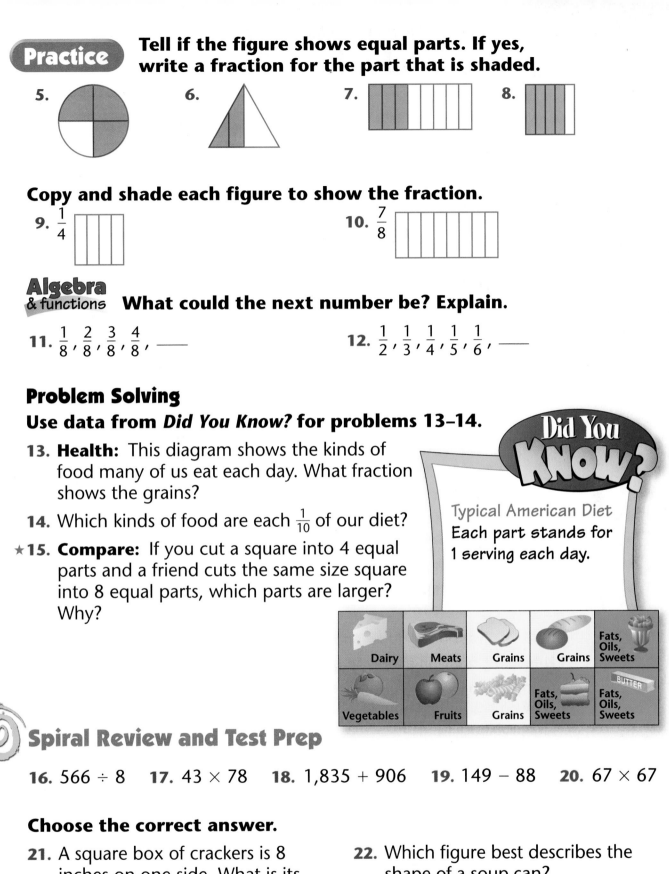

Did You KNOW?

Typical American Diet
Each part stands for
1 serving each day.

| Dairy | Meats | Grains | Grains | Fats, Oils, Sweets |
| Vegetables | Fruits | Grains | Fats, Oils, Sweets | Fats, Oils, Sweets |

Spiral Review and Test Prep

16. $566 \div 8$ 17. 43×78 18. $1,835 + 906$ 19. $149 - 88$ 20. 67×67

Choose the correct answer.

21. A square box of crackers is 8 inches on one side. What is its perimeter?
    - **A.** 16 inches   **C.** 32 inches
    - **B.** 24 inches   **D.** 64 inches

22. Which figure best describes the shape of a soup can?
    - **F.** Sphere   **H.** Cone
    - **G.** Pyramid   **J.** Cylinder

13·2 Explore Equivalent Fractions

Learn

Math Word

equivalent fraction
different fractions that name the same amount

You can use fraction strips to find equivalent fractions. Find another fraction equivalent for $\frac{1}{2}$.

Work Together

▶ Explore how to use fraction strips to model the problem.

You Will Need
• **fraction strips**

- Find the fraction strip to show $\frac{1}{2}$.
- Use two $\frac{1}{4}$ fraction strips to show $\frac{2}{4}$.
- Compare the $\frac{1}{2}$ and $\frac{2}{4}$ using the fraction strips.
- How do they compare? How does this help solve the problem?

| $\frac{1}{2}$ | |
| $\frac{1}{4}$ | $\frac{1}{4}$ |

▶ Use fraction strips to find as many **equivalent fractions** for $\frac{1}{2}$ as you can.

- List all of the equivalent fractions for $\frac{1}{2}$ that you find.
- Compare your list with others.

▶ Choose another fraction strip. List the equivalent fractions you find. Compare your list with others.

Make Connections

Here is how to show equivalent fractions for $\frac{1}{3}$.

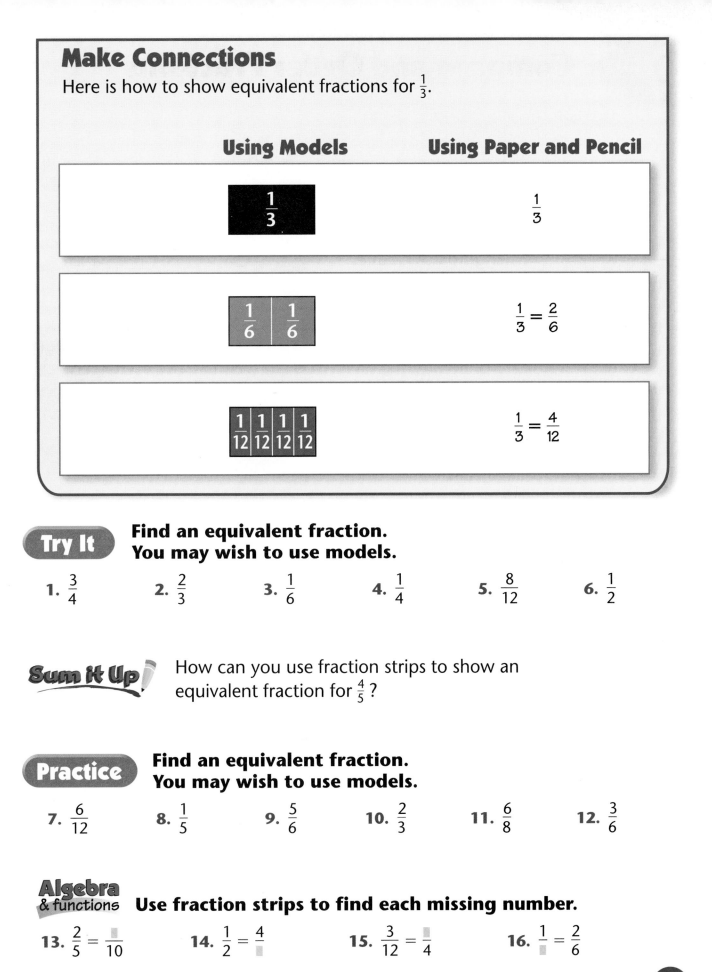

Using Models	Using Paper and Pencil
$\frac{1}{3}$	$\frac{1}{3}$
$\frac{1}{6}$ $\frac{1}{6}$	$\frac{1}{3} = \frac{2}{6}$
$\frac{1}{12}$ $\frac{1}{12}$ $\frac{1}{12}$ $\frac{1}{12}$	$\frac{1}{3} = \frac{4}{12}$

Try It   **Find an equivalent fraction.
You may wish to use models.**

1. $\frac{3}{4}$
2. $\frac{2}{3}$
3. $\frac{1}{6}$
4. $\frac{1}{4}$
5. $\frac{8}{12}$
6. $\frac{1}{2}$

Sum it Up   How can you use fraction strips to show an equivalent fraction for $\frac{4}{5}$?

Practice   **Find an equivalent fraction.
You may wish to use models.**

7. $\frac{6}{12}$
8. $\frac{1}{5}$
9. $\frac{5}{6}$
10. $\frac{2}{3}$
11. $\frac{6}{8}$
12. $\frac{3}{6}$

Algebra & functions   Use fraction strips to find each missing number.

13. $\frac{2}{5} = \frac{\blacksquare}{10}$
14. $\frac{1}{2} = \frac{4}{\blacksquare}$
15. $\frac{3}{12} = \frac{\blacksquare}{4}$
16. $\frac{1}{\blacksquare} = \frac{2}{6}$

Compare and Order Fractions

Algebra & functions

Learn

Jenna and Martha are making fruit smoothies. Jenna uses $\frac{1}{4}$ cup of fruit juice, and Martha uses $\frac{3}{4}$ cup of fruit juice. Who uses more fruit juice?

There's more than one way!

You can compare the fractions to solve this problem.

Method A

Use fraction strips to model and compare $\frac{1}{4}$ and $\frac{3}{4}$.

| $\frac{1}{4}$ |

| $\frac{1}{4}$ | $\frac{1}{4}$ | $\frac{1}{4}$ |

$\frac{3}{4} > \frac{1}{4}$

Method B

Use a number line to compare $\frac{1}{4}$ and $\frac{3}{4}$.

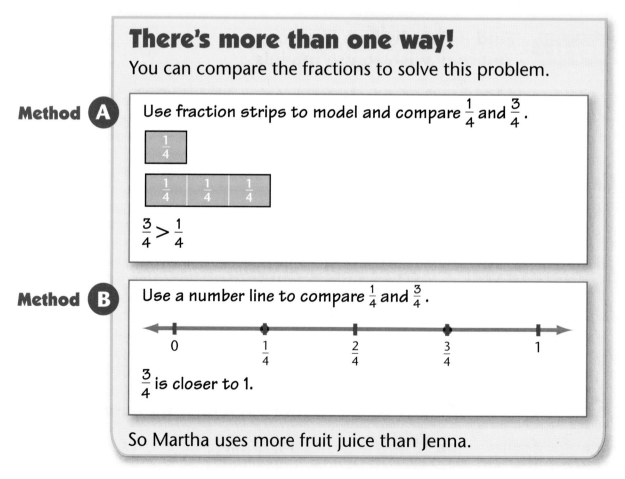

$\frac{3}{4}$ is closer to 1.

So Martha uses more fruit juice than Jenna.

Boris uses $\frac{5}{6}$ cup of fruit juice to make his fruit smoothie. Lana uses $\frac{2}{3}$ cup of fruit juice, and Garry uses $\frac{3}{4}$ cup of juice. Who uses the most fruit juice in a fruit smoothie?

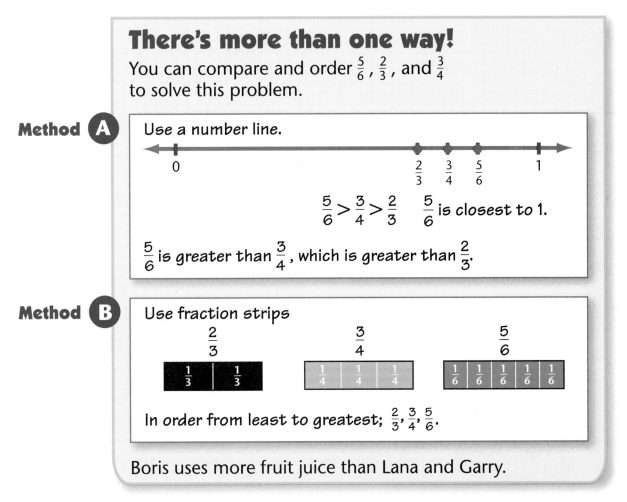

There's more than one way!

You can compare and order $\frac{5}{6}$, $\frac{2}{3}$, and $\frac{3}{4}$ to solve this problem.

Method A Use a number line.

$\frac{5}{6} > \frac{3}{4} > \frac{2}{3}$ $\frac{5}{6}$ is closest to 1.

$\frac{5}{6}$ is greater than $\frac{3}{4}$, which is greater than $\frac{2}{3}$.

Method B Use fraction strips

In order from least to greatest; $\frac{2}{3}$, $\frac{3}{4}$, $\frac{5}{6}$.

Boris uses more fruit juice than Lana and Garry.

Try It **Compare. Write >, <, or =.**

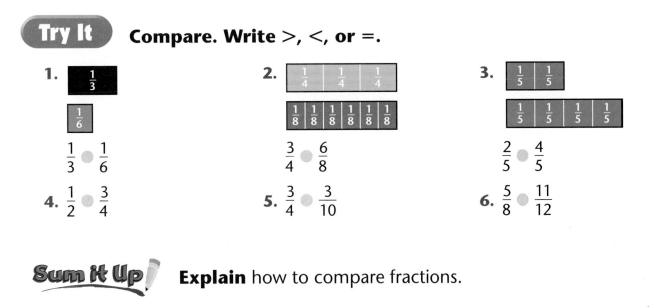

1. $\frac{1}{3}$ ⬤ $\frac{1}{6}$

2. $\frac{3}{4}$ ⬤ $\frac{6}{8}$

3. $\frac{2}{5}$ ⬤ $\frac{4}{5}$

4. $\frac{1}{2}$ ⬤ $\frac{3}{4}$

5. $\frac{3}{4}$ ⬤ $\frac{3}{10}$

6. $\frac{5}{8}$ ⬤ $\frac{11}{12}$

Sum it Up **Explain** how to compare fractions.

Compare. Write >, <, or =.

7.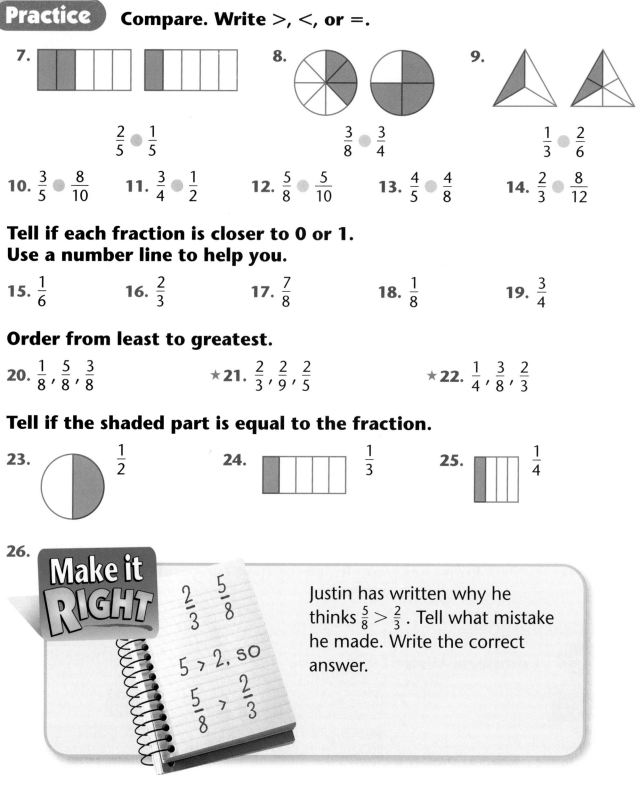

$\dfrac{2}{5}$ ● $\dfrac{1}{5}$

8.

$\dfrac{3}{8}$ ● $\dfrac{3}{4}$

9.

$\dfrac{1}{3}$ ● $\dfrac{2}{6}$

10. $\dfrac{3}{5}$ ● $\dfrac{8}{10}$ 11. $\dfrac{3}{4}$ ● $\dfrac{1}{2}$ 12. $\dfrac{5}{8}$ ● $\dfrac{5}{10}$ 13. $\dfrac{4}{5}$ ● $\dfrac{4}{8}$ 14. $\dfrac{2}{3}$ ● $\dfrac{8}{12}$

Tell if each fraction is closer to 0 or 1.
Use a number line to help you.

15. $\dfrac{1}{6}$ 16. $\dfrac{2}{3}$ 17. $\dfrac{7}{8}$ 18. $\dfrac{1}{8}$ 19. $\dfrac{3}{4}$

Order from least to greatest.

20. $\dfrac{1}{8}, \dfrac{5}{8}, \dfrac{3}{8}$ ★21. $\dfrac{2}{3}, \dfrac{2}{9}, \dfrac{2}{5}$ ★22. $\dfrac{1}{4}, \dfrac{3}{8}, \dfrac{2}{3}$

Tell if the shaded part is equal to the fraction.

23. $\dfrac{1}{2}$

24. $\dfrac{1}{3}$

25. $\dfrac{1}{4}$

26. **Make it RIGHT**

$\dfrac{2}{3}$ $\dfrac{5}{8}$

5 > 2, so

$\dfrac{5}{8} > \dfrac{2}{3}$

Justin has written why he thinks $\dfrac{5}{8} > \dfrac{2}{3}$. Tell what mistake he made. Write the correct answer.

Problem Solving

27. **Health:** A survey found that about $\dfrac{2}{5}$ of the women surveyed choose foods for a healthy diet. Is this close to one? Explain.

28. **Collect Data:** Survey students in your class to find out their favorite foods. Make a bar graph. Compare your results.

Use data from the graph for problems 29–30.

29. **Science:** Apples are solid. They can be used to make liquids. Are more apples used to make juice or applesauce?

 30. **Explain** how you can use a number line to compare the amount of apples sold fresh to the amount used to make applesauce.

31. Claudio and Tara are each reading the same book. Claudio has read $\frac{3}{5}$ of the book. Tara has read $\frac{1}{2}$ of the book. Who has read more?

32. Jen baked for $\frac{3}{4}$ hour. Jason baked for $\frac{1}{2}$ hour. Who baked longer?

★33. **Logical Reasoning:** Tim, Rudy, Luke, Nori, and Lita each eat an apple, a banana, a bran muffin, a cup of yogurt, or carrot cake. Use the clues to tell which dessert each person eats.
Clues:
Tim did not have fruit, yogurt, or a muffin.
Rudy has a red fruit.
Luke does not have fruit.
Nori's dessert is baked in an oven.

How Apples are Processed and Sold in the United States

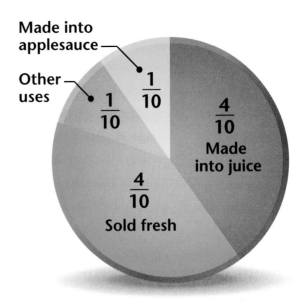

Spiral Review and Test Prep

Name each figure.

34.

35.

36.

37.

Choose the correct answer.

38. What is the volume of this figure?
   A. 6 cubic units
   B. 12 cubic units
   C. 8 cubic units
   D. 14 cubic units

39. The Martins buy 1 pizza. There are 8 slices in each pizza. All 4 members of the Martin family each eat 2 slices. How many slices are left?
   F. 12
   G. 6
   H. 832
   J. 0

Chapter 13 Fractions and Probability **539**

13·4 Parts of a Group

Learn

Jordan is looking at a plate of muffins. What part of the group of muffins is corn muffins?

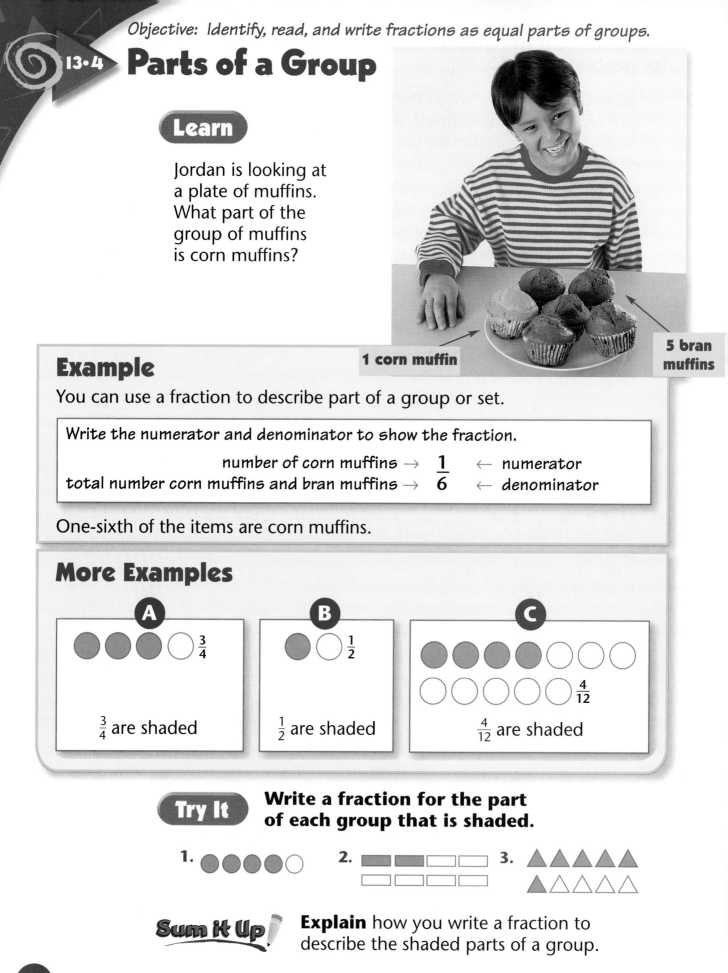

1 corn muffin

5 bran muffins

Example

You can use a fraction to describe part of a group or set.

Write the numerator and denominator to show the fraction.

number of corn muffins → **1** ← numerator

total number corn muffins and bran muffins → **6** ← denominator

One-sixth of the items are corn muffins.

More Examples

A

$\frac{3}{4}$

$\frac{3}{4}$ are shaded

B

$\frac{1}{2}$

$\frac{1}{2}$ are shaded

C

$\frac{4}{12}$

$\frac{4}{12}$ are shaded

Try It Write a fraction for the part of each group that is shaded.

1. ●●●●○

2. ▮▮▯▯ ▯▯▯▯

3. ▲▲▲▲▲ ▲△△△△

Sum It Up **Explain** how you write a fraction to describe the shaded parts of a group.

Write a fraction for the part of each group that is shaded.

4.  5.  6.

Copy and shade each set to show the fraction.

7. $\frac{3}{4}$ ▢▢▢▢ 8. $\frac{1}{3}$ ◯◯◯ 9. $\frac{5}{6}$ △△△△△△

Algebra & functions **What could the next shape be? Explain. Then write a fraction for the part of the set that is shaded.**

10.  ____

Problem Solving

Use data from the picture for problems 11–13.

11. **Art:** In this painting, two of the pieces of fruit near the pitcher are apples and three are oranges. What fraction tells the part of this group that are apples?

★12. **Language Arts:** Write a paragraph involving fractions to describe the painting.

Still Life with Apples and Oranges, by Paul Cézanne

13. Mara's ticket to the museum costs $6.95 and Mile's ticket costs $2.35 more than Mara's ticket. How much did they spend altogether?

 Spiral Review and Test Prep

14. $432 \div 6$ 15. 6×754 16. $\$12.14 \times 2$ 17. $356 + 12 + 785$

Choose the correct answer.

18. What is the area of this figure?

A. 24 sq units   C. 12 sq units
B. 16 sq units   D. Not Here

19. Kyle has 15 small boxes of cereal. If he divides them evenly among his 5 friends, how many boxes will each friend get?

F. 2   H. 11
G. 3   J. 21

13•5 Explore Finding Parts of a Group

Learn

You can use 2-color counters to explore finding parts of a group.
What is $\frac{1}{4}$ of 12?

Work Together

▶ Work with a partner to explore finding the fraction of a number. Find $\frac{1}{4}$ of 12.

You Will Need
• **2-color counters**

- Make 4 equal groups using 12 counters.

- Find the number of counters in 1 group.

- What do the 12 counters stand for?

- Why did you make 4 equal groups?

- What do the number of counters in 1 group represent?
  So $\frac{1}{4}$ of 12 = 3.

▶ Use counters to find the fraction of the number.

$\frac{1}{2}$ of 14 $\qquad$ $\frac{1}{5}$ of 20 $\qquad$ $\frac{5}{6}$ of 12 $\qquad$ $\frac{2}{3}$ of 15 $\qquad$ $\frac{5}{8}$ of 24

Make Connections

Here is how to show the fraction of a number.

Find: $\frac{1}{3}$ of 15

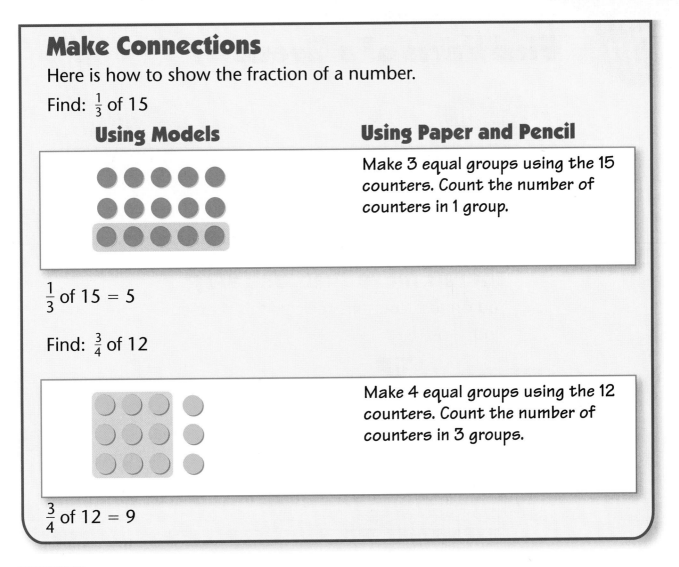

Using Models	Using Paper and Pencil

Make 3 equal groups using the 15 counters. Count the number of counters in 1 group.

$\frac{1}{3}$ of 15 = 5

Find: $\frac{3}{4}$ of 12

Make 4 equal groups using the 12 counters. Count the number of counters in 3 groups.

$\frac{3}{4}$ of 12 = 9

Try It   **Use counters to find each fraction of a number.**

1. $\frac{1}{4}$ of 8
2. $\frac{1}{2}$ of 6
3. $\frac{2}{3}$ of 9
4. $\frac{4}{5}$ of 10
5. $\frac{3}{4}$ of 16

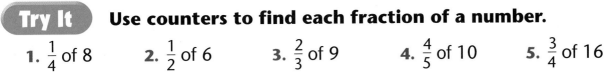 How do you decide how many equal groups to make with counters to find the fraction of a number?

Practice   **Find each fraction of a number. You may wish to use counters.**

6. $\frac{1}{4}$ of 16
7. $\frac{1}{6}$ of 6
8. $\frac{5}{6}$ of 18
9. $\frac{3}{10}$ of 20
10. $\frac{1}{5}$ of 10

11. **Analyze:** You know that $\frac{7}{10}$ of 30 counters are red. How many counters are not red? Explain.

Find Parts of a Group

13·6

Learn

At a science club meeting, members eat $\frac{2}{3}$ of the oranges in this bag. How many oranges do the members eat?

18 Large Oranges

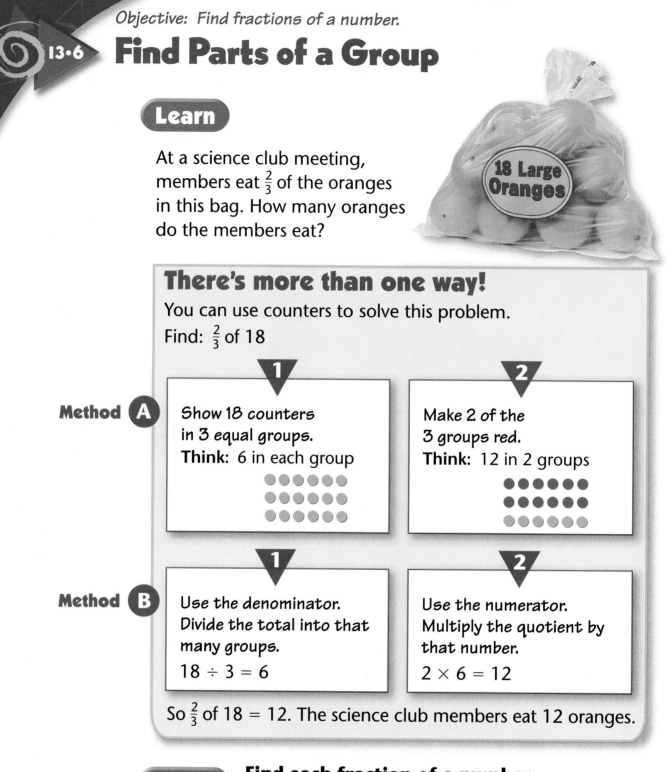

There's more than one way!

You can use counters to solve this problem.

Find: $\frac{2}{3}$ of 18

Method A

1

Show 18 counters in 3 equal groups.

Think: 6 in each group

2

Make 2 of the 3 groups red.

Think: 12 in 2 groups

Method B

1

Use the denominator. Divide the total into that many groups.

$18 \div 3 = 6$

2

Use the numerator. Multiply the quotient by that number.

$2 \times 6 = 12$

So $\frac{2}{3}$ of 18 = 12. The science club members eat 12 oranges.

Try It

Find each fraction of a number. You may wish to use models.

1. $\frac{1}{5}$ of 10
2. $\frac{2}{3}$ of 12
3. $\frac{3}{4}$ of 8
4. $\frac{2}{2}$ of 2
5. $\frac{1}{2}$ of 16

Sum it Up

Explain how to use the numerator and denominator when finding the fraction of a number using counters.

Find each fraction of a number.

6. $\frac{3}{8}$ of 16   **7.** $\frac{2}{3}$ of 6   **8.** $\frac{5}{6}$ of 12   **9.** $\frac{4}{5}$ of 20   **10.** $\frac{1}{4}$ of 16

Algebra
& functions   **Use the model to find each missing number.**

11. $\frac{2}{3}$ of 9 = ▧   **12.** $\frac{3}{4}$ of ▧ = 12   **13.** ▧ of 8 = 6

Problem Solving

Use data from the table for problems 14–15.

14. Grayson's Farm sold $\frac{2}{3}$ of the apples in the first hour of the sale. How many apples is this?

★**15.** Hector bought $\frac{1}{2}$ of the bananas and $\frac{3}{4}$ of the grapes. Did he buy more bananas or grapes? Explain.

16. **Create a problem** that you can solve by finding the fraction of a number. Solve it. Ask others to solve it.

Fruit Sale

Kind	Number Donated
bananas	16
pears	20
apples	18
grapes	12

Spiral Review and Test Prep

Identify each figure.

17.    **18.**   **19.**

Choose the correct answer.

20. Jessie puts her carrot cake in the oven at 2:20 P.M. It must bake for 45 minutes. What time should she take it out of the oven?

   A. 1:45 P.M.   **C.** 2:45 P.M.
   B. 2:55 P.M.   **D.** 3:05 P.M.

21. Adam needs to find the area of a square. He measured one side to be 8 inches long. What is the area of the square?

   F. 58 sq in.   **H.** 64 sq in.
   G. 62 sq in.   **J.** 68 sq in.

Objective: *Use prior knowledge to check for reasonableness of a solution.*

Problem Solving: Reading for Math
Check for Reasonableness

Cookies for Sale!

Read ▶ Lani baked a dozen oatmeal cookies. She put raisins in $\frac{3}{4}$ of the cookies. How many cookies have raisins?

READING SKILL ▶ **Use Prior Knowledge**

Sometimes, you must use what you already know to solve a problem.

- **What do you know?** Raisins are in $\frac{3}{4}$ of the dozen cookies.

- **What prior knowledge will help solve this problem?** 12 items = 1 dozen

- **What do you need to find?** How many cookies have raisins

MATH SKILL ▶ **Check for Reasonableness**

An answer is reasonable if it makes sense.

Plan ▶ You need to find $\frac{3}{4}$ of 12. Use your knowledge of fractions.

Solve ▶ 4 groups of 3 = 12. Raisins are in 3 of the groups. 3 groups of 3 cookies = 9 cookies.

Check the reasonableness of your answer. Half of the cookies is 6 cookies. Since $\frac{3}{4} > \frac{1}{2}$, 9 cookies with raisins makes sense.

Look Back ▶ • How could you check your answer?

Sum it Up! How does checking for reasonableness help solve problems?

Solve. Check for reasonableness.

1. Al bought a loaf of banana bread at the bake sale. He cut the banana bread into 8 slices. Al's friends ate $\frac{3}{4}$ of the bread. How many slices did they eat?

2. Wayne made 12 slices of carrot cake for the bake sale. He put coconut frosting on $\frac{2}{3}$ of the carrot cake slices. How many slices had coconut frosting?

Use data from the graph for problems 3–7.

3. Another person bought $\frac{5}{6}$ of Carlos's bags of munchie mix. How many bags of munchie mix did the person buy?

4. Sharon sold $\frac{2}{3}$ of her muffins in the first hour of the sale. How many of her muffins were sold?

5. A customer bought $\frac{3}{5}$ of Nan's granola squares. How many squares did the person buy?

6. Bud put peanuts in $\frac{1}{4}$ of his pretzel treats. How many pretzel treats did not have peanuts?

7. At the end of the sale, 1 pretzel treat, 1 bag of munchie mix, 1 granola square, and 1 muffin were left. Carlos writes a fraction to represent each amount. How are his fractions alike? How are they different?

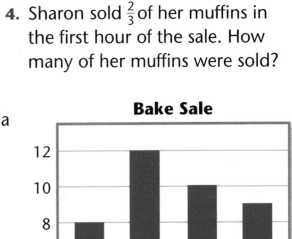

Bake Sale

Item vs *Student* (Bud, Carlos, Nan, Sharon)

Problem Solving

Spiral Review and Test Prep

Choose the correct answer.

A total of 20 items were for the bake sale. Of those items, $\frac{2}{5}$ were pies. How many items were pies?

8. Which of these statements is true?
   A. There were 20 pies sold at the sale.
   B. $\frac{2}{8}$ of the pies were sold.
   C. $\frac{3}{5}$ of the items were not pies.

9. A reasonable answer for this problem would be
   F. greater than 20.
   G. less than 4.
   H. greater than 4 but less than 10.

13·8 Mixed Numbers

Math in ACTION

Learn

Math Word

mixed number
a number that has a whole number and a fraction

Kelly and Kevin mix $1\frac{1}{2}$ cups of milk with cake mix, pudding, and whipped cream. How can they show and read $1\frac{1}{2}$?

Chef Kelly McHugh and Kevin Dempsey bake in her restaurant.

Example

You can draw a picture to show $1\frac{1}{2}$ as a **mixed number**.

Draw a picture.

$1\frac{1}{2}$ cups means
1 whole cup + $\frac{1}{2}$ cup.

Read: one and one half

1 whole cup + $\frac{1}{2}$ cup

More Examples

A

Two and one half

B

Three and one fourth

C

Two and two thirds

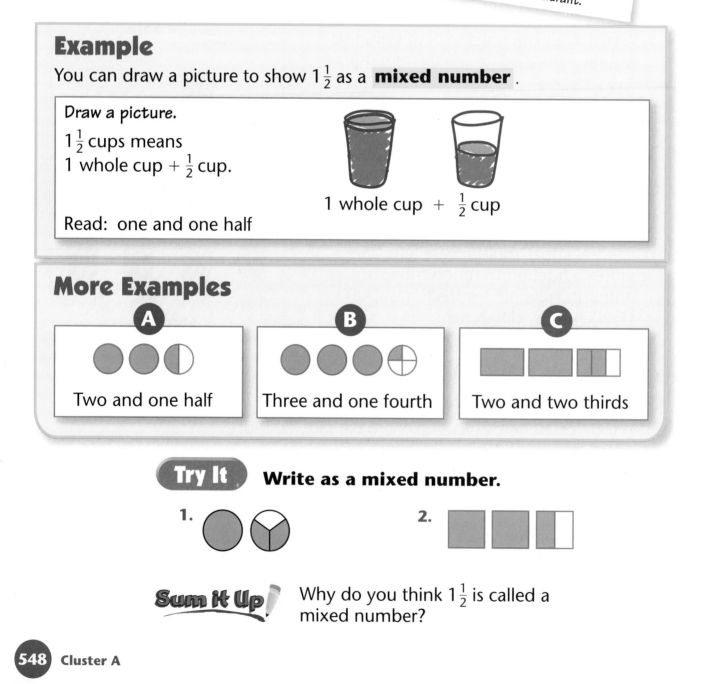

Try It   **Write as a mixed number.**

1.

2.

Sum it Up   Why do you think $1\frac{1}{2}$ is called a mixed number?

Practice · Write as a mixed number.

3.

4.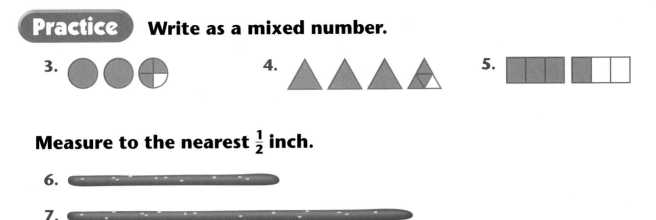

5.

Measure to the nearest $\frac{1}{2}$ inch.

6.

7.

Draw a model of each mixed number. Then, write each mixed number in words.

★**8.** $2\frac{1}{4}$

★**9.** $1\frac{2}{3}$

★**10.** $1\frac{3}{8}$

Problem Solving

Use data from the table for problems 11–12.

11. **Music:** How many beats are in this line of music?

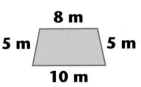

12. **Create a problem** using the data from the table. Use mixed numbers. Solve it. Ask others to solve it.

Numbers of Beats for Notes	
o = 4 beats	♩ = 1 beat
𝅗𝅥 = 2 beats	♪ = $\frac{1}{2}$ beat

13. **Analyze:** How many fourths are in 1? How many fourths are in 2? Draw a diagram to show your answers.

Spiral Review and Test Prep

Find each perimeter.

14.
16 in.   16 in.
24 in.

15. 15 cm
10 cm

16. 8 m
5 m   5 m
10 m

Choose the correct answer.

17. Al wants to buy 4 slices of pizza for $1.75 each. How much money does he need?

A. $4.75   C. $6.75

B. $5.00   D. $7.00

18. Meg eats a small bag of nuts. About how much does she eat?

F. 6 ounces   H. 60 ounces

G. 6 pounds   J. 60 pounds

Write a fraction for the shaded part. (pages 532–533, 540–541)

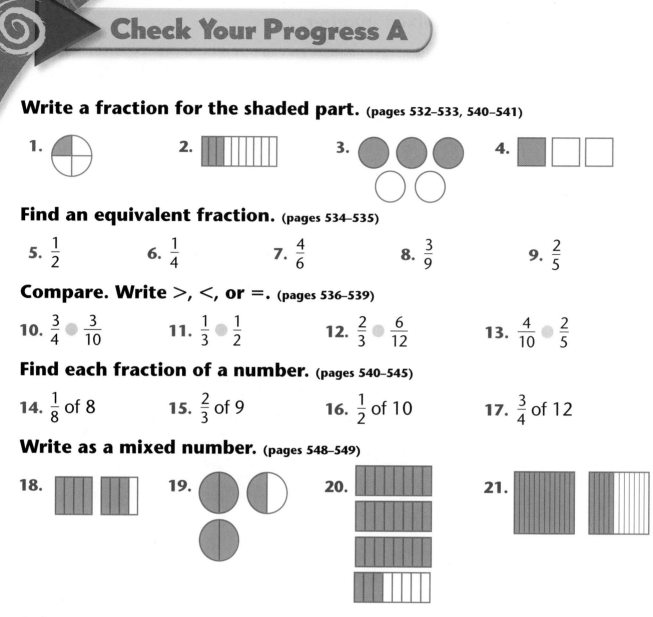

1.

2.

3.

4.

Find an equivalent fraction. (pages 534–535)

5. $\frac{1}{2}$

6. $\frac{1}{4}$

7. $\frac{4}{6}$

8. $\frac{3}{9}$

9. $\frac{2}{5}$

Compare. Write >, <, or =. (pages 536–539)

10. $\frac{3}{4}$ ● $\frac{3}{10}$

11. $\frac{1}{3}$ ● $\frac{1}{2}$

12. $\frac{2}{3}$ ● $\frac{6}{12}$

13. $\frac{4}{10}$ ● $\frac{2}{5}$

Find each fraction of a number. (pages 540–545)

14. $\frac{1}{8}$ of 8

15. $\frac{2}{3}$ of 9

16. $\frac{1}{2}$ of 10

17. $\frac{3}{4}$ of 12

Write as a mixed number. (pages 548–549)

18.

19.

20.

21.

Solve. (pages 548–549)

22. Morgan and Wes have the same size box of raisins. Morgan eats $\frac{1}{2}$ of his raisins. Wes eats $\frac{1}{3}$ of his raisins. Who eats more? Explain.

23. There are 12 students in line for lunch. One-fourth of them choose a salad. How many students choose salad?

24. There are 8 nuts left in a pack. Three of the nuts that are left are peanuts. What fractional part of the nuts are not peanuts?

Journal

25. **Explain** how to use counters to find $\frac{1}{4}$ of any number. Give an example.

Additional activities at
www.mhschool.com/math

TECHNOLOGY LINK

Model Equivalent Fractions

Sergio and his friends are sharing a pizza. The pizza is cut into 6 pieces, so each piece is $\frac{1}{6}$ of the pizza. If Sergio ate $\frac{1}{2}$ of the pizza, how many pieces did he eat?

You can model the number of pieces of pizza Sergio ate using fraction strips.

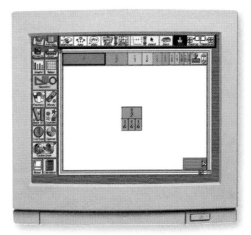

- Stamp out a $\frac{1}{2}$ fraction strip.
- Stamp out $\frac{1}{6}$ fraction strips under the $\frac{1}{2}$ fraction strip.
- The model shows that $\frac{1}{2} = \frac{3}{6}$.

How many pieces did he eat?

Use the computer to model each fraction. Then find one fraction that is equivalent to the given fraction.

1. $\frac{1}{3}$ **2.** $\frac{4}{8}$ **3.** $\frac{3}{9}$ **4.** $\frac{3}{12}$

5. Analyze: How do fraction strips help you find equivalent fractions?

Solve.

6. Maria made a carrot cake. She cut it into 12 pieces, so each piece is $\frac{1}{12}$ of the cake. She gave $\frac{1}{3}$ of the cake to her brother. How many pieces did she give to her brother?

7. Mrs. Arnez cut a long piece of ribbon into 8 smaller pieces, so each smaller piece is $\frac{1}{8}$ of the long piece. She gave 2 of the smaller pieces to her niece. What fraction of the long piece of ribbon did she give to her niece?

For more practice, use Math Traveler™.

13·9 Explore Adding Fractions

Learn

You can use fraction strips to explore adding fractions.

What is $\frac{2}{3} + \frac{1}{3}$?

Work Together

▶ Explore adding fractions.
Find: $\frac{2}{3} + \frac{1}{3}$

- Use fraction strips to model the problem.

- Record your work in a number sentence.

You Will Need
- **fraction strips**

| $\frac{1}{3}$ | $\frac{1}{3}$ | | $\frac{1}{3}$ |

▶ Use fraction strips to find the sum. Write it as a fraction with the least denominator, if possible.

$$\frac{1}{5} + \frac{2}{5} \qquad \frac{1}{3} + \frac{1}{3} \qquad \frac{2}{8} + \frac{3}{8} \qquad \frac{1}{4} + \frac{2}{4}$$

- What happens to the denominators of the fractions you added?

- What happens to the numerators of the fractions you added?

Make Connections

Here is how to add fractions and write the sum with the least denominator.

Find: $\frac{3}{12} + \frac{5}{12}$

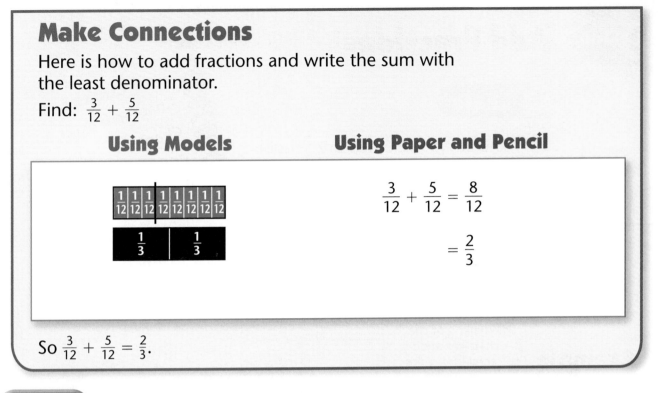

Using Models	Using Paper and Pencil

$$\frac{3}{12} + \frac{5}{12} = \frac{8}{12}$$

$$= \frac{2}{3}$$

So $\frac{3}{12} + \frac{5}{12} = \frac{2}{3}$.

Try It **Add. You may wish to use fraction strips.**

1. $\frac{1}{4} + \frac{1}{4}$

2. $\frac{1}{9} + \frac{2}{9}$

3. $\frac{3}{12} + \frac{7}{12}$

4. $\frac{1}{6} + \frac{1}{6}$

5. $\frac{1}{5} + \frac{3}{5}$

6. $\frac{3}{5} + \frac{3}{5}$

7. $\frac{1}{3} + \frac{1}{3}$

8. $\frac{7}{12} + \frac{3}{12}$

9. $\frac{6}{10} + \frac{4}{10}$

10. $\frac{2}{5} + \frac{4}{5}$

Sum it Up! How do you use fraction strips to rename a sum as an equivalent fraction with the least denominator?

Practice **Add. You may wish to use fraction strips.**

11. $\frac{1}{6} + \frac{2}{6}$

12. $\frac{2}{8} + \frac{4}{8}$

13. $\frac{9}{10} + \frac{2}{10}$

14. $\frac{4}{9} + \frac{2}{9}$

15. $\frac{1}{5} + \frac{1}{5}$

16. $\frac{4}{12} + \frac{4}{12}$

17. $\frac{1}{8} + \frac{2}{8}$

18. $\frac{2}{8} + \frac{2}{8}$

19. $\frac{3}{7} + \frac{4}{7}$

20. $\frac{3}{8} + \frac{4}{8}$

21. $\frac{1}{8} + \frac{2}{8}$

22. $\frac{3}{6} + \frac{4}{6}$

23. $\frac{1}{6} + \frac{4}{6}$

24. $\frac{7}{10} + \frac{4}{10}$

25. $\frac{5}{8} + \frac{2}{8}$

26. **Analyze:** When you add a fraction to a fraction, is your answer always a fraction? Give an example to support your answer.

13·10 **Add Fractions**

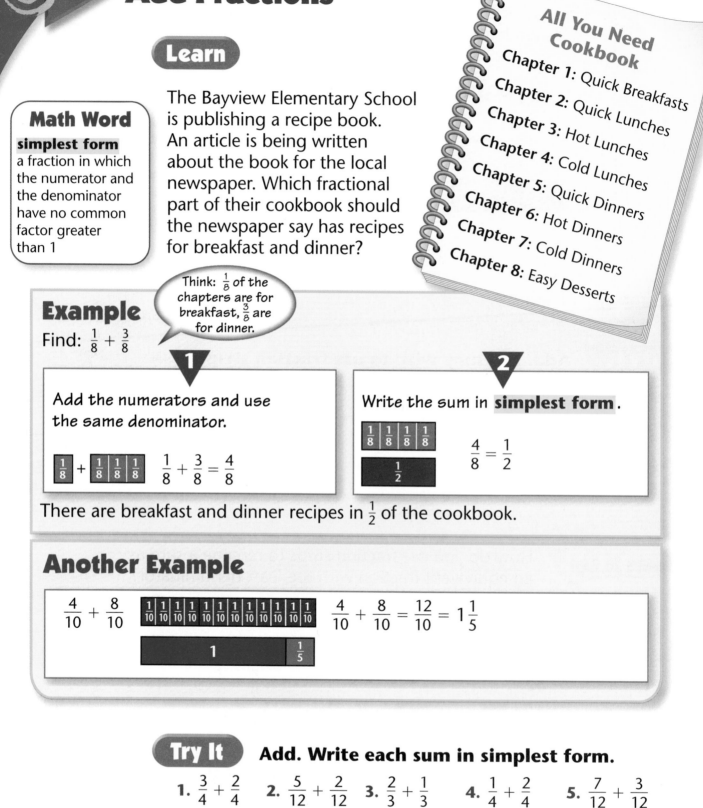

Learn

Math Word

simplest form
a fraction in which the numerator and the denominator have no common factor greater than 1

The Bayview Elementary School is publishing a recipe book. An article is being written about the book for the local newspaper. Which fractional part of their cookbook should the newspaper say has recipes for breakfast and dinner?

All You Need Cookbook
Chapter 1: Quick Breakfasts
Chapter 2: Quick Lunches
Chapter 3: Hot Lunches
Chapter 4: Cold Lunches
Chapter 5: Quick Dinners
Chapter 6: Hot Dinners
Chapter 7: Cold Dinners
Chapter 8: Easy Desserts

Think: $\frac{1}{8}$ of the chapters are for breakfast, $\frac{3}{8}$ are for dinner.

Example

Find: $\frac{1}{8} + \frac{3}{8}$

1

Add the numerators and use the same denominator.

$\frac{1}{8} + \frac{3}{8} = \frac{4}{8}$

2

Write the sum in **simplest form**.

$\frac{4}{8} = \frac{1}{2}$

There are breakfast and dinner recipes in $\frac{1}{2}$ of the cookbook.

Another Example

$\frac{4}{10} + \frac{8}{10}$

$\frac{4}{10} + \frac{8}{10} = \frac{12}{10} = 1\frac{1}{5}$

Try It Add. Write each sum in simplest form.

1. $\frac{3}{4} + \frac{2}{4}$ 2. $\frac{5}{12} + \frac{2}{12}$ 3. $\frac{2}{3} + \frac{1}{3}$ 4. $\frac{1}{4} + \frac{2}{4}$ 5. $\frac{7}{12} + \frac{3}{12}$

Sum it Up **Explain** how you would find $\frac{5}{8} + \frac{5}{8}$.

Add. Write each sum in simplest form.

6. $\dfrac{3}{10}$
$+\dfrac{8}{10}$

7. $\dfrac{5}{12}$
$+\dfrac{2}{12}$

8. $\dfrac{1}{4}$
$+\dfrac{2}{4}$

9. $\dfrac{2}{5}$
$+\dfrac{2}{5}$

10. $\dfrac{9}{10}$
$+\dfrac{3}{10}$

11. $\dfrac{3}{4}$
$+\dfrac{2}{4}$

12. $\dfrac{7}{10} + \dfrac{1}{10}$

13. $\dfrac{1}{7} + \dfrac{4}{7}$

14. $\dfrac{3}{4} + \dfrac{3}{4}$

15. $\dfrac{3}{8} + \dfrac{4}{8}$

16. $\dfrac{3}{6} + \dfrac{4}{6}$

★17. $\dfrac{1}{5} + \dfrac{2}{5} + \dfrac{1}{5}$

★18. $\dfrac{2}{12} + \dfrac{4}{12} + \dfrac{3}{12}$

★19. $\dfrac{1}{2} + \dfrac{1}{2} + \dfrac{1}{2}$

★20. $3 + \dfrac{1}{3} + \dfrac{2}{3}$

Algebra
& functions Find each number.

21. $\dfrac{5}{10} + \dfrac{\blacksquare}{10} = \dfrac{7}{10}$

22. $\dfrac{1}{8} + \dfrac{3}{8} = \dfrac{4}{8} = \dfrac{\blacksquare}{2}$

23. $\dfrac{3}{\blacksquare} + \dfrac{4}{9} = \dfrac{7}{9}$

Problem Solving

Use the data from *Did You Know?* for problem 24.

24. **Measurement:** How many yards was the kappa maki?

25. **Health:** Raw tuna is another fish that is often used in Japanese meals. A chef uses $\dfrac{1}{8}$ of a pound for each serving of a dish. If the chef makes 3 servings, how much of the tuna does the chef use?

26. **Generalize:** How can you tell if the sum of two fractions is greater than 1 whole?

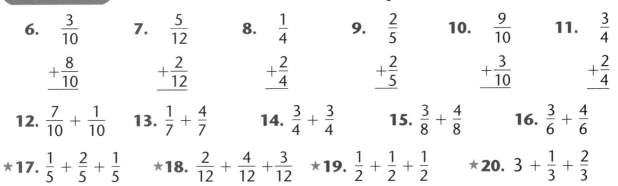

Did You KNOW?

Six hundred members of the Nikopaka Festa Committee made the largest sushi roll, a kappa maki (cucumber roll), that was 3,279 feet long at Yoshii, Japan, on October 12, 1997.

Spiral Review and Test Prep
Find an equivalent fraction.

27. $\dfrac{4}{12}$

28. $\dfrac{8}{10}$

29. $\dfrac{6}{12}$

30. $\dfrac{1}{3}$

31. $\dfrac{1}{4}$

Choose the correct answer.

32. Don makes 24 cookies. Robbie makes 12 more cookies than Don. How many cookies do they make altogether?

   A. 36   **B.** 60   **C.** 72   **D.** 48

33. Which number makes this number sentence true?
   $12 - 7 = 15 \div \blacksquare$

   F. 3   **H.** 10
   G. 5   **J.** Not Here

13·11 **Explore Subtracting Fractions**

Learn

You can use fraction models to subtract fractions.

What is $\frac{7}{12} - \frac{2}{12}$?

Work Together

▶ Explore subtracting fractions.
Find: $\frac{7}{12} - \frac{2}{12}$

- Use fraction strips to model the problem.

- Record your work in a number sentence.

You Will Need
- **fraction strips**

$$\boxed{\frac{1}{12}\ \frac{1}{12}\ \frac{1}{12}\ \frac{1}{12}\ \frac{1}{12}\ \cancel{\frac{1}{12}}\ \cancel{\frac{1}{12}}}$$

▶ Use fraction strips to find each difference. Simplify.

$$\frac{7}{10} - \frac{2}{10} \qquad \frac{11}{12} - \frac{5}{12} \qquad \frac{7}{8} - \frac{4}{8} \qquad \frac{3}{4} - \frac{2}{4} \qquad \frac{2}{6} - \frac{1}{6}$$

- What happens to the denominators of the fractions you subtracted?

- What happens to the numerators of the fractions you subtracted?

Make Connections

Here is how to subtract fractions and show the difference in simplest form.

Find: $\frac{7}{8} - \frac{1}{8}$

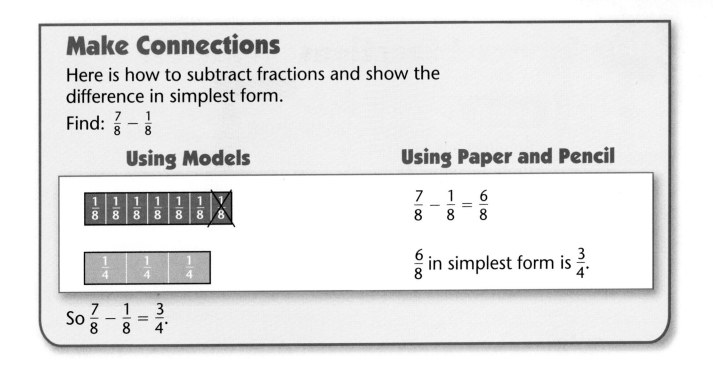

Using Models

Using Paper and Pencil

$$\frac{7}{8} - \frac{1}{8} = \frac{6}{8}$$

$\frac{6}{8}$ in simplest form is $\frac{3}{4}$.

So $\frac{7}{8} - \frac{1}{8} = \frac{3}{4}$.

 **Subtract. You may wish to use fraction strips.**

1. $\frac{6}{10} - \frac{2}{10}$

2. $\frac{5}{6} - \frac{2}{6}$

3. $\frac{8}{9} - \frac{5}{9}$

4. $\frac{5}{8} - \frac{2}{8}$

5. $\frac{7}{8} - \frac{5}{8}$

6. $\frac{3}{4} - \frac{2}{4}$

7. $\frac{1}{2} - \frac{1}{2}$

8. $\frac{7}{12} - \frac{4}{12}$

Sum it Up **Explain** how you can use fraction strips to find $\frac{3}{4} - \frac{1}{4}$ and write the difference in simplest form.

Practice **Subtract. You may wish to use fraction strips.**

9. $\frac{4}{6} - \frac{3}{6}$

10. $\frac{7}{8} - \frac{2}{8}$

11. $\frac{9}{10} - \frac{7}{10}$

12. $\frac{6}{9} - \frac{3}{9}$

13. $\frac{4}{5} - \frac{3}{5}$

14. $\frac{6}{12} - \frac{3}{12}$

15. $\frac{3}{4} - \frac{1}{4}$

16. $\frac{5}{8} - \frac{3}{8}$

17. $\frac{5}{6} - \frac{1}{6}$

18. $\frac{7}{8} - \frac{3}{8}$

19. $\frac{3}{6} - \frac{1}{6}$

20. $\frac{8}{12} - \frac{2}{12}$

21. $\frac{4}{6} - \frac{2}{6}$

22. $\frac{5}{8} - \frac{2}{8}$

23. $\frac{7}{10} - \frac{4}{10}$

24. **Analyze:** How could you use models to find $\frac{1}{2} - \frac{1}{4}$?

13·12 Subtract Fractions

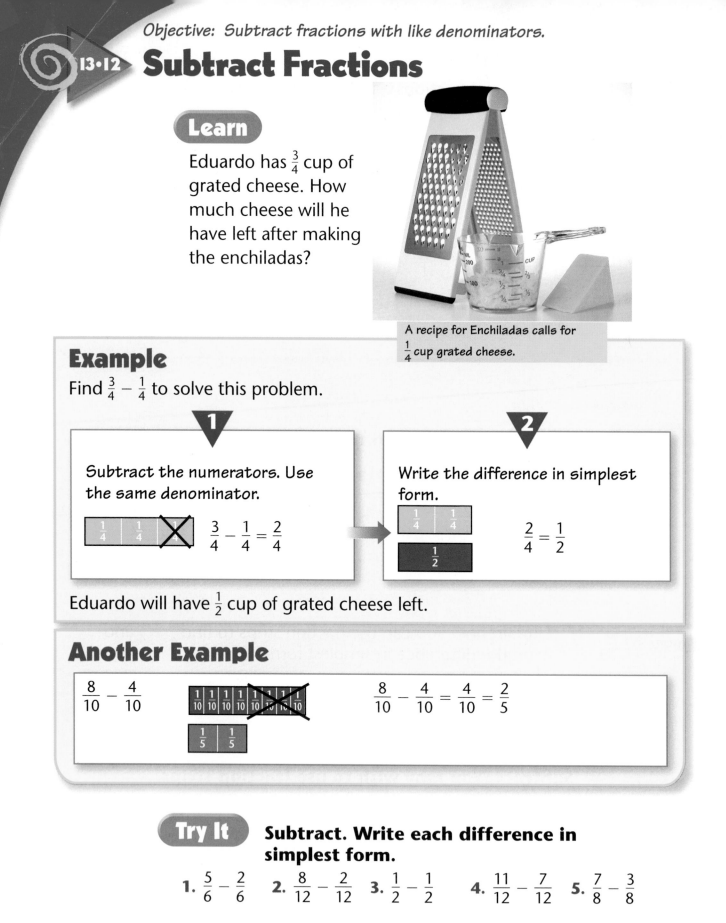

Learn

Eduardo has $\frac{3}{4}$ cup of grated cheese. How much cheese will he have left after making the enchiladas?

A recipe for Enchiladas calls for $\frac{1}{4}$ cup grated cheese.

Example

Find $\frac{3}{4} - \frac{1}{4}$ to solve this problem.

1

Subtract the numerators. Use the same denominator.

$$\frac{3}{4} - \frac{1}{4} = \frac{2}{4}$$

2

Write the difference in simplest form.

$$\frac{2}{4} = \frac{1}{2}$$

Eduardo will have $\frac{1}{2}$ cup of grated cheese left.

Another Example

$$\frac{8}{10} - \frac{4}{10}$$

$$\frac{8}{10} - \frac{4}{10} = \frac{4}{10} = \frac{2}{5}$$

Try It
Subtract. Write each difference in simplest form.

1. $\frac{5}{6} - \frac{2}{6}$
2. $\frac{8}{12} - \frac{2}{12}$
3. $\frac{1}{2} - \frac{1}{2}$
4. $\frac{11}{12} - \frac{7}{12}$
5. $\frac{7}{8} - \frac{3}{8}$

Sum it Up Explain how you find $\frac{7}{9} - \frac{4}{9}$ in simplest form.

Subtract. Write each difference in simplest form.

6. $\dfrac{4}{10} - \dfrac{2}{10}$ 7. $\dfrac{4}{6} - \dfrac{1}{6}$ 8. $\dfrac{4}{5} - \dfrac{1}{5}$ 9. $\dfrac{8}{11} - \dfrac{5}{11}$ 10. $\dfrac{5}{8} - \dfrac{1}{8}$

11. $\dfrac{9}{10} - \dfrac{1}{10}$ 12. $\dfrac{4}{7} - \dfrac{4}{7}$ 13. $\dfrac{6}{8} - \dfrac{2}{8}$ 14. $\dfrac{6}{9} - \dfrac{4}{9}$ 15. $\dfrac{5}{6} - \dfrac{2}{6}$

★16. $\dfrac{15}{30} - \dfrac{8}{30}$ ★17. $\dfrac{12}{17} - \dfrac{7}{17}$ ★18. $\dfrac{14}{25} - \dfrac{3}{25}$ ★19. $\dfrac{17}{21} - \dfrac{15}{21}$

Algebra & functions **Compare. Write $>$, $<$, or $=$.**

20. $\dfrac{6}{8} - \dfrac{2}{8} \bullet \dfrac{5}{8} - \dfrac{1}{8}$ 21. $\dfrac{8}{9} - \dfrac{2}{9} \bullet \dfrac{2}{3} - \dfrac{1}{3}$ 22. $\dfrac{3}{4} - \dfrac{2}{4} \bullet \dfrac{7}{8} - \dfrac{1}{8}$

Problem Solving

Use data from the recipe for problems 23–25.

23. You have $\frac{3}{4}$ cup of chopped tomatoes. How much will you have left after making Mexican Bean Bake?

★24. Which ingredient do you use more of in this recipe: salsa, lettuce, or tomato? Explain.

25. **Create a problem** using the data from the recipe.

Journal 26. **Compare:** How are adding and subtracting fractions with the same denominators alike? How are they different?

Mexican Bean Bake

$\frac{1}{2}$ cup	baking mix
1 cup	refried beans
2 tablespoons	green chilies
$\frac{1}{3}$ cup	salsa
2 ounces	cheddar cheese
$\frac{1}{2}$ cup	shredded lettuce
$\frac{1}{4}$ cup	chopped tomato
2 tablespoons	yogurt

Spiral Review and Test Prep

Write the fraction for the shaded part of each group.

27. ⬤⬤⬤⬤⬤◯◯◯   28. △△△▲   29. ▭▭▭▭▭

Choose the correct answer.

30. Sally sells 320 cheese sticks. Each serving has 4 cheese sticks. How many servings are sold?

   A. 80   C. 40
   B. 60   D. Not Here

31. A large muffin pan has 4 rows of 6 muffin holders. How many muffins can the pan hold?

   F. 10   H. 24
   G. 14   J. 36

Objective: Determine if outcomes are likely, unlikely, certain, or impossible.

13·13 Probability

 **Learn**

Math Word

probability the chance that an event will occur

There are 6 yellow raisins and 1 brown left in the box. Latisha is about to pick one. Is it *likely, unlikely, certain,* or *impossible* that she will pick a yellow raisin from the box? a brown raisin?

Example

You can draw a picture to help you determine the likelihood, or **probability,** of an outcome.

It is *certain* that Latisha will pick a raisin.

It is *impossible* that she will pick a green raisin.

It is *likely* that she will pick a yellow raisin.

It is *unlikely* that she will pick a brown raisin.

 Try It Use the words *likely, unlikely, certain,* or *impossible* to describe the probability.

Picking a
1. piece of fruit
2. red apple
3. yellow apple
4. banana

 **Explain** how you decide if picking an item of a certain color is likely or unlikely.

Use the words *likely, unlikely, certain,* or *impossible* to describe the probability.

Picking a

5. red grape

6. grape

7. raisin

8. green grape

Draw a spinner for each probability.

★9. Likely to land on a 4

★10. Unlikely to land on an even number

Problem Solving

Use data from the spinner for problems 11–14.

11. Whenever you buy a child's lunch at Burger World, you get to spin the spinner for a prize. Is it likely or unlikely that you will win a teddy bear when you spin?

12. What fraction of the spinner can the spinner stop on for you to win a teddy bear?

13. Sofia hopes she will get a poster for a prize. How can you describe the probability that she will get what she wants?

14. **Compare:** Which is more likely, getting a basketball or getting a joke book? Explain.

Spiral Review and Test Prep

15. 6 × 1,258   16. 3,408 − 476   17. 468 + 329   18. 520 ÷ 5

Choose the correct answer.

19. Which polygon has 6 sides?
    A. Pentagon   C. Octagon
    B. Hexagon   D. Rectangle

20. A floor has 5 rows of square tiles and 7 columns of square tiles. How many square tiles make up the area of the floor?
    F. 12   H. 30
    G. 24   J. 35

13·14

Objective: Organize and display the results of probability experiments.

Explore Finding Outcomes

Learn

You want to find out what the results would be if you flipped a coin 20 times. You can use a 2-color counter to explore the results of probability experiments.

Math Word

possible outcomes any of the results that could occur in an experiment

Work Together

▶ Use a 2-color counter to model the **possible outcomes** of probability experiments.

You Will Need
• **a 2-color counter**

• What are the possible outcomes for tossing the counter?

The probability, or chance, that the counter will be red is 1 out of 2 equally likely possible outcomes. You can write the probability as a fraction.

$\dfrac{1}{2}$ ← number of chances it will be red
← total number of possible outcomes

Results	
Counters	Outcomes
🔴	卌 卌 I
🟠	卌 IIII

• Toss the counter 20 times.
• Record the results in a tally chart.
• What are the total results for each outcome?
• How could you show these results in a different way?

Toss a coin 25 times. Spin a 0–5 spinner 50 times.
• What were the possible outcomes for the coin toss? for 0–5 spinner spins?
• Are the outcomes of both experiments what you expected? Why or why not?

Make Connections

A number cube with the numbers 1–6 was rolled 25 times.

Here are two ways you can record the outcomes.

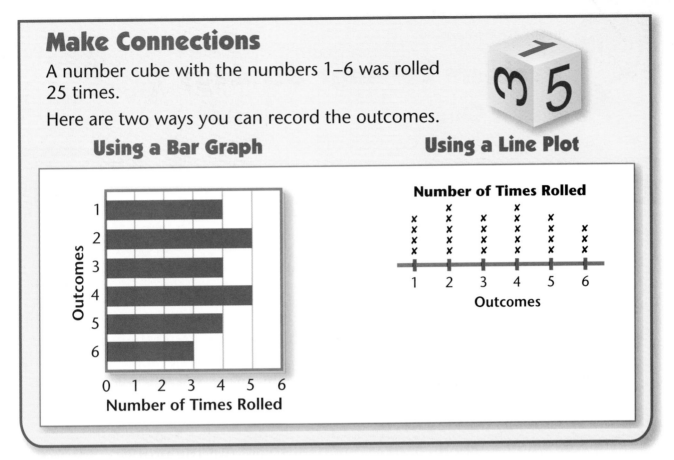

Using a Bar Graph

Using a Line Plot

 **Try It** List the possible outcomes for each. Then do the experiment and record the outcomes in a line plot and a bar graph.

1. Toss a coin 10 times.

2. Roll a 1–6 number cube 20 times.

 **Sum it Up!** There are 2 white cubes, 4 red cubes, and 1 blue cube in a bag. Which color cube are you most likely to pull from the bag? Explain.

Practice List the possible outcomes for each spinner. Then make the spinner and do the experiment. Record the outcomes in a line plot and a bar graph.

3. Spin the spinner 15 times.

4. Spin the spinner 20 times.

Chapter 13 Fractions and Probability

Objective: Predict the number of times an event will occur in an experiment.

Problem Solving: Strategy
Act It Out

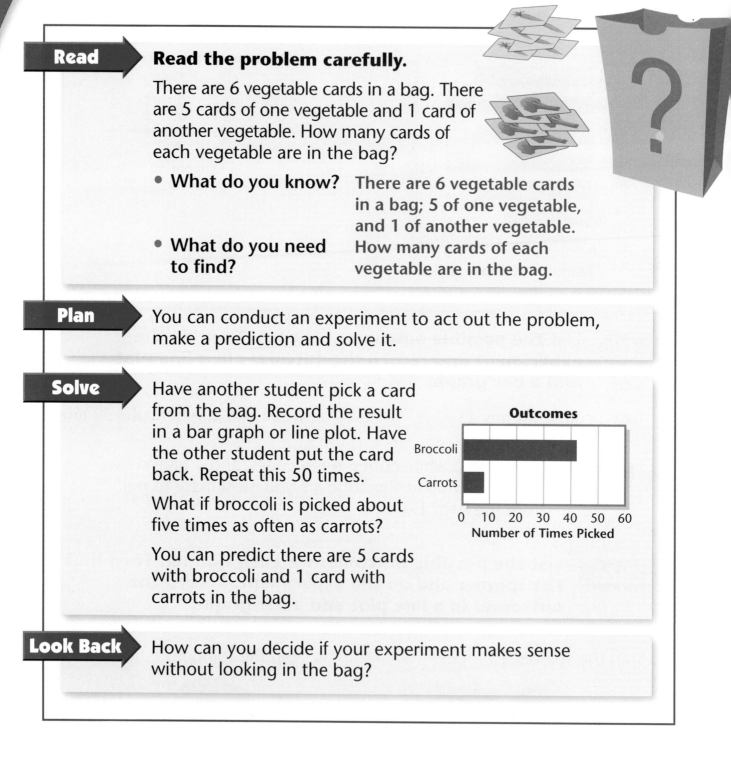

Read ➤ **Read the problem carefully.**

There are 6 vegetable cards in a bag. There are 5 cards of one vegetable and 1 card of another vegetable. How many cards of each vegetable are in the bag?

- **What do you know?** There are 6 vegetable cards in a bag; 5 of one vegetable, and 1 of another vegetable.

- **What do you need to find?** How many cards of each vegetable are in the bag.

Plan ➤ You can conduct an experiment to act out the problem, make a prediction and solve it.

Solve ➤ Have another student pick a card from the bag. Record the result in a bar graph or line plot. Have the other student put the card back. Repeat this 50 times.

Outcomes

What if broccoli is picked about five times as often as carrots?

You can predict there are 5 cards with broccoli and 1 card with carrots in the bag.

Look Back ➤ How can you decide if your experiment makes sense without looking in the bag?

Sum it Up! How can you use the results of an experiment to make a prediction?

Use data from the bar graph for problems 1–3.

Experiment Results to Predict Fruit Cards in a Bag

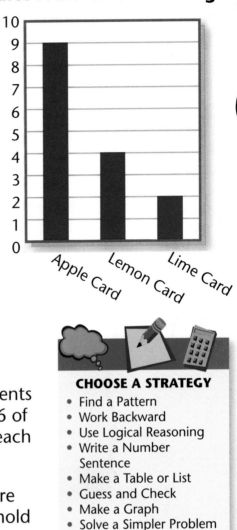

1. Which fruit card was picked most often from the bag?

2. How many times was a fruit card picked from the bag?

3. **What if** there are a total of 7 cards in the bag. How many of each fruit are there? Explain your reasoning.

4. Place 6 of one fruit card and 1 of another in a bag. Trade bags with a partner. Conduct an experiment to predict which cards and how many of each are in the bag. Compare results.

Mixed Strategy Review

5. Mr. Wing is getting 5 bags ready for his students to conduct an experiment. He wants to put 6 of one fruit card and 2 of another fruit card in each bag. How many fruit cards does he need?

6. There are 36 eggs in several cartons on a store shelf. Some cartons hold 6 eggs and others hold 8. How many of each carton are there?

CHOOSE A STRATEGY
- Find a Pattern
- Work Backward
- Use Logical Reasoning
- Write a Number Sentence
- Make a Table or List
- Guess and Check
- Make a Graph
- Solve a Simpler Problem

7. Alan and Josh write the letters of each of their names on cards and place them in different bags. They take turns picking one letter at a time from their own bag. The first player to pick a vowel wins. Is this a fair game? Explain.

8. **Create a problem** that you can solve by conducting an experiment. Solve it. Ask others to solve it.

★9. Rachel uses a spinner to conduct an experiment. The spinner lands on red 15 times, white 3 times, and black 3 times. Draw a picture to show what the spinner probably looks like.

10. **Analyze:** Rachel made up a game with her spinner. She says that she gets 1 point each time the spinner lands on red. The other player gets the point if the spinner lands on white or black. Is this game fair? Why or why not?

Problem Solving

13·16 A

Problem Solving: Application
Decision Making

You Decide!

Which platter will you use for your party?

You are planning a party for 6 people. You can make your own food platter or order one that is already prepared.

Prepared Platter

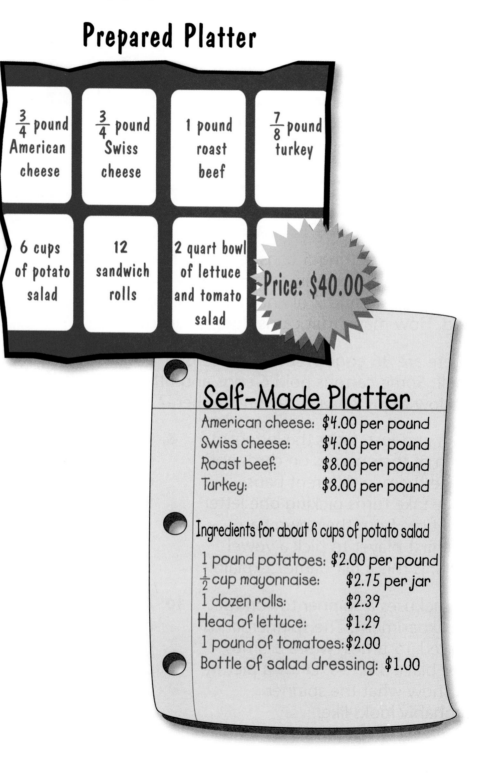

$\frac{3}{4}$ pound American cheese	$\frac{3}{4}$ pound Swiss cheese	1 pound roast beef	$\frac{7}{8}$ pound turkey
6 cups of potato salad	12 sandwich rolls	2 quart bowl of lettuce and tomato salad	Price: $40.00

Self-Made Platter

American cheese: $4.00 per pound
Swiss cheese: $4.00 per pound
Roast beef: $8.00 per pound
Turkey: $8.00 per pound

Ingredients for about 6 cups of potato salad

1 pound potatoes: $2.00 per pound
$\frac{1}{2}$ cup mayonnaise: $2.75 per jar
1 dozen rolls: $2.39
Head of lettuce: $1.29
1 pound of tomatoes: $2.00
Bottle of salad dressing: $1.00

Read for Understanding

1. How many pounds of meat do you get in the prepared platter?

2. How many pounds of cheese do you get in the prepared platter?

3. How is the prepared platter the same as a self-made platter? How are they different?

4. How many sandwiches can each guest have if you choose the prepared platter?

5. Which is there more of on the platter, roast beef or turkey?

6. How much potato salad would you make if you make $\frac{1}{2}$ as much as the prepared platter has?

7. If you buy a pound of American cheese, a pound of Swiss cheese, a pound of roast beef, and a pound of turkey, how much will you spend?

8. Which is there more of on the prepared platter, turkey or Swiss cheese?

Make Decisions

9. How much will rolls cost if you make your own platter and want the same number as the prepared platter has?

10. If you decide to buy $\frac{3}{4}$ of the number of rolls that come with the prepared platter, how many rolls will you buy? Will that be enough for your party? Explain.

11. How much will it cost if you decide to make 6 cups of your own potato salad? (Note: You will need to buy the jar of mayonnaise.)

12. Here is a recipe for a tomato and lettuce salad. How much will it cost to make? (Note: You must buy the whole bottle of salad dressing.)
    1 head lettuce
    $\frac{1}{2}$ pound tomatoes
    $\frac{1}{4}$ cup salad dressing

13. How much will the same amount of meats and cheeses that are in the prepared platter cost if you make your own platter?

14. Make a list of what you need to know to decide which platter is better for your party.

Your Decision!

Which platter did you choose for your party? Why?

13·16 B

Problem Solving: Math and Science
Which ball bounces best?

You expect a basketball to bounce well, otherwise how would you dribble it? But what about a baseball or volleyball?

Some balls bounce better than others. In this activity, you will determine which balls bounce best.

You Will Need
- basketball
- baseball
- volleyball
- meterstick

Hypothesize

Which ball do you think will bounce best—a basketball, a baseball, or a volleyball?

Safety

Be careful when standing on a step-stool.

Procedure

1. Work in a group.
2. Drop the basketball from 1 meter above the floor.
3. Measure how high the ball bounced on its first bounce.
4. Repeat with the baseball and the volleyball.

Use data from the graph for problems 9–12.

Students Buying School Lunches

9. How many more students bought lunch on Friday than on Monday?

   A. 1 more   C. 25 more

   B. 15 more   D. 35 more

10. If every student in the school bought lunch on Friday, what is the probability that 145 students will buy lunch the following Monday?

    F. Unlikely   H. Certain

    G. Likely   J. Impossible

11. On which day did the fewest students buy lunches?

    A. Monday   C. Wednesday

    B. Tuesday   D. Thursday

12. On which day did 15 more students buy lunch than on Wednesday?

    F. Monday   H. Thursday

    G. Tuesday   J. Friday

13. Janine buys 12 muffins. There are twice as many corn muffins as bran muffins. How many corn muffins does she buy?

    A. 2   C. 8

    B. 4   D. 10

14. Mel bought roast beef, ham, and turkey. He also bought a loaf of white bread and rye bread. How many different kinds of sandwiches can he make if he only puts one kind of meat on one kind of bread?

    F. 3   H. 6

    G. 4   J. Not Here

15. Lily leaves home and drives 10 blocks in her car to the grocery store. She then walks north 2 blocks to the post office. Finally, she walks 3 more blocks north to the florist. How many blocks must she walk to get to her car?

    A. 8   C. 6

    B. 7   D. 5

16. In Store A a box of Fruity O's cereal costs $1.75. In Store B you can buy 3 boxes of Fruity O's for $5.10. How much less does 1 box of Fruity O's cost in the store that sells it for less? Explain your method.

CHAPTER 14

Relate Fractions and Decimals

Theme: Inventions and Discoveries

Use the Data
Inventions Around the World

Invention	Country
Vacuum	England
Microwave	United States
Lawn mower	England
Compact disc	United States
Piano	Italy
Videodisc	Netherlands
Sewing machine	United States
Loom	Egypt
Bicycle	Germany
Paper	China

Source: Kids' Almanac

- What fraction of these inventions was invented in the United States? How can you write this as a decimal?

What You Will Learn
In this chapter you will learn how to

- identify fraction and decimal equivalents.

- read and write decimals to hundredths.

- compare and order decimals.

- add and subtract decimals.

- use strategies to solve problems.

Additional activities at
www.mhschool.com/math

Objective: Use models to make the connection between fractions and decimals.

Explore Fractions and Decimals

Math Words

decimal a number that uses place value and a decimal point to show tenths and hundredths

decimal point a period separating the ones and the tenths places in a decimal

 Learn

You can use graph paper to explore fractions and decimals.

Work Together

▶ Use graph paper to find what part of a dollar 50¢ is.

You Will Need
• graph paper
• colored pencils

• There are 100¢ in $1.00. Make a grid 10 rows by 10 columns so that there are 100 small squares.

• Shade 50 small squares to show 50.

• There are 50 out of 100 squares shaded. There are 5 out of 10 columns shaded.

• Write a fraction for the part that is shaded.

Write a fraction.

Write: $\frac{50}{100} = \frac{5}{10}$

Read: fifty hundredths equals five tenths

Write a **decimal** .

Write: $\frac{5}{10}$ = 0.5

Read: five tenths   **decimal point**

▶ Use 10-by-10 grids to model each money amount. Then write a fraction and decimal.

75¢   30¢   25¢   80¢

Make Connections

You can write equivalent fractions for a decimal.

50 cents = $0.5 = \frac{50}{100} = \frac{5}{10}$

Using Models

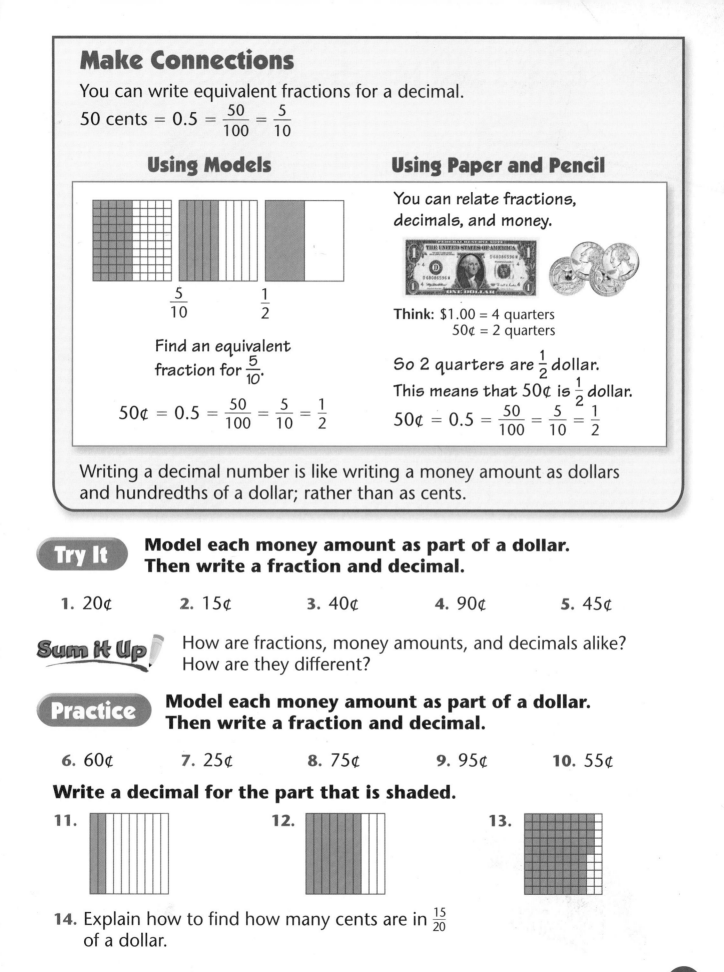

$\frac{5}{10}$ $\frac{1}{2}$

Find an equivalent fraction for $\frac{5}{10}$.

$50¢ = 0.5 = \frac{50}{100} = \frac{5}{10} = \frac{1}{2}$

Using Paper and Pencil

You can relate fractions, decimals, and money.

Think: $1.00 = 4 quarters
50¢ = 2 quarters

So 2 quarters are $\frac{1}{2}$ dollar.
This means that 50¢ is $\frac{1}{2}$ dollar.

$50¢ = 0.5 = \frac{50}{100} = \frac{5}{10} = \frac{1}{2}$

Writing a decimal number is like writing a money amount as dollars and hundredths of a dollar; rather than as cents.

Try It Model each money amount as part of a dollar. Then write a fraction and decimal.

1. 20¢   2. 15¢   3. 40¢   4. 90¢   5. 45¢

Sum It Up How are fractions, money amounts, and decimals alike? How are they different?

Practice Model each money amount as part of a dollar. Then write a fraction and decimal.

6. 60¢   7. 25¢   8. 75¢   9. 95¢   10. 55¢

Write a decimal for the part that is shaded.

11.   12.   13.

14. Explain how to find how many cents are in $\frac{15}{20}$ of a dollar.

14.2 Tenths and Hundredths

Learn

Math Word

equivalent decimals
decimals that name the same number

Shahid invented a toy glove with fingertips that light up and glow in the dark! If a toy company wants to pay Shahid 90¢ for every toy sold, what part of a dollar is 90¢?

Shahid Minapara lives near San Francisco, California.

Example 1

You can make a model to show 90¢.

Think: 90¢ = 9 dimes
$1.00 = 10 dimes

9 out of 10 parts are shaded.

You can write this amount as a fraction.
Write: $\frac{9}{10}$
Read: nine tenths

You can write this amount as a decimal.
Write: 0.9
Read: nine tenths

More Examples

Write as a fraction and as a decimal.

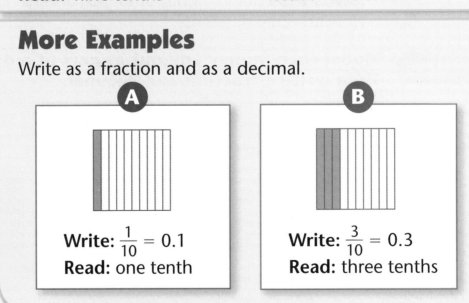

A
Write: $\frac{1}{10} = 0.1$
Read: one tenth

B
Write: $\frac{3}{10} = 0.3$
Read: three tenths

The Young Inventors Club sends out newsletters about inventions such as Shahid's. It costs about 64¢ to make and mail each newsletter. How can you write this amount in different ways?

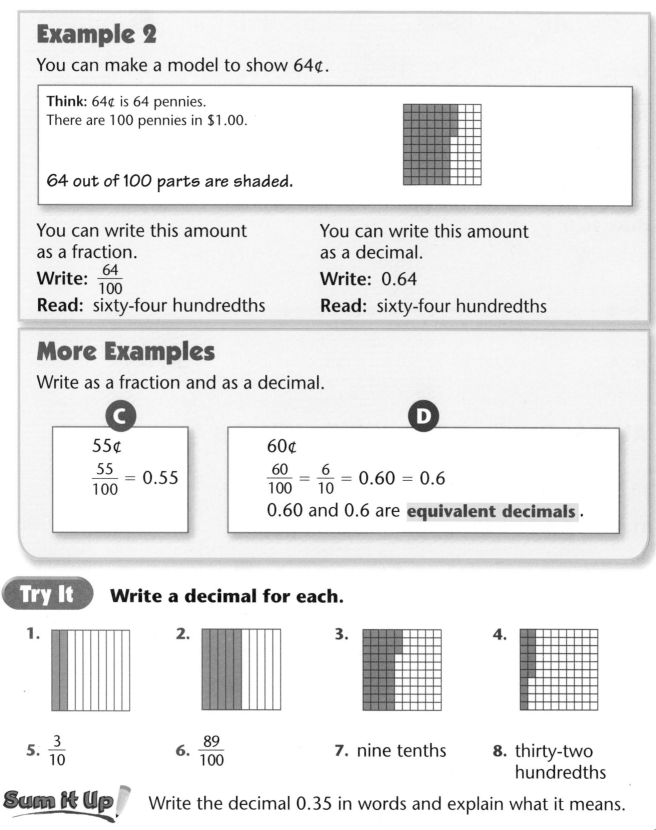

Example 2

You can make a model to show 64¢.

Think: 64¢ is 64 pennies.
There are 100 pennies in $1.00.

64 out of 100 parts are shaded.

You can write this amount as a fraction.
Write: $\frac{64}{100}$
Read: sixty-four hundredths

You can write this amount as a decimal.
Write: 0.64
Read: sixty-four hundredths

More Examples

Write as a fraction and as a decimal.

C

55¢

$\frac{55}{100} = 0.55$

D

60¢

$\frac{60}{100} = \frac{6}{10} = 0.60 = 0.6$

0.60 and 0.6 are **equivalent decimals**.

Try It **Write a decimal for each.**

1.
2.
3.
4.

5. $\frac{3}{10}$

6. $\frac{89}{100}$

7. nine tenths

8. thirty-two hundredths

Sum it Up! Write the decimal 0.35 in words and explain what it means.

Write a decimal for each.

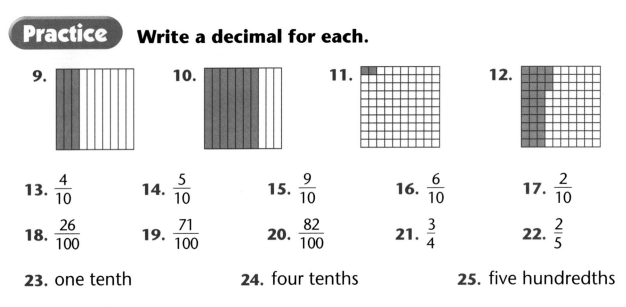

9.   **10.**   **11.**   **12.**

13. $\frac{4}{10}$ **14.** $\frac{5}{10}$ **15.** $\frac{9}{10}$ **16.** $\frac{6}{10}$ **17.** $\frac{2}{10}$

18. $\frac{26}{100}$ **19.** $\frac{71}{100}$ **20.** $\frac{82}{100}$ **21.** $\frac{3}{4}$ **22.** $\frac{2}{5}$

23. one tenth   **24.** four tenths   **25.** five hundredths

Write a decimal for the point. Tell whether it is close to 0, $\frac{1}{2}$, or 1.

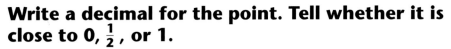

26. A   **27.** B   **28.** C   **29.** D

Describe and complete the following skip-counting patterns.

30. 0.1, ▮, 0.3, ▮, 0.5, ▮, 0.7, 0.8, ▮, 1.0

31. 0.16, ▮, 0.12, 0.10, ▮, 0.06, ▮, 0.02

32.

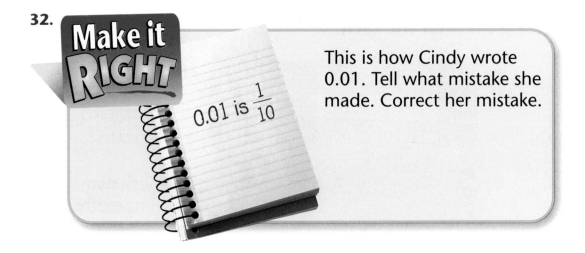

Make it RIGHT

0.01 is $\frac{1}{10}$

This is how Cindy wrote 0.01. Tell what mistake she made. Correct her mistake.

Problem Solving

33. Art: An artist working on the Young Inventors Club newsletter is designing a logo. He made this sketch. How many parts of the grid are shaded? Write a decimal.

34. How many parts of the grid are yellow? red? Write these numbers as decimals.

35. Analyze: How many hundredths are in 3 tenths?

★**36.** Remember that it costs 64¢ to make and mail the newsletter. How much would it cost for 10 newsletters? for 100?

37. There are 10 writers in the Young Inventors Club. Three are girls. Write a fraction and decimal for the number of girls.

38. Collect data from your classmates about how far they live from school using tenths.

39. It takes 100 pennies to make a dollar. What fraction of a dollar is a dime? a quarter? Write each amount as a decimal.

40. Mr. Lott's gasoline tank is $\frac{3}{8}$ full. Does he have more or less than half a tank left?

41. Paige buys 3 boxes of film on sale. Each box holds 5 rolls of film. How many rolls of film does Paige buy?

42. Mark wants to play basketball or soccer. If 3 of his friends want to play basketball and 5 more want to play soccer, are they more likely to all play basketball or soccer?

43. There are 5 boats on the Water Mill ride. Each boat holds 12 people. How many people can ride at one time?

Spiral Review and Test Prep

44. 5×32

45. $9\overline{)68}$

46. $\$8.47 + \$4.76$

47. $\frac{3}{4} + \frac{1}{4}$

Choose the correct answer.

48. Which is true?

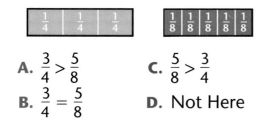

A. $\frac{3}{4} > \frac{5}{8}$ C. $\frac{5}{8} > \frac{3}{4}$

B. $\frac{3}{4} = \frac{5}{8}$ D. Not Here

49. Which describes the likeliness of picking a peach from a bag of apples?

F. Certain   H. Unlikely

G. Likely   J. Impossible

14·3

Decimals Greater than One

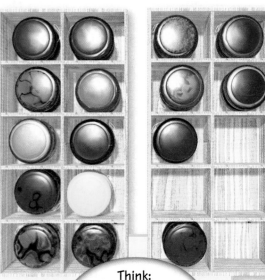

Learn

Pedro is a yo-yo champion. He keeps his yo-yos in special boxes. What part of the 2 boxes are filled with yo-yos?

Think: one whole box and 6 out of 10 parts of the second box

Example

You can write a mixed number or a decimal.

Mixed Number	Decimal
Write: $1\frac{6}{10}$	Write: 1.6
Read: one and six tenths	Read: one and six tenths

One and six tenths of the boxes are filled.

Another Example

Write: 1.13 or $1\frac{13}{100}$

Read: one and thirteen hundredths

Try It Write each decimal.

1.   2.   3.

4. $4\frac{62}{100}$ 5. $3\frac{8}{10}$ 6. $7\frac{48}{100}$

Sum it Up Explain how to write a mixed number as a decimal.

Write each decimal.

7.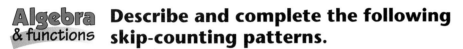

8.

9.

10. seven and fifty-seven hundredths   11. nine and three tenths

12. 0 ————————————— 1   13. 3 ————————————— 4

14. $8\frac{3}{10}$ 15. $6\frac{72}{100}$ 16. $5\frac{36}{100}$ ★17. $1\frac{1}{2}$ ★18. $3\frac{3}{4}$

Algebra & functions **Describe and complete the following skip-counting patterns.**

19. 3.20, ▪, 3.22, ▪, 3.24, ▪, 3.26   20. 2.15, 2.25, ▪, ▪, 2.55, ▪, 2.75

Problem Solving

Use data from *Did You Know?* for problem 21.

21. What is an example of an amount of money you might get if you sold one of these valuable dolls?

★22. Pedro bought a yo-yo for $7.89 and string for $1.29. How much change did he get from a ten-dollar bill?

 23. **Analyze:** Do 3.5 and 0.35 name the same number? Draw models with your explanation.

One of the most valuable toys is a 1959 doll. It is worth at least $3,000 and no more than $5,000.

Spiral Review and Test Prep

24. 133×5 25. $6\overline{)213}$ 26. $\$6.04 - \$0.38$ 27. $\frac{7}{8} + \frac{7}{8}$

Choose the correct answer.

28. Which group of fractions is in order from least to greatest?

   A. $\frac{2}{9}, \frac{6}{9}, \frac{4}{9}$ C. $\frac{2}{9}, \frac{4}{9}, \frac{6}{9}$

   B. $\frac{6}{9}, \frac{4}{9}, \frac{2}{9}$ D. $\frac{4}{9}, \frac{2}{9}, \frac{6}{9}$

29. What is the perimeter of a square 4 meters on a side?

   F. 8 meters   H. 16 meters
   G. 12 meters   J. Not Here

14.4 Compare and Order Decimals

Algebra & functions

Learn

Have you ever heard of an ERA, or earned run average in baseball? It is a decimal that tells how many earned runs a pitcher allows his or her opponent to score. Which pitcher has the lower ERA?

Compare the decimals to solve the problem.

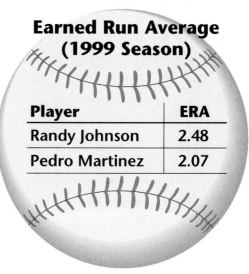

Earned Run Average (1999 Season)

Player	ERA
Randy Johnson	2.48
Pedro Martinez	2.07

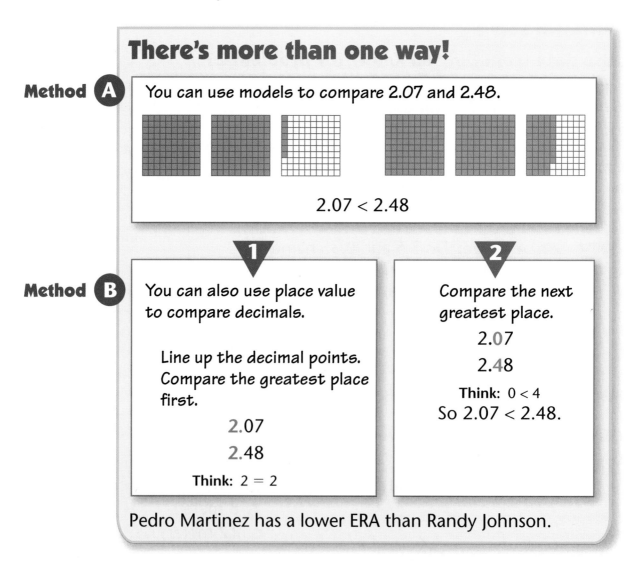

There's more than one way!

Method A

You can use models to compare 2.07 and 2.48.

2.07 < 2.48

1

Method B

You can also use place value to compare decimals.

Line up the decimal points. Compare the greatest place first.

2.07
2.48

Think: 2 = 2

2

Compare the next greatest place.

2.07
2.48

Think: 0 < 4
So 2.07 < 2.48.

Pedro Martinez has a lower ERA than Randy Johnson.

The table shows the ERAs for the top three pitchers in the American League. Write their averages in order from least to greatest.

Earned Run Average American League Pitchers (1999 Season)

Player	ERA
David Cone	3.44
Pedro Martinez	2.07
Mike Mussina	3.50

There's more than one way!

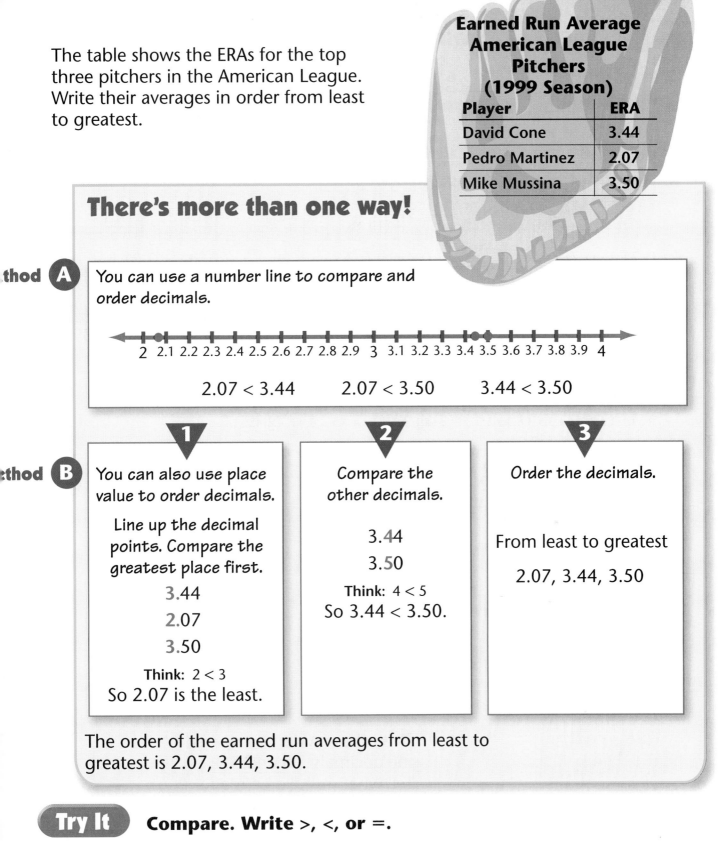

Method **A**

You can use a number line to compare and order decimals.

2 2.1 2.2 2.3 2.4 2.5 2.6 2.7 2.8 2.9 3 3.1 3.2 3.3 3.4 3.5 3.6 3.7 3.8 3.9 4

2.07 < 3.44   2.07 < 3.50   3.44 < 3.50

Method **B**

1

You can also use place value to order decimals.

Line up the decimal points. Compare the greatest place first.

3.44

2.07

3.50

Think: 2 < 3
So 2.07 is the least.

2

Compare the other decimals.

3.44

3.50

Think: 4 < 5
So 3.44 < 3.50.

3

Order the decimals.

From least to greatest

2.07, 3.44, 3.50

The order of the earned run averages from least to greatest is 2.07, 3.44, 3.50.

Try It **Compare. Write >, <, or =.**

1. 0.70 ● 0.7   **2.** 3.2 ● 3.02   **3.** 0.56 ● 1.09   **4.** 0.9 ● 0.86

Sum It Up How can you tell when a decimal is greater than or less than another decimal?

Compare. Write >, <, or =.

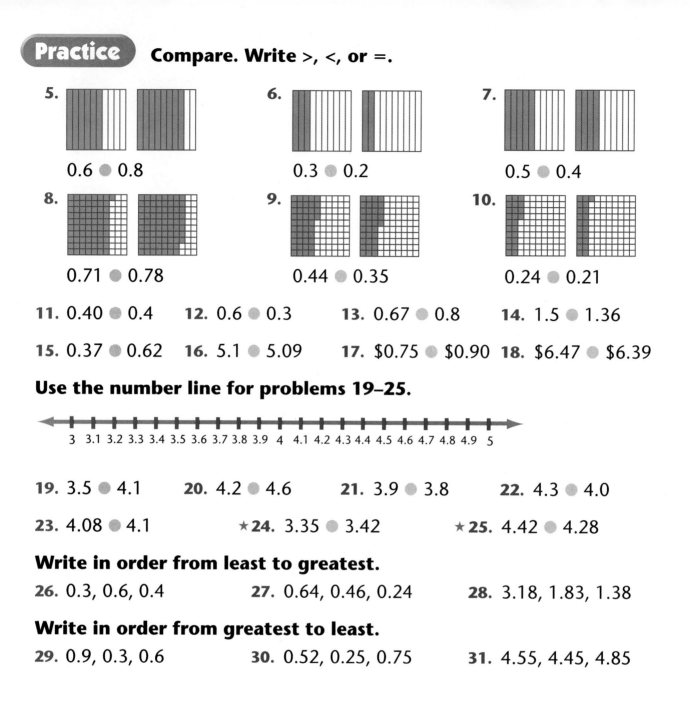

5. 0.6 ● 0.8

6. 0.3 ● 0.2

7. 0.5 ● 0.4

8. 0.71 ● 0.78

9. 0.44 ● 0.35

10. 0.24 ● 0.21

11. 0.40 ● 0.4   **12.** 0.6 ● 0.3   **13.** 0.67 ● 0.8   **14.** 1.5 ● 1.36

15. 0.37 ● 0.62   **16.** 5.1 ● 5.09   **17.** $0.75 ● $0.90   **18.** $6.47 ● $6.39

Use the number line for problems 19–25.

3 3.1 3.2 3.3 3.4 3.5 3.6 3.7 3.8 3.9 4 4.1 4.2 4.3 4.4 4.5 4.6 4.7 4.8 4.9 5

19. 3.5 ● 4.1   **20.** 4.2 ● 4.6   **21.** 3.9 ● 3.8   **22.** 4.3 ● 4.0

23. 4.08 ● 4.1   ★**24.** 3.35 ● 3.42   ★**25.** 4.42 ● 4.28

Write in order from least to greatest.

26. 0.3, 0.6, 0.4   **27.** 0.64, 0.46, 0.24   **28.** 3.18, 1.83, 1.38

Write in order from greatest to least.

29. 0.9, 0.3, 0.6   **30.** 0.52, 0.25, 0.75   **31.** 4.55, 4.45, 4.85

32.

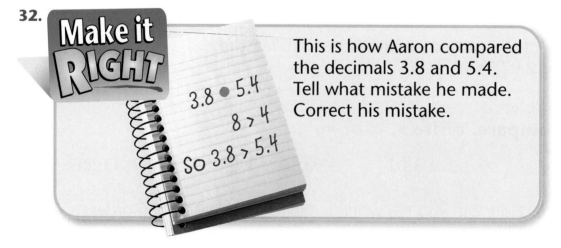

Make it RIGHT

3.8 ● 5.4
8 > 4
So 3.8 > 5.4

This is how Aaron compared the decimals 3.8 and 5.4. Tell what mistake he made. Correct his mistake.

Problem Solving

Use data from the table for problems 33–36.

Earned Run Average National League Pitchers (1999 Season)

Player	ERA
Kevin Brown	3.00
Mike Hampton	2.90
Randy Johnson	2.48
Kevin Millwood	2.68
John Smoltz	3.49

33. Which pitcher had the lowest earned run average?

34. Which pitchers had an earned run average less than 3?

35. Social Studies: The pitcher with the highest earned run average played for Atlanta. Who is he?

36. Create a problem using the data from the table. Solve it. Ask others to solve it.

Use data from *Did You Know?* for problems 37–38.

37. How many years passed between the pitchers' lowest earned run averages?

38. Whose lowest earned run average was lower?

39. Compare: How is comparing and ordering decimals like comparing and ordering whole numbers? How is it different?

Did You KNOW?

Between 1926 and 1939, Lefty Grove won the pitching title 9 times. His lowest earned run average was 2.07 in 1931. Roger Clemens won the pitching title 6 times in the 1990s. His lowest earned run average was 1.93 in 1990.

Spiral Review and Test Prep

40. $\frac{5}{8} - \frac{1}{8}$

41. $\frac{1}{6} + \frac{5}{6}$

42. 70×8

43. $42 \div 6$

44. $59 \div 8$

Choose the correct answer.

45. Linda is working on a science project. She adds $\frac{1}{4}$ cup of one liquid to $\frac{1}{4}$ cup of a different liquid. How much is this altogether?

   A. $\frac{1}{2}$ cup   **C.** $\frac{2}{8}$ cup

   B. $\frac{1}{4}$ cup   **D.** 1 cup

46. Which describes this shape?

   F. Right triangle   **H.** Acute triangle

   G. Obtuse triangle   **J.** Not Here

Problem Solving: Reading for Math
Choose an Operation

Car Club Holds Meet

Read

Eric is building a model car to compete in the Crazy Car Contest. He buys wheels for $2.39 and wire for $1.25. How much change will Eric get from a five-dollar bill?

READING SKILL ▶ **Make a Judgment**

When you make a judgment, you decide something based on what you know and the information given in the problem.

- **What do you know?** Wheels cost $2.39; wire costs $1.25; he paid with a five-dollar bill.

- **What do you need to find?** How much change he will receive

- **What judgment is called for?** Decide what operation to use

MATH SKILL ▶ **Choose the Operation**

Understanding what the problem is asking you to find can help you to **choose an operation**.

Plan

Add to find the total cost.
Subtract to find his change.

Solve

Add. $2.39 + 1.25 = 3.64$ Subtract. $5.00 - 3.64 = 1.36$
Eric receives $1.36 in change.

Look Back

- Is your answer reasonable?

How do you decide to add to solve a problem? to subtract?

Practice **Solve. Tell how you chose the operation.**

1. Rosa spent $3.76 on model parts. Emma spent $2.89. Who spent more on model parts? How much more?

2. Bob sold a model car he made for $45.85. Jedd sold his model car for $23.37 more than Bob's car. How much did Jedd sell his car for?

Use data from the list for problems 3–8.

3. Beth bought decals and wheels. How much did she spend?

4. Will paid for his paintbrush with a ten-dollar bill. How much change should he receive?

5. What is the difference in the cost between paint and wire?

6. Cal bought 3 paintbrushes. How much did he spend?

7. In May, the Crazy Car Club had 19 members. In June, 12 more people joined the club and 5 members dropped out of the club. How many members did the club have at the end of June?

8. Carla bought every item on the list. How much did she spend?

Cost of Equipment	
Item	**Cost**
Decals	$2.75
Paint	$1.89
Paintbrush	$3.35
Wheels	$2.39
Wire	$1.25

Spiral Review and Test Prep

Choose the correct answer.

Lee spent $4.55 on supplies for his invention. Rick spent $1.85 more than Lee. How much did Rick spend on supplies?

9. Which of the following statements is true?
   A. Lee bought Rick's supplies.
   B. Lee spent less than Rick.
   C. Rick spent more than any other club member.

10. Which operation can you use to solve the problem?
   F. Addition
   G. Subtraction
   H. Multiplication

Write a decimal for the part that is shaded. (pages 584–591)

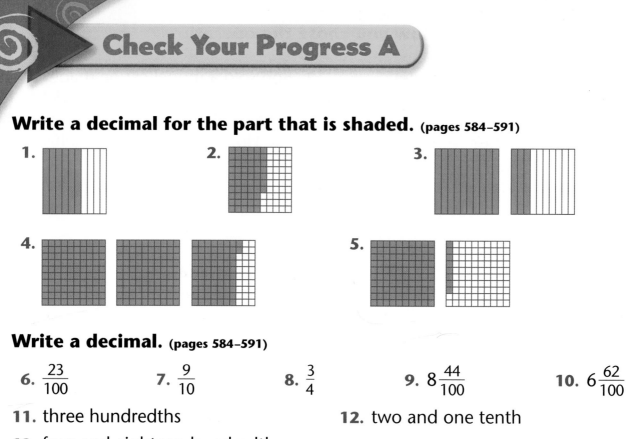

1.

2.

3.

4.

5.

Write a decimal. (pages 584–591)

6. $\dfrac{23}{100}$

7. $\dfrac{9}{10}$

8. $\dfrac{3}{4}$

9. $8\dfrac{44}{100}$

10. $6\dfrac{62}{100}$

11. three hundredths

12. two and one tenth

13. four and eighteen hundredths

Compare. Write >, <, or =. (pages 592–595)

14. 0.6 ● 0.5

15. 0.36 ● 0.63

16. 3.1 ● 3.10

17. 5.54 ● 5.45

Write the decimals in order from least to greatest. (pages 592–595)

18. 0.2, 0.4, 0.1

19. 0.26, 0.16, 0.46

20. 1.8, 1.5, 1.6

21. 3.35, 3.04, 2.37

Solve. (pages 584–597)

22. Parts for Nora's invention cost $7.65. How much change should she receive from a ten-dollar bill? Explain how you chose the operation to solve the problem.

23. There is a rock display at the museum. One rock is 16.5 centimeters wide. Another rock is 16.2 centimeters wide. Which measurement is greater?

24. At the Discovery Museum, 7 out of 10 exhibits are about science. Write this number as a decimal.

Journal

25. **Explain** how to order decimals less than one. Give examples.

Additional activities at
www.mhschool.com/math

City	Average Annual Snowfall	Rank

Use the Internet

Ms. Griffin's class is gathering data on the average annual snowfall for different cities in the United States. They need to find data for three different cities. They need to be sure that each city has a different average annual snowfall than the other two cities. They will use the data they collect to complete the table. How can they use the Internet to gather the data?

- Go to www.mhschool.com/math.

- Find the list of sites that show weather data.

- Click on a link.

- Find the data on average annual snowfall. Choose three cities for which data is given.

- Copy the table. Write the names of the cities you chose in your table.

- Record the average annual snowfall for each city in the table.

- Rank the cities from 1 to 3. Use 1 to rank the city with the greatest snowfall. Use 3 to rank the city with the least snowfall.

1. How much greater is the average annual snowfall in the city ranked 1 than in the city ranked 2? in the city ranked 2 than in the city ranked 3?

2. **Analyze:** Why does using the Internet make more sense than using another reference source to find the data needed to complete the table?

For more practice, use Math Traveler™.

14·6 Explore Adding Decimals

Learn

You can use graph paper to explore adding decimals. What is 1.2 + 1.4?

Work Together

▶ Use 10-by-10 grids to make models.

You Will Need
- graph paper
- colored pencils or crayons
- scissors

Use a blue pencil to color one set of grids to model 1.2.

Start from the end of the 1.2 model. Use a red pencil to color grids to model 1.4. Write a decimal for the total amount shaded.

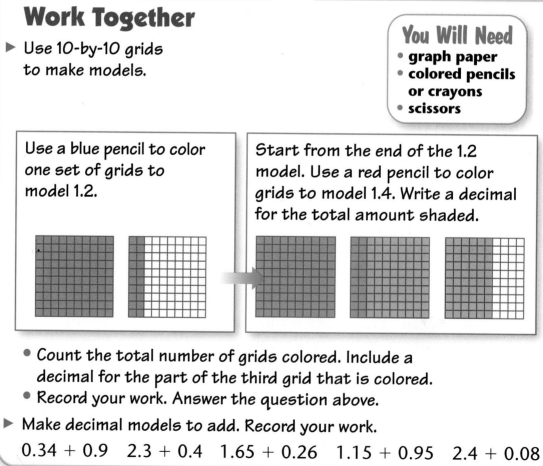

- Count the total number of grids colored. Include a decimal for the part of the third grid that is colored.
- Record your work. Answer the question above.

▶ Make decimal models to add. Record your work.

   0.34 + 0.9   2.3 + 0.4   1.65 + 0.26   1.15 + 0.95   2.4 + 0.08

Make Connections

Here are two ways to show how to add decimals.

Find: 1.68 + 1.54

Using Models

Using Paper and Pencil

Start with the hundredths, then add each place. Regroup as needed. Remember to place the decimal point in your answer.

$$\begin{array}{r} 1.68 \\ +1.54 \\ \hline 3.22 \end{array}$$

1.68 + 1.54 = 3.22

Try It   Add. You may wish to use models.

1. $\begin{array}{r} 0.3 \\ +0.8 \\ \hline \end{array}$

2. $\begin{array}{r} 1.5 \\ +1.7 \\ \hline \end{array}$

3. $\begin{array}{r} 2.44 \\ +1.09 \\ \hline \end{array}$

4. $\begin{array}{r} 0.96 \\ +1.52 \\ \hline \end{array}$

5. $\begin{array}{r} 2.5 \\ +4.3 \\ \hline \end{array}$

6. $\begin{array}{r} 3.34 \\ +2.46 \\ \hline \end{array}$

7. $\begin{array}{r} 4.72 \\ +3.87 \\ \hline \end{array}$

8. $\begin{array}{r} 3.09 \\ +0.98 \\ \hline \end{array}$

Sum it Up   Tell how you use models to add 1.04 and 0.97. Then solve.

Practice   Add.

9. $\begin{array}{r} 0.9 \\ +1.4 \\ \hline \end{array}$

10. $\begin{array}{r} 0.14 \\ +0.67 \\ \hline \end{array}$

11. $\begin{array}{r} 1.23 \\ +0.38 \\ \hline \end{array}$

12. $\begin{array}{r} 1.62 \\ +1.27 \\ \hline \end{array}$

13. $\begin{array}{r} 0.86 \\ +0.74 \\ \hline \end{array}$

14. $\begin{array}{r} 1.20 \\ +0.76 \\ \hline \end{array}$

15. $\begin{array}{r} 2.60 \\ +0.30 \\ \hline \end{array}$

16. $\begin{array}{r} 1.40 \\ +0.35 \\ \hline \end{array}$

17. $\begin{array}{r} 0.4 \\ +0.1 \\ \hline \end{array}$

18. $\begin{array}{r} 2.65 \\ +4.76 \\ \hline \end{array}$

19. $\begin{array}{r} 2.7 \\ +2.8 \\ \hline \end{array}$

20. $\begin{array}{r} 4.09 \\ +1.97 \\ \hline \end{array}$

21. **Generalize:** How is adding money amounts the same as adding decimals?

Objective: Add decimals.

14·7 Add Decimals

Learn

The Boyd family is on their way to Discovery Village. They have already traveled 1.6 miles when they see the sign. How many miles is the Boyds' trip altogether?

**Discovery Village
1.8 miles ahead**

Example

Find: 1.6 + 1.8

1

Line up the decimal points. Add the tenths. Regroup if necessary.

$$\begin{array}{r} \overset{1}{1}.6 \\ +1.8 \\ \hline 4 \end{array}$$

Think: 10 tenths = 1 one.

2

Add all the ones. Place the decimal point in the sum.

$$\begin{array}{r} 1.6 \\ +1.8 \\ \hline 3.4 \end{array}$$

The Boyd family travels 3.4 miles.

More Examples

A

$$\begin{array}{r} \overset{1}{0}.45 \\ +1.36 \\ \hline 1.81 \end{array}$$

B

$$\begin{array}{r} \overset{1\,1}{6}.95 \\ +3.47 \\ \hline 10.42 \end{array}$$

C

$$\begin{array}{r} 3.20 \\ +4.56 \\ \hline 7.76 \end{array}$$

Try It Add.

1. $\begin{array}{r} 1.4 \\ +3.7 \end{array}$

2. $\begin{array}{r} 5.4 \\ +2.5 \end{array}$

3. $\begin{array}{r} \$0.78 \\ +\ 0.13 \end{array}$

4. $\begin{array}{r} 6.35 \\ +3.39 \end{array}$

5. $\begin{array}{r} \$6.06 \\ +\ 4.20 \end{array}$

Sum it Up How is adding decimals like adding whole numbers? How is it different?

6. 2.59
+4.82

7. 6.74
+6.38

8. $6.05
+ 7.49

9. 7.3
+8.8

10. $0.84
+ 0.27

11. 1.3 + 7.2
12. 0.6 + 0.9
13. $1.34 + $5.93
14. 8.04 + 3.52
15. 0.48 + 0.27
16. 3.98 + 2.36
17. 0.68 + 3.84
18. 7.63 + 4.45
★19. 0.23 + 1.22 + 0.63
★20. 1.6 + 5.4 + 0.2
★21. 0.52 + 0.24 + 3.22 + 4.51
★22. 3.4 + 5.2 + 0.3 + 1.5

Algebra & functions **Copy and complete.**

23. 4.1■
+3.28
7.41

24. 3.6
+■.5
10.1

25. 5.93
+6.49
■.42

26. ■.48
+1.25
1.73

27. 5.66
+3.1■
8.84

Problem Solving

28. Scott buys a book on inventions. The book costs $9.56. How much does he spend for two books?

29. Admission to the museum is $6.95. Parking costs $3.75. How much does it cost for 4 people to park and go to the museum?

★30. **Time:** It takes you 2.25 hours to drive to the museum. How many minutes is this?

31. **Language Arts:** The name *crayon* comes from French words for "oily chalk." If 8 crayons in a box of 64 are all different shades of red, what fraction of the box is this?

32. **Create a problem** where you have to add using decimals.

33. Ian buys 6 bags of rolls. Each bag holds 5 rolls. How many rolls does Ian buy?

Spiral Review and Test Prep

34. $0.48 + $0.09
35. 7 × 613
36. $\frac{5}{10} + \frac{3}{10}$
37. $\frac{7}{12} - \frac{5}{12}$

Choose the correct answer.

38. A floor is 123 feet long. How many yards long is the floor?
   A. 10 yards
   C. 159 yards
   B. 41 yards
   D. 369 yards

39. Find: $\frac{3}{4}$ of 32
   F. 8
   H. 24
   G. 12
   J. Not Here

Objective: Solve a complex problem by solving a simpler problem first.

Problem Solving: Strategy
Solve a Simpler Problem

The Museum of Inventions

$7.95 Adults

$5.95 Children

$5.95 Senior Citizens

$5.25 Each for groups of 25 or more

$4.50 Parking

Read

Mr. and Mrs. Washington and their three children visit The Museum of Inventions. How much do the Washingtons spend on admission and parking?

- **What do you know?**
- **What do you need to find?**

There are 3 children and 2 adults. The total cost of admission and parking

Plan

You need to find out three things to solve the problem.
- How much do they pay for admission?
- How much do they pay for parking?
- How much do they pay for everything altogether?

Solve

You can sometimes see how to solve a problem by first solving a simpler problem. Try using smaller or easier numbers instead of the numbers in the original problem.

	Cost for adults	Cost for children	Cost for parking	
	2 × $8.00	3 × $6.00	$5.00	
Total Cost	$16.00 +	$18.00 +	$5.00	= $39.00

Now solve the original problem in the same way.

	2 × $7.95	3 × $5.95	$4.50	
Total Cost	$15.90 +	$17.85 +	$4.50	= $38.25

Look Back

Is your answer reasonable?

Sum it Up! How can using simpler numbers help you solve a problem?

1. The Washington family takes the train to the museum. Each train ticket is $4.75. How much do they pay for admission and train tickets?

2. The family has lunch in the museum cafeteria. Lunches cost $3.65 and drinks are $0.95. How much do they pay altogether for lunch?

3. Look back at the admission prices. How much money would the family save on admission if they went to the museum as part of a group of 30 people?

4. The museum is 0.4 mile away from the train station. The diner is 1.7 miles beyond that. A family walks from the train station to the museum, then to the diner, and then back to the train station. How far does the family walk?

Mixed Strategy Review

5. The museum is 42 miles away. It costs about $0.32 each mile to drive and $4.50 to park. The train tickets are $4.75 each way. The family is trying to decide whether they should drive or take the train. Which way would cost less? how much less?

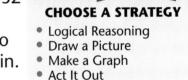

CHOOSE A STRATEGY
- Logical Reasoning
- Draw a Picture
- Make a Graph
- Act It Out
- Make a Table or List
- Find a Pattern
- Guess and Check
- Write a Number Sentence
- Work Backward
- Solve a Simpler Problem

6. **Measurement:** The museum wants to rope off a space that is under construction. It is a rectangular space with sides that measure 12 feet and 14 feet. How much rope do they need?

Use data from the pictograph for problems 7–9.

Favorite Exhibits

Inventors' Workshop ☺ ☺ ☺ ☺ ☺
Movie Mania ☺ ☺ ☺ ☺ ☺ ☺ ☺
Music Maker ☺ ☺ ☺ ☺
World of Magnets ☺ ☺ ☺

Each ☺ stands for 10 people

7. The museum took a survey to see which exhibits guests liked most. How many people did they survey altogether?

8. How many more people liked Movie Mania than World of Magnets?

9. **Create a problem** using the data in the pictograph. Solve it. Ask others to solve it.

14·9 Explore Subtracting Decimals

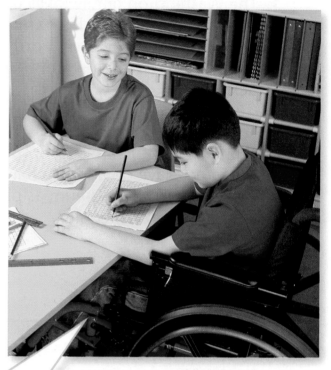

Learn

You can use graph paper to explore subtracting decimals.
What is 3.6 − 0.8?

Work Together

▶ Use 10-by-10 grids to make models.

You Will Need
• **graph paper**
• **colored pencils or crayons**

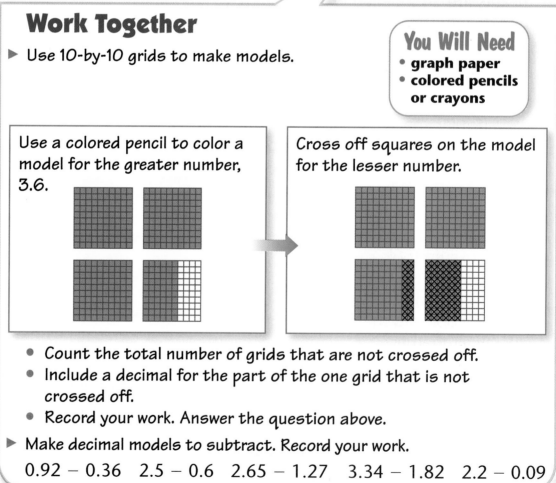

Use a colored pencil to color a model for the greater number, 3.6.

Cross off squares on the model for the lesser number.

• Count the total number of grids that are not crossed off.
• Include a decimal for the part of the one grid that is not crossed off.
• Record your work. Answer the question above.

▶ Make decimal models to subtract. Record your work.

0.92 − 0.36   2.5 − 0.6   2.65 − 1.27   3.34 − 1.82   2.2 − 0.09

Make Connections

Here are two ways to show how to subtract decimals.

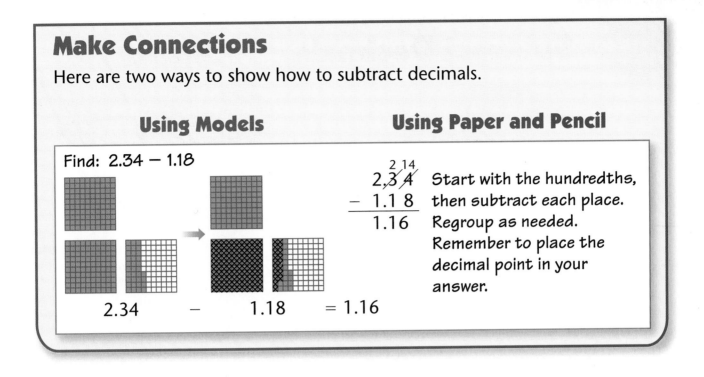

Using Models

Using Paper and Pencil

Find: 2.34 − 1.18

$$\begin{array}{r} \overset{2\ \ 14}{2.\cancel{3}\cancel{4}} \\ -\ 1.1\ 8 \\ \hline 1.16 \end{array}$$

Start with the hundredths, then subtract each place. Regroup as needed. Remember to place the decimal point in your answer.

2.34   −   1.18   = 1.16

Try It   **Subtract. You may wish to use models.**

1. 0.6
   −0.2

2. 1.8
   −1.1

3. 2.67
   −1.05

4. 0.89
   −0.38

5. 2.62
   −1.54

Sum it Up   Why do you model the greater number first?

Practice   **Subtract.**

6. 2.90
   −1.20

7. 1.7
   −0.87

8. 0.84
   −0.47

9. 1.39
   −0.46

10. 0.85
    −0.28

11. 1.70
    −0.45

12. 4.09
    −1.19

13. 0.94
    −0.68

14. 2.6
    −0.88

15. 0.9
    −0.3

16. 0.4
    −0.1

17. 2.35
    −1.15

18. 2.5
    −1.7

19. 4.56
    −3.64

20. 4.2
    −1.4

21. **Explain** how you know when to regroup.

14·10 Subtract Decimals

Learn

The first go-cart was invented when someone put a lawnmower engine on a cart. How much more power does a 3.5 horsepower go-cart engine have than a lawnmower engine?

Engine power is measured in horsepower.

2.75 horsepower

Example

Find 3.5 − 2.75 to solve the problem.

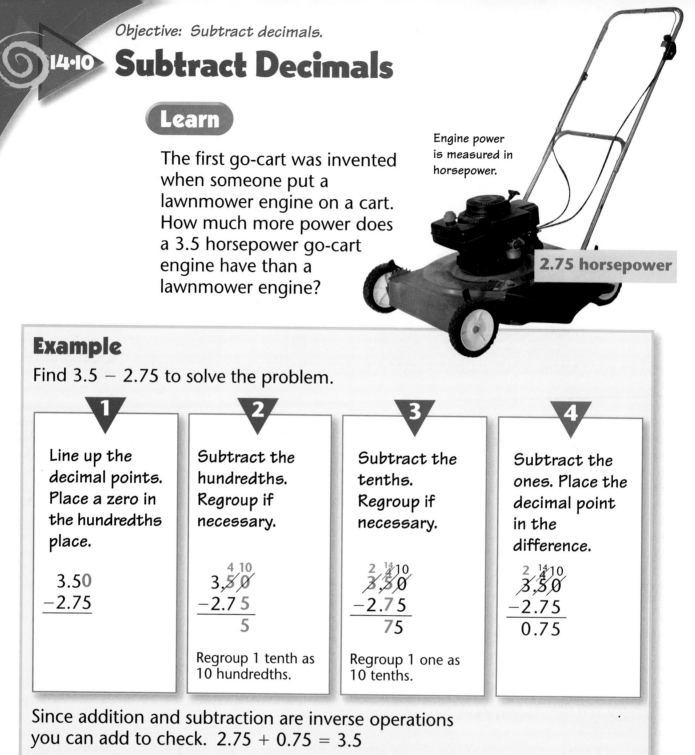

1

Line up the decimal points. Place a zero in the hundredths place.

$$3.50$$
$$-2.75$$

2

Subtract the hundredths. Regroup if necessary.

$$3.\overset{4\ 10}{5\!\!\!/0\!\!\!/}$$
$$-2.7\ 5$$
$$\overline{5}$$

Regroup 1 tenth as 10 hundredths.

3

Subtract the tenths. Regroup if necessary.

$$\overset{2\ \ 14\ 10}{3.\!\!\!/5\!\!\!/0\!\!\!/}$$
$$-2.7\ 5$$
$$\overline{75}$$

Regroup 1 one as 10 tenths.

4

Subtract the ones. Place the decimal point in the difference.

$$\overset{2\ \ 14\ 10}{3.\!\!\!/5\!\!\!/0\!\!\!/}$$
$$-2.75$$
$$\overline{0.75}$$

Since addition and subtraction are inverse operations you can add to check. 2.75 + 0.75 = 3.5

The go-cart has 0.75 more horsepower than the lawnmower.

Try It Subtract.

1. 3.4 − 1.7 **2.** 6.8 − 2.7 **3.** 0.76 − 0.37 **4.** 6.52 − 1.29

 How is subtracting decimals like subtracting whole numbers? How is it different?

5. 6.7 − 3.4   6. $8.15 − $2.39   7. $0.77 − $0.58   8. 8.90 − 6.86

9. 46.36 − 5.58 10. 8.3 − 5.2   11. 0.9 − 0.5   12. $7.54 − $3.92

13. 7.06 − 2.18   14. 0.8 − 0.36   15. 4.64 − 2.37   16. 0.75 − 0.34

17. (5.3 + 1.3) − 3.8   ★18. (3.4 + 7.6) − 4.2

★19. (8.2 + 1.1) − 3.3   ★20. (3.1 + 4.8) − 5.1

Algebra & functions **Copy and complete.**

21.	22.	23.	24.	25.
7.3▨	8.9	5.87	▨.65	4.53
−3.25	−▨.4	−2.26	−4.24	−3.1▨
4.09	3.5	▨.61	5.41	1.35

Problem Solving

Use data from the table for problems 26–28.

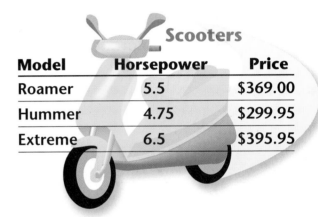

Model	Horsepower	Price
Roamer	5.5	$369.00
Hummer	4.75	$299.95
Extreme	6.5	$395.95

26. How much more power does the Roamer have than the Hummer?

27. What is the difference in price between the most and least expensive model?

28. **Create a problem** using the data in the table. Solve it. Ask others to solve it.

29. **Compare:** How is subtracting decimals like subtracting money? How is it different?

Spiral Review and Test Prep

30. $\frac{1}{2} + \frac{1}{2}$ 31. $68.42 + $5.21   32. $3\overline{)\$1.26}$ 33. $3.45 × 6

Choose the correct answer.

34. What is a certain event?
   A. Spin 3
   B. Spin 4
   C. Spin 5
   D. Not Here

35. Jody is inventing a new recipe. She puts $\frac{3}{8}$ teaspoon of garlic powder and $\frac{5}{8}$ teaspoon of pepper in the dish. How much spice is this?
   F. 1 teaspoon   H. $\frac{8}{16}$ teaspoon
   G. $\frac{2}{8}$ teaspoon   J. $\frac{1}{2}$ teaspoon

14·11 A Problem Solving: Application
Decision Making

You Decide!

Which buy is the best?

Central City School is planning a Discovery Day. Children will perform experiments, make things, and take objects apart to see how they work.

The principal needs to buy some supplies. You need to decide where to buy the most affordable supplies for 20 students.

Central City School

Supplies Needed for Discovery Day
- batteries
- magnets
- paper towels
- foil trays
- markers
- film

PRICE LIST

Item	Dave's Grocery store Price	Main Street Market Price
Batteries	package of 2 batteries $1.50	package of 4 batteries $2.88
Magnets	package of 3 magnets $1.56	package of 5 magnets $2.75
Paper towels	package of 4 rolls $3.20	package of 6 rolls $4.68
Foil trays	single tray $0.59	package of 3 trays $1.80
Markers	package of 2 markers $1.78	package of 4 markers $3.32
Film	single roll $2.29	package of 4 rolls $8.40

Read for Understanding

1. How much do magnets at Dave's Grocery Store cost? How many magnets are in this package?

2. How many rolls of paper towels come in the package from Main Street Market? How much does the package cost?

3. Which store has the package with 3 foil trays? What is the price?

4. How many markers come in each of the packages?

5. How many batteries come in the package from Main Street Market? What is the price?

6. What is the most expensive item on the list? Tell how you know.

Make Decisons

7. How much would 1 roll of paper towels cost if you shop at Main Street Market? at Dave's Grocery Store? Which costs more?

8. How much would 1 battery cost if you buy it at Dave's Grocery Store? at Main Street Market? What is the difference in price? Which store has the the best buy for batteries?

9. How much would 1 roll of film cost at Main Street Market? at Dave's Grocery Store? Which store has the best buy for film?

10. How much would 1 foil tray cost if you buy the package at Main Street Market? What is the difference between this price and the price of a single tray at Dave's Grocery Store?

11. How much would it cost for 1 magnet if you shop at Main Street Market? at Dave's Grocery Store? Which store has the better buy?

12. How much would 1 marker cost at Main Street Market? at Dave's Grocery Store? Which store costs more? How much more? Which store has the best buy for markers?

13. Which store has the best buy for foil trays? How much would you save if you bought 6 individual trays instead of two packages of 3 trays?

What is your recommendation for the principal if she wants to buy the most affordable supplies for 20 students? Explain.

14·11 B

Problem Solving: Math and Science
How does distance affect how many baskets you make?

A basketball player can score three points by making a basket from far away.

In this activity, you will discover whether it is harder or easier to make baskets as you get farther away from the basket.

You Will Need
- **paper ball**
- **trash can**
- **ruler or meterstick**

Hypothesize

Of ten tries, how many baskets will you make from 1.5 meters away? from 4 meters away?

Procedure

1. Work with a partner. Take turns.
2. Stand 1.5 meters from an empty trash can.
3. Try 10 shots. Record how many go in.
4. Repeat step 3 from 3 meters, 4.5 meters, and 6 meters.

Copy and complete the chart to record the number of baskets you made at each distance. Express your answer as a decimal.

Distance	Attempts	Baskets	Shots Made (as a decimal)
1.5 m	10		
3 m	10		
4.5 m	10		
6 m	10		

Conclude and Apply

- At which distance was it easiest to make baskets? Explain.

- Put the decimals in the table in order from least to greatest.

- When you were four times as far from the basket, was it four times harder to make the shots?

- Make a bar graph to display your data. Talk about what it shows.

- How does your success at making baskets compare with that of the NBA teams?

Did You KNOW?

The NBA players make an average of approximately 0.44 baskets for each 2-point shot during the season.

Problem Solving

Going Further

1. Design and complete an activity to find the longest distance you can be from the basket and still make at least one shot in 10.

Add. (pages 600–603)

1. 3.63
   +4.37

2. 2.85
   +8.19

3. $8.08
   + 4.22

4. 9.2
   +7.4

5. 5.47
   +3.21

6. 2.4 + 5.8   7. 0.5 + 0.2   8. 3.45 + 2.62   9. 0.32 + 1.48

10. 0.3 + 0.4 + 0.7   11. 0.2 + 0.7 + 0.9

Subtract. (pages 606–609)

12. 8.8
    −4.3

13. 4.79
    −3.25

14. $7.95
    − 3.49

15. 6.03
    −4.56

16. 5.50
    −1.48

17. 0.79 − 0.28   18. 3.84 − 3.18   19. 0.95 − 0.46

20. 5.07 − 3.68   21. 0.32 − 0.11   22. 2.38 − 1.24

Solve. (pages 600–609)

23. A fruit tray was served at the Inventors Club meeting. It had 2.4 pounds of melon, 1.8 pounds of grapes, and 3.2 pounds of berries. How many pounds of fruit were on the tray?

24. At Discovery Day children can experiment with clay. Heather uses 2.6 kilograms of clay to make a sculpture. Arlen uses 3.5 kilograms of clay. Who uses more clay? How much more?

Journal 25. **Analyze:** Why can you use addition to check the answer to 1.96 − 1.89?

Additional activities at
www.mhschool.com/math

Extra Practice

Tenths and Hundredths (pages 586–589)

Write a decimal for the part that is shaded.

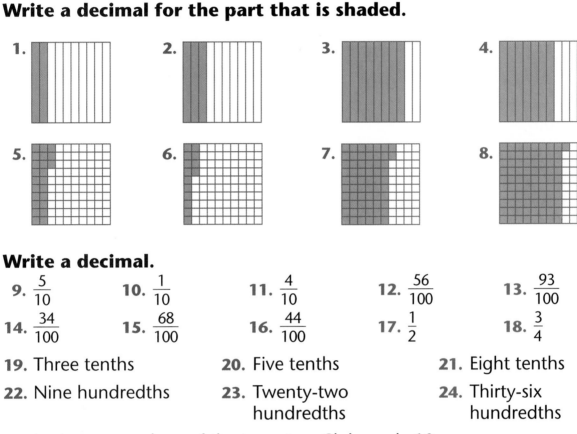

1.

2.

3.

4.

5.

6.

7.

8.

Write a decimal.

9. $\frac{5}{10}$

10. $\frac{1}{10}$

11. $\frac{4}{10}$

12. $\frac{56}{100}$

13. $\frac{93}{100}$

14. $\frac{34}{100}$

15. $\frac{68}{100}$

16. $\frac{44}{100}$

17. $\frac{1}{2}$

18. $\frac{3}{4}$

19. Three tenths

20. Five tenths

21. Eight tenths

22. Nine hundredths

23. Twenty-two hundredths

24. Thirty-six hundredths

25. Last year members of the Inventors Club made 10 new inventions. Four were toys. Write a decimal to show the part of the inventions that were toys.

Decimals Greater Than One (pages 590–591)

Write each decimal.

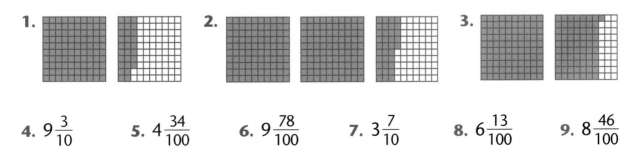

1.

2.

3.

4. $9\frac{3}{10}$

5. $4\frac{34}{100}$

6. $9\frac{78}{100}$

7. $3\frac{7}{10}$

8. $6\frac{13}{100}$

9. $8\frac{46}{100}$

10. seven and thirty-nine hundredths

11. two and nine tenths

Extra Practice

Compare and Order Decimals (page 592–595)

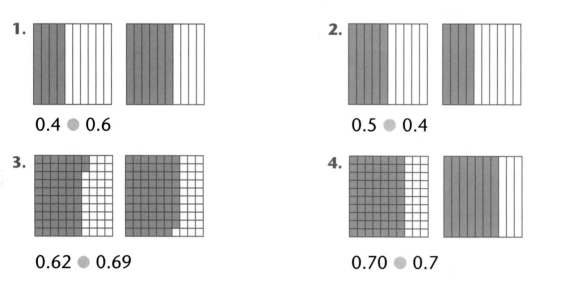

1. 0.4 ● 0.6

2. 0.5 ● 0.4

3. 0.62 ● 0.69

4. 0.70 ● 0.7

5. 0.80 ● 0.8   **6.** 4.1 ● 4.09   **7.** 0.87 ● 1.01   **8.** 0.8 ● 0.79

Write the decimals in order from least to greatest.

9. 0.26, 0.62, 0.52   **10.** 0.37, 0.24, 0.46   **11.** 2.23, 1.23, 1.32

Write the decimals in order from greatest to least.

12. 4.4, 4.8, 3.8   **13.** 5.43, 5.34, 4.35   **14.** 7.19, 7.91, 1.79

Problem Solving: Reading for Math
Choose an Operation (pages 596–597)

1. Bud's model car costs $3.40. Tom's car costs $1.90. How much do the cars cost altogether? Which operation will you use?

2. Jan's supplies cost $2.80. Sue's supplies cost $1.70 less than Jan's. How much do Sue's supplies cost? Which operation will you use?

Extra Practice

Add Decimals (pages 600–603)

1. 5.7
   +6.5

2. 0.91
   +0.19

3. $7.25
   + 3.19

4. 4.55
   +5.69

5. 4.73
   +3.36

6. 2.4 + 4.8

7. 0.4 + 0.8

8. $3.48 + $4.98

9. 6.02 + 4.79

10. 0.37 + 0.46

11. 2.76 + 3.43

12. 0.93 + 2.66

13. 6.18 + 3.42

14. $0.29 + $0.82

15. 4.60 + 3.78

16. 8.58 + 5.47

17. 4.85 + 6.33

Problem Solving Strategy: Solve a Simpler Problem (pages 604–605)

Solve.

1. Mrs. Hira's class is inventing games. She buys some supplies for the project. She buys 4 bags of marbles and 2 boxes of plastic chips. How much does she spend?

2. How much would she spend for 2 boxes of index cards and 2 boxes of markers?

3. How much would it cost to buy 2 bags of marbles and 1 each of the other items?

Bag of Marbles	$1.79
Box of Plastic Chips	$2.29
Box of Markers	$5.99
Box of Index Cards	$3.49

Subtract Decimals (pages 606–609)

1. 7.1
   −4.6

2. 8.3
   −4.6

3. $7.80
   − 3.94

4. 7.74
   −3.89

5. 5.06
   −3.27

6. 6.4 − 4.1

7. 0.8 − 0.3

8. $6.37 − $2.14

9. 9.09 − 4.36

10. 0.67 − 0.39

11. 5.46 − 2.72

12. 0.93 − 0.44

13. 4.56 − 2.73

Chapter Study Guide

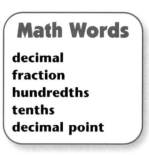

Language and Math

Complete. Use a word from the list.

1. In the number 9.4, the 4 is in the ____ place.

2. A ____ has a numerator and denominator.

3. A ____ always has a number to the right of the decimal point.

4. In the number 4.92, the 2 is in the ____ place.

Math Words

decimal
fraction
hundredths
tenths
decimal point

Skills and Applications

Identify fraction and decimal equivalents. (pages 584–585)

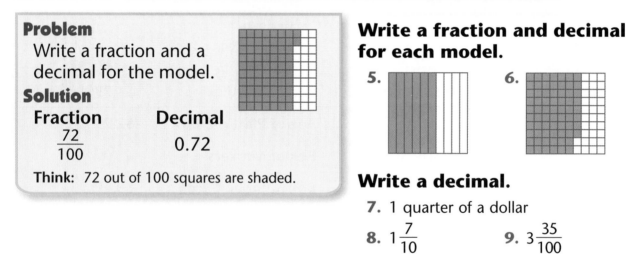

Problem
Write a fraction and a decimal for the model.

Solution

Fraction	Decimal
$\frac{72}{100}$	0.72

Think: 72 out of 100 squares are shaded.

Write a fraction and decimal for each model.

5.　　　　　6.

Write a decimal.

7. 1 quarter of a dollar

8. $1\frac{7}{10}$　　　9. $3\frac{35}{100}$

Read and write decimals to hundredths. (pages 584–591)

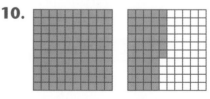

Problem
Write a decimal for the part that is shaded.

Solution

Think: 3 out of 10 parts are shaded.
　　　30 out of 100 parts are shaded.

Read: three tenths; thirty hundredths

Write: 0.3 = 0.30

Write a decimal for the part that is shaded.

10.

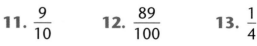

Write a decimal.

11. $\frac{9}{10}$　　12. $\frac{89}{100}$　　13. $\frac{1}{4}$

14. Five and six tenths

15. Nine and fifteen hundredths

Compare and order decimals. (pages 592–595)

Problem
Order from least to greatest:
3.45, 3.68, 2.45.

Solution
Line up the decimals.
Compare each place.

Ones	Tenths	Hundredths
3.	4	5
3.	6	8
2.	4	5

Order from least to greatest.
2.45, 3.45, 3.68

Compare. Write >, <, or =.

16. 0.3 ● 0.6   17. 0.64 ● 0.46

18. 1.23 ● 1.43   19. 3.6 ● 3.60

20. 5.49 ● 5.42   21. 2.35 ● 2.38

Write the decimals in order from least to greatest.

22. 4.2, 4.1, 3.7

23. 6.8, 6.5, 6.0

24. 5.84, 5.48, 5.68

Add and subtract decimals. (pages 600–603, 606–609)

Problem
3.5 + 2.6   6.74 − 3.45

Solution
Line up the decimal. Add or
subtract. Write the decimal point.

$$\begin{array}{r} \overset{1}{3.5} \\ +2.6 \\ \hline 6.1 \end{array} \qquad \begin{array}{r} \overset{6\,14}{6.\cancel{7}\cancel{4}} \\ -3.45 \\ \hline 3.29 \end{array}$$

Add or subtract.

25. $\begin{array}{r} 5.92 \\ +3.40 \end{array}$ 26. $\begin{array}{r} 6.30 \\ -3.22 \end{array}$ 27. $\begin{array}{r} 7.13 \\ +2.96 \end{array}$

28. 4.0 − 0.85   29. 2.27 + 4.54

30. 7.33 − 2.59   31. 0.9 + 0.3 + 0.6

Use strategies to solve problems. (pages 596–597, 604–605)

Problem
In two races, Ana's car went 6.5
feet and 7.75 feet. Burt's car went
6.75 feet and 7.25 feet. Whose
car had the greater total distance?

Solution
Use simpler numbers first.
7 + 8 = 15 7 + 7 = 14 15 > 14
Now use the original numbers.
6.5 + 7.75 = 14.25
6.75 + 7.25 = 14.00
14.25 > 14.00
Ana's car went the greater total
distance.

Use data from the chart for problems 32–33.

Rainfall Amounts (in Inches)					
Mar.	Apr.	May	June	July	Aug.
4.2	5.3	2.6	2.1	0.6	0.8

32. How much more rain did March
and April have than May and June?

33. How much more rainfall did the
Spring (March, April, and May)
have than the Summer (June,
July, and August)?

Chapter Test

Write a decimal.

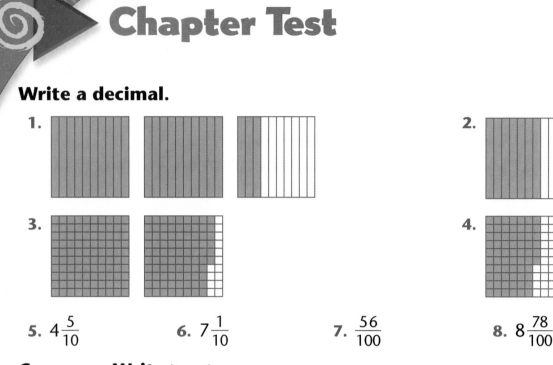

1.

2.

3.

4.

5. $4\frac{5}{10}$

6. $7\frac{1}{10}$

7. $\frac{56}{100}$

8. $8\frac{78}{100}$

Compare. Write >, <, or =.

9. 6.3 ● 6.7

10. 4.32 ● 5.32

11. 8.41 ● 8.14

Write the decimals in order from greatest to least.

12. 3.8, 2.9, 3.6

13. 7.63, 7.36, 8.03

14. 5.42, 5.24, 5.44

Add or subtract.

15. 5.7
   $+1.8$

16. 6.0
   -3.9

17. 6.47
   $+6.08$

18. 7.86
   -5.77

19. 3.9 + 4.6

20. 9.2 − 4.8

21. 4.09 − 2.78

22. 8.33 + 4.16

Solve.

23. A book about inventions costs $13.63. This includes tax of $0.64. How much is the book without tax?

24. The Hubble telescope is a great invention that lets us see far out in space. The main body of the telescope is 13.12 meters long and 4.27 meters wide. What is the difference between the length and width?

25. Rosa mixes two materials for an experiment. One material is 0.6 kilogram and the other is 1.25 kilograms. What is the total mass of the materials?

Performance Assessment

Your aunt gives you $25 to spend on your new puppy. With this amount, you need to buy a collar, a tag, and grooming tools. You can use the amount left over to buy more puppy items.

Choose your items from this catalog. Add up your three main purchases. Then decide what you will buy with the leftover money.

Copy and complete the chart to record you purchases.

Plastic Collar	$6.71
Nylon Collar	$5.49
Gold Tag	$4.98
Silver Tag	$3.98
Comb	$2.56
Brush	$3.79
Ball	$0.79
Box of Treats	$2.64
Teddy	$4.26

Item Bought	Price per Item	Number of Items	Total Amount

Journal

A Good Answer

- shows a completed chart.
- includes collar, tag, and grooming tools.
- shows what was purchased with the leftover money.

Portfolio

You may want to save this work in your portfolio.

Enrichment

Russian Abacus

You may have seen a Japanese abacus before. The Russian abacus is a little different—it lets you show decimals.

A Russian abacus is called a *schoty* (SHOH-tee). The picture shows what a schoty looks like. The schoty is showing 36.5.

The beads have been moved to the left to show the correct number. For example, there are 3 tens, 6 ones, and 5 tenths in 36.5.

thousands
hundreds
tens
ones
decimal point
tenths
hundredths

Write the number shown by each abacus.

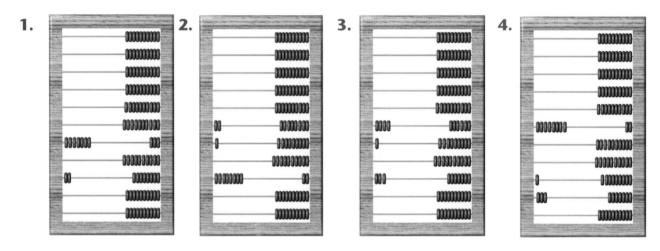

1.   2.   3.   4.

Describe how you could show these numbers on a *schoty*.

5. 2.05   6. 104.1   7. 67.52   8. 921.4

9. **Generalize:** Do you think a schoty would be better to use than a calculator? Explain.

Test-Taking Tips

S.O.S.

Sometimes the numbers in a problem make it seem harder than it actually is. It may help to **use simpler numbers**.

Josh ran 3.25 miles today and 2.75 miles yesterday. How far did he run altogether?

A. 1.75 miles   C. 6 miles
B. 5 miles   D. 6.75 miles

Use whole numbers in place of the decimals to make it easier to know how to solve the problem. Josh ran 3 miles and then 2 miles. You can add to find how far he ran altogether.

Now go back and add the original numbers.
3.25 + 2.75 = 6.00 or 6

Check the answer choices: 6 is there. The correct choice is C.

Check for Success

Before turning in a test, go back one last time to check.

☑ I understood and answered the questions asked.

☑ I checked my work for errors.

☑ My answers make sense.

**Choose the correct answer.
Use simpler numbers to help you.**

1. Phil ate $\frac{5}{8}$ of a pie. John ate $\frac{3}{8}$ of another one. How much more did Phil eat?

   A. $\frac{2}{8}$ C. $\frac{3}{4}$

   B. $\frac{2}{4}$ D. $\frac{8}{8}$

2. Kayla had $2.75. She saved $5.35 more. How much does she have now?

   F. $7.00   H. $8.10

   G. $7.05   J. $8.35

3. Which number can be added to 3.44 to make 6.24?

   A. 1.8   C. 3.85

   B. 2.8   D. 4.80

4. Jenna bought $2\frac{1}{2}$ pounds of apples, $1\frac{1}{2}$ pounds of cherries, and 3 pounds of pears. How many pounds of fruit did she buy in all?

   F. 6 pounds   H. $7\frac{1}{2}$ pounds

   G. 7 pounds   J. $8\frac{1}{2}$ pounds

Test Prep

Spiral Review and Test Prep
Chapters 1-14

Choose the correct answer.

Number Sense

1. Which multiplication fact makes the sentence true?

   $6 \times 7 >$ ▮

   A. 9×4 **C.** 6×8
   B. 5×9 **D.** 8×8

2. Which sum is about 1,200?

   F. $408 + 621$ **H.** $567 + 632$
   G. $678 + 733$ **J.** $488 + 534$

3. Jake has made $785 so far selling his new invention. How much more does he need to make $1,000?

   A. $315   **C.** $215
   B. $225   **D.** $115

4. There are 32 members in the Inventors Club. They will work in groups to make a new invention. How could they make equal goups?

   F. 2 groups   **H.** 4 groups
       of 15   of 9
   G. 8 groups   **J.** 6 groups
       of 4   of 6

Measurement and Geometry

5. Harold works on his invention for 80 minutes each day. If he ends at 5:20 P.M., what time did he begin?

   A. 4:20 P.M.   **C.** 4:00 P.M.
   B. 3:50 P.M.   **D.** 4:10 P.M.

6. Jeff sent his new invention to a company on May 6. One week later Jeff got a call from the president of the company. On what date did he get the call?

   F. May 13   **H.** May 16
   G. May 12   **J.** May 20

7. Which is *not* true?

   A. A square has exactly 4 equal sides.
   B. A circle has exactly 2 equal sides.
   C. A square is a rectangle.
   D. A triangle has exactly 3 sides.

8. A toy inventor is working on a new game board. There are 64 blocks on the game board. The blocks are placed in an equal number of rows and columns. How many columns are on the game board?

   F. 4   **H.** 7
   G. 6   **J.** 8

9. Identify the rule:

Rule: ■	
Input	Output
4	12
6	18
8	24

A. Add 3.
B. Multiply by 3.
C. Add 8.
D. Multiply by 4.

10. Which number makes the sentence true?

$(4 + 10) + 16 = 4 + (■ + 16)$

F. 30
G. 16
H. 14
J. 10

11. Which symbol belongs in the ●?

$56 ● 8 = 7$

A. +
B. ×
C. −
D. ÷

12. Owen studied the growth of a plant. At the beginning of the experiment, the plant was 4 inches tall. It grew 2 inches each week. How tall was the plant after 5 weeks?

F. 7 inches
G. 9 inches
H. 10 inches
J. 14 inches

Use data from the chart for problems 13–16.

The cellular telephone is a popular invention. Here are rates from 4 different companies.

Price for 1-Minute Call		
Company	Daytime	Nighttime
A	$0.42	$0.32
B	$0.45	$0.25
C	$0.33	$0.28
D	$0.35	$0.35

13. What is the difference between the daytime and nighttime price for company B?

A. $0.30
B. $0.20
C. $0.10
D. $0.05

14. How much would a 2-minute daytime call cost with company C?

F. $0.90
G. $0.84
H. $0.66
J. $0.56

15. Which company has the greatest difference between daytime and nighttime calls?

A. Company A
B. Company B
C. Company C
D. Company D

16. **Create a problem** using information from the chart. Explain how you solved it.

Glossary

(Italicized terms are defined elsewhere in this glossary.)

A

acute angle   An *angle* that is less than a *right angle*. (p. 492)

acute triangle   A *triangle* with all *angles* less than a *right angle*. (p. 492)

addend   A number to be added. (p. 46)

A.M.   A name for the time from 12 midnight to 12 noon. (p. 134)

angle   A figure formed when two *rays* or lines meet at the same point. (p. 486)

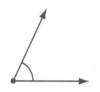

area   The number of square units needed to cover a region or figure. (p. 510)

array   Objects or symbols displayed in rows and columns. (p. 184)

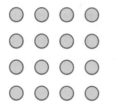

B

Associative Property of Addition   When adding, the grouping of numbers can change but the *sum* is the same. (p. 50)
Example: (4 + 5) + 2 = 11
　　　　　4 + (5 + 2) = 11

Associative Property of Multiplication   When multiplying, the grouping of the numbers does not change the *product*. (p. 246)
Example: 3 × (6 × 2) = 36
　　　　　(3 × 6) × 2 = 36

bar graph   A graph that shows data by using bars of different lengths. (p. 156)

base   The flat *face* on which a *3-dimensional figure* can rest. (p. 480)

C

capacity   A measure of dry or liquid volume of a container. (p. 436)

centimeter (cm)   A metric unit for measuring *length*. (p. 448) (See Table of Measures.)

certain   An event will definitely happen. (p. 560)

circle   A closed, *2-dimensional figure* having all points the same distance from a given point. (p. 487)

closed figure   A figure that starts and ends at the same point. (p. 490)

Commutative Property of Addition   When adding, the order of the numbers can change but the *sum* is the same. (p. 46)
Example: 12 + 15 = 27
          15 + 12 = 27

Commutative Property of Multiplication   When multiplying, the order of *factors* does not change the result. (p. 184)
Example: 7 x 2 = 14
          2 x 7 = 14

compatible numbers   Numbers that are close to the original numbers in a problem and easy to divide mentally. (p. 406)

cone   A pointed, *3-dimensional figure* with a circular base. (p. 480)

congruent   Same shape and same size. (p. 500)

cube   A *3-dimensional figure* with six square faces. (p. 480)

cubic unit   The *volume* of a *cube,* one of whose sides is the given unit of *length.* (p. 512)

cup (c)   A customary unit for measuring *capacity.* (p. 436) (See Table of Measures.)

cylinder   A *3-dimensional figure* with two *congruent faces* that are *circular.* (p. 480)

— D —

decimal   A number that uses *place value* and a *decimal point* to show tenths and hundredths. (p. 584)

decimal point   A period separating the ones and the tenths places in a *decimal.* (p. 584)
Examples: 0.8, 2.1, 27.64

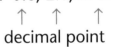

decimal point

decimeter (dm)   A metric unit for measuring *length.* (p. 448) (See Table of Measures.)

Degrees Celsius (°C)   Unit for measuring temperature. (p. 460)

Degrees Fahrenheit (°F)   Unit for measuring *temperature.* (p. 460)

denominator   The number below the bar in a *fraction.* It tells the number of equal parts in all. (p. 532)
Example: $\frac{5}{6}$ ← denominator

diameter A line touching 2 points on a *circle* and passing through the center of the circle. (p.487)

digit Any of the symbols used to write numbers—0, 1, 2, 3, 4, 5, 6, 7, 8, 9. (p. 4)

dividend A number to be divided. (p. 272)

division An operation on two numbers that tells how many groups or how many are in each group. (p. 268)
Example: 2 ← quotient
divisor → 3)‾6‾ ← dividend

divisor The number by which the *dividend* is divided. (p. 272)

E

edge A *line segment* where two faces of a 3-dimensional figure meet. (p. 481)

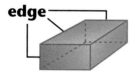

elapsed time The amount of time it takes to go from start to finish. (p. 140)

endpoint The point at either end of a *line segment*. The beginning point of a *ray*. (p. 486)

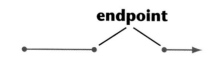

equilateral triangle A *triangle* with three sides the same *length*. (p. 492)

equivalent decimals *Decimals* that name the same number. (p. 586)
Example: 0.3 and 0.30
1.2 and 1.20

equivalent fractions Different *fractions* that name the same amount. (p. 534)
Examples: $\frac{1}{2}$ and $\frac{2}{4}$
$\frac{4}{6}$ and $\frac{2}{3}$

estimate To find an answer that is close to the exact answer. (p. 60)

expanded form A way of writing a number as the *sum* of the values of its *digits*. (p. 4)
Example: 536 can be written as 500 + 30 + 6.

F
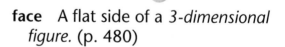

face A flat side of a *3-dimensional figure*. (p. 480)

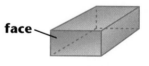

fact family A group of related facts using the same numbers. (p. 90)
Example: 5 + 3 = 8   3 + 5 + 8
8 − 3 = 5   8 − 5 = 3

factors Numbers that are multiplied to give a *product*. (p. 178)
Example: $5 \times 6 = 30$
$\uparrow$ $\uparrow$
factors

foot (ft) A customary unit for measuring *length*. (p. 434) (See Table of Measures.)

fraction A number that names part of a whole or group. (p. 532)

Examples: $\frac{1}{2}, \frac{3}{4}, \frac{5}{6}$

---G---

gallon (gal) A customary unit for measuring *capacity*. (p. 436) (See Table of Measures.)

gram (g) A metric unit for measuring *mass*. (p. 452) (See Table of Measures.)

---H---

half hour Amount of time equal to 30 *minutes*. (p. 138)

hexagon A *polygon* with six sides and six *angles*. (p. 490)

hour (h) Unit of time equal to 60 minutes. (p. 138)

---I---

Identity Property When one of the two *addends* is zero, the *sum* is the same as the other *addend*. (p. 46)

Identity Property of Multiplication The *product* of any number times one is that number. (p. 200)

impossible An event that cannot happen. (p. 560)

inch (in.) A customary unit for measuring *length*. (p. 434) (See Table of Measures.)

intersecting lines *Lines* that meet or cross at a common point. (p. 486)

is greater than (>) Symbol to show that the first number is greater than the second. (p. 8)
Example: $5 > 3$

is less than (<) Symbol to show that the first number is less than the second. (p. 8)
Example: $14 < 19$

isosceles triangle A *triangle* with two sides the same *length*. (p. 492)

key Tells how many items each symbol stands for. (p. 154)

kilogram (kg) A metric unit for measuring *mass.* (p. 452) (See Table of Measures.)

length The measurement of distance between two *endpoints.* (p. 434)

likely An event will probably happen. (p. 560)

line A straight path that goes in two directions without end. (p. 486)
Example: ⟵————⟶

line of symmetry A *line* on which a figure can be folded so that both sides match. (p. 504)

line plot A graph that uses Xs above a number line to show data. (p. 152)

line segment A straight path that has 2 endpoints. (p. 486)
Example: •————•

liter (L) A metric unit for measuring capacity. (p. 450) (See Table of Measures.)

mass The amount of matter in an object. (p. 452)

meter (m) A metric unit for measuring *length.* (p. 448) (See Table of Measures.)

milliliter (mL) A metric unit for measuring capacity. (p. 450) (See Table of Measures.)

minute (min) Unit of time equal to 60 seconds. (p. 134)

mixed number A number that has a whole number and a *fraction.* (p. 548)
Example: $6\frac{3}{4}$

month A unit for measuring time equal to about 30 days. (p. 142)

multiple The *product* of a number and any whole number. (p. 356)

multiplication An operation using at least two numbers to find another number, called a *product.* (p. 178)

multiplication sentence A math statement that uses an equals symbol. (p. 180)

net A flat pattern that can be folded to make a *3-dimensional figure.* (p. 481)

numerator The number above the bar in a fraction. It tells the number of parts. (p. 532)
Example: $\frac{4}{5}$ ← numerator

obtuse angle An *angle* that is greater than a *right angle.* (p. 492)

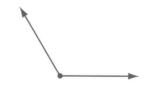

obtuse triangle A *triangle* with one angle greater than a *right angle.* (p. 492)

octagon A *polygon* with eight sides and eight *angles.* (p. 490)

open figure A figure that does not start and end at the same point. (p. 490)

ordered pair A pair of numbers that gives the location of a point on a map or grid. (p. 158)

ordinal number A number used to tell order or position. (p. 143)

ounce (oz) A customary unit for measuring *weight.* (p. 438) (See Table of Measures.)

parallel lines *Lines* on a plane that do not cross. (p. 486)

parallelogram A *quadrilateral* with opposite sides *parallel.* (p. 494)

pattern A series of numbers or figures that follows a rule. (p. 52)
Examples: 2, 4, 6, 8, 10, 12, 14

pentagon A *polygon* with five sides and five *angles.* (p. 490)

per For each. (p. 408)

perimeter The distance around an object or shape. (p. 508)

period Each group of three digits in a place value chart. (p. 6)
Example: 639, 271

Thousands Period			Ones Period		
Hundred Thousands	Ten Thousands	Thousands	Hundreds	Tens	Ones
6	3	9	2	7	1

pictograph A graph that shows data by using symbols. (p. 154)

pint (pt) A customary unit for measuring *capacity.* (p. 436) (See Table of Measures.)

place value The value given to a *digit* by its place in a number. (p. 2)
Example: In 5,349, the 3 is in the hundreds place and has a value of 300.

P.M. A name for the time from 12 noon to 12 midnight. (p. 134)

polygon A *closed figure* with straight sides. (p. 490)

possible outcomes Any of the results that could occur in an experiment. (p. 562)

pound (lb) A customary unit for measuring *weight.* (p. 438) (See Table of Measures.)

prism A *3-dimensional figure* with two *parallel congruent bases* and *rectangles* or *parallelograms* for *faces*. (p. 480)

probability The chance that an event will occur. (p. 560)

product The answer in *multiplication*. (p. 178)
Example: $6 \times 3 = 18 \leftarrow$ product

pyramid A *3-dimensional figure* that is shaped by *triangles* on a *base*. (p. 480)

──────────── Q ────────────

quadrilateral A *polygon* with 4 sides. (p. 494)

quart (qt) A customary unit for measuring *capacity*. (p. 436) (See Table of Measures.)

quarter hour Amount of time equal to 15 minutes. (p. 138)

quotient The answer in *division*. (p. 272)
Example: $15 \div 3 = 5 \leftarrow$ quotient

──────────── R ────────────

radius A *line* from the center of a *circle* to a point on the circle. (p. 487)

ray A *2-dimensional figure* that has one *endpoint* and goes without end in one direction. (p. 486)

rectangle A *polygon* with four sides and four *angles*. The opposite sides are the same *length*. (p. 490)

rectangular prism A *3-dimensional figure* with six rectangular sides. (p. 480)

regroup To name a number in a different way. (p. 54)
Example: 42 can be regrouped as 4 tens and 2 ones or as 3 tens and 12 ones.

reflection (flip) A movement of a figure across a line, producing a mirror image. (p. 502)

related facts Basic facts using the same numbers. (p. 90)

remainder The number left over after dividing. (p. 398)
Example: $22 \div 7 = 3$ R1 ← remainder

rhombus A *quadrilateral* with 4 sides the same *length*. (p. 494)

right angle An *angle* that forms a square corner. (p. 486)

right triangle A *triangle* with one *right angle*. (p. 492)

rotation (turn) A figure that is rotated around a point. (p. 502)

round To find the value of a number based on a given place value. (p. 14)
Example: 27 rounded to the nearest 10 is 30.

scale Marks that are equally spaced along a side of a graph. (p. 156)

scalene triangle A *triangle* with no sides the same *length*. (p. 492)

skip-count To count by twos, fives, tens, and so on. (p. 5)

side One of the line segments in a polygon. (p. 490)

similar Same shape, may be different size. (p. 500)

simplest form A *fraction* in which the *numerator* and the *denominator* have no common *factor* greater than 1. (p. 554)

sphere A *3-dimensional figure* that has the shape of a ball. (p. 480)

square A *polygon* that has four equal sides and four equal *angles*. (p. 490)

square number The *product* of multiplying a number by itself. (p. 224)

square units The area of a square, one of whose sides is the given unit of length. (p. 510)

standard form A way of writing a number that shows only its *digits*. (p. 4)

sum The answer in addition. (p. 46)
Example: $6 + 4 = 10$ ← sum

survey A method of gathering data by asking people questions. (p. 152)

tally A way of counting by making a mark for each item counted. (p. 152)
Example: 卌 stands for 5.

temperature   A measurement that tells how hot or cold something is. (p. 460)

tessellation   Repeated shapes that cover a flat surface without overlapping or leaving any gaps. (p. 502)

3-dimensional figure   A figure in space. (p. 480)

translation   To move a figure along a *line.* (p. 502)

trapezoid   A *quadrilateral* with exactly one pair of *parallel* sides. (p. 494)

triangle   A *polygon* with three sides and three *angles.* (p. 492)

2-dimensional figure   A figure on a plane. (p. 484)

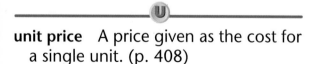

unit price   A price given as the cost for a single unit. (p. 408)

unlikely   An event that is not likely to happen. (p. 560)

V

vertex   The common point of the three or more *edges* of a *3-dimensional figure;* plural form is vertices. (p. 481)

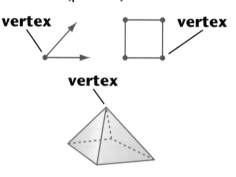

volume   The amount of space that a *3-dimensional figure* encloses. (p. 512)

W

week   A unit for measuring time equal to 7 days. (p. 142)

weight   A measurement that tells how heavy an object is. (p. 438)

Y

yard (yd)   A customary unit for measuring *length.* (p. 434) (See Table of Measures.)

Z

Zero Property of Multiplication   The product of any number times zero is zero. (p. 200)
Example: $57 \times 0 = 0$

Table of Measures

Customary

Length	Weight	Capacity
1 foot (ft) = 12 inches (in.)	1 pound (lb) = 16 ounces (oz)	1 cup (c) = 8 fluid ounces
1 yard (yd) = 3 feet, or 36 inches		1 quart (qt) = 2 pints
1 mile (mi) = 5,280 feet or 1,760 yards		1 gallon (gal) = 4 quarts

Metric

Length
1 meter (m) = 100 centimeters (cm)
1 decimeter = 10 centimeters
1 meter = 10 decimeters

Mass
1 kilogram (kg) = 1,000 grams

Capacity
1 liter (L) = 1,000 milliliters (mL)

Time

1 minute (min) = 60 seconds (s)
1 hour (h) = 60 minutes
1 day (d) = 24 hours
1 week = 7 days
1 year = 12 months (mo)

Temperature

32° Fahrenheit (°F) … Water freezes
212° Fahrenheit … Water boils

0° Celsius (°C) … Water freezes
100° Celsius … Water boils

Symbols

<	is less than	¢	cent	→	ray
>	is greater than	°	degree	∠	angle
=	is equal to	↔	line	(5, 3) ordered pair 5, 3	
$	dollar	—	line segment		

Index

P

Index

Index

Credits

Contents

◀ Calculator Handbook

Objective: Use the problem solving mode on the calculator to compare 3-digit numbers.

Comparing 3-Digit Whole Numbers

Mary and Elaine went bowling. Mary bowled a 132 and Elaine bowled a 125. Who had the higher score?

Using the TI-15

When comparing numbers you use > (greater than), < (less than), or = (equals).

132 ● 125

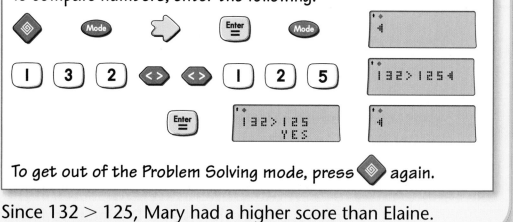

You can use the Problem Solving mode to compare numbers. To compare numbers, enter the following:

To get out of the Problem Solving mode, press ◈ again.

Since 132 > 125, Mary had a higher score than Elaine.

Practice **Use your calculator to compare.**

1. 296 ● 315 **2.** 450 ● 498 **3.** 536 ● 528 **4.** 760 ● 771

5. 983 ● 895 **6.** 520 ● 520 **7.** 127 ● 124 **8.** 643 ● 743

9. 845 ● 832 **10.** 974 ● 981 **11.** 444 ● 459 **12.** 940 ● 940

13. 123 ● 321 **14.** 561 ● 834 **15.** 693 ● 697 **16.** 805 ● 809

Solve.

17. Dale bowled a 117 and George bowled a 148. Who had the higher score?

18. Monica saved $258 in 4 months. Jerry saved $261 in 4 months. Who saved the most money in 4 months?